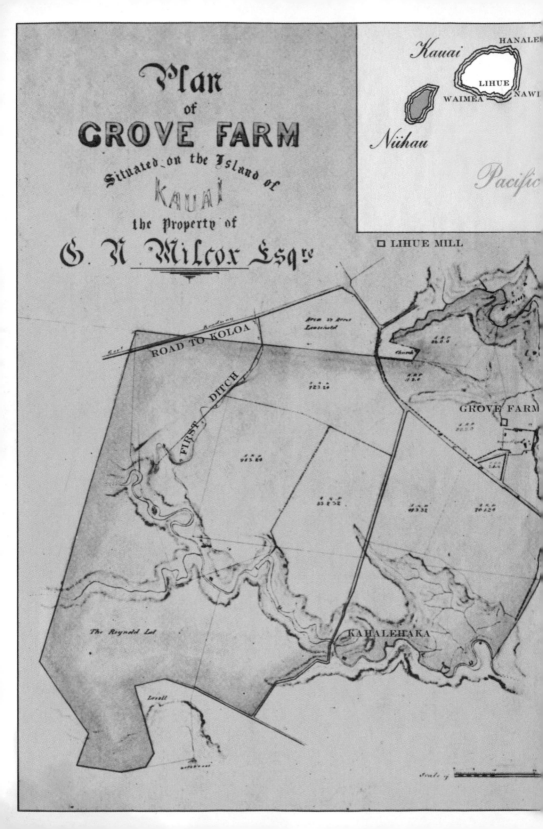

Plan
of
GROVE FARM
Situated on the Island of
KAUAI
the Property of
G. N. Wilcox Esqre

Kauai

HANALEI

LIHUE

WAIMEA

NAWI

Niihau

Pacific

□ LIHUE MILL

ROAD TO KOLOA

FIRST DITCH

Church

GROVE FARM

The Reynold Lot

KAHALEHAKA

Lovell

Scale of

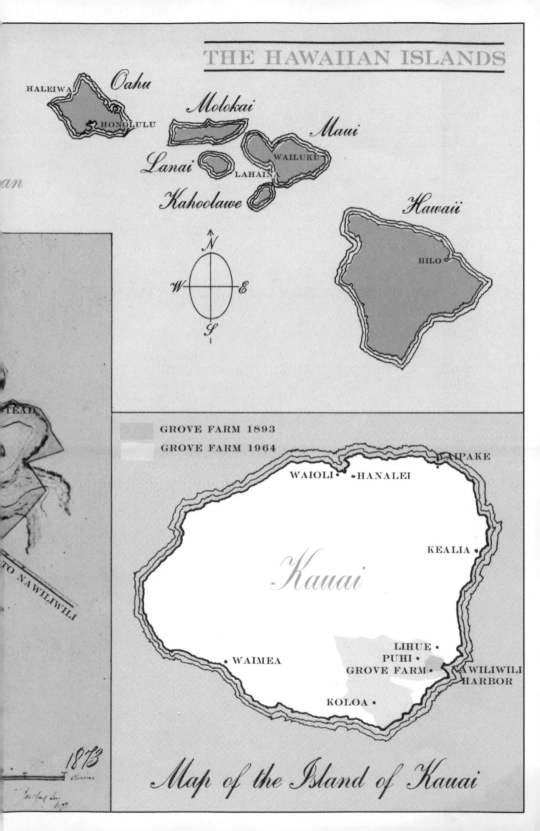

HALEIWA
Oahu
HONOLULU

Molokai

Maui

Lanai
WAILUKU
LAHAINA

Kahoolawe

Hawaii

HILO

N
W E
S

TEAD

TO NAWILIWILI

1873

GROVE FARM 1893
GROVE FARM 1964

WAIPAKE
WAIOLI HANALEI

KEALIA

Kauai

LIHUE
PUHI
GROVE FARM
NAWILIWILI
HARBOR

WAIMEA

KOLOA

Map of the Island of Kauai

Grove Farm Plantation

Grove Farm Plantation

THE BIOGRAPHY OF A HAWAIIAN SUGAR PLANTATION

By
BOB KRAUSS
with
WILLIAM P. ALEXANDER
Vignettes by Oliver Kinney

Third Edition

GROVE FARM Museum
LIHUE, KAUAI, HAWAII

Library of Congress Cataloging in Publication Data

Krauss, Bob.
   Grove Farm Plantation.

   Includes index.
   1. Grove Farm Company – History. 2. Wilcox, George Norton. 3. Sugarcane industry – Hawaii – Kauai – History. 4. Sugarcane industry – United States – Biography. 5. Plantations – Hawaii – Kauai – History. I. Alexander, William P., 1893- II. Title.
   HD9109. G76K72 1983   338. 1'7361'0996941   83-19298
   ISBN 0-9617174-3-2
   ISBN 0-9617174-2-4 (pbk.)

Publsihed by: GROVE FARM MUSEUM
   Post Office Box 1631
   Lihue, Kauai, Hawaii 96766

Printed and bound in the United States of America

Foreward to Third Edition

Since the first edition of Grove Farm Plantation in 1965, subsequent reprints and a second edition in 1983, the Hawaiian sugar industry and Grove Farm plantation have undergone massive changes. Sugar is no longer Hawaii's leading industry; only two plantations remain, one on Maui and one on Kauai. Grove Farm Company's focus changed from sugar to development, and in 2000 the company was sold.

The Trustees of Waioli Corporation, in making the decision to publish a third edition, recognize the original purpose of the book to be the story and growth of a sugar plantation, of George Norton Wilcox, its founder, and the people who contributed to its continuing operation. That operation having ceased to exist, it was decided that limiting the rest of the story to a brief epilogue would be most appropriate.

We would like to acknowledge Bob Krauss' research into the final phases of the original Grove Farm Company. His material has been donated to the Grove Farm Homestead museum archives where it is available for research purposes. Our gratitude is extended to him and those staff and trustees of the museum who contributed to this third edition.

Waioli Corporation Trustees
Ruth S. Smith, President

Grove Farm Homestead
Lihue, Kauai, Hawaii
August 2003

Foreword to Second Edition

In the original foreword written by Miss Ethel Damon for the first edition of *Grove Farm Plantation* in 1965, she gave credit to William P. Alexander and Bob Krauss for their research and admirable reconstruction of the life of George N. Wilcox. Since then the biography has been reprinted twice.

Seventeen years later the museum trustees of Waioli Corporation turned to Bob Krauss to ask him to continue the story of Grove Farm and bring it up to date. He has set down significant changes in the history of the sugar industry and in the development of Grove Farm plantation. His research through the records, including interviews with family members and others, has produced a fascinating and comprehensive up-date to *Grove Farm Plantation*.

RICHARD H. SLOGGETT, SR., President
Waioli Mission House and
Grove Farm Homestead Museums

Grove Farm Homestead
Lihue, Kauai, Hawaii
March 1983

Foreword to First Edition

George N. Wilcox's parents, Abner Wilcox and Lucy Hart Wilcox, were God-fearing people from Connecticut. They were among the early American Protestant missionaries to the Sandwich Islands, and were stationed first at Hilo, Hawaii. It was often my privilege to visit in George's home at Lihue, Kauai, and to chat with him of an evening. His niece, Miss Elsie Wilcox, agreed with me that some account of his life and work in establishing Grove Farm Plantation should be written.

Even in conversation he was interesting to the point of fascination, always accurate, often amusing and humorous. But when I asked him once whether he would be willing to let us put together and finally publish an account of his life and work, he demurred, saying that he would rather not have it done during his lifetime.

Now that Grove Farm has reached its Centennial Year it is eminently appropriate that the story should be told. William P. Alexander, manager at Grove Farm Plantation from 1937 to 1952, has worked diligently on building up a splendid body of research material, proceeding shoulder to shoulder with Bob Krauss in his admirable reconstruction of the life of George N. Wilcox and its relation to the development of Grove Farm Plantation.

Dr. William H. George, Professor of History at the University of Hawaii, was quick to place George N. Wilcox in the history of these Islands, and said to me once: "All of us know how intimately his life has been interwoven with the progress of Hawaii. He is one of the few surviving links between our generation and the pioneers who came from New England to bring the light of salvation to these Islands. I cannot but feel that he is more than a private citizen. He stands like the middle pier of a bridge, supporting a span from each shore. He represents an age that is gone; he lives happily in the present age; and he looks confidently into the future."

All seven of the Wilcox sons were brought up to know their Bible well. One might almost have seen George's whimsical smile as, in his 94th year, he left us to "carry on." Certainly more than one of us heard that last day of his life his quaint caution often given to the young fry in a cribbage game: "Let not him that putteth his armor on boast himself as he that putteth it off."

It was not easy to see him go.

ETHEL M. DAMON

Nu Hou
Grove Farm Plantation
Lihue, Kauai, Hawaii
July 1964

Mahalo

The authors of this book owe a large debt of gratitude to numerous historians, professional and amateur, in Hawaii who helped to gather, check, and edit the material in this story of a man and a sugar plantation.

In almost every chapter there are scenes that could not have been written without the specialized knowledge of many friends and professional associates. Foremost is Ethel Damon to whom the literature of Hawaii owes so much and without whose notes, as well as those of Elsie H. Wilcox, taken during conversations with George N. Wilcox over a quarter of a century ago, there would have been no book at all.

We wish to thank also Mabel I. Wilcox and Gaylord P. Wilcox who watched with patience and constant encouragement as their idea for a commemorative history of Grove Farm plantation grew into this volume.

The authors express sincere appreciation for the whole-hearted cooperation of the staffs of the following organizations: University of Hawaii, *The Honolulu Advertiser, The Garden Island, The Star-Bulletin* Printing Co., Mid-Pacific Institute, Experiment Station of the Hawaiian Sugar Planters' Association, Mission Children's Society, Archives of Hawaii, Hawaiian Historical Society, Library of Hawaii, Kauai Public Library, and, particularly, Grove Farm Company, Incorporated.

To the many, many others who contributed advice, information, criticism, and moral support we tender our deepest and warmest mahalo.

Bob Krauss
W. P. Alexander

Honolulu
February 1965

Contents

Foreward to Third Edition   v

Foreward to Second Edition   vi

Foreward to First Edition   vii

Mahalo   ix

Illustrations   xiii

PART I
The Missionary   1

PART II
The Youth   41

PART III
The Pioneer   117

PART IV
The Statesman   173

PART V
The Family   265

PART VI
The Plantation   331

Contents

PART VII

The Heritage 393

Epilogue 417

The Wilcox Family 423

Glossary 429

Index 431

Illustrations

Facing page

Abner and Lucy Hart Wilcox, 1855 16
Waioli home of Abner and Lucy Wilcox 17
Interior of kitchen in Waioli home 17
George N. Wilcox and Charles H. Wilcox as students
    at Punahou School 80
George N. Wilcox at time he entered Yale University 80
Judge H. A. Widemann, original owner of Grove
    Farm 81
George N. Wilcox at time he acquired Grove Farm .. 81
Thatched roof home of George N. Wilcox at Grove
    Farm, 1865 144
Lihue Plantation Company mill, 1865 144
Wilcox home at Grove Farm, 1874 145
Lihue Plantation Company mill and ox cart, 1880 .. 145
Palace of Princess Ruth Keelikolani 144
Grove Farm harvesting and hauling crews, 1887 144
Wilcox home at Grove Farm, 1886 145
Grove Farm office, 1885 145
Bark *George N. Wilcox* 208
Laysan Island in 1890's, showing guano deposits and
    gooney bird population 208
Inter-Island Steam Navigation Company dock, about
    1895 208
Sailing ships in Honolulu Harbor 208
Malumalu School for Boys 209
"Hapai-ko," hand-loading sugar cane into cars 209
A Fowler steam plow, 1893 209

Facing page

Robert W. T. Purvis, bookkeeper, Capt. Louis Ahlborn, Alfred Holly (Pele) Smith, and E. H. W. Broadbent, Grove Farm managers 240
Grove Farm showing Stable Camp and Lihue Plantation Company mill, 1905 272
First auto on Kauai 272
Harbor at Nawiliwili, Kauai, 1915 272
George Norton Wilcox, 1910 273
Lucy Etta Wilcox Sloggett, director; Henry Digby Sloggett, director and treasurer; Charles Henry Wilcox, general manager; and Ralph Lyman Wilcox, assistant to George N. Wilcox 272
First sled-type sugar cane planter 273
First wheel-type sugar cane planter 273
George N. Wilcox at ceremony marking connection of Koloa and Grove Farm Company's railroad systems, 1930 304
George N. Wilcox's first airplane flight, 1928 304
S. S. Mikahala on the Kauai run, 1915 305
S. S. Hualalai entering Nawiliwili Harbor, 1930 305
Plaque at Nawiliwili honoring George N. Wilcox . . . 305
Elsie Hart Wilcox, director and vice president; Mabel Isabel Wilcox, director and vice president; William Patterson Alexander, manager and vice president; and A. Hebard Case, treasurer and vice president, of Grove Farm 336
Koloa mill, 1948 337
Lihue Plantation Company mill, 1958 337
Grove Farm rock-crushing plant 336
Grove Farm limestone quarry 336
Mauka portion of Grove Farm fields, Haiku Division 337
Makai portion of Grove Farm fields, Haiku Division 337
Grove Farm Koloa mill, 1958 337

Facing page

Grove Farm's bulk seed cane planter, 1962 368
Aerial view of mechanical equipment used on Grove
    Farm, 1963 368
Grove Farm harvesting operation, 1964: Pushing cane
    into windrows, loading and hauling 369
Grove Farm Koloa mill, 1964 368
Nawiliwili Harbor, 1964 368
William Middleton Moragne, manager and vice presi-
    dent, and Gaylord Parke Wilcox, president of
    Grove Farm Company 369
Wilcox home at Grove Farm, 1958 369
Direct descendants of Abner and Lucy Hart Wilcox:
    Samuel Whitney Wilcox, director and vice presi-
    dent; Gerald Wilcox Fisher, director; Richard
    Henry Sloggett, Sr., director; and Albert Hart
    Wilcox, director and secretary 384
Office of Grove Farm Company, 1964 385
Grove Farm Company Board of Directors, 1963 385
Mabel I. Wilcox, 1970 412
Grove Farm Company Board of Directors, 1981 413

PART I

The Missionary

CHAPTER

1

Shortly before five o'clock in the morning on July 15, 1846, a sturdy little trading schooner coasted slowly on the inshore breeze into Waialua Bay on the northwest coast of Oahu, Sandwich Islands. The schooner was the *Emelia*, ninety-six tons. She was owned by M. Kekuanaoa, governor of the Island of Oahu, appointed by His Majesty King Kamehameha III, supreme ruler of this tiny Pacific Kingdom. The Hawaiian captain of the *Emelia* stood now on deck, gazing at the land as the schooner moved toward shore.

Clusters of native grass houses looked like haphazard haystacks in the indistinct light of first dawn. But the big stone church with its thatched roof, and the sturdy white-washed adobe walls surrounding the mission houses, stood out clear against the bleak landscape. There were gardens near the houses strung along the shore of the bay. Cattle grazed a short distance inland. Beyond this the land lay deserted, prairies of high grass and boulders broken by spiny-ridged mountains. As light spread across the sky, the jagged mountain skyline turned from black to mottled green.

Though the *Emelia* was small and her hull scarred from scraping reefs all over the Island chain, the captain had a grave expression on his brown face which gave evidence of the importance of his thoughts. Most of the time the *Emelia* was engaged in the work-a-day business of hauling cargo among the Islands: lumber, hardware, hides, produce for the whaling ships, a little sugar, and molasses. The ship's passengers were usually Hawaiians who slept on deck with their pigs, chickens, and dogs.

Today, however, the *Emelia* would carry passengers of a different kind, a missionary family moving to another station to the northwest on the island of Kauai. The captain didn't understand the missionaries, but he respected them. He knew that the timbers for the big stone church on shore had been dragged by hand from the mountains, that the coral for making mortar had been hauled from the bottom of the bay. He knew also that the church had blown down after years of back-breaking labor. The missionary had simply put his congregation to work rebuilding.

The captain was fond of saying that, in spite of their strange ways, the missionaries were useful. They knew how to grow new crops such as coffee and sugar and cotton, though anyone in his right mind could tell you that whaling would always be the chief business of the Islands. The missionaries taught everyone how to read, even the common people. They had brought doctors and medicines and tools. They knew the secrets of government and business that baffled so many Hawaiians. If only the missionaries could learn to smile. So the reason for the grave expression on the captain's face that morning was because he knew that he would probably forget himself and swear at his seamen while the missionary was on board. It was a painful thought.

The captain's worried expression faded as the *Emelia* eased up to the landing. With a quick glance at the landmarks on shore he bellowed to his Hawaiian deck hands, "Drop the mainsail and stand by the jib! Let go that anchor!" The anchor splashed into the still water, and the *Emelia* swung slowly into the breeze, waiting for her new passengers.

* * *

The day began for thirty-eight-year-old Abner Wilcox as it always did, at five o'clock in the morning when he slid his feet out from under the patchwork quilts and put them down on the cool, bare boards of the bedroom floor. When he and Lucy were married ten years before, she had always risen to pray with him. But it seemed that the Lord, who had blessed her with four babies since then, had more need of her strength than of her prayers. So Abner let her sleep.

Noiselessly, Abner padded across the room where Albert, the two-year-old, lay in his rocker crib. He was a handsome, delicate child. But the cross that weighed on their hearts was the deformity. Gently, Abner lifted the cover from the baby's feet. They lay relaxed in sleep, fully developed but twisted at each ankle. Abner knelt at a window set deep in the adobe wall. "Thy Will be done, Oh, Lord," prayed Abner. "But Thou knowest I do not wish to take the station at Waioli on Kauai. I have searched my heart and cannot find Your call to that place."

A rustle of bedclothes told him that Lucy was awake. Abner opened his eyes as Lucy laid her hand gently on his. She was a small, plump woman with dark hair and brown eyes. Even now Abner was almost ashamed of the pride he felt in having such a comely wife. She smiled at him. Then she knelt beside him and began praying in a soft voice. "Good and most merciful Lord, hear the prayer of my husband whose heart is sore. I know he feels that the mission is sending him to Waioli because others do not want to go, that he feels others do not want him here. If this be un-Christian, then may the others examine their own hearts for Thy Will."

Abner stirred uneasily, his mouth set in a disapproving line at her frankness. But Lucy continued, "Thou knowest that my husband is a teacher, Oh, Lord. Not a pastor nor a farmer nor a mechanic . . . although his work required him to be all of these things . . . but a teacher of the young. He is most contented when he is doing that. Remind him, Oh, Lord, that here at Waialua where we have labored alone without even a pastor, my husband has had to be all of the things he is not. But at Waioli there will be a pastor. There my husband is assigned to do the work he is fitted for. Though the climate be unhealthy and the baby will have no doctor, there my husband can teach. Perhaps, this is the call he seeks."

Lucy squeezed her husband's hand. Abner did not return her smile. It did not seem proper for her to speak about him in this soft, womanly way to the Lord. But Lucy had a knack of mixing the secular and the Sacred in such a way it was difficult to know the difference. Frowning, Abner was getting stiffly to his feet when six-year-old George burst into the room.

The words tumbled out breathlessly, "It's here, it's here! Charles and I saw the ship from the top of the wall. It's come to take us to Waioli!"

Lucy hushed him immediately. "George, the baby!" But it was too late. Baby Albert let out a hungry wail. Confronted by his startled parents and his squalling brother, the boy was horrified over what he had done. He was small and dark with his mother's eyes and coloring.

"See what your thoughtlessness has accomplished?" scolded Abner. But Lucy, who had quieted the baby in her arms, moved between the boy and his father. "It's the excitement, husband. We will all be more ourselves when we're settled at Waioli."

Abner nodded. "Nevertheless, he will spend fifteen minutes

in prayer to compose himself. We will leave you alone, George.
See that you do not stir from this room."

"Yes, father."

The boy knelt by the window and closed his eyes. But the
moment the door latch clicked shut, his eyes popped open.
Nimbly, he climbed into the window seat and stood on tip-toe
where he could watch over the five-foot adobe wall as the
Emelia came to anchor.

* * *

They had been packing busily for over a month, ever since
the General Meeting of the Sandwich Islands Mission, in Honolulu, where his fellow missionaries had voted to send Abner to
Waioli Station at Hanalei Bay on the island of Kauai, one hundred miles to the northwest. Without Brother Armstrong's
Negro butler, who had come from Honolulu to help, Lucy was
sure they would never have managed. It was astonishing the
things a family could collect in a few short years.

Abner's books alone had required two crates, the medicine
chest two more. There was a box of bed clothes and mosquito
netting, another with the whale oil lamps, coffee mill, nut-
meg grater, fire tongs, and butter churn. Lucy's wedding silver
went in with Abner's prized clock, which they had brought with
them ten years before from Connecticut. Then there were
beds, chairs, the desk and bookcase, the koa settee. And they
couldn't leave behind the red wagon that the Connecticut relatives had sent all the way around the Horn for Charles and
George.

As each new crate was added to the pile on the landing, the
Hawaiians made a great game of guessing what was in it. The
captain of the *Emelia* took one look and groaned. But it was
"Betsy Gray," the family mare, and her two colts, that finally
made him balk. Tucking his wad of tobacco in his cheek, he
explained firmly to Abner as the deck hands wrestled boxes

into the whaleboat, "The mission pay me to take one family with household goods up to Waioli on Hanalei Bay, Reverend. One family doesn't include a mare and two colts!"

It always irritated Abner to be mistaken for a minister. But this time, with his two oldest sons listening closely at his side, he swallowed a tart reply and said evenly, "Captain, 'Betsy Gray' is part of the family. It would break the boys' hearts if they had to leave her. I'm willing to pay the extra passage, if necessary."

"Maybe, that come pretty high."

"I doubt if you are the kind of man who would over-charge us, Captain."

"You right about that, Reverend. But you no can pay much either, eh?"

"That is correct."

The captain shifted uncomfortably to his other foot. "I no worry about the money, Reverend, I worry about the space. Where in the name of Jehov . . . sorry, Reverend, am I going to put a mare and two colts aboard the *Emelia?*"

"We might build a pen on deck, Captain. I assure you, my family will not set foot aboard your ship without Betsy Gray!"

The captain looked down at the two boys, a nine- and a six-year-old, flanking Abner. They stood big-eyed and worried, hanging on every word. The oldest had on a pair of pants with rings of unfaded color around the ankles where his mother had let the hem down. The youngest wore a shirt that was patched at the elbows. But they were scrubbed and mannerly. Mission kids, a new element in this land of bare, brown skins and lazy laughter.

"Is that right, boys?" asked the captain. "You no go along with me to Kauai unless I ship that mare and her colts?"

Both boys nodded decisively.

The captain sighed. "Maybe we better take the horses. But I think some people will be surprise at your family."

Then it was time to say good-by. Lucy cried, of course, as church members, all in their Sunday best, hardly a pair of shoes among them, kissed her cheek. The Hawaiian woman who had helped in their kitchen wept over little Albert. The girl who did their washing brought a bundle of food to eat on the ship. Abner's students lined up in uncomfortable, orderly rows as one of them made a farewell address. Each of the leaders of the congregation, huge men who dwarfed Abner's five-feet eight-inches, shook his hand with simple dignity.

To the herdsmen left in charge of the mission cattle, Abner gave last minute instructions in Hawaiian. "Remember, all of the cows that come fresh are to be driven to Honolulu to the mission dairy herd there. But don't run them or they'll dry up. The dry cows in Honolulu must be brought back here. I have counted 254 in our herd. You will account for that number to Brother Emerson when he comes."

With the native teachers of his outlying schools, Abner lingered longest. They were young men, all barefooted but wearing trousers and shirts as their marks of achievement. "I leave the work in your hands," Abner told them with his first show of emotion. "He has said, Go Ye and Teach All Nations. The people are thirsty for your knowledge. It is through you that this nation shall rise to greatness. I know you are badly paid and over-worked, my friends. But this has forever been the lot of teachers. I go with sadness. May we meet again in the Kingdom of Heaven."

The *Emelia's* whaleboat took them to the ship. They took turns climbing the ladder to the deck; Lucy handing up the baby first to Abner, nine-year-old Charles carrying Bushy, the tortoise-shell cat, six-year-old George lugging his pet turtle in a wooden bucket, and five-year-old Edward clutching a toy boat. The captain ushered them aft, just forward of the deck house where the koa settee had been lashed securely against the bulkhead.

To Lucy Wilcox he explained awkwardly, "All full up below so I had it put here. Maybe you and the Reverend and family would like to sit here out of the way while we cast off?"

"I am not a minister," said Abner irritably. "I am a teacher."

"This is very kind of you, Captain," added Lucy smoothly. "Come, children, perhaps he will help you with your things."

The captain gallantly filled his arms with bundles. He was about to aim a stream of tobacco juice over the side when Lucy smiled directly at him. He gulped in confusion, swallowing wad and all. As quickly as he could, he beat a retreat. "Hoist the anchor!" he bellowed in Hawaiian to relieve himself. "Stand by the jib! We're getting underway!"

The untidy old schooner swung slowly toward the open sea. The Wilcoxes sat in a row on the koa bench as the *Emelia* moved out of the bay. Abner's face was bleak. Lucy cuddled her baby, her heart full of compassion for her husband. Charles, George, and Edward sat in stair-step order, their eyes dancing with excitement over this journey to the new land.

* * *

It was a smooth crossing for the Kauai Channel, where currents eddying around the southern tip of Kauai and the northern end of Oahu to the south produce some of the most boisterous seas in the world. Lucy became terribly seasick. She always did. So, all day Friday and most of Saturday Abner was in charge of Edward and baby Albert. The two older boys were allowed on deck by themselves.

After the noon meal, when Abner sent Charles and George off to play, he repeated his usual words of caution. "Be careful and don't fall into the water. And I don't want you to speak to the natives on deck."

"Why can't we ever talk to the Hawaiians, father?" asked Charles, the oldest.

Abner answered impatiently, "I've told you before. We don't want you to learn bad habits from these people."

"Then why do we live in the Islands?"

"The Lord called me here, Charles, to lift up the heathen from their morass of sin. That was before you were born. Now that the Lord has given me sons, I cannot permit them to become contaminated with the wickedness of the heathen."

"But I don't think the natives are so wicked."

Abner's face clouded in anger. "That will be enough. You are not of an age to make such decisions. We will speak no more about it."

"Yes, father."

George, the next oldest son, followed his brother up on deck, grateful to get out of the stuffy cabin. He never argued with his father about wickedness and sin. It didn't do any good. At the age of almost seven, the boy had learned he could get more of what he wanted by doing instead of talking.

They were close in to the island, now, sailing smartly before a steady tradewind. The sunlight danced off the cobalt-blue water flecked with snowy whitecaps. Kauai rose up on the left, her mountains robed in jungle, the surf a ribbon of blinding white spray at the base of the grim coastline of cliffs.

George first saw to his turtle in the Hingham bucket, to make sure the cover was on tight. Yesterday, the turtle had escaped. Papa and Edward had found him crawling on a pile of chains. George removed the cover and squatted over the bucket to admire his pet. The turtle was already as big as a dinner plate. Its beady eyes stared unblinking at the boy. George pulled a morsel of taro from his pocket and held it between thumb and forefinger. The turtle nibbled without fear.

A deep voice rumbled from above, "You lucky boy. Not many people own a Galapagos turtle." It was the captain, so fat and rumpled. But his smile was friendly.

"A sea captain gave him to me," said George proudly. "This turtle came all the way from South America. He's going to get as big as a barrel. When I got him he fit just inside my hand."

"You plenty akamai. What are you going to be when you grow up?"

"A sailor," George announced without hesitation.

The captain was amused. "Maybe your father no like that.

Sailors smoke and drink and make plenty pilikia sometimes."

George answered thoughtfully, "I guess Papa wouldn't like that."

The captain reached down to pat the boy's head. "Your father's a good man. You better listen to him."

Then Charles called from the port side of the *Emelia,* "George, look at the waterfalls!"

They were rounding a bluff that guarded a blue bay ringed with tawny sand at the foot of an incredibly lush, green valley. Along the enormous crescent of beach there were a few coco palms and houses of thatch. Back farther, peeping through scattered trees, was the church, long and low with a thatched roof above plaster walls. Nearby were two frame houses where the missionaries lived. A sizable river flowed into the bay just around the bluff. The whole scene was framed in green mountains. Their craggy tops reached the clouds, and their steep slopes plunged to the valley floor. The folds and crags of these mountains were covered with a dozen shades of green that shifted into different patterns each time a cloud shadow moved across them. And among the mottled green folds were waterfalls, threads of white against the green, one after another, some spreading into gauzy ribbons, some disappearing into the jungle cliffs only to reappear below like faint spider webs in the distance.

George came running up. "I see three, no four!"

"There's another one over there," Charles added, pointing.

"Look on this side. Just look at them! I never saw so many waterfalls!"

"The name of this place is Hanalei Bay," the captain told them. "Over there is Waioli Mission. Waioli means Singing Water in Hawaiian. You listen to the waterfalls tonight, you'll see. But watch out for the rain and mosquitoes!"

The bustle brought Lucy and Abner on deck. She peered anxiously through the trees for a glimpse of their new home. Abner tried to pick out the school house, a thatched building near the church. Then they took the boys below to make them presentable. By the time they emerged once more, brushed and fitted out in their Sabbath clothes, the *Emelia* had anchored close to the mouth of the river. A large crowd of natives and a small cluster of white residents waited on the beach at the landing.

"There are the Johnsons!" cried Lucy, waving impulsively.

"It is better to preserve our dignity before the natives," Abner reminded her.

She answered warmly, "But, husband, there is dignity in a welcome between friends. I have hardly seen Sister Johnson since we sailed together from Boston ten years ago. Is it a sin to feel joy at the sight of familiar faces?"

The captain personally helped them into the boat. On shore, the greeting party included The Reverend and Mrs. G. B. Rowell, whose house the Wilcoxes were taking, obviously impatient to get their things on board and be on their way to Waimea, their new station on the other side of the island. There were the Johnsons with their brand new baby. Motherly Mrs. Johnson, half a dozen years older than her husband, was Abner's age. Brother Johnson, who had been teaching the school Abner would take over, was to be ordained a minister so that he could take the pulpit Brother Rowell was vacating. But most of the faces were strange: salty Captain Kellet, the port pilot; taciturn Charlie Titcomb, the Yankee coffee planter; and hundreds of staring Hawaiians. Abner stiffly acknowledged the introductions. They went on endlessly as each teacher from the country schools in the district and each church member came forward to shake hands. Half-way through, it began to drizzle, and before the hand shaking was over, the rain was torrential. Abner, refusing to take shelter, was soaked to the skin.

He began to cough before the party, splashing through the mud on horseback, reached the mission houses a mile away. Brother Rowell, looking back wistfully at his baggage still piled on the landing, tried to smile. "Well, here we are, Sister Wilcox. This is your new home. It was built by Brother William Alexander, the first missionary to Hanalei, ten years ago. He laid up the chimney with his own hands."

It was a square, frame house of two stories. A dining room had been added and then a pantry which connected the cookhouse to the main building. The cookhouse was thatched, but the roof of the main building was covered with solid sheets of grey zinc. Several were coming loose. As they stepped up the sandstone walkway and entered the sitting room, Lucy suddenly felt dejected. A small section of ceiling plaster, loosened by rain, came dribbling to the floor. Other sections, she could see, had been repaired after similar disasters.

Abner sneezed. Then he coughed once more. Lucy glanced at him with concern in her eyes.

"We've had exceptionally heavy rains this year," Brother Rowell apologized. "That ceiling has kept me jumping, and I just haven't found time to fix the roof."

Abner sneezed again. His hair was wet. He looked about the room unsmiling and said, "I plan to repair the roof as soon as we are settled, Brother Rowell. With God's help my wife and family will soon have dry shelter." Then he sneezed again. Lucy longed to touch his hand, but she knew he would never permit it.

CHAPTER
2

Abner had a hacking cough by the time he set out on Monday for his first day of school at Waioli. Brother Johnson stopped by after breakfast to walk with Abner through the rain, past the kukui trees in front of the house to the grass-thatched building nearby where forty-eight students were waiting. They sat on lauhala leaf mats spread on the dirt floor. Their desks were boards placed on blocks.

Brother Johnson led the way to the rough-hewn table at the far end of the room. "We have a dire shortage of text books, Brother Wilcox," he said apologetically. "But I don't imagine that makes Waioli much different from the schools at your past stations. However, this is probably the most remote station in the Islands. For that reason, many of the students are still quite primitive. Some of them never had seen a knife and fork until they came here."

Abner interrupted, "What subjects have you been teaching them?"

The younger man smiled. "Ah, yes, that's what really interests you, isn't it, Brother Wilcox. As you know, this is a Select School, that is, a school to which the most promising students are sent from Common Schools all over the island. Luckily, the Hawaiian government is now beginning to support the Common Schools, relieving the mission of that heavy burden. Our purpose here is to supply teachers for the Common Schools all over Kauai and to send exceptional scholars to the Seminary at Lahainaluna on Maui for basic college work. So, you see, the entire educational system of this island will rest upon your shoulders."

"Yes, yes, I know," said Abner impatiently. "And the subjects?"

"Well, in addition to reading, writing, and arithmetic, I've been able to give them classes in geography, geometry, astronomy, moral philosophy, and, for the best students, a one-hour class three times a week in English. Otherwise, the entire school is conducted in Hawaiian. Oh, yes, one other thing." Brother Johnson nodded toward a Hawaiian standing respectfully at the side of the room. "You are fortunate to have an assistant, a graduate of the Lahainaluna Seminary."

Abner's eyes ranged over the pupils, boys in their teens and young men in their twenties. He saw immediately that they were poorly dressed. All wore trousers and shirts, but some garments were so ragged that they served no purpose.

Brother Johnson sighed. "They don't look very handsome, do they? But the parents of these students can't afford anything better. Most of these boys arrive here owning two shirts and two pairs of pants. They board with Hawaiian families here at

Abner and Lucy
Hart Wilcox, 1855

Waioli home of Abner and Lucy Wilcox from 1846 to 1869

Interior of kitchen in Waioli home after restoration

Waioli, members of the congregation. Since the students work for their keep, they have precious little time to earn money for themselves. However, they do spend three afternoons a week of school time on the school farm to pay their tuition. You realize, of course, that your duties include superintending the farm, disposing of the produce, and keeping the accounts."

This time it was Abner's turn to sigh. "Yes, Brother Johnson, I know. I had thought when I left Connecticut that I had seen the last of farming. Now I'm doing more of it than ever. What have you planted this year?"

"We cultivate a large taro patch and four acres of yams, potatoes, beans, corn, and bananas. Actually, the school realizes very little from the farm because there is an insufficient market for our produce here, except when a whaling ship stops in the bay for provisions. . . ."

Brother Johnson obviously enjoyed talking with someone new, but Abner cut him short. "Yes, I understand. Now, may I meet my assistant, Brother Johnson, and get to work?"

"Of course, Brother Wilcox."

* * *

It was a full month after they landed at Waioli before Lucy finally had time to sit down and confide in a letter to her best friend, Sister Sarah J. Lyman, at the mission station in Hilo on the island of Hawaii, three hundred miles to the southeast. She wrote, "Rain, rain, rain. Mr. W. coughs and wheezes and feels completely down in body and mind, too. I do not think his health will ever be any better while he remains so low spirited. I do not feel that duty called us here—but, stop—I feel resolved to look on the brightest side. . . ."

The only physician on the island of Kauai, Dr Jared K. Smith, two days away in Koloa, prescribed cold showers for Abner. Lucy watched his diet, trying to get him to eat nourishing foods. But Abner continued to cough. Almost three months passed with no improvement. Lucy wrote to Sister Lyman, "It is all rain, rain now. Mr. W. complains almost constantly of a stricture and pain in the chest, expectorates a good deal and a good many times during the last six weeks blood. From the way he is affected after it, he is pretty sure it comes from his lungs. I keep up pretty good spirits, though I feel very much concerned about him. Our houses are so near the mountains that we have dampness and showers almost constantly. Yesterday and today it has rained almost all the time as hard as it can pour."

In time, the house was repaired so that it was warm and snug in spite of the rain. Finally, even the rainy season came to an end. Abner's cough lessened until it was only a minor irritation, but he couldn't seem to regain his strength. In her prayers Lucy told the Lord what she would not dare tell her husband, "Most gracious and understanding Father, please watch over Abner and give him peace. It is not the wetness that gives him sickness but his own dissatisfaction. He is hurt, Oh, Lord, and feels that he has been made an exile. He needs to hear Thy Call to this place. Please, let him hear It soon."

* * *

The boys were delighted with their new home. One morning Charles discovered that the second story veranda of their bedroom, the one with the post in the middle to hold up the floor, was a perfect place from which to spy on ships that sailed into the bay. From then on, the veranda was their crow's nest. There they spent hours watching the bustle aboard the big, weatherbeaten whalers that dropped anchor sometimes in the harbor. Their father was always glad when the ships sailed and his Hawaiian students could get their minds off of sailor's tales and back on arithmetic. But Charles, George, and Edward treasured every minute of a ship's arrival. From their lookout they could see the tall masts and intricate rigging, the crowd of excited Hawaiians on shore, the whaleboats plying back and forth with water casks and provisions.

Once in awhile a strange sailor or two, with that indescribable air of the open sea about them, would attend church on the Sabbath. This was a real windfall, for the Sabbath was the dullest day of the week. It began with prayers at home in the morning and continued with an interminable service in the thatched church. In the afternoon, their father conducted his own service at home where he read a chapter from the Bible, then asked everyone to kneel for prayer to be followed by a chapter which he read in the life of a missionary. After this they prayed again. Next came a sermon by their father, they all prayed once more, and then it was all over. For the rest of the day the boys were allowed to walk in the yard and look at the flowers. There was no running, tree-climbing, or talking in a loud voice. In the evening, each of the boys had to recite seven verses of scripture from memory. But a sailor or sea captain in church helped, almost as much as a dog fight during the sermon or a lizard running across the floor so that all the women squatting on the lauhala matting clutched their skirts around them.

Saturdays were much better. Often Abner would say, "All right, boys, let's go swimming." He had never learned to swim, but he was determined that his boys should have the opportunity. For safety, he made each of them wear a life preserver of air-tight gourds. Together they would tramp off to the Waioli River where the water was cool and mountain-fresh.

Next door, all of the Johnson children except one were girls. So the Wilcox boys made up for their lack of playmates by keeping pets. These animals always seemed to mind George the best. The boy, now a small and inexhaustible seven-year-old, had a firm, patient way with them. His turtle had grown too big to fit into a bucket. There was also the cat. And one day George came home with a black dog named "Smut," which Mr. Titcomb, the coffee planter, had given him.

"Smut" refused to stay at home, and every few days he would return to old man Titcomb's place up the river. Actually, the coffee planter was a year or two younger than Abner, but he was a gruff, outspoken Yankee with a sunburned face and fiery red hair. All of the children in the valley except George were afraid of him. One afternoon George came looking for "Smut" just as Mr. Titcomb, in his high boots and slouch hat, was mounting his big, black horse. Mrs. Titcomb, a pretty Hawaiian woman, called from the cookhouse, "Aloha, Keoki," to the boy. He waved back.

"What's the matter, ye lose that poi dog of yours again?" Mr. Titcomb asked brusquely.

"Well, he's not at home," George answered without flinching.

"Ain't ye got anything better to do than traipse around after a no-account dog?"

The boy nodded. "As soon as I get home I'm going to learn my Bible verses for the Sabbath."

Mr. Titcomb's lips curved in the hint of a smile. "That ye will, if I know your father. Well, there's time for other things, too. How would ye like to ride along with me to look at the coffee pickin'?"

George's eyes sparkled with excitement. None of his brothers had ever seen the coffee picking. But he hesitated. "Maybe I'd better ask first."

"Can't wait that long. You comin' or not?"

George took a deep breath, then nodded. Mr. Titcomb stepped into the saddle. He reached down with a wiry arm and lifted George up behind him. All thoughts of guilt were flooded away by the exquisite rush of new sensations as they started up the valley along the river to the coffee fields.

First they came to Titcomb's Landing where there was a scow used to ferry people and horses across the river. George knew that Hawaiians once earned money by taking people across in their canoes, then swimming their horses over. Papa said he'd still rather do it that way because the ferry scow was so rickety it frightened the horses.

Farther along they passed the grass thatched houses of the

Hawaiians, each house built upon a low platform of rock. The yards were fenced with hedges of thickly planted ti leaves or walls of stone to keep out the livestock, but the chickens, dogs, and pet pigs wandered in and out of the houses with no hindrance. Most of the men wore the malo, and the women, wraparounds. Some of the women, especially the old ones, didn't have on anything above the waist. Blushing, George guessed this must be one reason Papa didn't allow him to go out among the natives. Children ran about with no clothes at all; but none of them seemed the least embarrassed, and everyone waved and smiled at Mr. Titcomb as they passed.

"Friendliest people in the world," he observed as they rode along. "They'll give ye the shirts off their backs if ye don't have one. Don't know the meaning of saving against a rainy day. It ain't laziness. Not by their lights. It's common sense. The chiefs take whatever they want. If ye raise a good, fat pig and the chief sees it, all he has to do is say the word and it's his. If ye store up some fish against a famine and the chief he gets hungry for dried fish, he takes yours. If he don't, all of your relatives move in and eat it for you. If ye don't give it to them, ye are stingy and sinful because the worst sin these people know is selfishness. No, sir, for a kanaka it don't pay to save an' get rich. The smart Hawaiian, and there's plenty of them, mark my words, he earns himself just enough to live on every day. That way he doesn't make anybody jealous, and the chief leaves him alone. The way I see it, the kanaka ain't lazy, he's just smart."

It was a long speech for Mr. Titcomb, and George didn't understand all of it. But it helped pass the time as they made their way through patches of big-leaved, velvety, green taro growing in paddies bordered with sugar cane. Here and there a Hawaiian was standing thigh deep in the mud weeding a patch or pulling up enough of the big, potato-like tubers to feed his family.

Then they came to the coffee fields. The small, bushy trees, heavy with bright red berries, stood in orderly rows. Men, women, and children, all Hawaiians, moved along the rows gossiping as they stripped off berries and put them into lauhala mat bags. Mr. Titcomb rode among the workers, joking with some in Hawaiian, sending others back to pick berries they had missed. The coffee would all be carried to the mill farther up the river in bags suspended from poles carried on the shoulder.

Mr. Titcomb rode into another field nearby where the coffee was not quite ready for picking. Silent, he dismounted. George watched from atop the horse as Mr. Titcomb inspected the berries, then stopped and picked up a handful of soil, letting it trickle through his fingers. He remounted, and they sat looking over the broad acres of coffee stretching along the flat floor of the winding valley.

"One thousand acres of coffee," Mr. Titcomb said softly. "Mighty pretty, isn't it, son. I suspect all we New Englanders are farmers at heart, your father included, for all the books in that big cabinet of his. God knows, I never figured on growing coffee in Hanalei Valley when I took up watchmaking twenty years ago. Couldn't stomach it. So I went to sea. That didn't satisfy me, either."

"Were you really a sailor, Mr. Titcomb?"

"That I was. Until I saw these islands from a whale ship. I saw all the green things growing, and I said to myself, this is the place for me. Can't say I'm getting rich. Gone broke more times than not."

"What's gone broke?"

Mr. Titcomb chuckled. "It's like this, son. I left my ship in Lahaina on the island of Maui. Planted sugar cane. But the rats got it, and I went broke. Well, I moved over to Koloa on the other side of this island and planted cotton. It wouldn't grow, so I went broke again. Then I put in mulberry trees for raisin' silk worms, and the blight came. After I went broke, I moved over here. Mulberry grows like a weed in Hanalei. Sure enough, we had a good crop of mulberry trees. The silk worms thrived on it, and I even taught the Hawaiians to reel silk. At last, I had me a crop, a good one, top grade silk. But I couldn't sell it, so I went broke again."

"Why do you keep trying, Mr. Titcomb?"

"Well, son, I don't know. Probably for the same reason your father keeps trying to pound some learning into the heads of those Hawaiians in his school. Pure cussedness. But I'll tell you this. These islands are fertile as the Garden of Eden. There's a crop that's going to grow here that will make these islands rich beyond our dreams. Maybe it's coffee. I hope so. Whatever it is, I'll find it. Unless I die first."

"You won't, Mr. Titcomb."

The planter gave a noncommital grunt and urged his horse on the homeward path. To George's relief, his father did not ask where he'd been.

Shortly after that visit "Smut" was caught eating chicken eggs, and Abner insisted they get rid of the dog. Solemnly, George and his younger brother, Edward, trussed "Smut" fore and aft to a stick with strips of hau bark as they had seen Hawaiians carry pigs to market. They marched off to a clump of trees with the stick on their shoulders, "Smut" yowling indignantly between them. At the appointed place, they put the dog down and prepared to dash his brains out as they had seen Hawaiians do. But neither boy had the heart to strike the first blow. So they let "Smut" go. When Abner heard what happened, he gave the dog to a Hawaiian. Several days later George passed the Hawaiian's grass house to find "Smut's" hide on the ground near the imu where the family cooked its dinner in the underground oven. That evening George couldn't eat.

* * *

The fifth son was born September 19, 1847, a little over a year after the Wilcoxes had moved to Waioli Mission. They called the child Samuel Whitney, after the beloved pioneer missionary on Kauai who had died of consumption two years before. A daughter of Mr. Whitney stayed with Lucy during her confinement.

One night after their house guest had gone, Abner carried a candle up the steep, creaky stairs to the Prophet's Room, where he had his desk. It was called the Prophet's Room because here all the visiting missionaries slept. Here, also, Abner did his letter-writing at a large table with cubbyholes built along the rear edge. Downstairs, Lucy and the baby were asleep. Across the hall, the four boys had settled down for the night. Thoughtfully, Abner struck a lucifer match. It refused to light because the sulphur was damp. Impatiently, he struck again. The match spluttered into flame. Abner applied it to a small whale oil lamp. Then he selected a sheet of paper from a neat pile and a goose quill from a stand. Dipping the quill into a bottle of ink, he wrote swiftly in a legible but ungraceful scrawl:

"Waioli, Sandwich Islands
"Mr. Charles Wilcox
Harwinton, Connecticut
Dear Brother Charles,

The letter you wrote me dated February 23, 1845, and June 28, I received May 13, 1846. That is the only letter I have received from my friends since the reception of the box in the summer of 1844 . . . ."

Abner sat and stared into space. It would take the letter he was writing at least six months to reach the familiar old house in Harwinton. It was like writing to another planet.

"In relation to ourselves, I am able still to mention the loving-kindness of the Lord towards us. He has hitherto preserved all of us alive. And I may say, too, that we enjoy a portion at least of health. Neither Mrs. W. nor myself enjoys sound health. I have little doubt in regard to myself that, should I live, premature old age will come upon me. I have many infirmities upon me now."

Abner's pen stopped midway to the ink well. How many had come out in his company of missionaries on the barque *Mary Frazier* from Boston eleven years ago? Thirty-two. Of that number, one-fourth had died and only seventeen remained in the Islands.

"We now have five sons. The last was born the 19th of the past September. He was baptized in our own house last Sabbath and called Samuel Whitney. Our children are all well. The three oldest are of an age to perform some work, but we have little for them to do. They need to be brought up with some good farmer. They study their books some, and their parents are their only teachers. We have never allowed them to learn the language of the Sandwich Islanders. It is our endeavor to keep them away from the natives, for their influence on the children would be bad. What we shall do with them, or rather what the Lord will do with them, we know not. I hope these islands are not to be their home. . . ."

This thought had been with Abner for some time now. He knew it was on Lucy's mind, also. What would happen to the boys when they reached manhood in their backward islands? Where were the opportunities for earning a comfortable living, for finding a respectable wife? For himself, Abner longed for the privilege of intelligent conversation, of a forceful sermon delivered in English. How weary he was of his students' pranks, of the incredible void in the minds of all but one or two. And, in spite of all his patience and inhuman expenditure of energy, what good did it really do to fill that void? Of what value was geometry in this forgotten outpost? Abner reached for a new sheet of paper.

"With Charles, George, and Edward we have a school daily. Albert is too young to learn from books. Charles is now in his tenth year and has made considerable progress in geography and arithmetic. He is quite a reader of books and history. George is naturally rather slow but in other respects a bright and active boy. Edward learns more easily than George and can read and spell quite as well. Albert is a kind and affectionate boy of good mental capabilities. But he is unfortunate by being lame in his feet. He was born with curved feet, a deformity which seems to cleave to us. Who did sin, this child or his parents, that he was born with crooked feet?"

Frowning, Abner picked up the sheet of paper and read what he had just written. With a quick motion, he crumpled it in displeasure and reached for a clean sheet. When he was finished, he folded the letter into a small square and addressed it on the outside. His brow was furrowed with worry. Albert's deformity, he knew, was a terrible weight on Lucy's heart. If only there was something a doctor in the islands could do. Both Dr. Wood and Dr. Judd in Honolulu had made attempts. But Albert's feet remained as crooked as ever. In fact, neither doctor had really hoped for success since they were not skilled in the treatment of such cases.

Since Albert was born, Abner and Lucy had tried shoes to keep his feet straight; iron springs to stretch the muscles; and bandages. Nothing had helped. They had ordered an apparatus from Boston, only to be told that it could not be used successfully except by a skilled practitioner. But the same doctor had written to say that he could straighten Albert's feet by means of a surgical operation if they would bring the child to Boston.

With a rueful shake of his head, Abner drew his battered family account book out of its cubbyhole. He knew the figures on the inside pages by heart. His salary from the mission was $450 a year. For each child, he received an allowance of $30 for a total annual income of $600. Out of that he fed and clothed his family, kept his horses and other livestock, subscribed to magazines, and bought the books for his library which was Abner's most prized possession. In addition, he was constantly out of pocket for repairs to the house and the school. There was also the considerable cost of denim he bought every year to make shirts and pants for those students who couldn't afford them.

No use thinking of taking Albert to the United States for an expensive operation on that salary. Abner put the account book back into its cubbyhole. There was only one way to solve all of his problems: the futures of his sons, Albert's deformity, his own bad health at Waioli. But he had never even let himself contemplate this alternative. It was to quit the mission and ask the Board to send his family back to the United States. Other missionaries had done it. But could he? Where was his first duty, to his family or to the mission?

That night he tossed a long time before he went to sleep. For a full month he wrestled with himself. Then, on the night of November 18, 1847, Abner seated himself at his desk and, with his chin set firmly, reached for a sheet of paper. Rapidly, before his courage failed, he wrote:

"Waioli, Sandwich Islands

"Dr. Rufus Anderson, President
"American Board of Commissioners for Foreign Missions
Boston, Massachusetts
Dear Rev. Anderson:

Our fourth son, born in the spring of 1844, was born with club feet and has been a cripple ever since. . . ."

Abner poured out the story on paper, the first crushing knowledge of the deformity, the futile attempts to correct it, the insurmountable obstacle of distance from qualified medical help. He told about the lack of opportunities for his children, about his recurring cough. For all these reasons, he asked to be sent home. When the letter was finished, Abner sealed it before he had time to change his mind. The next day he put it aboard a trading schooner to begin its long and doubtful journey to Boston.

CHAPTER

3

The answer arrived in Honolulu one year and two months later. It took another month to reach Waioli Mission on Kauai. In February, 1849, Abner took the precious letter up the creaky stairs to the Prophet's Room where he could be alone. With trembling fingers, he slit open the envelope. The message was brief and sympathetic.

Mission funds were at a new low. In fact, the American Board of Missions in Boston had felt it necessary to advise the Sandwich Islands Mission that the Board was forced to gradually withdraw all support. It was hoped that the missionaries in the Islands would find the means to sustain themselves, ministers by their congregations, teachers by their students. However, because of Abner's special case, the Prudential Committee of the American Board had voted to pay the expense of an operation and passage to the United States for Abner's crippled child and one of the parents.

Abner was so disappointed he had hardly the courage to show the letter to Lucy. She read it carefully, then put it down with a worried frown. "Husband, I could never take little Albert on such a long journey alone."

"And I have no desire to return to the United States unless we can all go to stay," said Abner firmly.

Lucy sighed. "Perhaps it is not to be. If it is the Lord's will, I am content."

Abner's tone was bitter. "Others have been sent back, whole families. Why should we be refused?"

"Perhaps it is because you are needed here, husband," she said softly.

"I wish I knew."

Next spring, Abner's fellow missionaries in the Islands voted a resolution at their General Meeting in Honolulu recommending the return to the United States of Brother Wilcox and family for reasons of health. With this encouragement, Abner wrote another letter to Boston.

This time his sense of futility was greater than ever. The gold fever in California had hold of everyone. Charlie Titcomb and two other planters, Hermann Widemann and G. F. Wundenberg, were deserting their crops for a fling at quick fortunes in the gold fields. Most of Abner's best students and many church members were following their example. Worse still, epidemics brought in on the ships were rapidly thinning out the native population. Even in isolated Hanalei Valley, the number of Hawaiians was down almost a third.

Most discouraging of all to Abner was the growing conviction that his job here was finished. The Sandwich Islands were no longer a pagan but a Christian nation with churches dotting the landscape. Though destitute and backward, the native Hawaiian by and large exhibited a piety that compared favorably with more civilized peoples. The natives were also adopting Western ways, and all of those in authority used English almost as much as the native tongue. In fact, Abner in his lonely outpost on Kauai was among the few missionaries in the Islands still proficient enough to teach in Hawaiian. In the face of all this, Abner wrote, he felt his work no longer served the purpose which brought him to the Islands.

In January, 1850, the reply came back. Since Abner was

among the few missionaries in the Islands who still taught in the Hawaiian tongue, he was more valuable to the mission than ever. Though funds were low, the Board would underwrite a journey to Boston for the crippled child and one parent.

"Husband, it would not be right to reject an opportunity to cure Albert's deformity," Lucy said after she'd read the second letter.

"But which of us is to go with him?"

"You must go," she urged.

"No, you can look after him better."

"Not on a sea voyage. I get so horribly seasick."

"But I cannot possibly go. Who will look after the school, the farm, the herd?"

"I can do it," Lucy answered with spirit. "Don't forget, husband, that I was a school teacher before we were married. Brother Johnson will take some of your duties, I'm sure. And Edward is growing up enough to be a big help in the house."

Abner gave her one of his rare smiles. "Dear wife, it is too much for you. I would not think of it."

She smiled back, "Then, dear husband, I must tell you my secret. I cannot go because we will have a new Wilcox in the family before the year is out. It should be in July, I judge; and, unless I miss my guess, he'll be another boy. I've given up having a girl."

Lucy was right. They called the baby William Luther. Lucy was dangerously ill for three months before the baby arrived. Abner insisted he would not leave her. But, by fall, she felt stronger. He began making plans. On November 2, 1850, the family set out on the path from the house to the landing where a schooner waited to take Abner and Albert to Honolulu. The boy rode a horse for the first time by himself. He was six years old, a plump, handsome lad with a mouth that turned down like Abner's when he was in a sulk.

At the landing, Abner was awkward as usual. He stood stiffly beside Lucy as Edward, age nine, and Samuel, not quite three, clung to her skirts. Charles and George, ages twelve and almost eleven, were away at school in Honolulu.

"Give my love to the older boys when you see them," Lucy said. Her eyes were filled with tears.

"Yes, I will."

"And write as often as you can, dear husband."

Abner swallowed hard. "I shall. It is my hope that we will be back in a year or less if we are able to get return passage via the Isthmus of Panama."

"I will pray for you."

"And I for you."

Albert, frightened of being alone with his father, began to cry as the boat left the beach. On board the schooner, they stood at the rail. Abner waved once, a self-conscious farewell salute. But Albert kept waving to his mother and his brothers until they were tiny specks on the great arc of jungle-fringed beach in the Valley of Singing Waters.

* * *

They arrived in Honolulu four days later. The barque *Croton* that was to take them, together with other returning missionaries, to Boston was not due to sail for another month. Abner and Albert stayed in a room at Punahou School for missionary children where Charles and George were attending. A new problem arose almost immediately. Samuel Northrup Castle, one of the business agents for the Mission, brought the news to Abner. He was a tall, quiet man constantly harrassed by the job of trying to spread meager mission funds too thin. "Brother Wilcox, I have excellent news," he cried as they met on Fort Street in Honolulu. "It appears there is no longer a need for your long voyage to Boston."

Abner's jaw dropped. "How so?"

"I have just met a new doctor named Hardy. He arrived from New Bedford, where he had an extensive practice, only a few days ago. I was very impressed with him as I am sure you will be. He carries excellent letters of recommendation, one from our own mission president in Boston. Best of all, he is sure he can straighten little Albert's crooked feet."

Hope surged through Abner. But years of disillusionment made him ask, "What prompted him to come away so far?"

"He learned of Dr. Winslow's profitable practice at the seamen's hospital in Lahaina on the island of Maui where so many of the whaling ships come to provision. But the hospital is fully staffed, and he came on to Honolulu."

Brother Castle, a head taller than Abner, hurried him along the dusty street, dodging buggies and ox carts as they made their way between rows of box-like frame stores with false fronts. One block down, on the waterfront, the bowsprits of sailing ships tied to the docks aimed their spars into the heart of town. Brother Castle steered Abner into a stairway that led to an office overlooking the street.

Dr. Hardy was slightly younger than Abner, affable and poised. He seated his visitors, then took his place behind a large desk. He leaned back, placed the tips of his fingers together and said, "This is indeed a pleasure, Mr. Wilcox. Or is the proper address, Brother Wilcox? You shall have to teach me for I am a newcomer in your lovely land. My practice has been in New Bedford, Massachusetts. Of course, I have visited the hospitals in Boston and New York."

Abner asked, "Perhaps you are acquainted with Dr. Brown of Boston?"

"Of course," answered Dr. Hardy with a casual wave of his hand. "I believe Mr. Castle informed me that it is Dr. Brown to whom you are taking your son. I cannot say that I fully approve, Mr. Wilcox."

Bewildered, Abner said, "But I have investigated him thoroughly. He has a fine reputation. One of my friends spoke with him. The report he brought back . . ."

"Please, Mr. Wilcox, I wouldn't dream of disparaging Dr. Brown's integrity. He is a fine, honorable man. It is simply that his method of curing club feet is, shall we say, something less than completely successful."

"I don't understand."

"Mr. Wilcox, there are two methods of straightening a congenitally deformed foot. The most radical method is to sunder the tendons in the foot, then hold the foot in the correct position by means of a shoe or a brace until the tendons heal in that position."

"That is Dr. Brown's method," nodded Abner.

"That is correct. You must understand, however, that this is a new procedure. New methods don't always work. For example, Dr. Brown employs the use of ether during surgery. Why, five years ago such a thing was unheard of in the United States! Do you not hesitate to entrust the welfare of your child to such novel procedures?"

"What is your method?"

"Let me show you." Dr. Hardy rose smoothly to his feet and went to a cabinet. He took out a heavy, complicated framework of steel bars, leather straps and screws. "This brace is fitted to the child's foot. By turning up this screw, or any combination of screws, the foot can gradually be brought to the correct position."

"But is this not painful?" asked Abner.

"Unfortunately, it is quite painful. But it is safe. With this method you have only to wait until the tendons stretch and relax ino a normal position. This may take a year or more during which time the child suffers rather severe and constant pain. However, I feel quite sure I can cure any club foot if the parents will have the firmness to witness such pain for a considerable time."

"You see, Brother Wilcox, that's what I told you," Brother Castle broke in.

"Dr. Brown writes of effecting a cure within several months and that with relatively little pain," Abner said slowly.

Brother Castle answered with feeling. "But think of the long and dangerous voyage to which you are needlessly exposing your son. May I add, also, that the expense will be considerable. We are dealing with the Lord's money, Brother Wilcox. You have it in your power to effect a desperately needed economy."

"Could you subject your child to this torture, Brother Castle?"

The other missionary opened his mouth to speak, then closed it. After a time he said gently, "I understand your feeling, Brother Wilcox. Pray upon it, and give me your answer when you have made up your mind."

Within a few days Abner's dilemma was table conversation among all the mission families in Honolulu. Everyone gave advice. The mission wives told Abner to write to Lucy which he had already done, begging for her opinion. Brother Castle kept tactfully urging against the ocean voyage. Others suggested that, if they had to choose between a year of torture and doubtful surgery, they would drop all thought of a cure entirely. The Rev. Daniel Dole, principal at Punahou School, advised Abner to hurry and make up his mind one way or the other.

Meanwhile, the *Croton* was loading and almost ready to sail. No letter had arrived from Lucy. Desperately, Abner wrote, "Having been bandied and tossed about for so long, I feel rather inclined to go ahead." Still no answer. The sailing date was set for Saturday, December 7, 1850. Abner spent his spare hours on Friday pacing the waterfront hoping to spot a sail from Kauai. None came.

Saturday morning he prayed fervently. "Oh, Lord, am I exposing my wife and sons needlessly to a year of loneliness and hardship? Am I exposing Albert needlessly to a perilous voyage? If I am, Oh, Lord, tell me now before it is too late!"

His face was composed when he appeared on the dock an hour later, Albert's little hand firmly in his. As they were boarding, the boatswain turned them back. "Sorry, mister, we ain't sailin' this morning. Had a little collision with a ship leaving the harbor. Got to make some repairs."

That afternoon a boy put a letter into Abner's hand. It had arrived on board a small, decked boat with a schooner rig from Kauai. The letter was from Lucy. She wrote, "Dearest Husband, I think you should take Albert to Boston as we had planned for so long. Do not worry about us. We can manage."

Abner heaved a sigh of immense relief. The following Monday a group of missionaries, wives, and children sailed for Boston. The group included missionary pioneer Mrs. Lucy Thurston and her daughter, the Rev. Mark Ives, two teenage children of the missionary physician Dr. Dwight Baldwin, a son of the Rev. P. J. Gulick, and Abner and Albert Wilcox.

* * *

After so many years of anxiety, the operation on May 17, 1851, in Boston, seemed absurdly effortless. A few days after it was over, Abner wrote to Lucy, "The four external wounds show about as much as flea bites. On his right foot, Albert wears simply a lace boot with a spring on one side and on the other foot a curious and complicated apparatus hard to describe. . . ." Now there was nothing to do but wait until the muscles healed in the new positions.

Abner's optimism waned as summer came on, and he remained cooped up with Albert in a hot, little room in the downtown Boston boarding house for the patients of Dr. Brown. May dragged into June. Then June into July. Abner wrote nostalgically in his diary. "How I miss the tradewinds that make even the hottest days tolerable in Waioli."

The tendons in Albert's left foot healed too rapidly, causing severe pain when Dr. Brown tried to pull the foot into a normal position. Night after night, Abner held his sobbing son in his arms, trying to ease the pain. The doctor operated once more. Abner, hollow-eyed and exhausted, felt more alone in Boston than he ever had at Waioli. One bit of news gave him grim satisfaction. Toward the end of July a mother brought her daughter as a patient to Dr. Brown. The girl had club feet. She had been treated by Dr. Hardy, the mother said, who "left her feet more crooked than before he had nearly tortured the poor girl out of her mind."

The days dragged on, dreary, endless days of discouragement. Abner's spirits were at their lowest ebb when Dr. Anderson at Mission Headquarters called him to his office. The mission executive was a dynamic, decisive man with a direct gaze. He waved Abner to a seat and got right to the point.

"Brother Wilcox, the members of the Prudential Committee of the Board and I have been reviewing your case, and we have come to the conclusion that we may have been a bit hasty in denying your request to bring your family to the United States."

Abner couldn't believe his ears. Dr. Anderson went on.

"As you know, passage for you and your son came to only $250. This is quite reasonable. We don't expect the cost of the operation and your living expenses to total more than $250. We are grateful for every economy as the demands for funds to carry on the Lord's work increase every year. And, frankly, the churches are not contributing as they used to."

"Yes, I know that," said Abner, almost holding his breath in suspense.

"Now, then, it would seem that we can bring your wife and the rest of your family here almost as cheaply as we can return you and your son to the Sandwich Islands. Therefore, since you have expressed a desire to leave the mission, we now ask if you approve of this plan? Mind you, we have no desire to see you go. Without men like you, the work cannot progress. But you have earned a rest. What do you say?"

Abner swallowed. No words came. Dr. Anderson smiled. "I know it isn't easy. Why don't you pray on it, Brother Wilcox? Let me know when you have made up your mind. But I would appreciate having your answer as soon as possible."

Abner walked back to his room in a daze. At last it had come, his chance to be free of the unending work, of students who never wore shoes, of the remoteness from civilized conversation. By the time he reached his room he was deep in thought. If only he knew what Lucy wanted.

On August 12, Dr. Brown reported heartily that the end was in sight. "I think you may begin making plans to leave here, Mr. Wilcox. Albert is just about ready to take off that brace and put on his second shoe."

"Thank you, doctor," said Abner absently. He had been day-dreaming, wondering if Lucy had been able to keep order in the mission school.

As the time grew short, Abner became more and more absent-minded. His thoughts kept returning to the Valley of Singing Waters. How cool the breezes there, in spite of the heat! How satisfying the rich Hawaiian voices blending in a hymn on the Sabbath in that little thatched church!

He could picture Lucy, rosy-cheeked, preparing a meal for the boys. Well, she would no longer have to contend with a smoky fireplace. He was sending back an air-tight stove of the most modern design. He could see in his mind Charles and George riding their horses on the beach. There was a new saddle in one of the boxes he had sent to Lucy. And the turtle, now grown so big he couldn't get out of the pig pen where they'd put him for safe keeping after he'd wandered off several times. Abner knew he was homesick even for that ridiculous turtle.

But most often his daydreams returned to the thatched school. Had Lucy managed to provide the students with denim for pants this year? Were there enough books to go around? Had Lahainaluna Seminary taken his best students? More important, had Lucy succeeded in filling all the vacancies for teachers in the Common Schools? How desperately the Islands needed teachers!

Only a few days more. The doctor had pronounced Albert fit to be released for traveling on August 21. Abner had tried over and over to compose a reply to Dr. Anderson. If he went back to the Islands, what was to become of his children in that primitive land? If the mission withdrew its aid from the Waioli School, Abner wasn't even sure he could support himself. And yet, he found himself remembering the words he had used in his original letter to Dr. Anderson fifteen years ago asking to be sent out as a missionary.

How did that letter go? "I know it is a great thing to bid adieu to one's home and friends—it is trying in the extreme to give the parting hand to aged parents, to dear brothers and sister, to amiable companions and kind neighbors. And yet I think I covet the honor of helping to spread that Gospel which is one day to bless all nations."

He smiled, now, at those high flown words. How much of the Gospel had he been able to spread in a tiny valley on a speck of an island in the middle of the Pacific Ocean? How short had he fallen from the dreams he once had of educating a nation? However, he knew that in spite of everything, he still meant every word that he had written fifteen years ago.

At last he picked up his quill and wrote with a firm hand what was in his heart, "Now to speak plainly, I want to go back and labor as formerly. My family is there. They expect me. The natives expect me, too . . . Leaving out of account the welfare of our children, I think the preferences of Mrs. Wilcox and myself are decidedly in favor of spending our days at the Sandwich Islands. . . ."

He wrote for a solid half hour. Then he slipped the paper into an envelope and mailed it to the Rev. Rufus Anderson at Mission Headquarters.

* * *

As the schooner nosed in toward the landing, her young captain said, "Well, you're home, Mr. Wilcox. How does it feel?"

Abner let his eyes follow the graceful arc of beach, tawny

under the late afternoon sun. Through the coconut and kukui trees he could glimpse the familiar white house. Higher up, in the green folds of the mountains, he could follow the filmy tracery of the waterfalls. "It feels good, Captain," said Abner.

The anchor splashed down, and the schooner swung gently into the wind. Only a handful of natives clustered at the landing. It was the Sabbath. Lucy and the children, of course, would be at home. Besides, there hadn't been time for Abner to let her know he was back.

The captain cleared his throat delicately. "Goin' ashore to-day, Mr. Wilcox?"

He knew that the missionary company, back from Boston, had arrived in Honolulu on the Sabbath a week ago. Rather than break the sanctity of the Lord's Day, Abner and Albert Wilcox and Charles Gulick had stayed on board the ship until Monday. The captain had also heard the story of the shelf in Abner's house where all letters were kept that arrived on the Sabbath. They were never opened until the next day.

Abner hesitated. He looked wistfully at the white house where Lucy would be waiting. Then he squared his shoulders. "Yes, Captain, I think I shall go ashore today."

The captain smiled broadly. "And nobody is going to blame you for it, Mr. Wilcox. A year and five months is a long time."

It was an endless mile from the landing to the house. Abner had difficulty making the boys walk sedately as they must on the Sabbath. But, by the time they reached the gate, there was no holding them back. They went whooping into the house. A moment later, Samuel, now five years old, burst out of the door. He got as far as the sandstone steps and stopped, staring at his father. Abner stared back hungrily.

"My, you've grown, Samuel. Do you still have your turkey red dress?"

The boy stood, round-eyed, until Abner could almost touch him. Then he turned in fright and ran inside. But it didn't matter, for Lucy was there. For a long time there was only breathless, tender, teary confusion. Finally, she said, "Oh, dear, whatever am I going to fix for dinner for so many?"

But she managed. That evening Abner smiled fondly around the familiar table at his family. Then he folded his hands, and they all bowed their heads.

"We thank Thee, Oh, Lord, for preserving us on our long journey. We thank Thee also for the successful operation upon Albert's feet. But most of all, Oh, Most Merciful God, we thank Thee for reuniting our family under this roof tonight. Bless this Thy food. Amen."

As he picked up his fork, he turned to Lucy and said impatiently, "Now, tell me what has been happening in the school?"

PART II

The Youth

CHAPTER

4

Abner spent those first days getting to know the boys again. He showed little Samuel how to gather hala seed pods from an enormous, gnarled tree in the yard to burn in the new Franklin stove. To Edward's delight, Abner put him aboard the turtle and sent them plodding around the house. Abner even gave Charles and George permission to ride out alone on "Betsy Gray's" colts, now full grown horses.

He was so exuberant and carefree that Lucy waited a week before she showed him the letters from Mrs. Charlotte C. Dole, housemother at Punahou School in Honolulu and wife of the principal, the Rev. Daniel Dole. Abner read the letters and frowned. "Send for George," he ordered.

The boy was small for a twelve-year-old. He had an oval face with a rounded chin and a straight nose. His brown hair grew down to his ears in the fashion of the day. The twinkle in his eyes and the whimsy that turned up the corners of his mobile mouth gave him an elfin look. But his smile faded when he saw his father's face.

Abner said sternly, "I am sorry to hear, George, that you have caused Mrs. Dole anxiety. She writes that you purchased marbles without permission on the New Year. Surely you know that dancing and the playing of cards, chess, and marbles are not permitted in the school?"

"Yes, father."

"Do you also know the reasons for these regulations?"

"Dancing is immoral. Cards, chess, and marbles are used for gambling."

"That is correct. Mrs. Dole writes that she did not actually see you play with the marbles. I want to know, did you play marbles in your room?"

The boy answered quietly but firmly, "Yes, father."

"Have you an explanation?"

"No, sir. I just wanted to see what it was like to play marbles. We didn't gamble."

Abner began to speak, then paused in thought. "I respect your honesty, George, but I don't understand your disobedience. You have moral courage, yet you disobey."

"We are concerned about you, George," Lucy said softly. The boy hung his head.

Abner continued, "Mrs. Dole also writes that the next day you and some of the boys bought lemon and sugar for which you paid a rial. And that you drank it all in one day. Who gave you permission to do this?"

George bit his lip. "Must I have permission for everything, father? Mother gave me the money."

"I told him he could spend it as he wished," Lucy said quietly. "But, George, don't you think the rial could have been spent for something more worthwhile than lemon and sugar?"

"Yes, mother," the boy answered unhappily.

Abner glanced down at the paper in his hand. "Mrs. Dole also writes that you do not like to study and that you have kept your classmates back in geography. Is this true?"

George nodded.

"I hope you realize that the rest of our family does without many things so that you may have an opportunity for an education. The cost of keeping you and Charles in school comes to over two hundred dollars a year, more than one-third of my salary. Surely you owe it to us, if not to yourself, to study."

"Yes, father," said the boy. By this time he was miserable.

"Lately he has been doing better," Lucy said to Abner. "I think he has learned a lesson. You will try harder after this, won't you, George?"

"Yes, mother."

"Now run and play. Take a ride if you like. But be back for supper." With a worried smile, she watched him go. George was different from the others. Beneath his pranks and his teasing was a kind of quiet fury. She often wondered where it would lead him.

* * *

When it came time for Charles and George to go back to Punahou, Abner insisted that Lucy go along. "A few weeks in Honolulu will be good for you," he said. "You haven't seen a new face since Albert and I left for Boston. I can take care of things here." Lucy finally agreed.

On July 23, 1852, the two boys and their mother set out on a three-day voyage to Honolulu. They took with them home-made wooden chests filled with the new school clothes Lucy had been hand stitching for months, several bulging carpet bags, a Hingham bucket packed with food to eat on the way, and an enormous bag full of Waioli oranges. George got terribly seasick.

Though he had told no one, the boy had made up his mind to become a scholar. He wasn't quite sure how he would accomplish this. But once he set his mind to something he seldom gave up until it was done. On the first day of school, before dawn, he stumbled out of bed at the clang of the bell in the dining room in the old adobe building where the students roomed. He hastily pulled on his clothes and hurried outside to get his hoe and join the others in the short hike down the slope to the corn field. There Brother William Harrison Rice, a gaunt man with a painful cough, set the boys to work earning their tuition. Missionary children went to school free, but there was a charge of seventy-five cents a week for board. The school met expenses by growing taro, corn, bananas, cucumbers, and melons for sale in Honolulu.

George attacked the weeds with his new-found sense of high purpose. The other boys smiled at his enthusiasm. "You're really digging into your studies this year, aren't you, George?" called rangy Sam Alexander, a top student and Punahou's champion boxer.

George grinned back. "Watch me get an A in this course, Punahou-hoe-hoe-hoe-hoe!" The other boys picked it up, laughing in the pale dawn, their lusty young lungs sending the chant down the barren slope as their hoes moved in rhythm, "Punahou-hoe-hoe-hoe-hoe!"

It was an exhilarating moment. He was the smallest in his class, almost the smallest boy in school. It wasn't often he found a way to lead all the others.

At seven o'clock the bell rang, and George hurried back to his room to wash up for breakfast. He finished before Charles, who shared the small room, and got to the dining hall before any of his classmates. They lined up at the tables. Each student recited a verse from Scripture. Then they sat down to eat, the teachers in the center with the platters of food between them, the students at the ends of the tables where they couldn't help themselves. Instead, Miss Marcia Smith, in a stiff black dress with a small white collar, served them from the platters: a bit of taro, three slices of cucumber, half a slice of bread, and a tumbler of water.

George was the only boy who didn't ask for a second helping. When he poured water from the pitcher into his tumbler, he was careful not to spill a drop. Miss Smith, who wore her hair in ringlets and her mouth in an expression of disapproval, favored him with a smile. After breakfast there were morning prayers. Then George made his bed with unusual neatness and swept the room.

By nine o'clock, when the bell rang for classes, his mind was afire with lofty ambition. The students from Honolulu, all carrying their dinner pails, had arrived from across the plain. Some were on foot; some came by mule or horseback; some were in carriages driven by their parents. Most of the students were missionary children, although Punahou had been opened the year before to non-missionary children as well. The girls wore high, black, laced shoes with white stockings, hoop skirts, and ribbons in their hair. Most of the boys were dressed in made-over, tight-fitting trousers and short waist coats with patched elbows. Nearly all of them came to school barefooted.

They all assembled, over forty of them, in the first floor classroom of the new two-story, stone building that Brother Rice had built. It was a large room, about sixty by thirty feet with a twelve-foot high ceiling. The walls were covered with bookcases and cabinets where students stored their collections of land shells.

A hush fell over the group as the Rev. Daniel Dole, the principal, mounted the platform in the front of the room. He was a tall, slender, rumpled man who was reserved, extremely dignified, and very scholarly. With his best Latin students he was pleasant, even jovial. But students who mixed up the tenses of their verbs found him abrupt and impatient. George, who had seldom managed to please the principal, was afraid of him.

First there was a lengthy prayer. Then the principal lifted

his head. "It is my pleasure, students, to welcome you to Punahou's eleventh year. We are not a large school, and in our short history we have suffered many reverses. Yet, by God's Grace, we continue to prosper. You should take pride in the knowledge that you are attending the only English college preparatory school west of the Rocky Mountains." Here the principal permitted himself the ghost of a smile. "Unless, of course, you travel on to the British Isles."

The students laughed politely. A fierce loyalty to his school welled up in George's breast.

"We are an unusual school. Here at Punahou we teach you to till the soil. But we also teach you the classics, Latin and Greek, German and French. For those who wish it we teach algebra and geometry, geology and astronomy, composition and music. Here at Punahou, we plant the seeds of knowledge as you plant seeds in our gardens. There is value in both activities. Here we prepare you for the journey through life. Every lesson learned well at Punahou is a lesson in right living."

As the Rev. Dole paused for emphasis, George resolved to study as he had never studied before.

"However, you will not have the advantages here in the Islands that scholars have in the United States. We live in a half-civilized country lacking in refinement and culture. Indeed, our graduates now attending colleges in the United States have become known humorously as 'Cannibals.' William DeWitt Alexander, now studying at Yale, is known by his classmates as 'Fiji Aleck.' "

The students burst out laughing.

"Yet, those same classmates will find 'Fiji Aleck' a well-rounded scholar. I well remember a time at Punahou when this 'Cannibal' read several chapters ahead of his Latin class in order to see how 'Caesar' came out. That 'Cannibal' will make his mark someday. May you younger students of Punahou leave your marks just as high!"

As George walked out of the room, he had a clear picture

of himself as he left his "mark." He would be lean and scholarly like Mr. Dole. He would stand before a group of attentive professors and recite 'Caesar' until their mouths dropped open. But the inspiration did not last long. As his classes progressed, George's work was just as it had always been. Composition and spelling were a constant trial. He was inept at music. Languages baffled him. However, with numbers he did well, and he was fascinated by the classroom experiments of the older students studying astronomy or physics.

Classes ended at 4:30 P.M. Then, as the Honolulu students trudged home across the plain, the boarders got ready for supper. After the meal, the boys marched into the corn field with their hoes. When the first two stars were visible in the evening sky, they were allowed to go back to their rooms. There each student took his pail and fetched water from the spring for washing the next day. After that everyone settled down to study, that is, unless there was a meeting of the Debating Society. In that case, the members gathered in one of their rooms and argued until eight-thirty, when the bell rang. By nine o'clock the students were in bed.

The Punahou Juvenile Debating Society met on Wednesdays. George belonged to the Society, not because he enjoyed making speeches, but because it got him out of studying one evening a week. No matter how hard he tried, George couldn't make a speech. The moment he got up before an audience, his mind went blank. To make up for his shyness he had done a lot of clowning at the meetings. He'd been censured twice the year before by a vote of the older Society members for demoralizing the debates. This year he had behaved himself, but he still hadn't made a speech. So Charles was elected president for the winter quarter. That evening they selected as their next subject for debate: "Is tobacco more harmful than good?"

It was a daring subject. Not even the teachers were permitted to smoke at Punahou. But this time George was determined to get into the argument. As usual, he told no one of his plans.

The following Saturday he walked three miles across the plain to Honolulu, made a purchase, and walked back. By Wednesday night he was ready. The boys met quietly in Nathaniel Emerson's room. He wasn't there because it was his turn to churn butter for Mrs. Rice, who did the cooking. But the discussion went on without him.

Charles Wilcox made the first speech, boldly supporting the cause of tobacco. Samuel Conde, another missionary's son, spoke just as firmly against the "evil weed." One after another the boys got up and pitched into the argument. The debate grew hotter. By this time the speakers were waving their arms and pounding the table for emphasis. Finally, it was George's turn. The other speakers were startled to silence when he got up and made his way to the table. His expression was grave, but there was an elfin twinkle in his eye. Without speaking a word, he took a cigar from his pocket, struck a match to it, and puffed a large cloud of smoke toward his audience. Then he quietly sat down. A perfect uproar followed. Worse still, the cigar was cheap and vile smelling. George nearly gagged on it, and his eyes watered furiously. When the uproar subsided and the members took a vote, the tobacco side won.

*   *   *

Charles dressed as if he'd always just stepped out of a tailor shop. He wrote neat letters home from school regularly once a month. By 1854 he stood eighteenth on Punahou's list of some fifty students. George ranked twenty-eighth, four places behind Sanford B. Dole, son of the principal. George's shoes were usually scuffed. He hardly ever wrote home.

When he did write, it was about ships in Honolulu harbor. During class periods he would glance longingly out of the window and down the slope, past the clusters of grass houses and the native fish ponds, past the fringe of coconut palms on Waikiki Beach, and out to the cobalt-blue Pacific where as many as a dozen weather-stained whale ships sometimes ploughed majestically through the waves as they stood off and on outside Honolulu harbor, waiting for an anchorage. It seemed to George that he would never grow up.

Then, suddenly, everything changed. Early in 1857 the new president of the school, Professor Edward Beckwith, announced that he was closing Punahou for lack of funds. He was leaving immediately for the United States where he hoped to raise money, study advanced methods of education, and hire a new teacher. The news swept through the school like a grass fire.

That evening, after hoeing, nobody could get to sleep. After George had turned out the lamp and climbed into bed, he asked his brother in the darkness, "What are you going to do, Charles?"

The answer came promptly from across the room. "I'm going to ask Father if I can go to California."

George bounced up on one elbow. "What do you think he'll say?"

"He won't like it, but he'll let me go. This is my last year at Punahou. I'm almost nineteen, and I've got to leave some time. Mama's brothers have moved to California. I could stay with them."

"I'll go along," said George eagerly.

"Don't be silly. You have to finish school."

"I can come back when it opens again."

"You know father won't let you."

George sighed. "Just for once, I wish I was the oldest. How long do you think you'll stay?"

Charles paused. "I'm not sure I'll come back. The way I look at it, there's a future in California. Lots of people are making fortunes there. Here in the Islands . . . well, it's so backward. What kind of position can I get? Teaching school for three hundred dollars a year? Clerking in a store? They keep talking about sugar cane. But has anybody ever made it pay? It's just like tobacco and cotton and coffee and all the rest."

"Maybe so," said George doubtfully.

"Even men with experience can't get decent pay in the Islands. I could name you a dozen examples. Look at Mr. Rice. He spent ten years at Punahou experimenting with crops that might grow in this climate. Everybody says he's the best agriculturist in the Islands. Remember when his consumption got so bad the doctor told him to find an easier job and they offered him the managership on that new Peirce Plantation at Lihue? I found out what they're paying him, the best man in the kingdom. Four hundred dollars a year!"

George answered quietly, "Yes, but he gets his house free, and he can raise most of his food, and the plantation let him buy a sixteenth interest. He doesn't even have to pay it right away. They're taking it out of his salary. Someday . . ."

Charles snorted. "Someday! Someday before long that plantation will go broke like all the others. Everybody says so. Except Old Titcomb and he's lost his shirt so often he doesn't miss it. Now the blight's got his coffee, and he's right back where he started twenty years ago, planting sugar cane. Is that the kind of future you want me to look forward to?"

"I guess not."

"Well, I don't either. I want to go where there's a chance to get ahead. You can't blame me for that, can you, George?"

"No, I can't blame you," George answered. After his brother went to sleep, he lay awake for a long time staring into the darkness, a troubled frown on his face. He had been waiting so long to grow up. Now he had the uncomfortable feeling that it was happening to him. He wished it weren't so complicated. Most of all, he wished he could go to California.

CHAPTER
5

At first, Abner absolutely re-
fused to hear of Charles going to California. He said grimly,
"All of my life I have regretted my lack of a college training. I
am determined that my sons should not make the same mistake
if I can prevent it. Of all the boys, Charles, you have the quali-
ties of a scholar. I have always had high hopes for you. Your
mother and I have saved a small amount . . ."

"But, father, in California I can earn enough to pay my own
way to college."

Abner's face was bleak. "If you go to California, Charles, you
will never go to college."

"College isn't everything. At least, in California a person has
a chance to make something of himself. It's better than staying
here in the Islands. Anyway, I want to earn my own money. I'm
old enough."

"Mr. Rice has an opening in the plantation store at Lihue.
You could take that."

"Father, that's only a part time job," Charles replied impatiently.

"It is a start, my boy. And you will be living among God-fearing folk. In California you will surely learn the ways of the world more easily than those of God."

"I'll be staying with Uncle Albert and Uncle Miles Hart, father. Mama's brothers are God-fearing, aren't they?"

In the end, Abner gave up. But he turned to George and said, "We will ask Mr. Rice if you may have the position at the store."

Charles sailed for California from Honolulu on May 21, 1857, on the bark *Yankee*. George wasn't there to see him off. Instead, he had set out for the plantation early one morning. He rode "April Fool," a frisky mare. Edward and Albert walked along as far as the river crossing. Then George was alone. This time he didn't whistle. He remembered how gruff Mr. Rice could be when something didn't please him. George tried to picture himself in the store. How would he ever learn where everything was on the shelves? What if he couldn't remember the prices? The longer George rode, the more hollow his stomach felt.

He rode steadily along the short inland trail through the mountains instead of riding along the seacoast. But he didn't see the stately hardwood koa trees towering above the ferns. When he stopped to let "April Fool" blow beside a waterfall, the music of the stream fell on deaf ears. It was thirty miles to the settlement at Lihue. George covered the distance by late afternoon, but as he approached the plantation, he pulled "April Fool" to a slow walk.

Ahead he saw a thick grove of grey-trunked kukui trees with silvery-green leaves. Nearer, along the edge of a valley, was a long, low, white house with green shutters looking out on a vine-covered veranda. George knew this was "Koamalu," where the Rices lived. Beyond, he could see a village of flimsy bamboo huts with sugar cane thatching. Hawaiian plantation workers lived there. A homely, pock-marked Hawaiian came around the corner of the white house. When he saw George, he smiled broadly. This was Opunui, who had adopted the Rice family over twenty years before. George waved, feeling better. He dismounted and pushed open the gate. He walked to the door, squared his shoulders, and knocked. A pretty, brown-haired, fifteen-year-old girl opened the door. Her face, with wide-spaced eyes and a generous mouth, broke into a smile.

"Why, George Wilcox! What are you doing here?"

George smiled back shyly. The girl was Maria Rice, a few classes behind him at Punahou. "I'm going to work in the store. Didn't your father tell you?"

"He's so busy he forgets things. I'll scold him for it, you wait and see. Are you going to stay with us?"

"No, I think I'll stay upstairs over the store. That's what your father . . . "

"And what are you going to do for meals? I'll bet you don't even know how to fry an egg."

George shook his head, the color rising to his face. "I guess not."

Maria turned and called into the house, "Mother, George Wilcox is here. He's going to work in Papa's store. He'll eat here with us, won't he?"

"Of course, he will," a cheerful voice called from inside.

Maria turned back to George with a smile. "You see? Papa should be here soon. Why don't you come in and sit down?"

"Where is he?"

"He's down at the mill. I think the rollers got stuck again."

George shifted uncomfortably to another foot. He was always tongue tied when he talked to girls. "I'd better go tell him I'm here."

"Oh, pooh! It's too late to open the store today. Come in and tell us the news from Waioli."

The thought of gossiping with Maria and her sisters didn't appeal to George at all. "I'd better go," he blurted. Then he fled.

He turned his horse down the dirt road that followed the

edge of the valley. Below him he saw the placid mill pond, rushes breaking the surface at this end. At the far end of the pond stood the mill with its red brick chimney towering over the squat, warehouse-like factory. George pulled "April Fool" to a halt and sniffed the air. What was that faint smell, a sweet-sour odor like fermentation? Then he recognized it. Molasses!

He rode on past the village of bamboo huts, into the deep shade of the kukui grove, and out where two enormous grass-thatched, open-sided sheds overlooked the valley. An ox cart, piled with a mess of wet, crushed cane stalks, had just reached the top of the slope. Six oxen pulled heavily against their yokes as a husky Hawaiian urged them on, his bull whip cracking like pistol shots.

George watched the cart lumber into one of the sheds where Hawaiian women unloaded the cane trash. Other women were busy turning over piles of the wet cane already unloaded. George knew that this was a drying shed. Here the discarded cane stalks, with the juice squeezed out, were turned into fuel for the mill fires. Another ox cart appeared on the opposite slope of the valley, headed down to the mill. That must be a load of fresh cane coming in from the field.

George felt a tingle of excitement as he urged "April Fool" down the steep trail toward the mill. He had always been curious to learn by what magic those bulky loads of cane stalks were transformed into little, brown grains of sugar. As he came close he could hear the rush of water over the mill dam and the busy splashing of the water wheel. He tied "April Fool" and walked to the door of the mill. Stepping around a yoke of oxen, he recognized Mr. Rice, as gaunt as ever, huddled with a group of Chinese workmen around a pair of big stone rollers that were set up one over the other.

"Try it now, it's free!" shouted Mr. Rice.

One of the workmen pulled a long lever while two more jumped on the spokes of a heavy flywheel to start it turning. The rollers began to revolve slowly, much more slowly than the water wheel which drove them. Fascinated, George studied the gears which accomplished this. He watched curiously as a Chinese workman wearing a pigtail picked up an armful of cane stalks from a pile unloaded from the ox carts and fed the stalks by hand, a few at a time, into the rollers. Dirty cane juice, mixed with field dirt and bits of cane stalk, trickled into a catch basin below and ran off into a spout. George was so busy watching the grinding that he didn't notice Mr. Rice step up to him.

"Well, George, I see you got here, all right. What do you think of our mill?"

"It's a dandy!" George answered enthusiastically, his shyness forgotten.

Mr. Rice's raw-boned face was lined with fatigue, but he seemed pleased. "Our machinery is as modern as anything in the Islands. Those rollers weigh three and one-half tons . . . granite, shipped all the way from China. We use mostly water power, some steam. That's because we don't have enough water for a twenty-four-hour operation. Have to let it back up in the mill pond during the night."

George nodded in understanding. Mr. Rice went on, speaking as he would to another planter. "You see how we use pumps to take the juice to the clarifiers. From there the juice runs into the boilers. In most places, they scoop it all from one operation to another . . . "

The plantation manager broke off in a fit of coughing. "What are clarifiers?" George asked.

"Come here and I'll show you." They walked deeper into the mill to a battery of vats set over ovens. "Here's where we remove most of the impurities from the cane juice. The process is called clarification, and it's as tricky as threading a needle in the dark. First we mix in milk of lime . . . "

Mr. Rice smiled at George's bewildered expression. "That's a mixture of powdered lime and water. If you don't use enough lime the sugar grains won't form. If you use too much, the grains come out dark and the sugar doesn't bring such a good price. To make it even more difficult, no two batches of cane juice have the same sugar content so you have to keep changing the formula."

He would have moved on, but George held back to ask, "How does the lime work?"

"It coagulates the impurities. We stir it in gently, then slowly bring the juice to a near boil, then let it settle and scum it. After that we give the juice a quick boil for about ten minutes and let it settle again. In about thirty or forty minutes the clear juice can be drawn off the top."

George nodded eagerly. "I see."

"Want to take a look at the boiling house?"

George nodded again, his eyes sparkling with excitement. He was completely absorbed in this sequence of ingenious processes. Mr. Rice led the way into another big, barn-like room where five shallow iron pots, about six feet in diameter, flaring at the lips, were bolted together in a long row. The pots, diminishing in size, were set in a brick oven. An enormous Hawaiian, naked except for a loincloth, his skin glistening with sweat, threw chunks of wood and cane trash into the fire to keep it going.

The scene was like a painting by Rembrandt. In the late afternoon dusk, the flames threw weird, flickering shadows against the factory walls. The syrupy liquid in the pots bubbled and gurgled in violent agitation throwing up clouds of steam. Muscular Chinese workmen, as naked as the Hawaiian, handled long, oar-like sweeps with which they skimmed off the frothy scum that kept coming to the surface of the boiling juice.

A voice with a French accent shouted down from a platform above. "More wood, stoker! Give me heat! Now we are soon ready for the strike. This time it must be good. You lazy loafers, get ready!"

The man was swarthy and compact. He thrust a long pole into the last pot in the series, then lifted the pole, one end dripping cane juice. Skilfully he let some of the juice drip into a jar of water. It hissed for a moment. He reached in and lifted a hardened, taffy-like string of dark brown material to the light, rolled it between his thumb and forefinger.

"Make the strike!" he shouted dramatically. "Quickly, quickly! Do you want it to burn? Quickly, or we feed it to the pigs!"

One of the Chinese workmen ran forward with a long-handled wooden ladle. Smoothly, he scooped the boiling mass from the last pot into a spout that led to the next room. In a few moments the pot was empty. Then the workman began ladling juice from number four pot into number five, working at the same breakneck speed. Next, juice from pot number three went into pot number four. By the time he was finished, the man with the ladle had transferred the juice in each pot to the next. Then he filled pot number one with fresh cane juice. When it was all done, the man on the platform climbed down and stalked out of the mill giving Mr. Rice a curt nod as he passed. "Now I have my supper," he said without a glance at George.

Mr. Rice sighed as he watched him go. "That's Victor Prevost, a Frenchman from the Isle of Bourbon, the best sugar boiler in the islands. He's cantankerous, but we couldn't get along without him. Before he came we ruined more sugar than we made."

"What's so hard about boiling sugar?" George wanted to know.

"If you have ever watched your mother making taffy, you'll understand. Making sugar is just as ticklish. The whole purpose of boiling the juice is to transform it into sugar crystals, the maximum number of sugar crystals possible. To do that, the temperature has to be just right, about 288 degrees, the juice must be boiled the proper length of time, and the sugar boiler has to know exactly when the maximum number of sugar grains have formed. That's when it's taken off the fire and ladled into the cooling vats. It's called a strike."

"How does the sugar boiler know when to make a strike?"

Mr. Rice shrugged. "That's the art, George. If I knew, we wouldn't have to pay him. But Prevost is worth every cent. I just wish there were more men with such skills in these Islands."

George still wasn't satisfied. His eyes darted around the room in quick, perceptive glances. "Why are there so many pots?" he asked.

"You see how they get smaller as you go down the line? Well, as the juice gives off steam it gets thicker and the level drops below the rim of the pot. It's hard to skim off the scum when that happens. In a smaller pot, the level comes back to the top. By the time the juice reaches the last pot it has not only boiled off most of the impurities but has reached the proper density for forming sugar crystals."

George shook his head in admiration. The whole process was so simple, yet exciting. Here were men outwitting nature with her own weapons. Once before in his life he had felt this surge of excitement. That was the time, as a very young boy, when he had grasped the principle which permits a full-rigged ship to sail into the wind.

"I'll show you the centrifugal, and then we'd better hurry to dinner or Maria will scalp us," Mr. Rice said, hurrying George into another part of the mill. George recognized the small steam engine, but the purpose of the tub with the round, brass wire cage in the middle eluded him.

Mr. Rice explained, "The stuff that comes out of the boiling room is a mass of molasses and sugar grains all mixed together. The next step, after the stuff has cooled, is to separate the molasses from the sugar. Less than ten years ago, mill operators simply let the molasses run off. It was a slow tedious process; and by the time it was done some other fellow had usually flooded the market with his sugar, and the price was way down. A fellow named D. M. Weston from New England changed all that."

"You mean the man who started the Iron Works in Honolulu?"

"That's him. He was just a mechanic when he came to the Islands. But he had the good sense to apply the principle of centrifugal force to separating molasses from sugar. Watch!"

A workman spaded some of the sticky, black mass from a cooling vat into the brass cage. He tossed a few pieces of wood into the furnace of the steam engine, then pulled a lever. The brass cage inside the tub began to revolve slowly, quickly picking up speed. As it spun faster and faster, the black mass inside spread against the walls of the cage. Then the molasses began to seep through the screen. In a short time, only sugar crystals remained inside the wire mesh. The molasses had collected in the tub outside.

"We pack the sugar in half kegs for shipping," Mr. Rice said. "Kegs are more sturdy than native mat bags. The molasses goes through another boiling or two because there's still quite a bit of potential sugar in it."

That evening at the supper table, George scarcely heard Maria's teasing about being late, nor the chatter of the younger Rice children: twelve-year-old Emily, ten-year-old Willy, eight-year-old Mary, and three-year-old Baby Anna. Mrs. Rice, a slim, motherly woman who used to mend George's socks at Punahou, glanced at him several times. Finally, she asked, "Is anything wrong, George?"

"No, ma'am. I was just wondering how much all that machinery in the mill must have cost."

Mr. Rice smiled grimly. "More than you or I will ever have, George. That's what makes this such a risky business. If the crop is good and the price of sugar is up, the owners can make a potfull of money. But if it doesn't rain, or the cane borer gets you, or the price drops, or any one of half a dozen other things, you lose your shirt."

"I think I might like it."

Mr. Rice said dryly, "Well, I hope you like the store as well as you do the mill, because that's where you'll be spending most of your time."

George flushed. "Yes, sir," he said and went on eating.

*   *   *

George awoke before five o'clock in the morning in his little attic room over the store, eager to start his new job. His confidence had come back. He lay in bed for a few minutes daydreaming. He pictured himself in the store, wisely advising a customer which medicine to buy for a toothache. Then an even more appealing picture came into focus. He was waiting on Maria Rice, deftly slipping a bolt of calico off the shelf, as he had seen storekeepers do in Honolulu, and draping the fabric suavely over his arm. Maria was watching him in secret admiration. The daydreams faded immediately after breakfast when Mr. Rice said hurriedly, "George, this morning I want you to go down to Nawiliwili landing and meet the schooner when she comes in. I'm expecting a load of freight. Here's the order. See that nothing is left on board."

"Who's going to watch the store?" asked George.

Mr. Rice waved his hand impatiently. "You won't open the store until afternoon when the men get off work. Mornings I'll expect you to do odd jobs and help me with the plantation books. I know you are good with figures. That's the reason I gave you this job."

"Yes, sir," said George. So he was to be merely an errand boy.

"Oh, yes, and don't forget to ask the captain for the mail."

George rode "April Fool" into the valley, past the mill and up the other side where a small settlement of frame and grass houses stood on the plain overlooking the mill. About a mile beyond the settlement was the ocean. Mr. Prevost, the sugar boiler, and his wife lived on this side of the valley. The plantation stables were here, kept by a Hawaiian named Hoopii. A former landmark, the big Hawaiian church, had been torn down in 1853 and rebuilt across the valley, but the original bell still hung on its wooden frame where it now served as the plantation's work signal. A rutted dirt road led off to the left to the cane fields.

George rode straight ahead and a little to the right on another dirt road that sloped gently down to the sea. Here on the beach were more grass houses and a few coconut trees. The schooner was anchored in the bay. A gang of Hawaiians, all wearing the malo, splashed in and out of the water as they unloaded boxes and machine parts into an ox cart from a whale-boat moored about twenty feet from the beach. Nearby stood a tall, mustached man in a planter's outfit consisting of broad-brimmed hat, baggy coat, and knee high boots. A sailor wearing ragged trousers and a seaman's cap was directing the unloading. When he spotted George he called, "You from Peirce Plantation?"

George nodded. The planter glanced up, appraising the young man on the horse with sudden interest. George pretended not to notice.

"Better check this stuff against your order," said the sailor. George dismounted. He eyed the load of strange-looking boxes on the cart with a sinking heart. He didn't have the slightest idea what was in them. He hesitated, feeling foolish.

"What's the matter, boy?" asked the sailor.

"Nothing," said George.

"You're new, ain't ya?"

George's pride wouldn't let him admit it. "Oh, I've been around for a while," he said. He dug into his pocket for the order Mr. Rice had given him. When George glanced at the paper, he frowned in dismay. What was a bleeder valve? When he looked up, he saw an amused smile on the planter's face. George took a deep breath.

"All right, I'm ready if you are," he said briskly.

"Go ahead, it's all yours," said the sailor.

"Bleeder valve," George said distinctly.

"How's that?"

"I'm checking your cargo against the order," George answered tartly. "Sing out, please. Bleeder valve!"

"It's right there, can't you see it?" the sailor said pointing to what looked like a small metal faucet.

George ignored him. He made a check beside the item, then called, "Two dozen hickory shirts."

"They're over here," said the sailor reluctantly.

George made another check. "One hundred barrel staves."

"On the bottom," said the sailor.

George heaved a sigh of relief when he finished the list. As he was putting the paper in his pocket, the man in the planter's outfit walked over and held out his hand. "Nicely done, Mr. Wilcox," he said with a grin. His voice was deep with a marked German accent.

"Thank you, but I don't believe I know . . . "

"I'm Judge Widemann, Hermann to my friends," the tall man said pleasantly. "I also have worked in the plantation store. But I think you handle the job much better than I ever did." He chuckled. "Wait till I tell Charlie Titcomb how you faced down that third mate."

"Do you know Mr. Titcomb?"

The judge smiled. "Before I became respectable, we were in California together. Now I am trying out a few of my own ideas in agriculture and industry, when I'm not filling out government papers. My place is called Grove Farm. It's only a mile or so from the store. You must come to visit my wife and me one of these days. We would be delighted to have you. Charlie has told me about young George Wilcox. Now I see what he means."

"Thank you," stammered George. He shook hands and mounted "April Fool," his heart bursting with pride. He had almost reached the mill when he realized he'd forgotten to get the mail.

By the end of the month, George began to think even ten-year-old Willy Rice could handle his job in the store. If George took in over twenty dollars, it was a big week. Mostly he spent his time dusting and sweeping and trying to figure ways to keep the mice out of the cracker barrel.

He was squatting in front of the counter, feeding a handful of crumbs to a small dog that had wandered into the store, when a shadow fell across the floor. He looked up. Maria Rice stood above him, a severe frown on her pretty face.

"So that's how you spend your time, is it, George Wilcox, feeding our good food to every stray dog that comes in?"

George jumped to his feet, his face flushed. "I paid for the crumbs. There's no reason why I can't . . . " He saw the twinkle in her eyes, and his voice trailed off. Then she giggled. George smiled in embarrassment. He could never get used to her teasing.

At the age of fifteen, Maria had already taken over much of the housekeeping for her mother. She was a willowy girl with a direct gaze and a mischievous smile. At Punahou she had been three years behind George. He had hardly noticed her. Now he found it difficult not to.

"I know now why all the dogs around the plantation look so well fed," Maria said with a smile.

"They're hungry enough," George admitted ruefully.

Maria picked up a tortoise shell comb and admired it. "You didn't stay after supper last evening, George," she said casually. "Baby Anna missed playing dominoes with you."

"I was reading a book on soil chemistry that your father loaned me."

"George Wilcox, I declare! You prefer soil to our company!"

George squirmed uncomfortably. "I didn't mean it that way." He could never tell when she was teasing or serious.

"Well, you're forgiven. Father is pleased with your interest in the plantation. He said last night that 'That George Wilcox is a very able young man.' "

"I . . . I must thank him," stammered George, flustered by the compliment.

"You'd better not. He'll bite your head off. He's been working too hard again."

"I know."

Maria paused. It was mid-afternoon, and the flies buzzed drowsily in the warm silence. "What are you going to do when you finish Punahou, George?" she asked.

It was George's turn to pause. "I might go away."

"To college?"

"I'm afraid I'm not smart enough for college."

"Father thinks you are. He said once, 'That George Wilcox would make a fine engineer.' "

George frowned. "He never told me that."

"He forgets because he has so many things to think about. That's why I thought I would let you know."

Their eyes met. "Thank you, Maria," George said softly. He wanted to say more, but Maria suddenly blushed. Her gaze dropped and she fidgeted with the comb.

"My goodness, I almost forgot what I came for, talking away like this. Mother sent me for a box of saleratus."

"Oh, saleratus?" said George awkwardly. He went to the shelf where he kept the harness hardware. "Let's see now, saleratus . . . "

Maria giggled. "That's baking soda, you ninny! You might make a good engineer, George Wilcox, but you certainly don't know how to bake a cake." She was still laughing when she left the store.

* * *

In one way, George enjoyed working on the plantation books. There was a precision about the rows of neat figures that pleased him. It took him only a few weeks to pick up the bookkeeping system used by Mr. Rice. After that, George did the job without supervision. But the better he came to know the

Rices, the more his bookkeeping chores depressed him. Even George's inexperienced eye could see that the plantation was in serious financial trouble. The books showed losses due to bad crops for three years. One morning, he spent an hour looking up figures to satisfy his curiosity. When he had his result, he whistled. If his total was correct, the plantation had already cost the owners more than $100,000 since it began in 1851. No wonder Mr. Rice always looked so worried. His sugar plantation was losing money faster than even Old Titcomb's coffee fields.

Two mornings a week George would sit and make all the entries in the correct columns. He was continually amazed at the number of operations required to run the plantation and the expense each operation entailed. Just hauling the cane took six hundred oxen. They had to be caught, broken, driven, and fed. There were about twenty ox carts. To keep them in repair, the plantation maintained a blacksmith shop.

Running the mill required a completely different set of skills. The payroll included, besides the sugar boiler and his helpers, a machinist and a cooper who put together the kegs used for shipping sugar. Fuel was another item. A crew had to be kept for cutting timber in the mountains, another for drying wet cane in the trash house.

The Chinese workers had been brought in as an experiment almost five years before. Most of them worked in the fields, planting, cultivating, and harvesting cane. They were divided into gangs under supervisors, usually Hawaiians, called lunas, who took their orders from Mr. Rice. All of these workers had to be housed and fed.

There was one column of expenses that intrigued George more than the others. The entries had begun the year before, and the amount of money paid out was unusually heavy. The job, George knew, was the digging of a water ditch over five miles long, to irrigate the cane. Such a scheme was unheard of in the Islands. People called it "Rice's Folly." Some planters predicted that the water would soak into the ground before it reached the fields. But the gaunt, over-tired plantation manager was already hard at work lengthening the ditch to more than ten miles.

*   *   *

One morning at breakfast, in early fall, the plantation manager unexpectedly announced, "Now that the grinding is finished, we can all relax a little. George, it's time you took a tour of the plantation. How about riding along this morning to inspect the ditch?"

"Yes, sir!" said George, jumping out of his chair so fast that the whole family laughed.

The two of them rode easily down the dirt road, muddy from a night rain, toward the village of bamboo huts. It was the first time since George had come to the plantation that Mr. Rice wasn't in a hurry. The older man asked casually, "Well, how do you like working on a sugar plantation?"

"I like it. It's . . . interesting," George said truthfully.

Mr. Rice shot him a keen glance. "Yes, it is interesting. But it doesn't seem very promising, does it? Oh, I know what people are saying about this plantation. But we aren't ready to quit. Not just yet." The manager smiled to himself. "Do you know why I picked this job when I left the mission?"

The question embarrassed George. He said carefully, "It was for your health, wasn't it?"

Mr. Rice waved his hand in the familiar gesture of impatience. "Well, yes, the work at Punahou was just too much for Mrs. Rice, and the doctor said I'd better find something where I'd have more time for myself. But I had several offers before this one came along. One was from the government Land Commission at about $1,500 a year.

George's mouth dropped open. "You turned down $1,500 a year in Honolulu to come to Lihue?"

Mr. Rice chuckled. "That's right, and I'd do it again today.

One reason, I suppose, is because I'm a farmer at heart. Always have been. But it's more than that. I think the real reason I came here is because it's a chance to pioneer."

The horses were picking their way down the steep slope of the valley. "Look at those ox carts down at the mill. They had to be designed and built right here on this island. Do you know why? Because we couldn't import carts sturdy enough to stand up to these roads. We've had to develop our own heavy duty plows for the same reason. Did you know that there wasn't even a pair of working oxen on this island to pull the first plow at Koloa Plantation twenty years ago? Fifteen Hawaiians did it. Even now we have to catch and break wild cattle to the yoke. Can you imagine that happening in New England?"

George shook his head. Mr. Rice had never been in such a talkative mood.

"That's been one of the headaches at the mission. We've never been able to convince the Board in Boston just how primitive it really is out here. Look what's happening now to your father, for example. The Board is cutting off support on the assumption that he should be charging tuition to raise his salary. You know as well as I do that your father would be lucky to raise twenty-five dollars a year that way. We've made great progress in spreading religion here, but the economy is almost as primitive as it was fifty years ago."

George had never heard an adult speak so frankly about the mission. He listened carefully as the horses began plodding up the other side of the valley.

"What these Islands need is industry, jobs, ways for people to earn money so they can pay their preachers and teachers, or just go to the store and buy something. Somehow, we have to stimulate our economy or go back to living in grass houses. This plantation is my answer. We're making new jobs; we're tilling land that wasn't tilled before. We're putting this island to work. Let's ride over to the cane fields. I want to show you something."

Mr. Rice was certainly in a good mood this morning. "Come on," he shouted. George had to urge his horse into a trot to keep up. They rode by a gang of workmen digging the stump of a tree out of the middle of a harvested field. Eight oxen were pulling a big drill plow nearby.

Farther on, Mr. Rice waved his arm dramatically at the fields ahead. "Do you see anything unusual, George?"

They stopped their horses. In one field, the jointed stalks of cane grew taller than a man, in clumps of two dozen stalks to the clump. The clumps were so thick a man on horseback couldn't ride through them. The cane was a healthy, glistening green. But in the next field the cane grew in thin, sickly clumps.

Puzzled, George said, "That one field looks as though it's had rain, and the other doesn't."

Mr. Rice's eyes danced with excitement. "It's had water, all right, but not from rain."

"The ditch!" said George in sudden understanding.

Mr. Rice grinned broadly. "That's right, the ditch. Rice's folly. Well, there's the result. I'm the only sugar planter in these islands who doesn't have to depend completely on rain for his crop. Do you know what that means?"

George was caught up in the excitement. "Do I? Why, you'll never have to worry about a crop failure again. It's like money in the bank. The plantation can't help but make money now."

Mr. Rice laughed at George's enthusiasm. "There are plenty of other reasons for a crop failure, but I think we've solved the biggest single problem in the sugar industry here. Come on, I'll show you."

He was like a housewife with a newly wallpapered room. "You see, the ditch comes down from higher up where we tapped the stream. I'm trying to work out a system of connecting ditches and furrows to distribute the water into any part of the field. When we don't need it here, we can divert the water to the mill pond."

George studied a new field where water was running into furrows that led in straight lines across the uneven field. "How much water does the cane need?"

"That's a good question. I'm still not sure. If it gets too much water, it'll rot. If it doesn't get enough . . . Well, we'll just have to keep experimenting until we get the best results and can make the most economical use of the water. The heartening thing is that the ditch does work. Come on, we'll take a look at the head of it."

But George held back. "It doesn't work on the high ground. See the cane over there. It isn't as tall as the rest."

"Of course not. Water doesn't run up hill."

George frowned in thought. He turned to speak, but Mr. Rice was already riding up the main ditch. George started after him, then stopped. He looked back to study the field once more. He had thought of a way to distribute water evenly over the field and was sure his idea would work. But he didn't have the courage to mention it to Mr. Rice. Instead, he tucked the idea away in his memory. Someday, he might try it.

The ditch was about two and one-half feet wide and two and one-half feet deep. It curved and twisted endlessly up the slope, following the natural contour of the land, the water flowing in a musical murmur.

Soon they were in the timber. The ditch led in a snake-like path through the shadowy wilderness. They had already come three miles, skirting hills and ravines. It was wet here, a jungle of fern and koa. The ditch curved on ahead. At one spot George would have sworn the water was running up hill. At another, it flowed out of the damp, dripping mouth of a dark tunnel.

George forgot all about the dampness soaking into his boots, the mosquitoes swarming about his face. The ditch excited and baffled him at the same time, like an elusive mathematical formula. It was such a simple problem: take water from the mountains and bring it to the fields. But the solution made his head spin. How had Mr. Rice ever found a route for the water through these hills and gullies and dense jungle?

When they stopped to let the horses rest, Mr. Rice said, "What amazes me is that no other sugar planter has hit on this idea before. After all, the old Hawaiians built ditches to bring water down to their taro patches. Of course, most of them weren't on such a big scale."

George nodded. "I should think the biggest problem would be to decide where to dig the ditch."

Mr. Rice nodded emphatically in return. "Exactly! I've had a little practical engineering experience. It made all the difference. I tell you, it's skills we need in these Islands. A competent engineer would be a downright blessing around here. Come on, we haven't far to go now."

It didn't take long to reach the head of the ditch where the water flowed from a sparkling mountain stream. Then they turned around and headed back. George kept studying the course of the ditch, marveling each time it emerged sedately from what had seemed an impossible confusion of barriers. He didn't notice that Mr. Rice had begun to cough until they got back to the house and Mrs. Rice put her husband to bed.

"You must try not to let him get overtired," she told George gently.

"I'm sorry, ma'am," he said. But he really didn't hear her. His mind was on that magic ditch and the miracle of the green cane. The combination gripped him. It made such beautiful logic: man and nature working in harmony. He had learned something tremendously important today. A farmer alone could not have engineered the ditch. And to an engineer alone, the ditch would have no value. But when the farmer and the engineer were one? George decided he had a reason for going to college after all.

CHAPTER

6

George's plan to study civil engineering immediately ran into several obstacles. For one thing, Abner was not sure George's grades were up to college standards. "We will wait until the end of this school year and then ask Professor Alexander if he feels you are qualified to enter an engineering institution," Abner said finally.

Then there was the matter of money. George knew that his father had returned from the United States in 1852 with several thousand dollars he'd gotten for selling a farm he had tilled in Connecticut, before he became a missionary. Abner guarded the money as if it were the crown jewels, but he was not a shrewd businessman. He'd already lost some of his savings through a bad loan. Four hundred and fifty-five dollars had gone to buy sixty acres of land in Waioli because Abner was convinced that Hanalei Bay would soon become the most important port on Kauai. So far, the land had produced nothing but weeds. Abner had spent another nine hundred dollars for about six hundred acres of land in the rolling, grassy plateau called Koolau above Moloaa Valley, where the Wilcoxes were at least able to pasture their horses and the small herd of cattle which produced the family beef as well as a modest income from butter shipped to Honolulu.

George knew that whatever his father spent on his college education would come out of those funds so carefully hoarded against Abner and Lucy's old age. And this year the tuition at Punahou had gone up to twelve dollars a month for all students, including those from mission families. Now it would cost more to send one boy to school than it had to send two before. Over and over again, he told himself he had to find a way to earn his college expenses.

When Punahou opened again, he suddenly realized that he was one of the older boys. At eighteen he was still undersized, but it didn't matter so much now that he had learned to compensate for it. He swam just as well or better than the bigger boys, and because he was so quick, could outwrestle most of them. On weekend tramps up the bare slopes of Tantalus for land shells, George was usually one of the first to reach the top of the next ridge. He was still shy, especially around girls, though he concealed it carefully with a sense of humor. He would have been surprised to know that he was one of the best-liked boys in school.

As his confidence grew, he made more friends. There was Henry P. Baldwin from Maui, a stocky little fellow who had avoided the usual ducking in the pool on the first day of school by putting his back to the wall and offering to black the eye of the first boy who tried to throw him in. There was Albert Lyons from the remote mission station at Waimea, Hawaii, who was already sixteen when he entered Punahou that year. He'd arrived in a suit of country clothes without a necktie and a pair of homemade goatskin shoes that had never seen polish. The better-dressed Honolulu students stopped laughing when Lyons wrote his first composition, a brilliant essay on undersea geography. Their eyes popped when Professor Beckwith put Lyons in the most advanced Latin class. George, who had gone through the same agony of acceptance by the "townies," looked upon skinny, homely, little Albert Lyons as a conquering hero.

George studied hard that year, and his grades showed it. He felt sure now that he could master whatever courses college had to offer. If only he could think of a way to earn some money, a lot of money! The spring term was half over, and Abner had arrived in Honolulu for the annual General Meeting of the Mission when a sunburned man in his mid-thirties stopped by Punahou one mornng to ask for George. The grip of his calloused hand was firm when George met him outside of the classroom in the sun. "I'm Sam Wilder," the man said bluntly. "Are you George Wilcox?"

"Yes."

"I thought you'd be bigger," said Wilder thoughtfully. "You're just a little runt."

"Is that what you came to tell me?"

Wilder grinned. "No, it's not. Come on over here in the shade where we can talk." They sat down on the grass. Wilder came directly to the point. "I need a man to help me dig guano this summer on Jarvis Island, somebody who can get along with kanakas and keep a set of books. Are you interested?"

Suddenly George felt breathless. "What's guano?"

"Bird dung. Deposits of it have been building for thousands of years on the bird islands in the Pacific. It's used as fertilizer in the United States, brings anywhere from thirty to fifty dollars a ton at New York, costs ten dollars a ton to ship. Most of it has come from islands off Peru in the past. But the American Guano Company discovered a good deposit on Jarvis Island, about thirteen hundred miles due south, last year. Dr. Gerrit P. Judd is the agent in Honolulu. I'm the superintendent. A friend of yours, I believe, young Charlie Judd, works under me. He and another Punahou boy, Levi Chamberlain, are down there now."

"What would I do?" George asked eagerly.

"The American Guano Company bought 100,000 tons of guano on Jarvis. My job is to dig it, bag it, and get it out onto the ships. You'll be in direct charge of the operation once you learn the ropes. Jarvis is hot as Hades, dry, and lonely. It's the most miserable spot in creation. But you'll be able to earn enough to get started in college. I hear that's what you want."

George nodded emphatically, his eyes shining. "I'll have to ask my father."

"Well, you'd better ask him in a hurry. The *Josephine* sails for Jarvis tomorrow afternoon. You'll find me on board."

"I'll let you know this afternoon," George promised.

Abner hardly had time to object. He shook his head, a little dazed at the suddenness of it all. But he was there to wave goodby as the *Josephine* filled her sails outside Honolulu harbor at six o'clock in the evening, on Saturday, May 27, 1859. The voyage wasn't what George had expected. The trim little brigantine-rigged ship didn't have staterooms. Captain W. C. Stone, his first and second mate, and George, all slept in bunks built into the bulkheads of the main cabin where the officers smoked, played cards, and had their meals. When the Chinese cook brought in a Sunday morning breakfast of bacon and greasy potatoes with eggs scrambled in onions, George clapped his hand over his mouth and stumbled out of his bunk to the rail on deck.

Captain Stone was hardly George's idea of a deep-water sea captain. At night in the doldrums, when a severe squall hit the ship, the captain would calmly pull a slicker over his nightshirt and go up to take the helm. It wasn't until they reached Jarvis that George understood why the sailors kept bragging about Captain Stone's seamanship.

The *Josephine* set a sailing record on that trip, six days and thirteen hours from Honolulu to the mooring on the northwest side of the island. They sighted it at dawn. George scanned the horizon eagerly. All he could see was a tiny American flag floating above the water. Then two frame houses came into view, one with a roof shaped like a pyramid. Finally, he could see the island, a low mound of grey-green with a fringe of dazzling white beach and even more dazzling surf. Otherwise there was nothing but bleakness surrounded by the immense distances of the ocean.

The tall spars of a big, three-master speared the sky where she was tied up to moorings near the beach. Another large, clipper-built ship stood off the island under shortened sail. On shore, George could see the tiny figures of men scurrying about. Then, he saw a puff of smoke. Before the report of the saluting cannon reached his ears, an incredible thing happened. A million birds rose like a cloud of locusts above the island, their shrill, strange cries filling the air. Briefly they scolded the interruption, then settled back like an undulating blanket of feathers to their nesting places.

Now the *Josephine* was coming very close to the reef where the waves lifted their white teeth. Captain Stone was at the wheel. The wind blew briskly across the island from the southwest. The *Josephine* swung into the wind, her sails quivering. A Hawaiian poised on the bow, a manila line between his teeth. Gracefully, he dove over the side and swam powerfully for a large can buoy two hundred feet away. George glanced into the clear water. It was alive with sharks. He held his breath. But the sleek, grey monsters swam lazily alongside the ship, ignoring the man in the water.

Another danger arose. They were drifting closer and closer to the reef, still making strong headway against the wind. Unless the captain backed the sails to check their momentum, they would crash into the reef. George waited, his heart in his mouth. Still they drifted, closer, closer! He threw a glance at Captain Stone, tensed at the wheel and fiercely watching both the approaching reef and the man in the water who was now hauling the line through the eye of the buoy. Then the captain's arm shot up, glistening in the sunlight, and he bellowed, "Back the fore topsail!"

George could feel the weight of the wind as it checked their forward motion. A moment later the sails fluttered to the yards like limp rags. There was hurry and confusion on the deck. Finally, the captain nodded in satisfaction and walked to the rail.

"I've never seen such beautiful ship handling," George told him in a burst of admiration.

The captain smiled. "It's a nice problem of judgment, all right. If you back the sails too soon, you'll drift to windward and spend days beating back. If you don't back soon enough, you pile up on the reef . . . "

"Ahoy, George Wilcox!"

The shout came from a whaleboat skimming rapidly toward the *Josephine*. In it were two familiar faces. George recognized Charlie Judd and Levi Chamberlain. "Where's Sam Wilder?" Charlie shouted from the boat.

"He's coming down next trip," George shouted back.

Charlie grinned. "You know what that means. I'm going to work your tail into the ground until he gets here."

George grinned back. "You're not big enough," he boasted. Then he went below to get his things together.

* * *

The clang of the bell jolted him out of a heavy, sweating sleep. With a tremendous yawn, George sat up in bed. He pulled off a bedbug and pinched it between his fingers. Then he slid his feet into a pair of heavy, rawhide shoes. They'd been too big for him until Charlie Judd had told him to wear them in salt water. Now the leather had shrunk almost enough to fit his feet. In undershorts, he walked to the window and looked out.

The bedroom was on the second floor of a roomy frame

house that had been sent out, in sections, from New York the year before. There were living quarters above and store-rooms below. It was about the only touch of civilization on the island. He could see the workers' barracks a short distance down the beach. The brick cisterns, their only supply of fresh water, were in back. He could not remember a scene so bleak as this speck on the map of the Pacific. But at least now it was cool. In a few hours the flat glare of the equatorial sun would turn the barren surface of coral sand and coarse grass and bird droppings into a simmering, skin-scorching furnace.

The *Argo* was moored just under his window beyond the reef. The *Polynesia* was farther down where the *Josephine* had been tied up. Both the *Argo* and the *Polynesia* were clippers, rakish and beautiful, so out of place in this wretched end of the world. But George was grateful they were there. Without them he wasn't sure he would be able to keep his grasp on reality.

He turned from the window as Captain Hutchinson rolled up out of bed like a hairy elephant. The captain noisily cleared his throat as he scratched his ample stomach. He was in charge of laying the moorings and tending the boats. But he did more talking than anything else. In the next room George could hear the chemists stirring: Dr. R. H. Drysdale, a young fellow with a Southern accent, and Mr. Haig, just out of college and bright as a whip. Charlie Judd and Levi Chamberlain had another room.

George pulled on his pants and put on the clean shirt he'd mended the day before. Another day! He'd been on the island just one day less than a month. It had been the most monotonous, exasperating month of his life. He trooped downstairs to the cook house to get his cup of coffee. Breakfast would come later after they got the work started.

"Captain Morse on the *Polynesia* wants his loading speeded up," Charlie told George as they rinsed their cups in salt water and put them back on the shelves.

"He wants everything speeded up," grumbled George. Morse

was the youngest captain in the clipper ship fleet, a noisy, blustering fellow who was never satisfied with anything.

"Just the same, I want at least thirty tons delivered to the *Polynesia* today," Charlie said coldly.

George snapped back, "What are you so worried about? That's what he got yesterday."

"Then step it up today."

They glared at each other. George knew it was the monotony gnawing at their frayed tempers. Charlie had been riding him for a week, and George resented it.

"Anytime you think I can't do the job, just say so," growled George.

They were interrupted by an excited shout from the cupola atop the house. "Sail ho! It's the *Josephine*!"

Charlie turned to George. "All right, you want a job, you've got it. I'm going to catch up on the accounts, then meet the *Josephine*. I need Levi to help me. Today, you're in charge of the operation: digging, boating, loading, everything. Now get to work, and see that you get thirty tons of guano aboard the *Polynesia*!"

George was too angry to answer. He had never been in complete charge before, especially of the boating operation. He flared at the implication that he couldn't handle the job. The heat was building up when George, in a black mood, walked with his crew of Hawaiians to the center of the island where Dr. Drysdale had found the best guano deposits. The deposits were six inches to three feet deep, made up of an odorless, greyish-brown powder that caught in the hair of the nostrils and dried the throat and sifted into the scalp. Here in the center, the island formed a hollow. Dr. Drysdale said this area had once been a lagoon. Whatever it had once been, the hollow was now a hot, airless pocket of hell.

"We'll start here!" George ordered, waving his arm.

The natives went to work with a will. George never ceased to marvel at them. They existed on a pound of poi per day

Left: George N. Wilcox
and Charles H. Wilcox as
students at Punahou School
between 1850 and 1860.

Below: George N. Wilcox at
time he entered Sheffield
Scientific School, Yale
University, 1860

Judge H. A. Widemann, original owner of Grove Farm, 1865

George N. Wilcox at the time he acquired Grove Farm, 1865

for each man, plus the fish they caught and the birds' eggs they collected. They were never sick; and they worked, if you treated them right, from dawn to dusk without complaining. But today George was in no mood to be generous. He drove the men impatiently, not even giving them the usual rest periods to smoke their stubby pipes. In the boiling sun, they shoveled the guano into canvas bags, tied them at the top, and loaded them into wheelbarrows. Then they pushed their loads to the landing on the beach.

By mid-morning, after a hasty breakfast, the men were sullen. But George was too impatient to notice. At the tiny pier, he supervised the loading of a boat. This he had done before, making sure the weight was distributed evenly. But Charlie had never allowed him to steer a boat through the surf to the ships. Today was his chance. George counted the sacks, each weighing about 110 pounds, as they lowered them into the boat. When they'd loaded two tons of guano, he waved most of the natives back to the diggings. The six oarsmen hopped nimbly into the whaleboat. George leaped in after them and took the tiller.

"Pull away," he commanded.

From the first moment he realized his mistake. Steering the boat had seemed so effortless when he watched Charlie do it. Now he began to realize how much skill was involved. The gunwhales of the heavily loaded boat were only a few inches above the water. The slightest shift in weight caused the boat to tilt alarmingly. Even the movement of his rudder made the boat sway. He knew he should turn the tiller over to one of the boatmen, but his pride wouldn't let him. They were coming close to the line of surf where it broke over the reef. George steered for a small opening in the coral barrier where a boat could get through. The waves were much higher than they had appeared from shore. Their booming hiss filled his ears as they rolled toward the boat. It didn't seem possible that they could get through without swamping. Now it was too late to turn back. George steered straight into the next wave. He felt the bow rise sluggishly. The foam seemed to engulf him as the boat surged upward. He concentrated on holding the tiller steady. Then they were through it. George realized he was sweating. But the Hawaiians were rowing as calmly as ever.

By noon, his Hawaiians were within a few tons of filling the quota. They flopped in the shade of the veranda, spooning up globs of poi with their fingers and munching on dried fish. George shared the simple fare, sitting on a bench with a husky guano digger. The *Josephine* had tied up, and George could see that the crew had put the water casks over. The casks were usually lashed together and towed to shore by a ship's boat. This time they had been set afloat inside the reef, apparently to drift ashore.

"Something's wrong out there," George said after a moment. "Those casks are drifting on the reef. If they break up we're going to be mighty short of water around here."

No one moved. George got to his feet. "Come on, we'll get a boat and go after those casks."

The men looked up at him sullenly. The big Hawaiian on the bench said in his native tongue, "This is the time we eat. It is not time to work."

George's temper broke. "Without that water, we'll die like rats. Get up! That's an order!"

"All right, I'll get up, you smart little haole," the Hawaiian growled. He stood up and shoved, sending George sprawling into the sand. George heard the men laugh. Rage exploded inside him. He scrambled to his feet and rushed at his tormentor. The Hawaiian grinned, holding out his hands to fend George away; but George ducked inside the guard and threw his right fist. It caught the other man in the eye, all of George's wild rage behind it. The Hawaiian stumbled backward, crying in pain. But only for a moment. He snarled an oath and lunged. George side-stepped. snapping his left into the man's face, throwing the punches he had learned at school. It was amazingly easy. He ducked a wild swing and connected again with his right. Then someone pinned his arms from the back. George felt a moment of panic. The were ganging up on him. He twisted violently. But the man behind him was too strong. They were all yelling now and the big Hawaiian was coming at him. At the last moment, George twisted to one side and lashed out with his heavy shoe. He caught the man in the groin. The Hawaiian doubled over in agony.

Suddenly the yelling stopped. George felt his arms come free. The workers took to their heels for the landing where they scrambled into the boat and started after the water casks. George saw that the *Josephine's* long boat was approaching rapidly. That's what had saved him. Sam Wilder was at the tiller. A few moments later, he came running up.

"What happened?" he asked anxiously.

George pointed to the man on the ground. "I sent them after the water casks, and this one wouldn't go. He pushed me down. We had a fight."

Wilder looked from the bruised Hawaiian to George in amazement. "I'll say you did. Well, a few days in irons will cool this fellow off."

George frowned. "Irons?"

"That's the only way to teach them to obey. In a place like this you must have discipline, Wilcox, or there's always trouble."

"But he didn't really . . . "

"He struck you, didn't he? On this island, that's a crime. By George, you didn't get the worst of it, though, did you?"

"No," George replied. But his face was troubled as he watched the Hawaiian march away to prison.

* * *

When Charlie Judd and Levi Chamberlain sailed on the *Josephine* for Baker's Island, a thousand miles to the west, to take charge of the guano diggings there, Sam Wilder put George in complete charge at Jarvis. The only advice George got was, "There's maybe 250,000 tons of guano on this island. The American Guano Company owns 100,000 tons of it. Your job is to get it on those ships."

The first morning, George called the men together on the beach. The man he'd fought with was among them. George told the men in Hawaiian, "I'm not going with you this morning because nobody needs to tell you how to shovel guano in a sack, and you're all better boatmen than I am. Here are 130 bags. Take them, divide them any way you want, fill 'em, and boat them out to the *Gosport*. I'm going to help Captain Hutchinson repair that broken mooring. If you need me, whistle. When you're finished you can go fishing."

The men exchanged grins. They grabbed the guano bags and hurried off with their wheelbarrows. As George anticipated, they had all 130 bags on board the *Gosport* by midafternoon. They were expert fishermen and Jarvis, uninhabited for centuries, was virgin fishing ground.

George spent the day in the iron-mooring repair boat used for hauling the heavy anchors and chain out into the water. Jarvis Island was the top of an extinct volcano that rose from the ocean floor. A fringe of coral grew like a crown around the top of the undersea mountain. Beyond that fringe the bottom fell away so sharply that a ship's anchor would not hold. To provide moorings for the ships, an anchor had to be laid inside the reef, connected by a heavy chain to another anchor laid on the steeply sloping ocean floor outside the reef. From this anchor a chain came up to a large can buoy to which the ships made fast; and a third chain, connecting the anchor inside the reef directly to the buoy, provided additional holding power. The chains were constantly chafing through. It took all day to haul a chain broken on the reef and repair it.

Before dark George went to have a quick talk with his men about the fishing, their provisions, the work for the next day.

In making his rounds, George noticed that the big Hawaiian
he'd fought on the beach was injured. His hand was torn and
bloody. The man grinned sheepishly.

"I catch a shark instead of a fish," he explained.

"Better let me put something on it," George said.

"It's all right. I washed it in sea water."

George knew that the Hawaiians had their own remedies
and their own superstitions. The year before one of them had
come under a spell. He refused to eat until he died. It didn't
help to argue. So George left the barracks. But the hand grew
rapidly worse. It began to swell. Then it turned green. That
morning George found the Hawaiian lying listlessly in his
bunk. Looking at the swollen, discolored hand made George
feel sick. He forced a smile.

"Well, are you ready to use some haole medicine now?"

"No use," the man said feebly.

"Humbug! You've got a bad infection, that's all. I remember
once when I cut my foot and it turned red, my mother put on a
hot poultice. We'll try it."

The Hawaiian nodded. "You wait here," George told him
confidently. George had never made a poultice. He rummaged
in the pantry of the cook house until he found some linseed
meal. That might work. Then he cut out a piece of canvas
from the roll used for making guano bags. Now to get some hot
water. There was still some in the kettle on the outdoor fireplace, but he would need more. When he was ready, he had a
couple of the men help the sick man to the cook house. They
laid him on a wooden bench. George put a handful of dry linseed meal in a pan on the fire and added water. He stirred
until he had a mush that reminded him of oatmeal. Then he
packed several handfulls upon a strip of canvas.

"This will hurt," he said. "Do you trust me?"

The Hawaiian nodded. Gently, George applied the hot poultice. His patient winced. George knew the heat against the
soreness must be terribly painful. If only he had something to

make it easier for the man. He glanced rapidly over the pantry shelves. There was one bottle at the end that caught his eye. It was a large bottle, green, labeled "Red Precipitate." George had no idea what "Red Precipitate" was. The liquid appeared colorless. He pulled out the cork and smelled it. His eyebrows rose. No wonder the new cook, an Englishman just out of Oahu Prison, had been acting so strangely. He'd brought a supply of ti root whiskey.

George thrust the bottle at his patient. "Here, this is just the medicine you need."

The Hawaiian took a swallow. Then he grinned broadly and took a bigger gulp. Before he could drink more, George grabbed the bottle. "Save some for the next treatment."

On the following day the abscess opened and began to drain. By that time the green bottle was empty. George spent most of those two days tending the big Hawaiian who recovered rapidly once the poison was gone.

From that time on, the Hawaiians couldn't do enough for George. Every time they went fishing, they brought him the best of the catch. He never had to lift his voice to get them to work. After they had loaded ten hundred tons of guano aboard the clipper ship *Victory*, in nine and one-half days, Sam Wilder said, "For a little runt, you sure can make those kanakas work." But the cook never forgave him for finding his bottle of okole·hao.

* * *

George dropped his carpet bag into the boat, then hopped nimbly in after it. He made his way to the stern and took the tiller. Above, on the rickety pier, Sam Wilder and Captain Hutchinson waved their caps.

"Have a good trip," Hutchinson called.

"Hope you aren't too far behind in school when you get back," added Wilder.

"Don't worry," George waved once. "Pull away," he ordered.

The boat, loaded only with empty kegs, skimmed over the water. The sea was rough today with a booming surf coming over the reef. George smiled happily as the boat sliced into the wave. He was an expert steersman now, delighted to have one more opportunity to try his skill.

He handed his bag up to the deck of the *Josephine,* then climbed easily up the rope ladder. On deck, he stood and looked back. The six months had passed so quickly. The bleak, windswept island hadn't changed at all. The glare of the white sand still hurt his eyes, and the countless birds still wheeled and circled in their endless, effortless flight. The dreary buildings, surrounded by the litter of civilization, were just as dreary as ever. He kept looking as the *Josephine* wore about and set a course on the larboard tack, cutting close to the south corner of the island. George stood there until the island sunk into the sea and he could see nothing but birds circling over a desert of water. Then he faced eagerly in the opposite direction. He would be home by the middle of January. A few more months at Punahou and he would be ready for college.

CHAPTER

7

Have you written down the names of your relatives in Connecticut?" Abner asked for the hundredth time.

"Yes, father," George told him.

"Now, remember, your deportment will speak for our entire family. Your mother and I wish for your uncles and aunts to think well of you."

"I'll remember my manners, father," promised George.

"Be sure and do not lose your letter of introduction from Professor Alexander at Punahou. It was very kind of him to recommend you as a student in the Sheffield Scientific School at Yale."

"I have the letter packed in my trunk, father."

George looked uncomfortable as they stood together in the little stateroom aboard the *Frances Palmer*. He hoped Willy Gulick and Sam Alexander, who were also sailing on the ship, wouldn't come in while his father was lecturing him. Why couldn't Abner understand that he was grown up and didn't need to be fussed over like a school boy? His father was dressed, as usual, in a slightly frayed white shirt and soft black tie, with a black coat as shiny at the elbows as the black trousers were in the seat. George knew that because of this trip his father would be wearing the same suit for another two years.

"George, I took the trouble to write down for you the method you must use to procure funds at Yale. Apply to Mr. Gordon, Treasurer of the American Board in Boston. He will draw on my account with Castle and Cooke here in Honolulu."

"Yes, father, I know."

"I trust you feel the importance of making your savings go as far as possible. Your education at the best will be expensive, and I sometimes feel troubled lest my own funds fail."

"I'll be careful, father."

There was a commotion on deck. The ship's bell struck. Abner took a deep breath. There were tears in his eyes. "Goodby, my boy," he said. "I pray that you will come back to us." With a sudden, awkward movement, Abner embraced his son. That was the moment George's Punahou classmates, Sam Alexander and Willy Gulick, burst into the room. George flushed with embarrassment.

"Goodby, father."

Abner gave his son a final, emotion-filled handshake, then hurried up on deck and down to the pier. He was still standing there, erect and motionless, as the lines were cast off and the tall-masted vessel moved slowly away from the dock. George waved dutifully until a pier shed blotted out the tiny figure, then he turned eagerly to the exciting bustle around him. The date was July 18, 1860.

* * *

Events began to swim together. The voyage was one grand lark. As they crossed the Isthmus of Panama, on the first railroad cars George had ever seen, he had to pinch himself to make sure he wasn't dreaming. New York harbor was a forest of towering masts and the city a wonder of buildings and hurry and excitement.

He arrived at Harwinton, Connecticut, on September 5, to find twenty-one relatives, practically the entire relationship on his father's side, waiting for him. By coincidence, they had all met to celebrate the sixty-second birthday of Uncle Elias, Abner's oldest brother, in nearby New Hartford. George was sure he'd never remember all of the names.

His Uncle Charles shook his hand heartily. "All the way from the Sandwich Islands and arrived just today? Well, this is a pleasant coincidence. How I wish your father and mother might be here! Enrolling at Yale, are you? I know how students like to eat. You know, Nephew George, I think I will send you down a barrel of apples. Our trees are bearing so this year we don't know what to do with them all. How would you like that, my boy?"

"Very much, sir," said George politely.

His Aunt Olive kissed his cheek. "George Wilcox, a stranger in our midst. Yes, I do see the family resemblance. How nice to have you here! As soon as you get settled at Yale, I shall ask my husband to send you a barrel of apples. An apple a day, you know! They'll do you good."

"Thank you, Aunt Olive," George replied.

He met cousins until their names swam in his mind. At last it was all over, and he took the railroad car to New Haven. The trees that arched the streets, he learned, were called elms. He took a room at North 21 Whitney Avenue with a young man by the name of Edwin Purrington. The rent was much more than he had expected to pay, and the school was much smaller than he had anticipated. In fact, the engineering department at Yale wasn't even as large as Punahou. There was a drafting instructor and one engineering teacher, W. A. Norton, who lectured the first day on surveying. George listened eagerly.

"The oldest historical records in existence today, which bear directly on the subject of surveying, state that this science had its beginning in Egypt. Herodotus says Sesostris, in about 1400 B.C., divided the land of Egypt into plots for the purpose of taxation. The annual floods of the Nile River swept away portions of these plots, and surveyors were appointed to replace the bounds. These early surveyors were called rope-stretchers. Their measurements were made by means of ropes with markers at unit distances. As a consequence of this work, the early Greek thinkers developed the science of geometry. Heron stands out prominently for applying the science to surveying in about 120 B.C. He was the author of . . . ."

George sighed. He had expected to learn how to build bridges and irrigation ditches. Instead, he was getting more Greek history. He tore his gaze away from the window and tried to keep his mind on what the professor was saying.

The first barrel of apples arrived in November. The second in January. By that time George was so sick of apples he gave most of them away. He studied. He carried coal for the fire in his room. He wore an overcoat which he hated. And on April 14, 1861, he bought a newspaper which carried a very distressing news item. Fort Sumter was being bombarded, and a civil war had burst upon the nation.

* * *

The following summer, Abner dipped deep into his savings to send George's younger brother, Edward, to the United States to study mechanics. George received a worried letter from his father saying he hoped Edward's vessel would not encounter a

Confederate war ship. Edward arrived safely in September, and George went with him on the round of visits with the relatives.

For his roommate that year George chose a classmate, Ignacio MaMagia, from Oaxaco, Mexico. Nothing in George's experience had prepared him for such a friend. The Mexican did everything with a flourish. His English was a strange mixture of unusually large adjectives and misplaced verbs. He was a loquacious talker, a fastidious dresser, and his manners were impeccable. In artistic subjects he was brilliant. Mechanical things bored him. George could never understand why Ignacio had decided to study engineering. Oddly enough, the Mexican admired him tremendously.

One evening after supper Ignacio leaned back in his chair and yawned. "And so today, friend Wilcox, we have studied the mysteries of the steam engine and the use of the screw propeller. How dull!"

"No, it isn't. The steam engine is one of man's greatest inventions."

"And the screw propeller?"

"You heard Professor Norton tell us what the possibilities are when the principle is applied to ships."

Ignacio lit a slender, black cigar and sent a stream of pungent smoke up at the pictures of Jefferson Davis and Abraham Lincoln hanging side by side on the wall. Below the pictures stood a bookcase full of textbooks. An old wall clock ticked industriously across the room.

"My dear Wilcox, what do you intend to do with this plethora of knowledge that our illustrious Professor Norton is forcing into your skull?"

"I might use it to dig a ditch," George answered thoughtfully.

Ignacio turned to address the clock. "Gentlemen, I present to you the cream of the Sheffield Scientific School. Whither will his knowledge lead him? Is he to build the tallest structure in existence, the world's greatest bridge, the most fantastic engine man has ever seen? No, gentlemen, he intends to dig a ditch."

George chuckled. Ignacio got to his feet and began waving his arms. "Why has he studied for two years the marvels of engineering, the intricacies of modern machines? To dig a ditch, of course. Why else would one come half way around the world to attend Yale University . . . "

"Stop, stop," cried George, grabbing the waving arms. "You don't understand."

"Indeed I do not," grinned Ignacio, taking his seat once more. "There is a great deal about you I do not understand, my dear Wilcox. That is why you fascinate me."

"It isn't just the ditch," George began feeling his way, "it's all kinds of things that are going to happen some day in the Islands. There's so much to be done. You don't have any idea how primitive it is . . . " For five minutes he explained to Ignacio about the ox carts and poverty of the Hawaiians.

His friend listened, then commented with an engaging smile. "In my country it is primitive also. But these things need not concern us. Peasants have always lived this way. It is not the duty of the gentry to change the ways of God."

"But in my country there is no gentry. I'm a peasant, Ignacio . . . "

"Ridiculous. You are studing engineering, are you not? You speak properly; you dress decently. Hence, you are not a peasant."

"I'm studying engineering because I worked half a year digging guano to earn the money. My father is as poor as a church mouse, a school teacher in a mission that can't afford to keep him. I'll tell you something else. He hates Catholics."

Ignacio shook his head in amusement. "I cannot believe you. At this school of yours . . . how do you say it, Poonahoo? You tell me you and the other scholars worked in the fields before you went in to study geometry. Now you say that your father, a man learned in all things, hates Catholics. What sort of place is this Sandwich Islands?"

George laughed over his friend's bewilderment. "It's not easy to explain, Ignacio. The Islands are poor and helpless and backward. Yet they are beautiful and rich in so many ways. You only have to know how to admire the beauty and release the wealth."

"And how does this ditch of yours add to the beauty and wealth of your islands?"

George's eyes glowed. "It's a water ditch I saw once. It brought water ten miles from a mountain stream to a field of sugar cane. You should have seen that cane, Ignacio. Have you ever stood beside a field of healthy, growing sugar cane? It looks like giant grass, and you feel like a pigmy when you stand under it. It's the color of grass, too. The sun glistens on the blades of it, and the trade winds make it talk softly if you listen."

"Bless my soul, Wilcox, you are a poet," said Ignacio in admiration. "Who would have guessed?"

"But the important thing is that sugar cane will grow in the Islands, better than almost anywhere else. If only it can get water. It's like a pretty girl waiting for a man to come along and kiss her. Water! That's the magic word, Ignacio. And there's plenty of it in the mountains, gallons and gallons of it, fresh and sparkling. The peasant who knows how to deliver that water to thirsty sugar cane can become a prince!"

Ignacio smiled. "My dear Wilcox, you sound like a man in love."

George smiled ruefully in return. "Maybe I am, Ignacio. But I'm afraid this is one suitor who will never get to the altar. Digging water ditches costs money, lots of it. Now, if my father were as rich as yours . . . "

Ignacio chuckled. "You would be as irresponsible as I. Which reminds me, my friend, I am embarrassed by a lack of pocket money at the moment. Would it be convenient for you to lend me five dollars until I receive my next communique' from home?"

"Ignacio, you're impossible," George said grinning. "That makes seven dollars, doesn't it?"

"Thank you, Professor Wilcox, I believe it does. You shall have your money before the end of the term."

"I'm not worried," said George. He tackled his books. But that night, as he lay in bed, he thought of what he had told his friend. He'd never before been able to explain to another person how he felt about a field of sugar cane in the sun or how exciting it was to dream of bringing water to thirsty fields. With this awkward Wilcoxian shyness of his, he'd probably never be able to explain it again. But that was how he felt.

* * *

The Battle of Bull Run fanned the flames of patriotism to fever pitch at Yale, and all over New England young men were enlisting. Sam Alexander was talking about it. Cousin Charley Spaulding had gone off to war, Norfolk Company E, 11th Regiment. Below George's window a volunteer company of students marched by to the drill field. George had the fever as stong as the rest, but he knew how his parents felt about it. Abner had written:

"The North does not lack men. Then let those whose interests are more immediately concerned, and are allied to the country by birth, take the lead. I say, let the others be excused. If the North had not the men it might be different. You remember the words of Solomon—Proverbs 26:17—He that passeth by and meddleth with strife belonging not to him is like one that taketh a dog by the ears."

So George kept to his books. And now his two years were almost finished. Edward was in Norfolk working in a machine shop making guns. The war had provided him with just the kind of mechanical work he had hoped for. But George was torn. The trouble was, he kept getting too much good advice.

A cousin, Charles Welton, had gone to live in Elmwood,

Illinois, with an uncle who was a farmer there. Cousin Charles kept writing letters, in envelopes decorated with eagles and flags and red, white, and blue shields, about the great opportunities that lay in the West. In California, brother Charles promised him an opening as County Surveyor at one hundred dollars a year with a clear field to earn much more surveying town lots. George's relatives in Connecticut kept urging him to find work in an engineering office in New England, since there was so little outlet for his training in the Islands.

After George received his certificate on July 28, 1862, he made the rounds of engineering offices. August slipped away. Then September. The October frosts stripped the trees of their leaves leaving them in bleak nakedness. All of the engineering offices seemed so dreary, not nearly so exciting as watching Mr. Prevost make a sugar strike.

In November a letter arrived from Abner dated August 20. It explained that Robert C. Wyllie, an Englishman who had recently resigned as Foreign Minister for the Hawaiian government, was building a sugar mill and starting a large plantation in Hanalei. Mr. Titcomb was busy growing sugar and had a small mill. George read the news about the family. The part of the letter that caught his eye read, "I think you can find work at the Islands. If you come back, you can plant our land, and Mr. Titcomb lets me know of twelve or fourteen acres by the Hanalei River which he will let you plant, which cane when ripe he will grind at half shares."

It was a hard bargain, half of the profits in return for grinding the cane. Also, George had a strong suspicion that Hanalei Valley was far from the best place to grow sugar cane. Still, it was better than sitting in a stuffy office watching the snow outside. More important, it was the excuse he needed to take him home. He was as happy as a young colt just released from the corral.

CHAPTER

8

$\mathbf{A}$t first, George couldn't understand what was wrong. After stopping in California to visit Charles, he had arrived in Honolulu aboard the *Cambridge* on March 5, 1863. Now, as he stood on the deck of an untidy inter-island schooner, his eyes searched the familiar, lush landscape that framed Hanalei Bay. He found the church, the house, the Johnson house. But something was missing. The school! It was gone! Puzzled, he landed with his bags and boxes in the whaleboat. As he stepped ashore, a rider came galloping wildly down the beach shouting and waving his hat. It was Albert. He rode up and leaped off the horse.

97

"When I saw them putting the boat over, I knew it was you, George. It's about time you came back, you fancy dude, you!"

The brothers shook hands, grinning happily. Albert was heavier than George, a stocky, handsome young man of eighteen. He was dressed like a planter in a big hat and high boots. A downy mustache grew on his upper lip. George, at twenty-three, was leaner. He looked uncomfortable in a neat, dark suit and tie. He wore a bushy, black mustache. They clapped one another on the back, wrestling in high good humor.

"How are Father and Mother?" George asked.

Albert paused. "I hate to spoil your homecoming with bad news."

"What bad news?"

Albert kicked sand with his boot. "Father's school burned down night before last. I'm afraid it's just about finished him off."

"Why doesn't he rebuild it?"

"What with? The mission has stopped buying books and supplies. All father gets now is three hundred dollars a year pension."

The brothers rode double on the horse on the way to the house. They passed the black tangle of charred timbers. Abner's desk, with one leg burned off, stood forlornly amid the ruins. Their mother met them at the door. She wore a faded gingham dress and an apron. She was still plump but her hair, pulled straight back into a knot, was greying. George was startled to see how she had aged.

"George, George, I knew the Good Lord would send you back to us," she murmured as she hugged him. "Let me look at you. You're thinner. And older. But you haven't changed. Oh, it's so good to look into your face once more."

"Where's father?"

Her round face clouded. "He's holding classes in the church.

Did Albert tell you what happened? It's a terrible blow to your father, George. His life is tied up in that school."

"But isn't there something we can do?"

His mother pressed her fingers to her temples for a moment. Then took a breath and smiled. "It's a long story, and I think better when I'm busy. You sit down, and I'll tell you about it while I get something for you to eat."

George listened while his mother bustled between the pantry and the dining room. Shortly after he had left for college, the mission had withdrawn all support from Waioli School. For a long time his father had debated whether to give up or try to carry the load by himself.

"Of course, he decided to keep on," Lucy said proudly as she put George's cup before him. "But he had to let one assistant go. There just wasn't money enough. The school garden brings in a little. And some of the students bring things for their tuition. You never saw so many dried fish in your life."

"Is father well?" George asked.

"His body is well enough. It's his spirit that is sick. Oh, George, we can't let him give up now. Do you realize that fifteen of the school teachers on this island graduated from your father's school? For nearly twenty years, Abner Wilcox has been the public school system on Kauai. The Hawaiians don't have anyone else. They need him so desperately. Try to cheer him, George. I know you can do it."

Abner came in a few minutes later. He walked slowly, as if each step brought him pain. He hunched forward, now, peering ahead through the tops of his spectacles. George realized with a sense of shock that his father was an old man. Some of the keenness came back to Abner's gaze as he greeted his son with awkward warmth. He settled himself into a chair and gave George a long, steady appraisal. George smiled back.

"Satisfied, father?"

Abner cleared his throat. "We are indeed happy to have you

home again, George. However, your mother and I are gravely concerned over your failure to be received into the Church."

George squirmed uncomfortably. Like his father, many of his friends had experienced a sense of personal salvation at the hands of Jesus Christ in a sort of vision. But George had never felt such a religious experience, and he could not bring himself to go before a congregation to witness to something he didn't feel.

Abner continued, "As I wrote you, we feel you can profitably use your time planting cane with Albert on our land here at Waioli. You are welcome to live here with us, of course. It may be that you will be able to find employment as a surveyor . . . I trust you have acquired that skill . . . or as an outlet for your engineering training. I am sorry that I cannot offer you better prospects, but . . . "

"Father, what about the school?" George interrupted.

Abner seemed to wilt. His gaze wandered off. "Oh, yes, the school," he said vaguely.

"Will you build a new school?"

Abner sighed. "It seems unlikely. I have neither the funds nor the strength."

George said impatiently, "Well, I have the strength! And I know how to do the job. After two years in engineering school, I should be able to build a school house."

Abner smiled faintly. "That is good of you. But it takes money. I did manage to save quite a few of the timbers but . . . "

"Then you probably won't need as much money as you think. Have you asked the government for help? You don't think the Board of Education wants you to quit, do you? You've been saving them money for years training teachers for them. They can afford to help now. Why don't you take a trip to Honolulu and put it to them? If they'll pay for the materials, I'll rebuild the school house as good as new!"

For the first time, George saw hope in his father's eyes. Abner nodded slowly. "I think you may be right. I hadn't thought of the government. It would at least be worth a trip, wouldn't it?"

When George stepped into the dining room his mother hugged him happily.

* * *

George and a Hawaiian carpenter rebuilt the school with hand hewn timbers from the mountains and lumber purchased by the Board of Education in Honolulu. Abner paid the freight to Waioli. Members of the congregation thatched the roof of the new thirty-two by twenty-one foot structure in back of the church. It was finished almost in time for the General Meeting of the Mission in the spring. By that time, after working in the rain for days, George had come down with a fever.

His mother put him to bed in the Prophet's Room where he would not be disturbed by Samuel, now fifteen; Luther, now thirteen; or baby Henry, now five. There George lay, restless and impatient to get well. Coming home was so different from what he had imagined it would be. What good was his engineering certificate doing him now?

Lucy did her best to cheer him. She was full of news about his old Punahou classmates. Most of them were planting sugar cane now that the price was up and whaling had gone into decline. George Dole, the older son of the former Punahou principal, was assistant manager at the Koloa Sugar Plantation under Sam Burbank. Sam Alexander was back from a year at Williams College and had married Pattie Cooke. He was planting cane at Waihee, Maui after a year of teaching at Lahainaluna School. Henry Baldwin was planting cane with his brother, Dwight, at Lahaina, Maui. Only the younger Dole boy, Sanford Ballard, was going into a different field. He had decided to study law.

Each bit of news depressed George still more. His friends were already on the move. And he hadn't even started. He couldn't wait to get back on his feet. But Lucy wouldn't hear of it. "You have the rest of your life to be a success," she said soothingly. "A few more days won't matter."

She told him that Mr. Rice was dead and that Maria had married Paul Isenberg, a tall, business-like German who was now in charge of the plantation.

"It won't be the same without Mr. Rice," George said sadly. "And Maria married. I just can't believe it."

His mother asked casually, "Did you meet any nice girls in Connecticut?"

"Oh, yes, Cousin Nellie Catlin was very nice. And Sarah Spaulding was good about writing to me. I still have her letters. They are full of family news. I thought you might like to see them."

"Surely there was one girl besides your cousins who caught your eye during those two years," his mother said, teasing.

"Of course, there was," he replied, laughing, "But I was too busy and too poor to do much about it. Besides, I'm afraid girls don't think I'm very interesting, or handsome, or whatever it is they look for in a man."

"But you are handsome," scolded his mother. "And it's time you began thinking of marriage."

"I don't have time now."

"The Smith girls in Koloa are your age," mused his mother. "Perhaps we should take a little trip there to celebrate your return when you get well."

"When I get well, mother, I'm going to start planting cane. I'm afraid the trip will have to wait."

Lucy leaned over and kissed his forehead. "All right. Rest now so that you'll soon be well." She closed the door softly and slowly descended the creaky stairs, a small frown of annoyance on her face.

* * *

George's plans to become an independent cane planter went askew from the beginning. The soil in Hanalei Valley was sandy and thin. There was so much rain the seed cane often rotted in the ground. To remedy this, George and Albert planted the one-and-one-half foot long sections of seed cane, three joints to a section, in hills carefully built above ground level for drainage. They covered each section with about two inches of soil.

Most of the work the brothers did themselves with hoes and the blubber spade which the Hawaiians had adapted from whaling ships as an all purpose digging tool. They called it o'o.

But hand tools were no good for clearing off the jungle that covered all but a fraction of Abner's land. For that, George knew they needed oxen. Swallowing his pride, he took a job as luna on the new Wyllie plantation. He spent the summer cutting someone else's cane with a crew of Hawaiian and Chinese workmen. Then he cleared off the trash so that the ratoons could begin to sprout. It was brutal, drenching, exhausting work.

Within two weeks after he and Albert had planted their own cane, the first sprouts appeared. Then the hoeing began because the weeds seemed to grow faster than the cane. After cutting cane for Wyllie, then cultivating his own, George invariably reached home after dark, wet and muddy. After a brief supper, he would stumble to bed.

Meanwhile, he ordered a pair of ox cart wheels and an axle from a carpenter in Koloa named Wright. The price was sixty-five dollars—more than he would pay for an imported cart. But Wright's rugged, homemade carts lasted twice as long. By the time the wheels and axle were finished, George had the money from his foreman's job to pay for them. He could buy an old, second hand box for the cart for a few dollars. Yoke irons, bolts, and all, he could get at Hanalei for $2.50. But the ox bows and chains would have to come from Honolulu. George made one other investment, fifty dollars for a second-hand surveyor's compass which a friend found for him in San Francisco.

By September he was ready to clear land for planting more

cane, but his funds had run out. On his father's credit at Castle and Cooke, in Honolulu, he ordered goods to hire Hawaiian workmen: one dozen hickory shirts, one dozen calico shirts, one dozen coarse pants, one-half dozen rather better pants, three pea jackets, and one dozen thick shoes size eight and nine.

With eight men and rented oxen he began clearing land at the ford between the river and the road. When it rained, they worked in ankle deep mud, the oxen tugging hopelessly at the tree stumps. One particularly exasperating day, an erect figure came riding down the road. George immediately recognized his old friend, Judge Widemann. The German leaned from the saddle to shake George's muddy hand, then looked at his own in dismay.

"I heard you were back and hard at cane planting," Widemann said. "But I had no idea you were trying to grow it out of your ears."

"Am I that muddy?"

"You look like a log dragged out of a swamp." As he wiped his hand on a handkerchief, the German said, "I understand they taught you surveying in that engineering school of yours."

"That's right."

"Well, I need some surveying done when you're ready to quit stomping in the mud. I'm willing to pay cash. What do you say?"

George felt his fatigue disappear. "Give me two more weeks, Judge Widemann, and I'll survey the top of Mount Waialeale if you want me to."

*   *   *

The surveying took him all over the island. One day, when Judge Widemann was in the area, he rode along. "I want to see if I'm getting my money's worth," he said with a grin as he set out with George and his two young Hawaiian helpers.

The parcel of land to be surveyed belonged to a Hawaiian who had mortgaged his property. Now he couldn't pay back his loan, even though it was a small sum, considerably less than the

value of his property. Rather than see the Hawaiian lose everything, Judge Widemann was buying the land at a fair price. In
the same way, the German planter-politician had acquired
other plots that he really didn't want and couldn't afford. He
was very popular with the natives.

Their little cavalcade rode to a weather-beaten grass house
in a clearing. Dogs came to meet them, barking furiously.
Several pigs scampered into the bushes. A tiny, naked Hawaiian
child stood rooted to a spot near the door, both his mouth and
eyes wide open. As they dismounted, a muscular, middle-
aged Hawaiian emerged from the house. He greeted Mr. Widemann effusively, then shook hands solemnly with George.

In halting Hawaiian, for he had never learned to speak the
language well, George asked, "Where are the boundaries to
your kuleana?"

The Hawaiian waved vaguely with his hand. "Over there."

George smiled patiently. "Would you show me?"

"Why?" asked the native, suddenly suspicious.

Still smiling, George explained, "In order to buy your land,
Mr. Widemann must know how much there is . . . "

"Everyone knows how much there is. It has been in my
family since my grandfather. It was given to me by the King!"

These interviews were always painful to George. It was always the same, over and over again, the Hawaiian losing his
land, unable to understand what was happening to him.

"That is the old way," George said gently. "The new way is
different. We must measure your land and draw a picture of it.
Then Judge Widemann must take the picture to the land office.
If he does not have the picture, he cannot get title to the land."

The Hawaiian glanced at Widemann who shrugged, then
nodded. "It is the new way," he said apologetically. "The old
way is good enough for me. But it is not good enough for the
government."

Bewildered, the Hawaiian shook his head. "Come," he said.
He led the way to a taro patch. Pointing up the slope, he said,

"My land runs from the taro patch on this side of the auwai to the stream. From the stream to that rock. From the rock to the kukui tree, then down that gully to this line of taro patches."

The whole family watched George take the brass compass out of his saddlebag and fit it to the tripod. Judge Widemann also watched with interest as George set up the compass at the corner of the taro patch. Making sure the needle swung free, George flipped up the two sighting rods hinged to opposite sides of the compass. Erect, they stood at right angles to the glass cover of the instrument.

With great care, George sighted through the rods along the water ditch until the alignment of the rods was exact. Then he took a reading of the alignment from the needle of the compass. Into his canvas covered notebook he jotted down the reading, then another figure.

Looking over his shoulder, Judge Widemann asked, "What's that second figure for?"

"It's a correction for the magnetic variation. The compass needle doesn't point to true north, you know."

"Do all surveyors take the trouble to do it that way?"

"I'm afraid there are some in the islands who don't," George replied.

"What does that note about the weather mean?" asked Widemann, indicating a comment George had scribbled before he had set up his compass.

"Well, today is a sunny day. But if it were raining, and the visibility were poor, it might affect my measurements, make them less accurate. You're paying for my accuracy so you have a right to know under what conditions I'm working."

The tall German stroked his mustache with a thoughtful finger. "I'm impressed," he said.

"Thank you," George replied absently. "Now, I have to find out what kind of measurements my chainmen are getting. Excuse me."

Judge Widemann watched him with new interest as George

methodically worked his way around the parcel of land. Several times on the way home, the German seemed about to speak, as if he had a secret he found difficult to keep. But he maintained his silence as well as a look of pleased decision on his handsome face.

*   *   *

George chafed against the irritations of living at home where his parents watched over him as closely as they did their younger sons. His mother always wanted to know where he rode on weekends. His father checked George's expenditures and, even more exasperating, kept giving advice about how to grow sugar cane. George would have preferred to strike out on his own but he felt an obligation to stay home and help his father until he could support himself. The cane he had planted would not mature for at least another year.

Restlessly, George took a part time job as tax collector with Duncan McBride, a young Scotsman who had settled on Kauai. It had been almost a year and a half since George had earned his engineering certificate. Was all the expense and effort to be wasted after all? At Christmas he was moody and irritable. On the New Year, when the family exchanged gifts, he did his best to enter into the festive spirit. He only managed to worry his mother. But a few days later a letter from Judge Widemann, dated Grove Farm, December 27, 1863, put him on top of the world! The letter read, "If you can make it convenient to yourself, I should like you to undertake the supervision of the cutting of a water lead which I intend to commence before long. Be kind enough to consider this matter so that you can give me an answer when you come over."

A water ditch! He was getting an engineering assignment at last. Just the kind he had dreamed of. Not since Mr. Rice had built his ditch had anyone attempted such a project. And he, George N. Wilcox, would be the engineer! In an exuberant mood, he rode directly to Grove Farm, not even stopping to say hello to Maria and her husband, past the bamboo village, past the trash houses, past the Hawaiian church.

Judge Widemann and his Hawaiian wife lived just beyond the church on a bare, windswept bluff on the edge of the valley. The house was a long, rectangular building with a lofty, shaggy, grass-thatched roof. There was a cook house next door. Nearby George saw an old vat for storing kukui nuts where the enterprising judge had tried to extract the oil from the nuts for commercial purposes. There was also the foundation for what was to have been a saw mill for making barrel staves from native timber. One thing about Judge Widemann, if one idea didn't work, he had another ready to try the next day. Besides being the judge, tax assessor, road supervisor, government clerk, and Lihue's member of the legislature, he manufactured lime and tried to start a dairy in the valley below the house.

Mrs. Widemann greeted George at the door. She was a pretty woman, younger than her husband. Two wide-eyed children stared at George from the corner. The house had open rafters and was divided into small rooms by means of partitions that did not reach to the ceiling. It was an unpretentious place, rough hewn, but comfortable and snug.

Obviously, Judge Widemann's enthusiasm matched George's. He waved his guest to a chair but wouldn't sit down himself. Instead, he paced the room in his excitement. "This is a project I have long dreamed of, George. I've always known that Mr. Rice found the key to successfully growing sugar cane with that ditch of his. Lihue Plantation, that's what it's called now, is finally on its feet. Too bad Mr. Rice isn't here to see it. But I am, and there's no reason why I can't profit from it. In fact, I've wanted to put in my own ditch for years, but I haven't been able to figure a way to finance it until recently."

George nodded. The judge plunged on. "This is my plan. We'll use Hawaiian labor. They are my friends, those people. They deserve a chance to get in on this. In return for their labor, I will give them land, cane land, and they will share the water from the ditch. They will help me dig the ditch, and I will help them become cane planters. You see? I have already chosen my men. They have agreed."

George broke in eagerly. "Where are you going to tap the water? If I may make a suggestion . . . "

"Thank you, George, but that's already decided. I've had the best engineer in the Islands lay out the ditch, William Webster from Honolulu, the government land agent. He just finished the job. That's why it was time to send for you . . . why, what's the matter?"

George forced himself to smile. "Nothing. Webster is a fine engineer."

"I'm glad you think so because you'll be working with his plans. George, I want you to supervise the digging. You know the Hawaiians. They like you. And you have some engineering training. I'll pay you eighty dollars a month. What do you say?"

George turned his hat over in his lap, his dream demolished. So he was to be merely the construction foreman? But eighty dollars a month would get him out of debt to his father. "Thank you, Mr. Widemann, I'll do the best I can for you."

"Good, good! First thing in the morning we will ride up the line Webster laid out."

They started before breakfast at first light, riding toward the mountains along a newly blazed trail marked with pegs. The land, partly wooded, sloped gently upward into the forests at the foot of the mountains. It was an easy journey of about three miles, free of major obstructions. George could see that no tunneling would be necessary. Even digging would be easy because there were so few rocks in the soil. But as they approached the water source, a frown formed on George's face. He kept looking back along the route, measuring with his eye. Then he would peer ahead. By the time they reached the stream, he was deep in thought.

"Well, what do you think, George?" Judge Widemann asked enthusiastically. "Can you handle the job?"

George nodded. "Digging the ditch will be no problem. I don't even think we'll have to do any blasting. But . . . "

"What is it?"

George hesitated. Then he blurted, "The ditch is laid out wrong."

The judge frowned, then burst out laughing. "By golly, wait till I tell Webster. So he laid the ditch out wrong, did he? He'll get a kick out of that."

George flushed. "It isn't very funny. You won't get any water into your cane with this ditch."

Still grinning, the judge asked, "Very well, my expert engineer, tell me why not?"

"The grade is too gentle. There isn't enough fall to bring the water down. It'll soak into this porous soil before it gets to the cane."

Judge Widemann began to look annoyed. "I'm grateful for your opinion, George, but I'm quite sure Webster knows his job. When you've been an engineer as long as he has, you may think differently."

"But Mr. Webster hasn't had any more experience laying out an irrigation ditch than I have," George answered stubbornly. "Mr. Rice is the only one who's done it before. Maybe Webster miscalculated when he measured the grade. Do you know if he used a hand level or one on a tripod? For a ditch this size, I would say he should have allowed for a fall of at least one foot per 1,000 feet . . . "

By this time the judge was angry. "Don't you suppose Webster has sense enough to know that?"

"If he has the sense, he didn't use it. I can show you where this ditch should be, Judge Widemann. Don't throw your money away on this one . . . "

"That's enough!" snapped the judge, his face flushed. "I don't need a young smart aleck just out of college to tell me how to spend my money. I hired you to dig this ditch, that's all. You will follow Webster's plans exactly! Is that understood?"

"Yes, sir," George replied.

As they rode home in silence, he kept wondering if his judgment was correct or if he had spoken out of envy of Webster.

Every day, as he rode at dawn with his party of Hawaiian workmen to the ditch, George became more convinced that it would not bring down the water. But no one agreed with him. The men even teased him about it. So he kept his silence. The work kept him busy from dawn to sundown. He ate poi, salted fish, or jerked beef with the men. He lived with the Widemanns and sent most of his paycheck home every month.

By July the ditch was finished. Judge Widemann was on fire with eagerness. It was late in the day when they all stood at the end of the long, freshly dug trench, waiting for the first stream of water to flow into the freshly plowed field. The judge strode restlessly up and down, trampling the fresh dirt. After an hour, he impatiently mounted his horse and started up the ditch. George followed. They rode half a mile without seeing even a trickle of water.

"I can't understand what's the matter," the judge fretted. "Don't those men know how to turn the water into the ditch?"

They rode on. Here the ditch was muddy on the bottom. They kept riding. Water stood in puddles, soaking slowly into the soil on the bottom of the ditch. Farther up the slope there was more water. But it wasn't moving.

Judge Widemann pulled to a halt, his face grave. "I should have listened to you, George," he said slowly.

George shrugged. "I don't blame you for not listening. Frankly, I wasn't too sure myself. When you have so many variable factors . . . an uncertain water supply, a shallow grade, porous soil . . . it's easy to miscalculate."

The tall German sighed. "Well, there goes all that cane I wanted to plant. The only thing I can do now is pray for rain."

"I'm sorry, Judge Widemann."

*　*　*

At supper, the judge managed to joke about the fiasco. But George was glum. After supper they went out on the lanai for the judge's evening cigar.

"What are your plans now, George?" the judge asked.

"I guess I'll go back to Waioli."

"You've done a first rate job on that ditch. Oh, never mind the water. I've been watching you for some time, now. You have a good head on your shoulders and plenty of common sense. And you seem to be a fellow who likes to be his own boss. Am I right?"

"You're right," replied George, embarrassed by the praise.

"Good. Now let me speak frankly. As you know, I have a number of business interests besides Grove Farm that keep me occupied. Frankly, I would like to be relieved of some of the burden. And my wife is anxious to move to Honolulu. Would you consider taking this plantation off my hands?"

George sat stunned. "I don't understand."

"You are looking for a start. You couldn't ask for a better place than Grove Farm. Oh, I know it hasn't produced a great deal. But that's because I haven't had time to work it. For you, it would be ideal. I have four hundred acres of cane land, five hundred more in pasture for livestock. Lihue mill is only a mile away. Some planters haul their cane three times as far. You're within a mile and a half of the landing, and the house is in good repair. I even have a field plowed and ready to plant. As for water, well, you've proved you know more about where to put a ditch than I do."

George's head was spinning. "But I don't have any money. How can I . . . ?"

"That might be arranged, George. Suppose I loaned you the amount of the mortgage and arranged credit with Hackfeld and Company in Honolulu for expenses until your crop comes in? It would be a considerable risk, George, but I have learned to trust my judgment about people. I think you would make the loan good."

"At what rate of interest?" George asked.

"Twelve per cent, compounded quarterly."

George whistled. The judge shrugged. "I know it's steep, but it's the going rate. A few good crops and your worries are over. If you don't want to buy, I might lease the plantation to you . . . "

"But what if I can't get water down to the cane?"

"I think you can, and I'd be willing to help finance the ditch."

"I . . . don't know."

"Think it over," Judge Widemann told him as he rose to go inside. "There's no hurry. Let me know when you've decided."

That night George couldn't sleep. His own plantation! Judge Widemann made it sound so easy, the chance of a lifetime! But George's inner voice of common sense kept finding fault with the scheme. He had no mill. What if the new manager of Lihue Plantation decided not to grind his cane? His crop would be worthless. What if a second ditch failed as the first had? He'd be ruined. What if he couldn't meet the payments to Judge Widemann? He'd lose all the work and money he had put into the plantation. Even worse, he'd be saddled with debts it would take him years to pay.

The longer he thought about it the more he realized that the cards were all stacked against any chance of success. No wonder so many sugar planters went broke. Yet, a few were succeeding. George shook his head irritably, as if to clear it, and rolled over again, trying to get to sleep.

* * *

He went home, as uprooted as ever. In August, he received a letter from young Professor William D. Alexander, now president of Punahou, offering him Mr. Rice's old job at the school with a salary of $450 a year and board. Meanwhile, George applied for a job as teacher at Lahainaluna School on Maui where Sam Alexander had been for a year. But he wasn't eager about taking either position.

Abner advised him to be cautious about accepting Judge Widemann's offer. "He has no fencing for his cane, my boy. That will be a heavy expense. You must remember that it will be eighteen months before your first crop matures. How will you live in the meantime? Most important of all, there is no water. Don't forget that the first ditch failed. Even if you could finance a second ditch, how do you know it will work?"

George couldn't make up his mind. He was more restless than ever. He spent his days clearing new cane fields down the valley with his brother, and because he was irritable, he often argued with Albert, a headstrong young man. When the letter, dated October 28, 1864, came from Judge Widemann, George read it with relief. The judge still wanted him to buy or lease Grove Farm. But if the arrangements did not suit, would George at least manage the place on salary while the judge was away on business?"

The business was a well-paying position as temporary manager of the new Wyllie Plantation at Hanalei. George wrote back agreeing to talk it over. So George, on his way from Hanalei to Grove Farm, met the judge who was riding from Grove Farm to Hanalei. They dismounted under a spreading hau tree in a district called Waipake. The large, flat hau leaves rattled beneath their feet.

"Well, George, have you decided to take the plantation off my hands?" the judge asked jovially.

"No, I haven't," George replied, feeling uncomfortable.

"The offer still stands."

"I'd like to take it. I want to so bad I dream about it at night. But I just don't see how I can . . . "

"I know. Now let me be very frank. I have borrowed money on the plantation, and I need an income from it to pay my debts. But I don't have time to work Grove Farm. Would you consider managing the place? I'll pay you seventy-five dollars a month."

"I might," said George slowly.

"Let me make an alternative proposition. Why not lease the place from me? I'll charge you nine hundred dollars a year, payable semi-annually. Wait, wait, I know you have no money. But I think I know how that problem might be solved. I have had experience in these matters, you know."

George smiled.

"Once you bring the ditch down, I think Lihue Plantation would be glad to pay you two to three hundred dollars a year for turning the water into their ditch at night. Besides that, I believe I could turn into your hands employment such as surveying and the like that would pay, perhaps, $250 per annum and also, possibly, the Governor's clerkship which is worth another $250. In addition, I would finance the construction of a water ditch and arrange credit for your expenses with Hackfeld and Company."

"That's very generous, Judge Widemann."

The judge smiled. "Not generous if I get my investment back. And I have confidence that I will."

George hesitated. "May I work on a salary for a while? There's something I have to make sure of."

"Of course. I'll keep in touch with you."

They shook hands and rode in opposite directions. George felt much as he had that day he rode to his first job at the plantation store. But this time the stakes were so much higher!

He moved in with Mrs. Widemann and her mother who were busy getting the family ready to move. Every evening George would stand on the barren bluff beside the shaggy-roofed house and gaze up the gentle slope to the green mountains, jagged against the sky. Those mountains held a treasure of water. Could he bring it down to the cane by the time the rains stopped in the summer?

On weekends he rode far up the slope above the house with a Hawaiian helper. They always did the same thing. The assistant went ahead with a tall pole. He would stop at George's signal, holding the pole erect, and wait while George sighted carefully through a spy glass. Then he would move ahead with the pole and George would measure again. They worked their way up a slope, then worked down another way while George checked one series of sightings against the other.

As he worked, methodical hour after methodical hour, he always wrestled with the same problem. Could he bring the water to the cane by next summer in time to save the crop? It would mean using as much of the existing ditch as possible. He'd have to extend the upper end of it to get a better supply of water. Maybe he could bring the lower end out higher up the slope to give it more fall? But what if the porous soil soaked it up anyway?

At night he sat with a pencil and paper, figuring endlessly. No matter how closely he figured, his income from part time work did not come to nine hundred dollars a year. If he took the lease, the ditch had to work. And the location of the ditch was his decision to make this time. He was the engineer, the farmer, everything, just as he'd always wanted it.

One night in late November, 1864, he put the figures away and sat mulling over his survey notes. They showed that his ditch would bring down the water. Not as much as he had hoped, but enough, unless he was wrong as Webster had been.

Finally, he pushed aside the survey notes and took up his pen. In a hasty scrawl, he wrote, "Dear Judge Widemann, I have decided to lease Grove Farm on your terms provided you finance the water ditch as promised." He signed the note and stuffed it into a small envelope. Then he walked outside to the edge of the barren bluff overlooking the valley and stood in the starlight alone, not knowing if he felt like a frightened young school boy or a man who had just conquered the world.

PART III
The Pioneer

CHAPTER

9

The next day George rode in the rain, his horse splashing reluctantly up the muddy trail through the kukui grove. It was gloomy there, and dead trees marred the leafy scene. He passed the mill, shrouded and grey behind a screen of rain in the valley below. Water dripped from the brim of his black slouch hat. The back of his coat was soaked. But George saw none of this. He was too excited. His whole future hung on the next hour.

He had tossed all night trying to decide how he should approach Paul Isenberg about the milling contract. Now his mind was made up. He would neither beg nor take advantage of his long friendship with the Rices. All he would ask was a fair share of the products of his labor. Surely, Isenberg must agree to that. George was far from confident as he tied his horse to the fence in front of the sprawling white house, patted the animal's wet nose, and made his way up the walk.

Maria opened the door. She was very thin, dressed in a high-throated frock, her hair tightly pulled back into a bun. She held a baby in her arms.

"Come in, George, we've been expecting you," she said with a bright smile.

"You have?" he asked, startled.

"Of course, we've been neighbors for weeks, and you've never even said hello."

"Oh, I'm sorry," he said quietly.

He stepped into the familiar room, even more richly furnished than he remembered it: the koa bookcase, chairs of Chinese ebony, the Oriental panelling, a heavy three-legged table in the center. It all made his tiny room in the thatched house seem plain by comparison.

"Is Mr. Isenberg in? I'd like to see him . . . on business."

Maria made a little pout of disappointment. Her cheeks seemed flushed, and her eyes were unnaturally bright. "I'll call Paul," she said. "But sometime, George Wilcox, you must come for some other reason than business."

He grinned, "I will."

Then Mother Rice bustled into the room, her head shaking irritably. "Maria, you know you aren't supposed to be up. The doctor ordered you to rest. Now please give me the baby and go in for your nap."

"But mother, I never get to hold the baby. And we haven't seen George in ages . . . "

"I'm sure George will excuse you this time. Please, Maria, you'll have time for visiting later. Now it's important that you get well."

With a sigh, Maria gave her mother the baby, smiled at George, and went out of the room. Mother Rice, a small lace cap over her greying hair, nodded then to George. "Please forgive our rudeness, my boy. I'm so worried. First it was my brother-in-law, then my husband, and now Maria."

"Oh," said George. He couldn't think of anything else to say so he reached and awkwardly patted the work-worn old woman on a thin shoulder.

"You have come to see Paul?" she asked.

George nodded.

"He's working on his accounts in the office. Go right in. If you'll excuse me, I'll go tend to Maria."

Paul Isenberg rose to his feet as George opened the door. He was a powerfully built man, over six feet tall with massive shoulders and a deep chest. At twenty-eight he was only three years older than George; but his full beard, cut square just below his collar, and the flowing mustache gave him an air of importance that George's short, untidy mustache had never been able to achieve. Isenberg wore a well-tailored, black broadcloth coat and neatly shined shoes. George suddenly felt out of place in his rumpled coat with the baggy pockets and his mudspattered, knee-length boots. When Isenberg waved him to a chair, George sat with relief. Sitting down, Isenberg didn't tower over him so much.

"I understand Widemann has made you his overseer," said Isenberg casually in precise English with a marked German accent.

"I'm not his overseer any longer," George answered, a bit nettled. "I've decided to lease Grove Farm."

Isenberg toyed with his gold watch chain. He seemed amused. "So you have been bitten also. Well, you could have done worse."

"Grove Farm is a good investment," said George, more sharply than he'd intended.

"Without water, without a mill?" Isenberg said dryly.

"I can bring down the water."

"And your mill?"

"I don't have one but . . . "

"You wish to make a milling agreement with me. Is that it?"

"Yes," said George. This was not going the way he had hoped. He looked helplessly at his hands.

Isenberg continued smoothly. "You must understand the position of Lihue Plantation in such an arrangement. As a small planter, Wilcox, your investment is trivial: a few field hands, an ox or two, seed cane, perhaps a plow and an ox cart, and you are in business. This is precisely the reason so many hopeful men with insufficient capital start as you do hoping to make a fortune in sugar."

George flushed. Isenberg went on matter-of-factly.

"Most of them fail. And I can tell you why. The growing of sugar cane must be geared to the mill. For two reasons. First, a mill represents an investment of hundreds of thousands of dollars. The risk of such an investment is great. Second, the plantation can profitably grow only as much cane as the mill is able to convert into sugar that can be sold at a profit. A surplus of raw sugar has no value. At the moment we are growing as much cane as our mill can handle."

"But, couldn't you expand the mill?" said George hopefully.

"Expansion would be an added expense."

"And the increase in production would mean added income," George countered.

Isenberg answered blandly, "Any added income must be large enough to make an expansion profitable. And the amount of expansion must govern the amount of cane any independent planter would be allowed to grind at Lihue mill."

"Yes, I know that. But the more cane you grind the more money you'll make in the long run."

"It is not that simple. Remember, we can also lose money. Don't you Americans have a saying, 'the bigger they are the harder they fall?' "

George nodded, glum.

"This year we will manufacture approximately three hundred tons of sugar." The plantation owner stroked his beard thoughtfully. "By adding a vacuum pan we should be able to increase our output considerably. In that case, we might allow you, shall we say, forty acres."

George tried not to show his disappointment. "I had hoped for more. That will hardly pay my expenses."

Isenberg pursed his lips. "Here is something we might look

into. If you are successful in bringing additional water down from the mountains, and that remains to be seen, we would be interested in buying any surplus . . . if the price is right. In that case, I think you might be permitted to plant seventy-five acres."

"I could do that," said George hopeful again.

"Good, then it's settled. Now, as to the split, we will have to ask a straight fifty per cent of the sugar and molasses produced from Grove Farm cane. Is that satisfactory?"

"That seems a little high just to mill the cane . . . "

"All right, since you don't have but a few oxen, we will throw in the hauling and loading. But your men will cut the cane. Is that agreeable?"

George nodded.

"Just a few more details. We will charge you 65¢ each for the half kegs into which we will pack your sugar, 2¢ a keg for hauling from the mill to the landing in the bay, and 75¢ a month storage in our warehouse until the sugar is shipped. Oh, yes, molasses barrels will be charged to you at $1.75 each. Can you think of anthing else?"

George paused uncomfortably. "Yes, I'll need some seed cane."

"I'm sorry. I must ask you to buy from the natives. I do not wish to take from them a chance for income."

George continued doggedly. "Very well. But there's something else. I'll need men for digging the ditch. Would it be all right if I took some of your men when you don't need them?"

"How many will you need?"

"I figure about fifty for, maybe, three months. I hope to build up a labor force of my own as soon as possible. It's quite a problem."

Isenberg smiled thinly. "Labor is *the* problem on a sugar plantation. I have no men I can give you now, but it might be well to let you keep them busy during the slack season. But not before January. They earn 25¢ a day."

"Fair enough," said George, getting out of his chair. The meeting hadn't turned out as well as he had hoped, but it could have been worse.

The two men shook hands at the door. Before George turned to go, Isenberg said, "Wait a moment, there is a way I can turn a bit of cash your way, Wilcox. Are you taking over the herd of sheep Widemann kept on the slopes of Mount Kilohana?"

"Yes."

"Excellent! I will give you 50¢ a week for a quarter of good mutton. A steady diet of beef gets monotonous."

"It's a deal!"

The rain had stopped when George stepped off his horse at Grove Farm. He took a deep breath. He hadn't lost. But he hadn't won, either. He was bound to Lihue Plantation hand and foot. It gave him the same feeling of futility he'd experienced at Punahou School when Mr. Dole picked him out for a licking because he was the smallest. This time he couldn't fight back either.

His eyes followed the barren, rolling flat of the small plantation, a wasteland of brown mud and grey grass and lonely clumps of gnarled koa and kukui trees. Then he looked higher to the mist-shrouded mountains that embraced the land like a jagged, green necklace. In his mind he saw a clear mountain stream flowing into that waste land, turning it into a garden of tall, glistening cane.

Someday, he vowed, this would be his and he would be his own master. Until then, he would not be satisfied.

* * *

George awoke at five o'clock in the morning, instantly alert and impatient to begin working. He sat up in the cold darkness before dawn listening to the wind rustle the dry thatching above. A rooster crowed across the valley as he fumbled for a match to light the kerosene lantern. The flame cast a cheerless glow in the small room that had been Mr. Widemann's office.

Now it was crowded with supplies George had laid in hoping to exchange for labor: a brine barrel of salt salmon, a bolt of blue denim, a jar of epsom salts, and a bottle of castor oil. So far, there had been no workers to pay.

He pulled the nightshirt over his head and reached for his pants hanging on a hook because there were no closets in the grass house. Dressed, he picked up the lantern, his towel, and a scrap of soap. He hurried to the wash house on the edge of the valley, carrying water from a large wooden tub nearby. Finally, he made his way around the main house to the little cook house on the other side. Here he built a fire in the stove and put on a pot of coffee. When it was ready, he poured the steaming liquid into a heavy, white mug without a handle. Then he sat on the door sill sipping gingerly as the plantation yard came slowly into focus.

George was rinsing his cup, sparingly, for water had to be carried up from the stream in the valley, when an old Hawaiian woman padded silently into the cook house. She was Mrs. Widemann's mother, her majestic bulk covered by a simple mother hubbard.

"You are working too hard, Keoki," she told him in Hawaiian, her smile gentle and concerned. "There is no need to get up before the roosters."

"There is need when I can get no one to help me," he answered with a worried frown. "It has been two weeks since I took the farm, and I have built only a fence."

"You are too impatient."

"I can't help it," said George unhappily. He went after his horse pastured in the huge, treeless yard inclosed by a stone wall. George caught the long trailing rope and walked the animal to the harness shed set off from the north end of the main house. With quick, practiced motions he put on his saddle and buckled on the bridle.

He had not expected to find it so difficult to hire workmen. The natives who had helped him dig the ditch for Mr. Widemann were disillusioned by its failure. Now George felt like a man without arms. He stepped into the saddle and rode out onto the plain. His first field lay on the left, forty acres of virgin soil. Next year he planned to clear and plant thirty-five acres more. But he was helpless without workmen!

So every morning, in growing exasperation, he rode more than a mile across the plain to the shady seclusion of Kahale-haka Valley where grass houses nestled among mango and banana trees along a quiet stream. A pack of mongrel dogs announced his coming. Naked, sun-browned children came running out to wave at him. George waved back, grinning in spite of himself. At each house he stopped to inquire politely, "You want to work today?" The answer was always the same: a friendly grin with a shake of the head.

Discouraged, George returned to Grove Farm. He had breakfast with the Widemanns who were busy packing, then hurried to the field where he began setting fence posts. The sun was high when a Hawaiian rode up and dismounted. He was about thirty-five years old, wiry, and muscular. His white teeth flashed against the rich bronze of his skin in a wide smile.

"You are Keoki," he said, extending a calloused hand. "I am Pikau from Kilauea. I went to your father's school. He told me you are looking for men. I am a good man."

"I can use one," said George hopefully, wiping the sweat from his forehead with his sleeve. "What can you do?"

Pikau said proudly, "I can ride a horse. I can throw a rope. I can drive oxen. I can lay stone. I can fish. I can read, too, a little."

"Pikau, you're the answer to my prayer. You're hired! Twenty-five cents a day to start."

The Hawaiian clapped George on the back. "Good. You will be glad Pikau came today."

Immediately, George felt his discouragement vanish.

With his staff of one, he prepared the field for planting. Widemann had plowed and furrowed it the year before, but

George wasn't satisfied. Now he and Pikau plowed it again to break up the soil. George grew callouses on his hands from gripping the hardwood handles of the small, homemade plow as he steered it behind a yoke of plodding oxen. Next came harrowing to break up the clods. Like the plow, the harrow was made on the island; it had a frame of tough ohia wood with iron teeth set in the underside.

Pikau could do all the things he claimed and more. He knew how to weave hats from the stems of the cane tassels, he slaughtered and dressed a sheep every week, he could predict the weather and hypnotize chickens by drawing a line on the ground. And every so often he would disappear in the middle of the afternoon and come back the next morning with a basketful of fish.

The first Saturday George took him hunting in the mountains. They shot a wild pig. On the way home Pikau suggested innocently that he knew some good men who enjoyed the taste of pig. George quickly handed over the porker. A couple of days later, two more natives showed up for work.

The approach of January brought a new worry. In a week or two, the laborers at Lihue Plantation would be free to begin work on the ditch. But George had no way to transport them from their homes to the ditch every day. It would take at least an hour to walk the distance, then another hour to walk back.

George fretted, "We can't waste that much time. Pikau, I need horses, a whole lot of horses. But it would cost a fortune to buy them."

"How many horses do you want?"

"At least fifty to start."

Pikau thought a moment. "Lihue Plantation is rounding up wild horses and shooting the poor ones to save the pastures. Maybe we could buy the ones they're going to shoot?"

George slapped Pikau on the shoulder. "You're a good man! Why didn't I think of that?"

Pikau grinned. "I'm a good man, eh?"

"Do you think you're good enough to be my overseer at 50¢ a day when the digging starts?"

"Plenty good!" said Pikau without modesty.

A few days later George bought all the horses he could use for 12½¢ apiece.

* * *

He had been up since 4:30 A.M. The picks and shovels were piled where the men could each grab one. The bag of poi and bundle of jerked beef were ready for loading on a pack saddle. The January sky was turning grey when the workers arrived, all mounted on small, bony horses with Pikau proudly in the lead. George could hear them shouting and laughing long before they turned into the yard.

He counted about thirty workmen from Lihue plantation in addition to his own five full time laborers. It was not as many as he'd hoped for. He got into his saddle and sat impatiently while the workmen selected their tools, pushing and shoving in good humor. Then they set out over the rolling wasteland, climbing steadily into the wooded foothills.

The year before, when they were digging Mr. Widemann's ditch, George had joked with the men. Today he was too preoccupied for humor. With such a small crew, could he finish the ditch in time?

As he rode, he translated the problem into mathematics. A good man could dig five feet of ditch in a day. George had plotted about two miles of new ditch. Thirty-five men working six days a week could dig that much in two and a half months. Then allow a week or two for rain when they couldn't work. That meant finishing in April. April was late, but, with water, the cane might have enough time to form the sweet juice that produced sugar. Unless the cane was rich in sugar content, a crop would not pay expenses. Nobody knew for sure why some cane made a lot of sugar, some very little, except that the plant required lots of water and plenty of sun.

So George rode impatiently as they scrambled into and out of gullies, winding higher into the hills. When they reached the line of stakes in the ground, he was the first off his horse. He snatched a shovel and thrust the point into the ground. The workmen cheered as he tossed the first clump of dirt over his shoulder.

After that the weeks passed much too quickly for George. Once it rained for five days. The storm began one evening as he and the Widemanns were at supper. The gust of wind burst the door latch and knocked over a lamp. Mrs. Widemann's mother held the door while George nailed it shut.

His workmen were a constant source of hilarity and frustration. If the fish were running, only half of them showed up for work. One new man, an enormous fellow from a remote valley on the northern coast, had to be taught how to use a shovel. He had never seen one.

In order to shorten the route and save time, George decided to blast through a hillside rather than dig around it. He carefully supervised the hauling by muleback of two kegs of black powder. He dug the coyote hole himself, a tunnel into the hillside just large enough for one man, then a short cross tunnel for the powder. He placed the kegs in the cross tunnel, strung his fuse, and plugged the coyote hole. Then he shooed his workmen to a safe distance and lit the fuse.

At the last moment a Hawaiian came strolling down from the top of the hill. George waved frantically. The man waved back amiably and sat down on a rock a short distance above the tunnel to watch the explosion. When it went off, the man, rock, and all disappeared in a cloud of dust. George ran forward expecting to find arms and legs scattered over the hillside. The native picked himself up, dusty but perfectly whole, to quickly become the envy of every other man in the crew.

The most unexpected frustration was a water tunnel. Rather than dig a ditch all the way around a long ridge, George made up his mind to tunnel through it, a distance of about one hundred feet. The tunnel would save almost a week of digging, but the Hawaiians, even Pikau, refused to work in the darkness underground where the spirits of the dead might be lurking. George demanded, begged, cajoled. It was no use. Reluctantly, he put his men to work digging on the other side of the ridge.

Every day that break in his ditch exasperated George a little more. Then it began to worry him. If he couldn't get the tunnel through, the delay could put the whole project behind schedule. When the solution arrived, he did not recognize it. A young, short, chubby Chinese wearing a pigtail rode a mule into camp one day. He dismounted with surprising agility and crossed over to where George was checking the grade on a new section of ditch.

In very bad pidgin the bland little man said, "Come for make puka."

"Where you learn dig puka?" asked George.

"Californee. Long time me keiki come Frisco. Catchum hana hana railroad. Beeeeg mountain. Makum puka for track inside."

George looked skeptical. The man had told him that as a boy he had gone to California to dig railroad tunnels. "What's your name?"

"Kaipu," the man said.

"You haven't run away from Koloa Plantation, have you?"

The man shook his head firmly. George scratched his chin. The Chinese was the most unlikely looking construction worker he had ever seen, but George couldn't be choosey.

"All right, Kaipu. We'll give you a try."

"Fourteen dolla, please."

"Fourteen dollars! What for?"

"Make puka!" said Kaipu.

Pikau grinned at George. "He owes somebody fourteen dollars, Keoki. You pay him now and you'll never see him again."

"Make puka!" Kaipu insisted. "Fourteen dolla."

"It's a fair price," said George with a shrug. "Tomorrow I pay. You dig the puka."

They shook hands. The next morning at dawn, Kaipu showed up with another Chinese. They worked industriously all day. And the day after, in spite of Pikau's prediction. In two weeks the tunnel was finished. George kept the amiable little Chinese on as a part-time cook and field worker after the Widemanns moved away. The other Chinese remained also.

By March the ditch was still on schedule, and George turned his attention to plowing the furrows in his field. He had given this a lot of thought. On Lihue Plantation the furrows and feeder ditches ran in straight lines at right angles from each other in a geometrical pattern across the fields. But the system worked well only on level ground. Where there were slopes and ridges, the water all ran into the low areas leaving the upper elevations as dry as ever.

George's field was not entirely level. Now he made up his mind to put into practice the idea that had popped into his head that day he had looked at Mr. Rice's ditch so long ago. George's plan was to bring his main ditch in at the point of highest elevation. Then, using his surveyor's level, he laid out feeder ditches that followed the ridges. From the feed ditches he carefully staked out furrows that curved around the slopes in descending spirals instead of running straight down the hill.

The Hawaiian plowmen from Lihue Plantation watched these preparations with interest and amusement. Soon George was known as the dumb haole who couldn't make a straight line. On the day of the furrowing, a big crowd gathered on the fence. This was too good to miss.

It was Lono himself, Lihue's best handler of oxen, who brought the plow behind six yoke of oxen. The implement was a mammoth Burbank drill plow built of native hardwood with a double moldboard plowshare of iron bolted to the frame. Lono was an independent, cantankerous little Hawaiian fully aware of his reputation. He took one look at the curving lines of stakes and said in a loud voice, "You crazy!"

Lono's friends on the fence nudged one another, grinning.

"I'm hiring you to plow my furrows, not give advice," George answered. "All you have to do is follow those lines. They're six feet apart. Can you do that?"

"I get dizzy going in circles," said Lono. His audience snickered. From the corner of his eye, George saw Isenberg coming down the road, his big bulk dwarfing the horse.

Lono was enjoying himself hugely. He pointed down the slope for the benefit of his audience. "Keoki, I think you get mix up. That furrow down there bump into the other one." A sally of laughter followed his remark.

George felt his temper flare. "It's supposed to be that way. The furrows join at the end of the contour."

"Now you get me all mix up," said Lono. Isenberg dismounted at the fence as the Hawaiians howled in glee.

"All right, I'll plow it myself," George snapped.

Lono shrugged and walked away from the plow. As George grasped the wooden handles, the lead ox lay down. He was a big, dun-colored brute with enormous horns. George knew that Lono had done it. The little man knew every one of Lihue's five hundred oxen by name, which worked best together, which animal went on the off side. The oxen obeyed him like trained dogs.

"What's the matter, Keoki?" Lono asked innocently. Even Isenberg grinned.

George flushed. There was only one thing to do. He stepped behind the ox, twisted its tail and bit as hard as he could into the dirty, thick bristled hide. The ox scrambled to its feet.

"Hiiiiiyaaa!" George shouted, running back to take the plow handles. The oxen lumbered into motion. The heavy plow veered to the left. George threw his weight against the opposite handle. His audience was silent now, but George was too busy to notice. The enormous plow required not only strength but skill to hold. Doggedly, George plowed to the end of the furrow. Then he turned the plow back to Lono.

"That's the way I want it," he said firmly.

Lono had run out of argument. "Yes, Keoki."

Paul Isenberg walked over in his neat, black coat and a planter's hat. "Well, this is a new way to plow furrows," he said dubiously. "What do you call your system?"

"There isn't a name for it, I guess," George told him. "It just seems to me the water will be distributed more evenly if the furrows follow the contour of the slopes."

Isenberg shook his head. "I'll be interested to see if it works."

That evening George was tired and discouraged. He ate in silence. As Kaipu cleared the dishes, George sighed. "Everybody thinks your boss man pupule for making furrows in circles, Kaipu. What do you think?"

Kaipu shook his head with determination. "No pupule. In China same."

"What do you mean?" asked George with sudden interest.

"You go Canton. Plenty rice paddy. Plenty hill. Father, grandfather, his father make furrow same like you."

"On the contour?"

Kaipu nodded vigorously. "Long, long time, same, same!"

George answered gratefully, "Kaipu, you and I have a lot to learn from each other!"

*　　*　　*

There wasn't time to wait with the planting until the ditch was finished. So George drove an ox cart to the beach and around the bay to a Hawaiian settlement called Niumalu where the natives grew sugar cane, as a supplementary food crop, on the earthen dams that separated their taro patches. George carefully chose stands of healthy cane, making sure that they were original plantings and not ratoons.

He hired half a dozen Hawaiian women at the prevailing wage for female workers, $17\frac{1}{2}¢$ a day, to do the planting. "Cut it into two or three foot lengths," he told them. "The best part for planting is at the top of the stalk where the joints are close together. Sugar cane sprouts from the joints."

George supervised the planting. "Like this," he explained, taking a bundle of sugar cane sections from the ox cart. He walked along the furrow dropping the sections lengthwise in the furrow about a foot apart. "Now you do it," he told one of the women.

Then George took a hoe and lightly covered each section of cane with dirt. He handed the hoe to another worker. "You try it."

As the ditch neared completion, George became more and more restless. What if it failed after all? The project had already cost Mr. Widemann another thousand dollars. George knew now the judge had raised the money by borrowing from Paul Isenberg against Grove Farm. George's plantation expenses totalled almost one thousand dollars so far, advanced from Hackfeld and Co. in Honolulu. Well, in a week or two he would know if his theories worked. If they didn't the Hawaiians would never stop laughing.

In the middle of April, exactly as George had planned, the workmen finished building a small dam across the stream in the mountains. George was waiting impatiently below. Paul Isenberg was there, and Joseph Lovell the blacksmith, and young Willie Rice, now graduated from Punahou and in the hauling business. Hawaiians kept galloping up the ditch line to see if the water were coming. George waited in the hot sun, his eyes following the course of the ditch as it snaked across the plain and lost itself in the rugged green breast of Mount Kilohana. He resisted the temptation to ride up the ditch as Widemann had done.

Then a rider came galloping back. The water was moving! Now there was eagerness all around the field as they waited for the water. Again, George climbed into the ditch to make sure his crude, wooden barricade was secure in its slot. The barricade would divert the water into a feeder ditch where it could be fed into the furrows, a few at a time. When this section of the field had enough water, George could plug up the feeder ditch and open another. Or let the water run away into the sea. It was a good plan, if it worked.

Isenberg was at George's elbow as the water splashed against the wooden gate. The muddy stream turned obediently into the feeder ditch. Kaipu was waiting below. The stream of water was pitifully small.

"Stop it at the third furrow," George called.

Kaipu hastily dammed up the feeder ditch with dirt at a point just beyond the third furrow. The water stopped at this dam. As the tiny stream kept coming, the level of the water in the ditch rose almost to the level of the dirt dams that blocked the furrows.

"Open the furrows," George ordered.

Kaipu opened one furrow after another. Each time the water turned obediently into the furrow and moved slowly in a graceful arc around the very top of the ridge.

"Amazing," breathed Isenberg.

"Thank God," said George. "There isn't much water. But it follows the contour."

"Indeed it does." The other planter looked thoughtfully down at George. "I wonder if you would be interested in laying out the furrows in my fields like this, at a reasonable fee, of course."

George nodded happily. "I'll be glad to, Mr. Isenberg, but I'm afraid I'll be too busy on my own plantation for a while to work on yours." He touched his hat politely and walked away.

CHAPTER

10

George awoke with the feeling that something was wrong. It was almost five o'clock in the morning. The sky through the windows was pale grey. He lay still and listened. The sheep he'd pastured across the road were restless. He could hear them bleating. Puzzled, George got up and opened the door. His face clouded in anger when he saw that a dog was tearing at the carcass of a lamb. Snatching his Henry rifle from the wall, George ran into the yard, his nightshirt flapping around his legs. The dog began to run, with the lamb in its mouth, through the guinea grass toward the kukui grove. George stopped. He sighted carefully and fired. The dog stumbled, then fell in a heap.

George put his rifle away and got dressed. There didn't seem to be a day that went by without a new problem on his little plantation. Right now he was most worried about his supply of water. He kept an accurate record of rainfall, marking on his calendar the reading he took every morning on his homemade rain gauge out behind the house. The rains had been light in June. Now at the beginning of July, the dry season had begun. If the mountain streams that fed his ditch ran dry, those leafy green rows of juicy cane stalks in his field would turn yellow and dry. As he stepped out beneath the low overhang of thatching, his eyes searched the sky above the mountains for rain clouds. There were none.

With a sigh, he went to the cook house where Kaipu had his mug of coffee ready. George sipped gratefully. It was lonely living alone. He was glad that his younger brother, Sam, was coming to visit him next month.

George saddled his horse and rode to the field. The cane looked good, as tall as his waist, the stalks bursting with vigor and the leaves hanging in graceful adornment. George dismounted and picked up a handful of soil. It was very dry. He must tell Kaipu to be very careful with the water or there wouldn't be enough to go around.

Getting back into the saddle, George rode around the field. At one point he stopped, frowning. The weeds had gained a foothold here. Soon they'd choke out the cane. He must tell Pikau to take some of the men from clearing the new field and put them to hoeing.

Then he rode on to the new field. The clearing was going slowly, only started. Rocks from the ground were used to build stone walls. The trees would be cut up for firewood saleable to the mill. The stumps had to be blasted out. But the roots still could snap the shaft of a plow if the plowman wasn't careful.

His tour of inspection over, George rode quickly back to the house for a hasty breakfast of steak, poi, and coffee. Then he walked outside where his small crew was gathered for his instructions. It was now 6:00 A.M. He told Pikau about the weeds, Kaipu about the water. They were discussing the clearing of the new field, when a boy rode up with the news that the schooner had arrived.

"Good, that means you'll have two men to spare for hoeing, Pikau," George said. "I hired a couple of fellows from Honolulu. They should be on board that schooner."

"I hope they're worth the bounty," muttered Pikau. "My little boy works harder than the last bunch we got."

"We'll see," said George. "I'll go fetch them."

Bringing laborers down from Honolulu was a dubious undertaking. They always demanded a bounty in advance, and deck passage cost a dollar or two extra per man. Many of the men were deserters off whaling ships. But they were better than nothing at all. Maybe, with these two, he would be lucky. He wasn't. The first man was big, amiable, and obviously slow witted. The second was dark skinned and sullen. They mounted the extra horses George had brought and followed him to Kahalehaka Valley, where he had built a frame house with a thatched roof for his itinerant workers.

"It isn't fancy," he told them. "But mine isn't either."

The swarthy newcomer began to grumble. George ignored him. The men stowed their meager duffel bags under two of the bunks. Then George took them to the field. Kaipu was there looking worried.

"No water," he explained. "Ditch dry!"

George's heart sank. If the streams dried up so early in the season he might as well quit. But it didn't seem possible. More likely the ditch had gotten plugged up.

"Come on, Kaipu, we'll go take a look," George said irritably. As an after thought, he motioned for the unhappy new worker to follow. A complainer never made a work gang perform well. The man would do less harm out of earshot. The trio followed the winding course of the ditch until, in a heavily wooded valley, they found a tree fallen across the path of the water, spreading it into a hundred useless rivulets.

George looked pained. "I'd sooner go without a meal than see water go to waste like that," he said. Kaipu nodded. The other man gave a cynical grunt.

The three of them dismounted and walked around the tree. "One of us had better get down there in the ditch and put his back to the trunk while the other two pull from this side," said George. The new worker eyed the muddy ditch with distaste. Impatiently, George scrambled down into the mud.

"When I heave, you pull," he ordered.

Then minutes later the ditch was open and flowing freely once more. George was a muddy mess. The new worker had stopped grumbling.

* * *

It would have been pleasant to ride with Sam to swap stories with Willie Rice. The two of them together, spouting kanaka lingo like native politicians, were funnier than the legislative sessions in Honolulu. But after supper George waved good-by to his eighteen-year-old brother and took down the canvas-bound ledgers from their shelf.

He pulled a chair up to the table, dipped a steel pen in a bottle of ink, and wrote in his awkward scrawl half way down page eight of the cash book, in the center of the column: July 23, 1865. Then, consulting a notebook, he made the following entries:

Passage of 2 natives	$4.00
Poi money	2.50
Repairs on plows	2.00

He turned a page in his notebook and copied in another entry:

1 Retail License to H. Gilling	$51.00

Finally, he completed the cash book entries for the day with the last item, this one on the credit side:

Clerk's Salary $37.00

George stared proudly at the figure. After six months of working like a galley slave, he had finally upped his earnings to more than 50¢ a week from the sale of mutton, thirty-seven dollars all at one time. It was the first salary he'd received as government clerk. Filling out the papers and handling the money was a headache. But he had to have some cash!

Every time George added up the total he owed to Hackfeld and Company in Honolulu, he felt a touch of panic. He kept trying to economize, but the men had to be paid. He had to have tools and equipment. Joseph Lovell had charged $206.37 for carting stones cleared from his new field, another fourteen dollars for repairs to an ox cart, ten dollars more for making a bedstead for Sam to sleep in.

Figuring everything, his lease rent, advances for labor and equipment, George knew he was in debt nearly $1,500. He'd never seen so much money, much less owned it. With a good crop he had a chance of earning $3,000 to $4,000. But it would be another six months before his cane was ready to harvest. He sighed. Now he knew why so many small sugar planters gave up in despair. He flipped back through the pages of the cash book adding the amounts he'd spent on himself during the past six months.

1865

Jan.	21—Repairs on saddle	$ 3.75
Jan.	28—Cloth for coat	4.00
Mar.	11—Drawing paper	7.50
Mar.	11—Shoes	3.50
Apl.	22—Knife	.50
May	20—Gun repaired	2.00
May	30—1 pair boots	6.00
July	16—Shoes	5.00
July	16—Boots repaired	.75
		$33.00

The total gave him deep satisfaction. His clerk's salary covered his personal expenses with four dollars left over. He was paying his own way. When the crop came in, he'd be able to use every cent of the money to build the plantation.

George had just finished transferring the entries for the week from the cash book to the individual account books when Sam came back. The youth, bigger and heavier than George's 135 pounds, sprawled into a chair.

"Well, how much do you owe so far?" asked Sam cheerfully.

George winced, "If I told you, you wouldn't believe me."

"Willie Rice says you're a mighty cool gambler."

"Gambler?"

"That's right. You take over a farm that's up to its neck in mortgages, dig yourself an irrigation system that nobody's ever tried before, and then spend somebody else's money for twelve months before your crop is ready to harvest. If that isn't a gamble, what is?"

George scratched his chin for a moment. "I never thought about it like that before." He grinned at Sam and began putting away the books.

* * *

Sam went back to Punahou School late in August. It was in September that Willie Rice, a gangling nineteen-year-old, brought the news that George Dole of Koloa was back from his trip to the United States where he had attended the funeral of President Lincoln. On the following Sunday morning, George found himself riding with Willie across the island to the settlement of Koloa, once a whaling port, now a sugar plantation. The trail led through a wooded gap in the mountains, a park-like scene of lush foliage and grey, moss-mottled cliffs against the washed blue sky. But Willie hardly gave George time to enjoy the ride.

"I hear George's been all over the East, even in the South," chattered Willie. "He'll have plenty to talk about."

"George Dole usually does."

"Well, I don't mind. I want to hear how they feel about reciprocity back there. And annexation. Besides, there are plenty of other reasons for going to Koloa. Have you seen the Smith girls lately?"

"I guess not."

"Well, you're the only one. That Lottie is the prettiest girl on the island. Boy, is she popular!"

"Isn't she teaching in the mission school now?"

"That's right, she and her sister, Emma. But Lottie won't be teaching school very long, not with as many beaus as she's got. Come on!"

From the mountains the land sloped gently to the sea four miles away where the sparkling white surf broke on a rugged, black lava rock shore. The sweeping view stretched for miles on both sides. Koloa huddled far below: the mill, two churches, a school, several stores, and houses of adobe and thatch.

They arrived just in time for services at the "foreign" church where the Reverend Mr. Dole preached in English every Sunday. All other sermons on the island were in Hawaiian. Every seat in church was taken except in the very front pew where half a dozen students from the mission school for native girls were sitting in a prim row with their teacher. Nearby, Charles Neumann, the plantation cooper, sat at the new melodeon, ready to launch the first hymn.

George felt his ears burn as he led the way to the front, his shoes thumping on the bare board floor. There was really only room for one in the pew; but Willie squeezed in anyway, pushing George against a young woman in a high lace collar, her hair done in a stylish bun. The smooth roundness of her chin and the graceful curve of her neck were appealingly feminine.

"Hello, Lottie," Willie whispered loudly.

George would not have recognized her. He remembered Charlotte Smith as a girl in white stockings and pigtails. She smiled at Willie and then looked demurely at George. He smiled in return, and everything would have been fine if Willie hadn't whispered, so loud that everybody in church could hear, "This is George Wilcox."

At that moment the Reverend Daniel Dole arose and glared at George as he had years before at Punahou. George flushed and looked at the floor. He felt like a fool. All through the sermon he felt like kicking Willie. When it was over George had to shake hands with everybody outside. Mrs. Smith, wife of the pioneer missionary doctor on the island, put her hand on his arm. "You will come to the house for dinner, won't you? The Doles will be there. My goodness, it's been such a long time since we've visited. How are your father and mother? Why don't you walk me home and tell me all about them?"

"Yes, ma'am," said George.

Mrs. Smith patted his arm. "Come, Charlotte," she called. "George Wilcox is being kind enough to see us home. We mustn't keep him waiting."

Lottie turned away from Willie Rice, her long skirt swirling around her ankles. "I'm afraid I embarrassed Mr. Wilcox in church," she said with a smile.

"It wasn't your fault," George said quickly.

"You frowned so, I was sure you were very angry."

"No."

"Now you're frowning again."

"I frown when I'm embarrassed," he said unhappily.

For the first time, Lottie smiled warmly at him. "Well, that makes me feel better." George found himself smiling back. Willie Rice was right. Lottie Smith was the prettiest girl on the island. For some reason, his usual shyness didn't plague him as they walked down the dusty road, that is, not until they reached the house where the other boys broke into the conversation.

After dinner, the old folks set out to attend the native church because it "set a good example." Lottie and her sister dutifully went along to teach Sunday school. The young men stayed behind to argue politics. They were still arguing when the girls returned from church. Then it was time to go home.

"Why don't we all ride part of the way with Willie and George?" Lottie suggested. There was a merry scramble for the horses. Finally, they trooped out of the village leaving a cloud of dust. They laughed and joked all the way to the gap.

"Come back soon," called Lottie, waving.

George waved back. "We will."

He smiled as he and Willie rode slowly through the lengthening shadows. It had been years since he'd enjoyed himself so much.

"Wasn't that better than sitting at home with a newspaper?" Willie wanted to know.

"A lot better," George agreed. But before they reached Grove Farm his mind was already at work planning the plowing.

*   *   *

The days began to run together. And every day George awoke with a feeling of haste. There was so much to do! Now he was also tax collector: $1 for each horse, $1.50 for every dog, $2 school tax, $5 poll tax. Sometimes darkness caught him miles from home on a dusty back road. Then he would eat poi and jerked beef with the Hawaiians and sleep among the children and dogs and mosquitoes. Every paid up taxpayer received a receipt which he was required to show before voting at the next election. George spent hours keeping the accounts straight.

He took the job of road supervisor for three districts: Lihue, Anahola, and Hanalei, almost a third of the island. As a result, he spent several days a week planning road repairs, ordering materials and seeing that they got to the job, delivering poi to the workers. Once, when they ran short of taro, he sailed a boat with two natives to the remote valley of Kalalau on the north shore for a fresh supply.

Thatched roof home of George N. Wilcox at Grove Farm, 1865

Lihue Plantation Company mill, 1865

Wilcox home at Grove Farm, 1874

Lihue Plantation Company mill and ox cart, 1880

Palace of Princess Ruth Keelikolani, built in Honolulu
in 1881 from sale of lands to Grove Farm

Grove Farm harvesting and hauling crews, 1887, with
S. W. Wilcox on horseback (center)

Wilcox home at Grove Farm, 1886 (from drawing by Mrs. Margaret Gillin)

Grove Farm office, 1885

In November he spent three weeks surveying the island of Niihau, off the southwest coast of Kauai, for six dollars a day. For a time he was postmaster of Lihue, and the thatched farm house became a post office. He took any job that would help meet the mounting expenses of his plantation. And every night he sank wearily on his bed feeling that he had not done enough.

* * *

All summer the sugar cane had grown chest high, shoulder high, head high, drawing vigor from the musical stream of water that flowed obediently from the mountains across the plain to do its work in the field. The clumps of stalks thickened, then began to crowd one another until the field was a leafy, impenetrable green jungle. When the leaves shut out the sun, George sighed with relief. For the men could then be taken from hoeing and put to other tasks. That winter they planted the new field.

By February the first crop stood proudly, so tall that a man on horseback could not look over it. In March George brought Paul Isenberg to see. The big German nodded approvingly.

"We have been fortunate this year, Wilcox, no blight, no hurricane. I think we may show a profit on this crop."

The possessive "we" irritated George, but he merely said, "I'm ready to begin harvesting any time."

"Don't be impatient. These things take planning. Let me see, I think we'll make about ten tons of cane to the acre. Forty acres at ten tons each comes to four hundred tons. How much cane would you say an ox cart can carry?"

"A ton is a pretty good load."

"Correct. Now I will give you a lesson in the operation of a plantation. An ox cart moves at one mile an hour. Your field is about a mile from the mill, maybe less. Thus, it will require two hours for each ox cart to haul a load to the mill and return. With loading and unloading, each cart should be able to haul three loads a day. Therefore, one cart could do the job in, let me see, 133 days. That would be too slow. We will put twenty-five carts on the job and finish in five days."

"Fine, when can we start?" said George eagerly.

Isenberg shrugged. "I'll let you know. Lihue cane comes first, and we are late this year."

George fought down his exasperation. He received the twelve cane knives he had ordered from Hackfeld and Co. in February at one dollar each. Then he took his men to the field and showed them how to use the knives.

He slipped on a pair of gloves. "Now watch," he said, taking one of the heavy machetes. He bent over to grasp a stalk of cane in his left hand. With his right, he swung the cane knife in a crisp arc. "Cut as close to the ground as you can," he said. "That's where the best juice is. If you leave stumps, you'll waste a lot of the crop. But be sure to cut off the tassel. That's rubbish."

George surveyed his ragged little crew of about a dozen workers. Most of them were barefooted. Their pants were denim and their shirts nondescript. They wove their own hats from the leaves of the lauhala tree or from the stems of the cane tassels. Few of them could read, and he had to teach some of them how to perform the simplest tasks. But they were loyal, and they depended on him for their livelihood. He was determined not to fail them.

"The ox drivers will load their own carts," George explained. "It's your job to cut enough cane to fill those carts. If we get behind, there will be pilikia at the mill." The men nodded. "One thing more. When this job is finished, we'll have the biggest luau you ever saw!" The men grinned broadly.

Finally, the big day came. The colorful ox drivers, haughty and proud of their skill, drove the lumbering carts to the field. It took three yoke of oxen to pull a fully loaded cart.

George had started his own crew at daybreak. Each man received a pair of gloves and a file for sharpening his cane knife. Now they were moving slowly across the field, bent double, their knives flashing in the sun. It was brutal work, hot and dusty, and tiny, needle sharp splinters from the cane stalks had a way of getting under the workers' clothes.

Paul Isenberg rode up during the middle of the afternoon. He glanced with a disapproving frown at a man standing idly at the edge of the field. "Is that fellow smoking?"

George nodded.

"If he were my man I'd fire him for that. He'll burn the field."

"I let the men stop for a smoke now and then as long as they do it at the end of the rows," George answered mildly.

Isenberg gave him a sharp glance, then changed the subject. In spite of their inexperience, George's men managed to cut enough cane to fill the carts with enormous tangles of supple, juicy stalks. Each time one of those towering loads moved slowly off to the mill, George felt a moment of pride.

In five days it was done. The field was bare again. And it was time to celebrate. Pikau went fishing while George set out with his gun to hunt for wild pigs. The men gathered taro from their patches and shell fish from the sea while their families snared tiny, fresh water shrimp in the mountain streams.

George invited the ox drivers and the mill hands to the feast. The Isenbergs came with Mother Rice and Willie. The Doles and Smiths rode over from Koloa. They all complimented George on his success. Solomon Kamahalo even made a speech. Pointing proudly toward Paul Isenberg, Solomon told everyone they were lucky to have their haole nui. Then, pointing to George, the old Hawaiian said they were just as lucky to have their haole liilii. The crowd roared.

But George couldn't feel the excitement he'd expected. This year had been only a skirmish. He was still plowing someone else's land. His cane was going to someone else's mill. When Lottie came to say good-by, he realized that he'd hardly spoken to her.

"You didn't come back to visit us the way you said you would," she said. "Didn't you enjoy yourself?"

George felt instantly contrite. "I enjoyed myself very much," he answered. "But I've been so busy ever since . . ."

"It isn't good for you to think of the plantation all the time," she said seriously. Then she teased, "It isn't very flattering, either."

"You won't ever lack attention, Lottie, you're much too pretty," he said without guile.

"That's better. You will visit us soon, won't you?"

"Yes," he promised.

But even as he said it he knew that he had more important things to do first.

CHAPTER

11

In June, 1866, Hackfeld and Company sold George's sugar for $4,432. His advances totaled $3,484. He had cleared $948. When George received the news, he took a trip to Honolulu to settle his account and talk to Judge Widemann. The judge settled back in his chair under a shelf heavy with law books, and smiled at his visitor.

"Well, young man, you are to be congratulated. You are finally making Grove Farm pay. I tried for years to do that and didn't succeed."

"It's the ditch," said George modestly. "That's what I came to talk about."

"Yes, of course, the ditch. But Paul Isenberg tells me you have also improved the system of furrows. You have a good head on your shoulders. That's what it takes in this business."

"About the ditch, you see . . ."

The judge wasn't listening. "I have confidence in you. You're willing to take a calculated risk but not a foolish one. And sugar is full of risks. I suppose you know that the great Prince-

149

ville Plantation at Hanalei is almost bankrupt. An investment of at least a quarter of a million. I doubt if it will bring $50,000. You have been extremely fortunate.

"I realize that, Judge. That's why . . ."

"Sugar has a tremendous future in the Islands but it needs to be put on a more substantial footing," the judge continued. "We need better port facilities for loading and unloading. We need regular steamer service so that we can count on shipments to arrive. Most of all, we need a favorable market. The duty in San Francisco, plus shipping costs, is a major hardship."

"Yes, sir," said George, giving up.

"And the labor problem will get worse. Do you realize that the Hawaiians are dying at a rate of 2,000 a year? Hardly sixty thousand remain. As a sugar planter, I am concerned about who is to till the crops. But as a sentimentalist, I am more concerned about the Hawaiians and their tiny nation. What is to become of them?"

George listened respectfully. The judge was a man of many moods. Now the handsome head was sunk on his breast, the quicksilver mouth turned down with brooding. But a moment later he smiled again. "And now you have come to Honolulu to celebrate, eh?"

"No, I came to talk about the ditch."

"Yes, what about it?"

"I want to extend it, tap more streams. Now there's enough water for only the first forty acres. The other thirty-five acres look very bad. I don't think they will make a crop."

"I see."

"With enough water, I'm convinced Grove Farm can produce a crop of two hundred tons of sugar. But there's no sense in planting cane unless we can irrigate it. The investment will be worth every penny."

Judge Widemann nodded thoughtfully. "I think you are right, George. However, I am not in a position financially to invest more money. Is there any chance you might swing it alone?"

"I thought of it," George confessed.

"I'm willing to extend the lease to make it worth your while."

The younger man remained silent. With every step he took forward, it seemed that he took two in the opposite direction. By the time he extended the ditch to where he wanted it, he would spend at least a thousand dollars, more likely two or three. But without more water he might as well forget about being independent.

He sighed. "Let me think it over," he said finally.

Judge Widemann smiled. "Take all the time you want. The offer remains good. I like having you as a tenant."

* * *

In August, Lucy made her first visit to her son's new sugar plantation. As Abner waved from the doorstep with Luther, now sixteen, and Henry, eight, Lucy seated herself on the side-saddle, adjusted her wide-brimmed straw hat, and set off with George down the road. She kept her poise along every inch of the rough, fifty-mile trail even when George forgot himself at a river crossing and roundly cursed a native for mistreating his horse. It was the first time his mother had heard him swear. Lucy pretended not to notice.

When George tried to tell her about his system of irrigation she kept interrupting to ask about his meals, how often he washed his clothes, and what time he went to bed at night. But she was keenly attentive when he told her about visiting at Koloa. George's enthusiasm kept mounting the nearer they came. Finally, as they rode past Lihue mill and into the kukui grove near his house, he couldn't contain himself any longer.

"Grove Farm was named after this old stand of kukui," he explained. "The trees are dying out now but when the house was built in the early fifties, it must have been a beautiful spot.

Hawaiians began calling it Nu Hou after Mr. Widemann built a pump to bring water up from the stream in the valley to his cistern. They had never seen water go uphill before."

Lucy nodded. George plunged on, "As nearly as I can tell a man named Warren Goodale got first title to the land, in 1850, just after the mahele when foreigners were permitted to buy real estate. He sold it the same year to James F. B. Marshall for $3,000, to turn a quick profit, I suppose. Then Marshall sold it in 1856 to Mr. Widemann for $8,000. I'm not sure which of them built the house but . . ."

His mother wasn't paying attention. They had emerged from the shady grove into the glare of the sun on the grassy bank of the valley. The thatched house loomed ahead on the windswept bluff, alone and austere with only the shabby clutter of outbuildings for company.

George glanced at his mother. Then he looked back, with a frown, at his home. He had never realized before how dreary it appeared. No trees, just ox carts and piles of lumber. The thatching on his own highpitched roof was getting ragged.

"I haven't had time to do much with it, yet," he said hurriedly. "But I'm going to plant trees for shade. And some flowers by the house, maybe. When I get the new ditch in I'll be able to do more watering."

His mother was only half listening. "My, such a nice, big house," she said. "I like having a veranda all the way around like that. And the room! Why, you could easily raise a family here!"

George grinned. "Come on, mother. Sam is waiting for us. He promised me he'd have things cleaned up by the time you got here."

As they rode into the yard, Pikau hurried up to take the horses. Lucy, of course, made a big fuss over him. Then she turned her attention to Pikau's little boy, Kaili, who stood big-eyed as she knelt and stroked his head.

"What a handsome child! Pikau, I hope you are sending him to school."

"School in Lihue waste time," said Pikau with a shrug.

"But he must get an education. Why don't you let me take him along to Mr. Wilcox's Select School at Waioli?"

Pikau was embarrassed. "We have no place for him to stay."

"Why, he'll stay with us, of course. The house is getting empty with the boys all growing up. We'd love to have him. Would you like that, Kaili?"

The boy was too shy to answer. Lucy patted his head and went into the house. At the sight of an ash tray on the table she stopped.

"George, have you taken up smoking?"

"He smiled. "A cigar now and then. It's good for the digestion. How do you like my bachelor's den? I bought that wardrobe from the Widemann's so I'd have a place to hang my clothes."

Lucy sniffed. "Then what's that pair of trousers doing on that chair? My goodness, I've never seen such a mess. Don't you ever dust, George? It will take me a week to put this house in order."

A centipede fell from the thatching above and landed at her feet. She screamed as George stepped on the squirming creature. He kissed her cheek, chuckling. "Relax, mother. This is supposed to be a rest for you, remember?"

She pushed him away. "Stop this nonsense and fetch me a pail of hot water."

When she left more than a week later, the house was spotless and little Kaili, not at all happy about the new school, rode with her.

* * *

George became a frequent Sunday visitor at Koloa. He went along on picnics and horseback excursions along the seacoast.

Lottie was so popular he seldom had a chance to speak with her alone. But he had more pressing problems on the plantation than that of winning her attention. On September 15, 1866, he wrote to a cousin in Connecticut, "I find the sweets of single life will do very well, and I am so busy that I do not have time to go a-courting, so unless the girls come a-courting me there is not much chance for me."

At the end of September he discovered he was wrong. He made another trip across the island, and on the walk home from church, Lottie was more excited than he had ever seen her. "George, I have wonderful news!"

"What is it?"

"I'm going away."

George glanced at her, startled. "For good?"

"No, just to California. Maria must go for her health, and I am going with her. Mother says the change will do me good. I'm so excited!"

"How long will you be away?"

"Oh, months, at least. Will you miss me?"

"Yes, I will."

"I don't believe it. You hardly ever even notice me," she teased.

But he did miss her. Much more than he anticipated. He had come to depend on those few hours at Koloa for the companionship he didn't have time for during the week. Without Lottie's quiet humor and the way she had of making him forget his worries, it wasn't the same.

The winter rains came too late to save George's second crop of unirrigated cane, but the ratoons were doing well. With luck, he would be able to harvest about the same amount of cane as he had before. He was as busy as ever, but it was lonely in the big house, especially when the accounts were finished. George read a great deal, and when a stray cat appeared on the doorstep one morning, he fed it a saucerful of milk. From then on, the cat was a member of the household.

Early one stormy morning in December George found Paul Isenberg on the landing watching the natives load kegs of sugar. They carried each keg from shore to the longboat moored about twenty feet from the beach. When the boat was loaded, they rowed to the little schooner anchored in the bay. There they handed the kegs, one at a time, to the deck. It was tedious, time-consuming work.

The big German raised his hand in salute. "In weather like this one must watch the men so they will keep the kegs dry," he said.

George glanced at the schooner. She was the *Sally*, tugging heavily against her anchors as a strong wind from the south blew almost directly into the bay. "I'm not sure they should be loading at all. With a wind like this, the *Sally* might not be able to get out of the harbor."

"Oh, it's not that bad," said Isenberg.

The two of them stood in the wind. George finally asked the question that had been on the tip of his tongue. "Have you heard from Maria?"

Isenberg sighed. "Yes, she seems to be improving. Thank the Lord she writes often. The house is empty without her."

George hesitated. "And Lottie is getting along well, I suppose."

Isenberg shot him a shrewd glance. "She's getting along splendidly," he said. After a moment he added, "Since we are bachelors together, George, why don't you come to the house for a chat some evening. I have a bottle of brandy that will go well with your cigars."

"I'll do that," said George gratefully, as he turned to go.

He was half-finished with his breakfast when one of the stevedores rode up in a great hurry to say that the *Sally* was in pilikia. George shouted for Pikau as he leaped on his horse and galloped for the bay. One glance at the schooner told him what had happened.

The *Sally* was dragging her anchors. Little by little the wind was blowing her toward the shore where the waves dashed high against black lava boulders. Another two hundred feet and she'd be on the rocks. The only chance for the little vessel was to make sail and beat out of the harbor. But maneuvering past the point at such close quarters would take courage and skilful boat handling. The natives on board apparently refused to take the risk.

Pikau came galloping up with two of the men. "Come on," George shouted against the wind. "We're going to try and save her!"

They rode hastily around the bay. By this time the *Sally* was very close to the rocks. George waited until a huge wave had broken on the boulders, then he dove into the water. He got halfway to the ship before the next wave washed him back. Between each wave he gained a few feet. Finally, panting, he grasped a line trailing over the side and scrambled up on deck. Pikau followed.

Frightened faces stared at him. "Get the anchors up!" George bellowed. The crewmen hesitated. One man was ready to leap over the side. "Get back, damn you! We're going to make sail! Stand by to set the jib and the mainsail!"

Pikau called from the bow, "I can't get the big anchor up."

George shouted back. "Then slip it. Can you get the kedge up?"

"I think so," panted Pikau.

It would be very close. Thank God for Pikau, thought George, as he spun the wheel. They began to make headway, fighting to keep clear of the rocks. George found himself enjoying the contest as the spray whipped into his face. It was good to be on a deck again. Slowly, they edged past the point. Then they were clear. But a moment later the full force of the gale threw the *Sally* on her side sending the crewmen sprawling.

"Take in sail, all of it," George yelled.

Somehow they did it. The *Sally* righted herself. George turned the wheel back to the Hawaiian captain. He and Pikau launched the whaleboat. George took one of the oars as they started the heavy pull back to shore. Soon the schooner disappeared, hidden by the wild waves. George pulled grimly on his oar as the rain ran down his face, wishing he could work up enough courage to write to Lottie.

* * *

The homecoming in January was not a happy one. Now it was obvious that Maria would not recover. Lottie seemed remote in her sadness, and although she often came to visit Maria, George saw little of her. On Sunday noon, April 7, 1867, George wrote a hasty note to his parents and sent a rider galloping off with it.

"Mrs. Isenberg died last night, and the funeral comes off tomorrow at four o'clock. I send this at the suggestion of Mrs. Smith so that if any of the Hanalei folks wish to come over, they will have a chance."

Maria was buried on the edge of the valley overlooking the mill. George walked with Lottie back to the house, wishing he could tell her how much he had missed her. But this didn't seem the time. So he said, "I suppose you're teaching again?"

"Yes. How have you been, George?"

"The same. Too much to do and not enough time to do it."

"I've heard you've been asked to run for the legislature."

He grinned at that. "It's just talk. I'm not a politician."

"That's the best reason I can think of for you to run."

"I've never made a speech in my life. I wouldn't know how to begin."

"If you don't run, Willie Rice will," said Lottie tartly.

"That's fine. He'd be much better at it than I."

He knew he had displeased her. How could he explain that he must win his independence first, before anything else. He must not be like all the others, grinding their cane on half-shares, renting someone else's land, always living on the edge of debt.

George came near to failure that year. The price of sugar dropped almost 5¢ a pound. It was the irrigation ditch and his extra jobs that saved him. The lesson was clear. He had a choice of harvesting marginal crops year after year, or plunging more deeply in debt to extend the ditch. He decided to plunge, investing all of his savings to begin pushing the irrigation system farther into the mountains. Work had barely started when, on January 10, 1868, one of Honolulu's most prominent business firms, Walker, Allen and Company, went into bankruptcy. Several sugar plantations went down with it.

But the next crop was a little better, and the price of sugar inched upward a cent. George took an additional five year lease, then borrowed money to complete the ditch. As a result, he was busier than ever. That year Paul Isenberg took a trip to Germany to see his family. He took Mother Rice and his children with him. Albert Wilcox, who had been struggling grimly to grow cane at Hanalei, came to Lihue to manage the plantation in Isenberg's absence.

"How are father and mother?" George asked when his brother arrived.

Albert, short but more powerfully built than his older brother, shook his head. "Not very well, I'm afraid. Father's hands shake so he can hardly write a letter. But it's mother I'm really worried about. She's having headaches, and her ears hurt her."

"What is it?"

"Overwork," said Albert bluntly.

"Yes, I know. We should make her take a rest."

"I've tried. It doesn't do any good."

On his next visit, early in 1869, George found that his mother had suffered a slight stroke of paralysis. This time he made the proposal that he and Albert had agreed upon. His mother had always wanted to see her relatives in Connecticut once more. Now that the boys were grown, it was time to make the trip. By traveling on the new trans-continental railroad across the country, she and Abner needn't endure the tedious journey via the Isthmus of Panama. Luther, nineteen, would remain at Punahou School in Honolulu. Henry, eleven, would make the trip with his parents. Sam, twenty-two, who had a job as deputy sheriff, would stay at the old mission home and look after things. The older boys could help a little with expenses.

George didn't give his parents a chance to refuse. He kissed his mother's wrinkled cheek when they sailed and made her promise to rest as much as possible. A letter in Abner's handwriting arrived promptly on July 24, four days after they arrived in California to visit Charles and his family. Lucy was impatient to see her mother again. They remained only a week, and a week after that they arrived in New York. Henry stayed behind with Charles in California.

George smiled over the letters. They were so like his father. In the last one, Abner complained because the railroad had lost their trunks. That letter was dated August 6. "Your mother stood the journey well," it read. That was good. George hoped that her brothers and sisters would make a big fuss over her.

Then a short note arrived from Edward in Connecticut. George read a few lines. He read them again, stunned. Abner and Lucy were dead. They had come down with a fever; and both died unexpectedly, his mother on August 13, his father exactly a week later. They were buried side by side.

At first there was no grief, just numbness, and the sensation of being alone. The news spread quickly, and the mission families from all over the island came to offer sympathy, the Doles, the Smiths, the Rowells. George felt smothered in the center of such a sentimental gathering. As soon as he could, he slipped outside. There was comfort in the familiar, functional setting of his plantation yard. An ox cart had little beauty, but it was sturdy and dependable and seeing it there made him feel better. When he went back into the house, Mrs. Smith asked gently, "What are you going to do about little Henry, and Luther?"

George answered firmly, "They're my responsibility now. First, I'll go and get Henry in California. Then I'll have to see them both through school. It just means I'll have to manage a little better, that's all."

CHAPTER

12

Paul Isenberg returned from
Germany late in 1869 a different person. George had not
realized how heavily Maria's illness had weighed on her handsome husband until he brought back a new bride, a gentle
German girl with a shy smile and complete astonishment at the
life she found about her. Isenberg was exuberant.

"My friend, it is good to go away. It gives a man new perspective. I have been looking and listening. What I saw and heard
have convinced me that a boom in sugar is coming. One of these
days our friends in the United States will lower the duty. We
must be ready. Wilcox, it is time to expand!"

George nodded eagerly. This was exciting talk!

"The Pioneer Mill at Lahaina, Maui is grinding 10,000 tons
of cane a year with steam power. Why should Lihue not grind
an equal amount?"

George whistled.

"We can do it. But we must grow more cane. I intend to
extend my ditch to the Wailua River for more water, and I'd
like you to lay it out for me. Also, I want to know if you are
willing to double your acreage in cane?"

"I'm willing, all right," George answered happily.

There was the same excitement all over the Islands as 1870 began. Willie Rice ran for the legislature and won, taking the seat that Judge Widemann had held fifteen years before. Everyone discussed the report that the United States was considering a treaty of reciprocity that would allow Hawaiian sugar to enter the United States duty free. That year, as a result of his improved water supply, George's crop brought $12,000. He paid most of his debts.

It was as if a door were opening and he was about to step into his dream. His own plantation!

When he arrived in Honolulu, armed with a loan from Paul Isenberg, the town was alive with controversy. Sanford Dole, now a young attorney back from Williams College, was campaigning against the contract labor system used by plantations to hire Chinese coolies. Sam Wilder, going into the shipping business, and Sam Alexander, now growing sugar cane on Maui, were just as vocal in favor of the system.

At Judge Widemann's, as usual, philosophy preceded business. "I am opposed to this reciprocity scheme," the judge said with some heat. "Oh, I know that duty-free sugar would bring prosperity to the Islands, especially to sugar planters. But what is the inducement our friends hold out to the United States in return for such a favor? We offer Pearl Harbor as a coaling station. This is a proud little nation, George. We must not tamper with her sovereignty! I, for one, am not willing to trade independence for wealth. The next step would be complete annexation by the United States. I shudder at the thought."

"I came to see if you will sell me Grove Farm, not to argue politics," George said.

The judge's vexation vanished. "So you want to buy my farm? I've been wondering how long it would take you. Well, I'm willing to sell at a fair price, but this time I will need cash."

"What is a fair price?" asked George.

"With all the improvements . . . let me see . . . $12,000, how does that strike you?"

"I would say that's pretty good for a plantation that never made money until I took it over," George answered without rancor.

Judge Widemann chuckled. "I had confidence in you from the beginning. You see, I was right."

George hesitated. "To tell the truth, I don't have that much money. I can pay down $3,000 in my own money, and Mr. Isenberg is willing to take a mortgage on the land for $6,000. That's all I can raise."

"Well, if Paul Isenberg has that much confidence in you, I don't see why I shouldn't. I'll give you my personal note for the other $3,000 . . . at a proper rate of interest, of course. Let's say, ten per cent."

They settled on no interest for the first thousand, ten per cent on the remaining two thousand The papers were signed April 25, 1870. Judge Widemann shook George's hand. "Well, young man, you now own a sugar plantation. How does it feel? Would you like to go out and celebrate?"

George answered thoughtfully, "No, I don't think I'd better. I have to buy some fence wire and a saddle tree before I go back."

He told Lottie what he had done and she congratulated him. But he couldn't seem to tell her how he felt about her. Not until he was sure of his future.

One day he was stacking the magazines on his cluttered table when an old letter, dated March 21, 1870, dropped from the pages. It was a note from his brother, Sam, in Hanalei. Absentmindedly, George scanned the folded paper. One sentence leaped out at him. "You are a deuce of a fellow courting a whole year and then don't have the spunk to propose . . . "

George grinned wryly at the letter. Sam was right, of course. He often teased George about it. Well, it wouldn't be much longer. He'd be able to work off the debt soon. Then Grove Farm would be his, and he'd be in a position to give Lottie what she deserved. George slipped the letter carefully back into its envelope. It would be something to smile over in later years.

* * *

The summer clouds were far below them. Breathing heavily, they struggled up the steep, rocky slope through the mist. The five Hawaiian guides, four men and a woman, were shivering in the cold. The botanist, Dr. Heinrich Wawra, climbed gamely, but he was tiring. George paused to smile encouragement at the scientist, then he forged ahead, excitement in his eyes.

He was always most contented tramping through the mountains, usually with his Henry rifle over his shoulder. Up here on the jungle-covered slopes he could forget himself, Lottie, the plantation, everything but the unspoiled scene around him. He found adventure in exploring the faint, forgotten trails of the old Hawaiians, in the discovery of an unnamed plant or an unmarked water source.

This was the most exciting adventure of all. For years he had been wanting to try climbing the misty, treacherous summit of Mt. Waialeale, the mysterious mountain that stood in the center of the island, its peak almost constantly shrouded in rain clouds. The Hawaiians told numberless stories of spirits that lurked on the mountain, of the shrine that was built there, of the sacrifices that must be offered.

Such mumbo jumbo never aroused George's interest, but the challenge of the mountain did. So in 1870, when the Austrian botanist, Dr. Wawra, from a visiting warship, asked him to help make an attempt on the mountain to collect botanical specimens, George jumped at the chance. They had started from the Isenberg's home about noon and camped the first night, at the base of the cliffs, in a banana-leaf hut which the Hawaiians made. Next day they climbed to a little flat place near the rounded knob toward the northeast side of the mountains. Here they spent another night.

By that time Dr. Wawra's enthusiasm was spent. He told George he would have to turn back in the morning. Dawn broke unusually clear. George begged the scientist to climb for just a few more hours. "It's only a little way to the top," he said. "You'll never get this chance again, especially in such clear weather!"

Against his will, Dr. Wawra went on. And now they were almost there. In his impatience, George strode on ahead of the others, dragging the thin air into his lungs, his muddy boots slipping on the wet rocks. He bent forward, leaning against the slope. Suddenly he pitched forward almost on his face. The slope had flattened out. He was at the summit!

A scene of misty, swampy desolation, broken by jagged lava boulders, lay before him. In the center was a long, oblong lake. Puddles stood everywhere. The bushes were drenched. Though the clouds had lifted, the rocks glistened from recent rain.

Panting, George waited for the others. Very few climbers had ever reached the summit from the Wailua side the way he had brought Dr. Wawra. Even most of the Hawaiians had forgotten the trail.

While the scientist scuttled about collecting plants, George scouted for Hawaiian relics. He found a prehistoric ditch that drained this greatest of all water sources on the island down the Wailua side of the mountain, apparently forming a watershed for the Wailua and Wainiha rivers. The ditch was filled with moss about a foot deep. George found the sacred rock, large and low, where Hawaiians had left seed leis for the spirits of the mountain. George took the seed leis as souvenirs and left a 50¢ piece instead.

In a short while they started back and, after sliding nearly all the way down the mountain, reached Lihue about ten o'clock that night. Although George was mud from head to toe, he couldn't remember ever being so pleased with himself.

*   *   *

Out of habit, he checked the bleak November sky for rain as the seven Chinese waded ashore. He wondered if they were as curious about him as he was about them. Almost all of his other workers were local Hawaiians who lived on the island, or itinerant laborers from Honolulu. Kaipu was the exception, and he seemed as Hawaiian as the rest. But with fields to open and additional acres to harvest, George desperately needed more men than he could hire at home. So he had contracted for seven of the Chinese who were flooding into the Islands from that strange land across the sea. These men were not Cantonese. They were bigger, rawboned, with a look of alert competence about them in spite of their ridiculous pigtails.

There were all sorts of theories about these Oriental laborers. Some planters claimed they were excellent workers. Some insisted they were worthless. George had heard that the Chinese coolie was docile, argumentative, adaptable, unadaptable, loyal, untrustworthy. These men, he decided, didn't appear to be any of these things. They just looked confused and a little frightened, the way he'd felt that first day at Punahou. The thought cheered him. Maybe he and the Chinese would get along after all. "Kaipu, tell them to get in the ox cart," George told the cook.

The little Cantonese barked an order, and the men climbed into the cart. A mill hand from Koloa Plantation watched in amazement. He laughed uproariously. "Since when are those coolies too good to walk?" he wanted to know.

"Never mind," George answered evenly. "I'll treat my men the way I please."

"You start coddling them, and you'll ruin it for everybody else!"

"Out of my way. Hiiiiiyaaa!"

"Don't say I didn't warn you!" the man shouted after them.

George smarted from the insult all the way across the plain to Kahalehaka Valley. There the men climbed out, looking curiously about the clearing under a mango tree where George had built a wooden house with a thatched roof for them beside the stream.

"Do they pick up your lingo pretty good, Kaipu?" George asked.

The small Chinese nodded. "Sabe plenty!"

"Then you'll be in charge of these men from now on. Is that all right with you?"

"Kaipu boss man?"

"That's right, you're the boss. Will you tell them that?"

Kaipu launched into a harangue, pointing first to George, then to himself. The men listened, nodding. They watched George with new interest.

"Now tell them this. I've paid their passage from China plus an advance in wages and agents' fees that come to $154 per man. That's a total of $1,078 paid out in advance before I've got a lick of work out of any of them. They've signed for three years at twelve dollars a month, and I expect each man to earn his money."

Kaipu fired a volley of Chinese at the new men. They listened impassively.

"One more thing," George added. "Maybe they've heard about whippings on plantations around here? Well, no man has ever been whipped on Grove Farm. And no man ever will be. That's a promise. No man is forced to work if he's honestly sick. But I expect every man to work as hard as I do. And if anybody has a complaint, bring it straight to me. Tell them that! Then have them start clearing the new field."

Satisfied, George drove back to the house. He had just finished supper that day when the whole troop of Chinese marched into the yard and came to a determined halt in front of the house. His heart sank. He hadn't expected trouble so soon.

"Kaipu, come here," he called as he walked out to the veranda.

One of the workers held a bowl of poi in his hand. He burst into a torrent of language that left George mystified. The men were obviously upset. But George couldn't make out why. Another Chinese snatched the bowl and spooned up some of the purple paste inside with his finger. He took a mouthful, then spat it out in disgust. The whole group began talking and gesticulating. Kaipu finally appeared at the door.

"Can you figure out what's wrong?" George asked. "It looks to me like they got hold of a bad batch of poi."

Kaipu shook his head. "Batch plenty good. Poi plenty bad. Chinamen want rice."

"But that's silly! Everybody I know eats poi."

"In China, no poi," said Kaipu firmly. "Rice!" The cook addressed a few words to the workers in their own tongue. They nodded vehemently. Then, one by one, they took a mouthful of poi and spat it out in violent dislike.

George scratched his head. "All right, tell them we'll find some rice tomorrow. And if they like, they can plant their own. How's that?"

Kaipu conveyed the message to the men. They brightened immediately. The Chinese on Grove Farm proved to be very good workers when they were treated with consideration. But from that day on George had a reputation for coddling his men.

*   *   *

The year 1870 was gone almost before it began. There was so much to do. George surveyed a ditch for Paul Isenberg and began planning ways to bring down more water for his own fields. He cleared land, fenced it. And he never stopped his everlasting round of road building, tax collecting and book-keeping.

His trips to Koloa continued. By this time everybody from Lihue to Koloa knew why. But he never quite got around to proposing marriage. He wasn't ready. Not yet. Next year's harvest was bigger than ever. And that summer, Lottie spent several months in Honolulu. It was lonely without her.

When she came back, he crossed the gap once more, lighthearted and eager. Maybe this time! She was particularly radiant in church that morning. Outside, she hurried over to him.

"George, it's good to see you again. I have wonderful news, and I want you to be the first to know. I'm going to be married."

He made himself smile. "That's fine, Lottie. Who's the lucky man?"

"Alfred . . . that is, Judge Hartwell. Remember, he's come here for court several times. Oh, George, I'm truly happy."

"I'm glad," he said

George remembered the young judge as a handsome man with a decisive manner and educated views on all sorts of topics. Lottie was lucky. Few girls in a remote village like Koloa were able to marry as eligible a bachelor as the brilliant judge.

There was a great lot of good-natured teasing. George took it, smiling. At the dinner table he listened to the girls compliment Lottie.

"Imagine marrying the youngest general in the Union Army during the Civil War! And a Phi Beta Kappa. How did you manage it?" And, "I wonder what it's like to be the wife of a supreme court justice?"

So the day ended very differently from what he had intended.

* * *

It helped to work. And no one on the plantation worked longer or harder than the owner. Every morning he arose before dawn to sip coffee from the familiar white sailor's mug without a handle. Then he made a circuit of the plantation: testing the soil, checking the ditch, planning the day. When a worker got sick, George treated the man himself. He knew their wives, their children.

One day a Hawaiian field hand asked him for an advance of three dollars to buy a pair of shoes. George looked suspiciously at the splayfooted giant. "Didn't I give you three dollars last week for a pair of shoes?"

The Hawaiian grinned sheepishly and hung his head like a naughty child. George lost his temper.

"You went out and got drunk, didn't you? Well, you're not going to make a fool out of me again. You're fired! Get out!"

The man blinked in alarm, then shambled unhappily away. George's anger evaporated as quickly as it had come. He had known the Hawaiian for years, a likeable fellow who never complained. His only weakness was liquor, illegal to natives. He had a big family and children in school.

George cleared his throat. "Hey," he called. The man looked back. "Never mind what I said." He reached into his pocket and flipped the man a fifty-cent piece. "Go out and celebrate. But be sure to get to work on time tomorrow!"

The Hawaiian grinned and hurried away. It took the others only a short while to detect George's weakness. The trick was to make him angry enough to fire you. Then he would be sorry and give you whatever you asked.

On April 24, 1872, George paid off his $3,000 debt to Judge Widemann. In November he allowed himself the luxury of a case of Norway beer. The following year he finally gave up the road supervisor's job. That November he bought a new Henry rifle for $32.10 and 1,000 cartridges, $13.50. In 1874 he climbed Mt. Waialeale once more, this time with two boyhood chums, George Dole and Fred Smith.

He re-thatched the house and planted ironwood trees, introduced from Australia, as a windbreak. One day he noticed a switch in the hand of Kahele Laweleka, the mail carrier who took letters once a week from Lihue to Hanalei.

"Let me see that," said George.

It was a branch from a mulberry tree. He recognized it from those that Old Titcomb had once grown. He planted it in the yard and up it came. For Pikau he built a new house below in the valley. After all, the overseer was bossing more than two dozen men not counting the construction crew. They planted and harvested two hundred acres of cane a year.

George was alone on June 2, 1874, when he took the familiar ledger from the shelf after supper. He settled himself beside the lamp. Opening to page 194, he read the last few entries: 2 bags Portland cement, 1 small side-hill plow, one barrel ale, 2 cases coal oil, 6 cases pilot bread.

Then he took up his pen and added an item in the same awkward scrawl: Payment to P. Isenberg of Note and Mortgage on Grove Farm, $6,000.

He put down the pen and stared at what he had written. The last ten years of his life were compressed into those few words. Well, he had done it. Grove Farm was his. At thirty-five, he was probably the most successful young sugar planter in the Islands. In a few years he might even be wealthy.

A house cat came in through the open door and rubbed against the chair. George reached down to stroke it, moving his hand from the head along the back and on to the end of the tail. The animal's meow sounded plaintive in the quiet, cluttered room.

George glanced into the shadows. The things he had chosen were all around him; the battered surveyor's compass, his hiking boots, the box of cigars, his books, the Henry rifle, a well-thumbed pile of Harper's Weekly, and a wrinkled heap of newspapers. Here, at last, he was his own man, the complete and absolute master. It was what he had always wanted. Now he wondered if it was enough.

PART IV

The Statesman

CHAPTER

13

The day was warm for October, but George didn't notice the heat as he watched the whaleboat move briskly toward the landing, oar blades glistening in the sunlight. He had remembered to shine his shoes and to brush his suit. Still, he was nervous. He had been living alone for a long time. Was he making a mistake now?

It had seemed like a good idea when Sam and his Punahou sweetheart set their wedding date, October 7, 1874, to invite them to live at Grove Farm. There was a job open for Sam as sheriff of the Island, and George needed someone he could depend upon to run the plantation when he went to Honolulu. Besides, it was lonely living by himself. The couple had agreed to come, and here they were, after the wedding in Hilo.

A brawny Hawaiian carried the young woman ashore as easily as if she were a doll. Sam Wilcox, in a new suit with a black bow tie slightly askew, rode to shore on the back of another native. The girl hastily adjusted her bonnet as Sam hurried her eagerly forward.

"Well, here she is. The new Mrs. Wilcox!"

George shook hands.

"She won't bite you," Sam said with a grin.

George couldn't think of anything to say to his brother's wife. She was a tiny thing with brown hair and eyes. She wore dainty gold earrings and a smart, close-fitting, high-necked dress with a long flaring skirt. "The carriage is this way, Mrs. Wilcox," he said.

"Please, call me Emma."

George turned the team up the short-cut to Grove Farm. He kept his eyes on the plodding horses as they climbed the steep, rutted trail. Beside him, Emma exclaimed about the scenery.

"Is that your sugar cane?" she asked, pointing to a field ahead on the left.

George nodded briefly.

"Then we're on Grove Farm."

George didn't answer.

"That is certainly healthy looking cane," exclaimed Emma.

"It's the new Lahaina variety."

"What in the world is Lahaina variety?"

George explained, "It came from Tahiti. But it's called Lahaina cane because that's where it was introduced in the Islands. At first we just planted what cane we could get from the Hawaiians. Then we discovered that those varieties seem to decline in yield. This Lahaina cane is higher in sugar content and grows more vigorously."

"I had no idea you needed to know so much to run a sugar plantation," said Emma in admiration.

George didn't understand how it happened. Before they reached the house he was explaining why the mynah bird from India had been introduced to control caterpillars. Sam began to yawn but Emma hung on every word. She seemed so interested that George showed her the shop where he made his own harness, the new cistern he had built to save carrying water from the valley, and his rain gauge. He explained, "You see, I run water in from the irrigation ditch, then let the dirt settle to the bottom. The water tastes fine. Would you like to see how we cure the wood for making ox carts?"

Emma touched her forehead with a tiny handkerchief. "I'd like to see the house first, if you don't mind," she said politely.

"Oh! Yes, of course."

"Do you have a vegetable garden?" she asked as they walked around the house.

"There isn't much time for that," George answered. "But we can always get bananas or breadfruit or oranges."

"We'll have a garden," said Emma firmly. "Can you get flour here?"

"Well, it's usually full of weevils. So we eat poi and saloon pilot crackers."

"Potatoes?"

George shook his head. "But we butcher beef or pork or mutton when we want fresh meat. And there's plenty of salt beef curing in the storehouse."

He showed Emma the south half of the house, Judge Widemann's old office and a small bedroom, where she and Sam would make their home. She glanced briefly around the austere rooms, then slipped off her bonnet.

"I know you men have things you want to discuss, so you can

just leave me alone. I'd like to straighten up a little, then fix supper."

"Don't worry about that. Mrs. Isenberg has trained a new cook for you. He'll be glad to . . . "

Emma answered with unexpected spirit. "George Wilcox, from now on the cooking will be my responsibility. And tonight I plan to do it myself."

George had to admit the meal was a great improvement over the salt beef and crackers Kaipu usually put before him. There were flowers on the table. And from somewhere Emma had produced real silverware and linen napkins.

Sam was in the middle of an amusing story when the cats came trooping in. Without thinking, George cut bits of meat from his plate and handed them down to his pets. He looked up as Sam stopped midway in his story. Emma was staring with amusement at George who flushed. "They keep me company," he said, embarrassed.

It had been an excellent meal and now to make it complete George took out a cigar. This was one of the pleasures he permitted himself every day, a good cigar after supper. He puffed contentedly, turning the air blue with pungent smoke. He had built only an inch of ash on the cigar's tip when he realized that Emma had turned pale. Sam looked embarrassed.

"Is something the matter?" asked George, bewildered.

His brother blurted, "Emma can't stand cigars in the house. They make her sick."

She tried to smile. "I'm sorry, George."

"No, no, that's perfectly all right," he said hastily, crushing out the cigar. "I can smoke out on the veranda." But it wasn't quite the same. And as he sat under the rustling grass eaves, alone with his cigar, he knew that his bachelor days were over.

*   *   *

The sugar boom that Paul Isenberg had predicted was like an exciting dream at first. By the end of 1874, when George counted his earnings, he thought he'd made a mistake. The total for the year was an amazing $22,800. In the same year he renewed a lease, for twenty-five years, of a 10,000-acre tract of land adjoining Grove Farm that was known as Haiku. This was a royal estate, reaching from the mountains to the sea, owned by Princess Ruth Keelikolani, a high chiefess who lived in Honolulu. In 1874 George also made his first plunge in Honolulu real estate, about $3,000 down and $7,000 in mortgages on a large slice of land called Kewalo, between Honolulu harbor and Waikiki beach. There was nothing on the property but a cemetery. Yet, everyone told him he couldn't miss if he put his money in real estate. Why, Honolulu was already a city of 35,000 and expanding every year!

It was all very exciting and a little unreal. But a conversation with Paul Isenberg late in 1875 quickly re-established George's perspective. It had been ten years since George had gone to seek his first milling agreement. Now, as an established planter, he confidently asked for a little better share of his crop and an increased acreage. Isenberg seemed disappointed.

"You are doing very well as it is, Wilcox. Aren't you satisfied?"

George answered carefully. "You still take one half of my crop for your share. But your expense for grinding comes to only one-eighth of what it's worth. That's much better than I've been able to do."

Isenberg chuckled. "Ahhh, I see you've been studying."

George nodded. "I don't want to be unfair. But I think I deserve a higher percentage of my crop. My men buy goods from your store. I've helped you lay out your ditch system . . . "

"Wilcox, I know how you feel," said Isenberg heartily, "but business is business. Your men have to buy their goods somewhere. I am paying you well for your work on the ditches. And without my mill . . . " Isenberg spread his hands, "you would have no plantation at all."

"My plantation has been very profitable for you," George said evenly.

"Don't be so impatient. This sugar boom has just begun. One day soon the United States will remove the duty on our sugar. I can give you many reasons why. Those people in America are sentimental about our small kingdom, for one thing. For another, a few of their politicians are intelligent enough to see the value of having an outpost in the Pacific that is friendly to America. They do not like our sending sugar to Australia. It builds commercial ties with Britain. Believe me, Wilcox, the reciprocal trade agreement we have heard so much about is not far off! And when it comes, your income could easily be doubled. Be satisfied. Don't you Americans have a saying, a man should not grow too big for his trousers?"

"Britches," grumbled George.

"There is nothing personal in this, Wilcox. I admire your ability, and I value your friendship. But one cannot let personal feelings influence business transactions. The important thing is I have a mill, and you do not."

George walked out of the room holding tight to his temper. He was beaten. Unless he bought his own mill, he would remain firmly in the grip of Lihue Plantation. His dependence on Lihue rankled more than the money. If only he could find a way to build his own mill!

He knew the idea was preposterous, but it wouldn't go away. One night instead of reading the new issue of the *Sugar Planter* he wrote to the Iron Works in Honolulu. To his surprise, he received a prompt answer dated January 3, 1876. And the price, for a mill and machinery, was not so much as he'd expected, $27,740. But that would be only part of the expense. He'd have to build up his herd of oxen, buy more ox carts, and hire more men to drive them in order to get his cane to the mill. To meet those expenses he would need to expand his acreage and extend his ditches. He could spend $75,000 before he milled his first stalk of cane. One unprofitable crop and he might lose everything.

Those were exactly the doubts expressed in Honolulu by Hackfeld and Company manager, J. C. Glade, when George asked for credit. Glade, a genial but shrewd business man, ended by telling him, "So many planters have failed because they over-reached themselves. I would not want that to happen to you, though I know how you feel about your milling contract."

George answered quietly, "I would rather fail than spend the rest of my life taking orders."

Glade sighed. "Well, I think you're a good risk. We'll back you."

The men at Hackfeld's advised George that the best milling equipment was manufactured in Scotland. In June, he sailed on the steamer *Moselle* for Bremen, Germany. There he learned from Hackfeld's agent that he must go to Glasgow, Scotland to make arrangements for the procurement of the milling machinery. The agent sent George off on a five-day holiday on the Rhine while he arranged an appointment with Mr. William Renny Watson of Mirrlees, Tait and Watson, makers of fine machinery in Glasgow.

Mr. Watson drove George to his town house, offered him a selection of nearly a dozen different kinds of cigars, and then bustled him off on a holiday through the Highlands of Scotland while he studied George's order for a small, compact, and inexpensive sugar mill. They settled on a trim little unit of the latest design that would manufacture six tons of sugar a day. The rollers, steam driven, were about three-and-one-half feet long by two feet in diameter. There was a vacuum pan for sugar boiling, steam driven centrifugals for separating the sugar from the molasses, and the juice was fed by pumps through the whole system. The mill could easily handle all of the cane that Grove Farm would grow for many years to come.

When George started home on the sleek, new steamer, *Germanic,* the doubt began to set in. Across the Atlantic, over the Continent by rail and on down to Hawaii by steamer, he worried. If sugar took a slump now, he was ruined. So the jubilation in Honolulu provided a pleasant welcome. At last, the elusive Treaty of Reciprocity with the United States had passed the Congress. By the end of the year, Hawaiian sugar would enter the United States duty free. Island sugar planters would reap a bonus of two cents on every pound of raw sugar, a bonanza to the industry. Already a California sugar refiner, Claus Spreckels, was in Honolulu buying up all the sugar he could get at prices undreamed of before.

At Hackfeld and Company, J. C. Glade greeted George with unaccustomed respect. "You certainly bought your mill at the right time. If you aren't careful, you'll be a millionaire before long."

George shook his head. "That's not why I bought the mill." He took the first steamer for Kauai to wait for the arrival of his machinery. A few days later he was working on his accounts at a plain, wooden table by the window when his dogs began to bark. Paul Isenberg, as tidy as ever, walked into the little office and took a straight-backed chair. They talked about the crops and the weather.

Then Isenberg said casually, "I understand you have bought a mill?"

George nodded.

Isenberg smoothed his mustache with his forefingers. "I have under-estimated you, Wilcox, and I apologize. May I congratulate you on an extremely smart stroke of business."

George answered with s shrug. "You wouldn't change the milling agreement."

"I see now that was a mistake, and I am willing to correct it," said Isenberg slowly. "There is no reason for the two of us to compete when we have worked so well together in the past."

He paused. "What if I met your terms for a new milling agreement and at the same time offered to buy your mill at a profit?"

George blinked.

Isenberg continued smoothly. "I would like to develop that section up the coast called Hanamaulu. It is fine cane land. All it needs is water, and that can be brought in. But it is too far by ox cart from my mill. Your new mill would be just the thing. So you see, Wilcox, I am being honest with you. I can put your mill to good use and afford to give you a good price for it."

George hesitated.

"Your life will be much simpler without a mill to worry about," Isenberg added.

"Let me sleep on it."

When Sam heard what had happened, he was jubilant. "You've got Isenberg right where it hurts," he chortled. "Without Grove Farm cane he'll lose a fifth of his crop."

After supper, he couldn't seem to concentrate on the newspaper. And he didn't sleep well. All he'd wanted was a fair percentage of his crop. Now he was embroiled in a power play that could hurt both Grove Farm and Lihue. George rolled over and stared through the mosquito netting out of the window. Every success seemed to bring more worry than satisfaction.

Another thought troubled him. He felt responsible for his brothers. Henry had just finished at Punahou, and George was determined to send his youngest brother to college. Luther in Honolulu was earning his living as a Hawaiian interpreter in the courts. George sent him money regularly. Sam and Emma were as dependent on Grove Farm as George himself. And there was Albert, going bankrupt on a hopeless plot of cane land in Waipa, the valley next to Hanalei. It was Albert's failure that gave George his idea. The more he thought about it, the better it seemed. Satisfied at last, he went to sleep.

Isenberg listened anxiously to George's decision. "I'll sell you the mill on these conditions. I want nine-sixteenths of my crop instead of one half. And I want my brother Albert to grow the cane for the new mill."

"That's an interesting proposition," said Isenberg thoughtfully.

"He's a first class sugar planter. Remember what a good job he did for you at Lihue when you were away? But that land of his at Hanalei just won't grow cane. At Hanamaulu he'd have a chance."

"I think he might work out very well. What kind of arrangement do you have in mind?"

"I want a contract specifying that Albert will supply all the cane for the new Hanamaulu mill for the next twenty years."

Isenberg's eyebrows went up. "That will start him very nicely. All right, I accept the terms."

They settled on a price for the mill, and finally, Isenberg got to his feet. He was in an expansive mood. "I'd like to ask one question. You might have made this very difficult for me. I am grateful that you did not. But I am curious, why didn't you?"

George explained what to him seemed so simple. "All I ever really wanted was a better milling agreement. Now I've got it." But he had learned a lesson. That day he began to build a reserve fund for buying another mill if he ever needed one again.

* * *

He was always so busy he scarcely noticed the changes taking place on Grove Farm. Emma's first baby had been born on January 3, 1876. The child was a boy, and Sam named him Ralph. Now the little family centered around the baby. George sometimes felt like an intruder. He drew more within himself. But it was his idea to install an electromagnetic telephone link with Koloa so that Emma could call Dr. Smith when the baby got sick. Willie Rice, who was married and had a growing family, also installed a telephone. The only other telephone system in the Islands was a private line on Maui.

The instrument quickly became a nuisance because Hawaiian mothers from miles away came to call poor Dr. Smith. When the old man seemed reluctant to ride all the way over the mountains, the mothers would make their babies cough over the telephone to show Dr. Smith how serious it was.

It was engineering that took up much of George's time now. His reputation as an irrigation expert had spread. He contracted with Isenberg to lay out and build another ditch. And George had hardly returned from Scotland when a letter, dated September 25, 1876, arrived from a Punahou classmate, Sam Alexander, now growing sugar cane on Maui with another Punahou graduate, Henry Baldwin.

The two of them were planning the biggest irrigation project yet attempted in the Islands, a seventeen-mile-long ditch that would bring water from the wet slopes of Mount Haleakala to Haiku Plantation on the arid north coast. "Were it possible," wrote Sam, "I would beg of you to come up here to Haiku and help us engineer the new ditch. I know that you are not much of a letter writer, but I want you to sit down and give me all the information on the subject of ditching you can . . . "

The project intrigued George because the water had to be gotten across several formidable gulches. One, the Maliko gulch, was three hundred feet deep and eight hundred feet wide. Sam planned to syphon the water across in an eighteen-inch pipe made of boiler-iron riveted together. George nodded in approval. But he just didn't have time to help much with the Haiku ditch.

Soon there was another baby on the way. This time George decided they would have to build an addition on the house. For Sam and Emma he drew plans for a four-room, one-story building that would join the north end of the main house leaving space for the veranda between. For himself, George planned a little cottage about one hundred feet off the south end of the house. And while they were at it, he said, they might as well take off the thatching and put on shingles.

By the end of the summer in 1877, sailing schooners were unloading lumber, kegs of nails, doors, tongue-and-groove flooring, redwood shingles. August moved into September. George and Sam worked with the men, trying to finish before the baby came. By October, they were both worried. Mrs. Isenberg came to call on Emma every day, holding her skirts carefully away from the buckets of paint, wincing every time a hammer struck a nail. Emma bore it all more patiently than the men. By October 9, when Dr. Smith came hurrying over from Koloa, the house was finished, and George was at loose ends. The women were all busy whispering and scurrying back and forth. Dr. Smith didn't have time to talk. Even Sam had a job. At least, he could hold Emma's hand. But for George there was nothing.

At last, one of the women thrust little Ralph into his arms and told him, for goodness sake, to take the baby for a walk. George set out across the yard, gingerly holding the solemn, big-eyed boy. They made a circuit of the new cistern, out around the storehouse and the harness shed, the carpenter shop, and the machine shed where the plows and harrows were stored.

The baby clung confidently to George's neck, and at the water trough where ohia logs were soaked for making bullock cart tongues, Ralph reached up to pull George's short beard. George stared down at the boy, and Ralph stared back in unblinking appraisal.

"You're not afraid of me, are you?" said George softly.

The baby smiled, and George awkwardly patted his head. They grinned at each other. Then they walked on, and George found himself delaying their return. Finally, Sam came hurrying across the yard. "It's a girl this time," he said proudly.

"Is Emma all right?"

"She's fine."

"Congratulations!"

Ralph reached for his father, impatiently wriggling out of George's arms. George gave him up, and as they walked back to the house, he felt a stab of the loneliness that he thought he had long ago learned to control.

* * *

There had never been a boom in Hawaii that remotely resembled the wave of prosperity that swept over the Islands in the wake of reciprocity. New sugar plantations began popping up like mushrooms. Some failed almost immediately, like the one on the Island of Hawaii where two crackpot Englishmen tried to use wind power to run their mill. Other plantations made huge profits from the beginning. The most ambitious of all belonged to the multi-millionaire sugar refiner from California, Claus Spreckels, who had an engineer busy on Maui surveying a thirty-mile-long irrigation ditch.

Profits came so easily that George began to feel breathless. The Island of Kauai, on the remote northwest end of the chain, had always suffered from bad shipping service. To improve the service, George bought a one-fifth share in a schooner operated by Captain T. R. Foster of Honolulu. To George's surprise, the investment became an immediate money-maker. So he bought into another schooner.

In the spring of 1878, George received two important visitors at Grove Farm. They were dapper Judge Widemann and the manager of Hackfeld and Company, J. C. Glade. They had come all the way from Honolulu to ask his help.

"To be perfectly honest, George, I'm sorry now that I let Grove Farm go," the Judge explained. "I'd like to get back into sugar. As Mr. Glade knows, I have been interested for some time in a new plantation with excellent prospects at Waianae on Oahu. However, my financial resources are not equal to the task. Mr. Glade and I have come to interest you in the proposition."

Glade nodded. "It promises to be a profitable operation, and my company is interested in participating. You can give us two things we want. One is the financial stability that the Judge here is unable to offer. The second is your experience in irrigation and your knowledge of milling equipment."

"How much money do you need?" George asked.

The Judge answered, "Forty thousand."

"Whew! That's too steep for me."

"Don't let that figure scare you," said Glade easily. "The Judge is not asking you to put up the money, simply to stand security for it if we finance the plantation."

"Maybe we'd better look at the land," George said slowly.

They sailed into Honolulu harbor on June 27, 1878, aboard the brand new steamer, *Kilauea Hou*. George counted half a dozen new buildings going up. He could feel the excitement in the air. Luther, cheerful and loaded with gossip, met them on the dock.

"You're just in time for the big news," he told them. "The whole town is talking about it. Claus Spreckels and King Kalakaua are hatching some kind of deal for water rights on Maui. They say the King is ready to sign over the rights if Spreckels covers his gambling debts."

Honolulu was in the grip of the sugar fever. George caught it, too, when he learned at Hackfeld's that sales of his sugar for the last quarter had earned him $30,000. The first person he ran into on the street as he left the building was Sam Wilder, his old boss on Jarvis Island. They shook hands enthusiastically.

"I hear you're a shipping tycoon now," George said with a grin.

"Wilcox, you're just the man I want to see," Wilder answered with his characteristic bluntness. "I need a loan and I'm willing to pay top interest to get it. 'Shipping is growing so fast I just can't keep up with it. I'm putting on more steamers. Fast, regular service. That's what these Islands need."

George nodded in agreement.

"You never saw anything like it. I bought the *Likelike* last year. This year it was the *Kilauea Hou*. The *Mokolii* is on the ways in San Francisco. You should get a piece of it. Somebody has to ship all that sugar, and I'm the man who can do it. What do you say?"

"How much do you need?"

"Seven thousand for, say, two years."

"I'd like to help you, Sam," said George. "Give me a few days to see what I can do."

"Thanks, George, you'll never regret it!"

The town was alive with rumors, but nobody expected the thunderbolt that fell a few days later, on the night of July 1, 1878. Luther gave George the details. Claus Spreckels, the boastful little millionaire, had been drinking champagne with King Kalakaua and a few cronies including Sam Parker in a room at the fancy new Hawaiian Hotel back of Beretania Lane. Some time after midnight, the King sent for his messengers. He ordered them to rout the Ministers of his Cabinet out of bed and have them dismissed. Among the Ministers was Lottie's husband, Judge Hartwell, who had been Attorney General of the Kingdom and the chief opponent of the Spreckels water petition. Nothing like this had ever happened before.

J. C. Glade was furious. "This man Spreckels must be stopped," he stormed as he paced his office the next day. "He acts as if he owned the Islands."

"He's a smart businessman," George agreed.

"That's not what I mean!" snapped Glade. "It's his bull-headed attitude. Do you know the story of what happened on Maui two years ago while you were away? It's typical of Spreckels. He went up there looking for a sugar plantation, and Sam Alexander was courteous enough to show him the Island. That was the time when Alexander and Baldwin were planning their Haiku ditch. What did Spreckels do? He tried to steal their water rights!"

"I see what you mean."

"Well, he didn't get away with it. So he's bribed Kalakaua to lease him some of the most valuable water rights in the Islands for five hundred dollars a year." Glade banged on his desk. "They're worth five times that!"

While the heads of Honolulu's biggest sugar agencies fumed about this free wheeling new competitor, the newspapers praised Spreckels for his enormous investment in Hawaii, half a million already, probably three or four million before he got his plantation in operation. Judge Widemann supported Spreckels, and Sam Wilder was enthusiastic about the stimulus a man like Spreckels would give to business in Hawaii.

George wasn't surprised when the King appointed Samuel G. Wilder Minister of Interior in the new Cabinet. On July 8, the lease was signed, giving Spreckels extensive water rights on Maui. The next day George loaned his friend, Sam Wilder, $7,000. George also agreed to borrow $40,000 from Hackfeld at six per cent interest and loan it to Widemann at eight per cent to finance Waianae Plantation. Then he returned to Kauai, weary of the frantic maneuvering for advantage in Honolulu.

But he couldn't seem to stop making money. Kekaha Sugar Company was a good example. Paul Isenberg was looking for a way to set his brothers up in the sugar business. George had the same idea. So they all pooled their resources to buy a mill from Mirrlees, Tait and Watson, in Scotland. Kekaha plantation, on the southwest coast of Kauai, became a gold mine, and Sam and Albert profited handsomely. But so did George! Waianae Plantation did even better.

In 1879 Paul Isenberg finally gave in to his wife and moved his family back to Germany. Before he left, he offered to sell George his interest in Lihue Plantation and the opportunity to become one of the most powerful sugar magnates in the Islands. This time George said, "No." He was satisfied with what he had.

CHAPTER

14

With the children in bed, the noises in the old house gradually diminished for the night. Tatsy, the slender Japanese house boy, had made his rounds lighting the lamps. In the parlor, where Mr. Widemann's office and a tiny bedroom had been, Emma sat in a corner beside the gleaming center table stacked with magazines. Sam sat on the other side of the table, deep in a armchair, the November 22, 1879, issue of the *Pacific Commercial Advertiser* spread out before him. In a chair across the room, George read the *Scientific American.*

Sam rattled his paper impatiently. "Listen to what the *Advertiser* has to say about the election next year. 'So far as present appearances indicate, the same apathy on the part of foreign-born voters on this subject that has prevailed for years past still exists.' "

"I agree," said George. "It's no wonder so many jackasses get elected."

Sam looked up. "Then why don't you do something about it? They're looking for a good candidate from this district."

George said "Humph!" and went back to his magazines.

Sam had struck uncomfortably close to home. For months, Willie Rice, now the Hon. William H. Rice, veteran of the Legislatures of 1870, 1872, and 1873, had been urging George to run for office. And when George visited Honolulu, he got the same argument from W. O. Smith, Lottie's younger brother, now a successful attorney.

"I'm a farmer, not a politician," George told him.

W. O. Smith was young and slender, with deep-set eyes like his father. "That's why you should run," he answered. "It takes as much brains to operate the government as it does a plantation. Some of the politicians in the Legislature now can hardly read and write. Good God, are you satisfied to see the Judiciary and Education Committees in hands like that?"

George shrugged. "You worry too much. Everything has worked out all right so far."

"Everybody used to live in grass houses, too. But this is 1880, and it's time the men who are building this country took a hand in running it. Don't you ever worry about what those comedians in the Legislature are going to do next?"

"It doesn't matter. The King can veto what they do. He'll listen to reason."

But George wasn't as sure of that as he had once been. King Kalakaua, genial and sophisticated, had started well in 1874 when he was elected to the throne after the death of King Lunalilo. The new King appointed good ministers, promoted the interests of his Hawaiian subjects, and worked hard for the Reciprocity Treaty to stimulate business. It was the midnight champagne party incident with its overtones of bribery that had shaken George's confidence.

Now the King had embarked on what seemed to George to be a rather foolish program of establishing the Islands as the major power in the Pacific. Kalakaua's party was campaigning for a $10,000,000 loan that would provide for fortifying Diamond Head, an extinct crater at the foot of Waikiki Beach; establishing a large army and a powerful navy; and building hospitals, a marine railway and roads all over the Islands. Simple arithmetic told George that the interest alone on such a note would be more than half the combined revenues of the entire Kingdom.

By the middle of January, George had reluctantly agreed to run. But he could never arouse enough courage to make a speech. When a voter asked him what he thought about the King's $10,000,000 loan, George said it would be more sensible to talk about building a pier at Nawiliwili Bay so the stevedores wouldn't always have to wade into the water. One of the unscrupulous campaign techniques in use that year was the buying of tax receipts. Before he was allowed to vote, every man had to present a receipt to show that he had paid his taxes. Dishonest candidates "bought" receipts for a few pennies from unsophisticated Hawaiians who believed that they must vote for the man who "owned" their tax receipts. George countered with a proposal to buy back any voter's tax receipt so long as that voter marked his ballot without a feeling of obligation to either candidate. One of his biggest supporters was Paul Puhiula Kanoa, son of the old governor of Kauai, whom George had established as an independent sugar planter adjacent to Grove Farm.

At 8:00 A.M. on Wednesday, February 4, 1880, all voters over twenty who had paid their taxes began streaming to the polls where candidates harangued and sang songs and provided feasts in return for support. George seemed colorless beside his Hawaiian opponents. But when the polls in the

Court House closed at 5:00 P.M., he had won a majority of 240 of the 410 votes cast. He was one of three white men elected to the Legislature of 1880. He was forty years old. On Oahu, Sanford Dole was defeated, as was Judge Widemann on Maui.

*   *   *

Luther laughed at the sight of George standing uncomfortably for inspection in his new suit. "Stop acting as if the pins were still in it."

"Does it fit all right?" George asked.

"You look better than the Minister of Finance."

"Then we'd better get started. It's a long walk."

Luther threw up his hands. "Walk! A member of the Legislature doesn't walk to hear the King's message. He rides in a carriage!"

So they rode in a carriage. George was glad to have his lighthearted brother with him that day. Everybody liked Luther, especially the Hawaiians. In the courts, where his amazing ability to translate colloquial Hawaiian into English made him indispensable, judges leaned heavily on his interpretations of cases involving natives. From the courts he had moved to the Legislature where that bilingual body appointed him interpreter year after year. Luther knew everyone by his first name, including judges and legislators. And he shared George's enthusiasm for sailing. The two of them often went out in Luther's trim little yacht, the *Pauline*, for an afternoon of racing. Then they'd sit with other yachtsmen and tell tall stories until late into the night.

But today was too serious for joking. Other carriages were going in the same direction along the dusty, tree-shaded streets. There were narrow sidewalks in front of the frame, false-fronted stores in the business district. But beyond Alakea Street the new, grey concrete-block Government Building and, farther on, venerable old Kawaiahao Church, built of coral slabs, stood on an almost open plain. Inland from the Government Building, the walls of King Kalakaua's ornate new palace were going up on a bare vacant lot. George shook his head in disapproval at the expensive pile of building materials.

"Who does Kalakaua think he is, the King of England?" he said irritably as their carriage became part of a long procession leading into the entrance to the grounds of the Government Building.

"The Czar of Russia," said Luther, chuckling. "He'd like to hold his own coronation, you know."

"What!"

"Why not? The natives will love it. One thing the King knows how to do is throw a party." Luther sighed at George's frown. "Now don't start complaining about the Hawaiians. God knows, they don't have many reasons to celebrate any more."

George started to answer, then stopped. He sighed, too, and nodded at Luther. They were passing between ornate gate posts which supported elaborate, wrought iron gates. Beyond the entrance two rows of the King's Household Guards stood in gaudy uniforms, presenting arms. The Government Building, Aliiolani Hale, was a two-story rectangular building with wings on each side, Gothic columns flanking the entrance and a clock tower in the middle between the wings. More guards stood at attention on the steps outside the massive, arched doorway. Inside were stately rows of feather kahilis, polished hardwood poles topped by cylinders of intricately woven feathers of brilliant yellow and red. The tall kahilis were symbols of Hawaiian royalty. Between each pair of kahilis was an enormous basket of flowers.

In the right wing, the members of the Cabinet had their offices; also the judges, Governor of Oahu, Marshall, Police, records keeper, and the heads of the Bureaus of Instruction and Health, were located in that wing.

The left wing, where the Legislature sat, was a scene of primitive splendor and happy confusion. The legislators were smothered in wreaths of fresh flowers and engulfed by well wishers. Brown-skinned women in regal, highnecked holokus with trains, hair trailing in profusion or put up in glistening black piles and secured by tortoise shell combs, and men in stiff suits and squeaky shoes, all were wearing flower leis, singing, back-slapping, and shouting to one another in high good humor.

Luther elbowed his way through the crowd, introducing George to other members of the Legislature. There was picturesque George W. Pilipo, an aging Hawaiian preacher known as the Lion of North Kona for his fearless attacks against the Kalakaua regime; and a bland-faced young Hawaiian from Hilo, James Nawahi, with a calculating look in his eyes; and James Hoapili Baker, the King's candidate, a pompous, part-Hawaiian. Most striking of all was Walter Murray Gibson of Maui, a tall, gaunt man with sharp, deep-set eyes and a flowing, prematurely grey beard. His rich voice rang with the sincerity of an evangelist, but George felt uncomfortable around him. One of the few law makers that George already knew was towering Paul Isenberg, appointed a Noble in the upper house by the King six years before. Isenberg had come back to attend the Legislative Session and to look after his plantations.

At noon the legislators took their seats, and guards hastily cleared the floor of spectators. A moment later the band outside launched into the impressive strains of "Hawaii Ponoi," the national anthem. Then King Kalakaua, in a splendid uniform glittering with gold braid and medals, marched into the chamber with his guard. He was a portly man with a handsome face behind a carefully tended mustache and mutton chop whiskers, and intelligent brown eyes.

The King made his way to the throne, draped with a golden feather cloak. There he turned and read the brief message his Cabinet had prepared for him. In a pleasant, resonant voice, free of formality, he proclaimed prosperity for the land, announced that treaties had been negotiated with Germany and

Denmark, asked for funds to build a sewage system for Honolulu, recommended the construction of railroads and tele-
graphic communications, and assured the legislators that the
finances of the Kingdom were in excellent condition. Then he
declared the Legislative Session open. It was all over in less
than half an hour, and then everyone went home to celebrate.

* * *

George Wilcox was in his seat for the second day of the
session, Monday, May 1, promptly at 10:00 A.M., eager to begin
the business of making laws. His eagerness gradually turned to
frustration. First, the Hon. Godfrey Rhodes moved that the
Hon. J. Mott-Smith take the chair. Then the Rev. M. Kuaea
gave a long prayer. After that came the minutes. Next the
clerk droned through the roll call.

George fidgeted at his desk as the Minister of Interior moved
that a Committee on Credentials be appointed by the chair.
When the committee withdrew, the rest of the members gossiped. Then the committee came back, and the Hon. L. Aholo
moved that its report be adopted. Next His Honor, the Chief
Justice of the Supreme Court, entered the hall to swear in the
legislators.

To George, these formalities seemed endless. Finally, they
elected a permanent chairman. Then a vice-chairman. Then a
sergeant-at-arms, a messenger, a chaplain, a janitor. It took
three ballots to elect a clerk. Luther was made interpreter by
acclamation. At the end of the day, George was at the end of his
patience.

That evening, he took a long walk along the waterfront, past
the rows of rakish bowsprits, the deserted open air market that
would be a beehive the next morning, into Chinatown. He
enjoyed the strange odors, the confusion of tongues. And it
helped to rub shoulders with simple, honest working people.
On the way back George saw a blind man wearing shaded
glasses. An alert little dog guided the man as he crossed the

street. Impulsively, George stepped forward and put a coin in the man's hand. "God bless you," the man said. And George felt better.

The next day he was appointed chairman of the Accounts Committee and a member of the Judiciary Committee under the chairman, Walter Murray Gibson. And the day after, bills began pouring in. One of the first was a proposal to license the sale of opium. It was assigned to the Judiciary Committee.

From then on George felt like a dragon killer. If he cut off one head, seven more grew in its place. He was horrified at some of the proposed legislation. Hoapili Baker spent most of his time promoting the $10,000,000 loan and figuring ways for legislators to tap the treasury for expenditures. A suave Italian, Celso Caesar Moreno, who was very close to King Kalakaua, was lobbying for money to subsidize a steamship line between Hawaii and China, and for $1,000,000 in gold to build a trans-Pacific cable to Shanghai. Walter Murray Gibson, competing for the King's favor, introduced a bill to authorize $10,000 for the coronation of Kalakaua. George, with seven others including Pilipo, the Lion of North Kona, took the unpopular stand. They voted "No" and lost twenty-three to eight.

But the session didn't lack humor. One day a Hawaiian legislator made a long-winded, ten-minute speech. Luther repeated it in English in a little over one minute. The legislator got up and protested, "I talked longer than that!" Luther answered, "Oh, yes, but I interpreted all you said." The other members roared with laughter.

Late every afternoon, George took his walk along the waterfront, and, almost always, he passed the blind man with his little dog. Each time George went through the ritual of dropping a coin in that hat and receiving a grateful, "God bless you," in return. The little act helped erase his growing disillusionment with the processes of government.

On July 27 George voted wearily against raising the salaries of Cabinet Ministers from $10,000 to $12,000. He was on the losing side. The next day he voted against a $24,000 subsidy for Moreno's China Steamship Line and lost again.

In the Judiciary Committee, the opium bill received support from the Hawaiian members. Walter Murray Gibson took a self-righteous stand but rode with the crowd. The committee submitted a majority report favorable to the bill and on July 30, the Legislature passed it nineteen to fourteen. George and the Lion of North Kona voted "No." To George's relief, King Kalakaua vetoed the bill.

It got worse! On Thursday, August 5, Hoapili Baker introduced a resolution providing all legislators and their families free steamship passage to and from Honolulu. The chairman ruled the resolution out of order. Later in the day Baker's $10,000,000 loan bill got its second reading. When Pilipo got up and asked Baker if he knew anybody with $10,000,000, everyone laughed.

Sometimes George found it difficult to take the whole thing seriously. Yet, it was actually happening! To his relief, the loan bill was indefinitely postponed the next day, twenty-three to nineteen. But it popped up again on August 10, with Walter Murray Gibson as sponsor. This time it was defeated decisively, twenty-seven to eleven.

The final blow came on August 12 when the Legislature was asked to pay off $30,000 of a $40,000 loan made by Claus Spreckels to the King two years before. The notes were dated the same day Spreckels had been awarded the lease for his water rights on Maui. Only five others, including the Lion of North Kona, voted "No" with George Wilcox.

Finally, on August 14, it was all over, and genial King Kalakaua, in a short speech, congratulated the Legislature on its fine work. An hour later he fired his Cabinet and appointed one headed by the Italian lobbyist, Caesar Moreno, who had promised the King he could float the $10,000,000 loan in China. To

George, it was incredible! But this time Kalakaua had gone too far.

The foreign offices of Britain, the United States, and France flatly refused to recognize the appointment. Two other Cabinet members refused to serve with Moreno. A mass meeting headed by Sanford Dole and George Pilipo voted to send Dole and Pilipo with a note of protest to the King. Meanwhile, a mass meeting of Hawaiians supported the King against the haoles. Threats of rioting increased until, three days later, King Kalakaua capitulated and dismissed Moreno.

By that time, George was thoroughly disgusted with the whole sordid farce of Island government. Before he left he took one last walk along the waterfront. This time he followed a different route than he usually took later in the day. On a strange street he passed a familiar figure walking the other way and smoking an expensive cigar. He didn't recognize the blind man at first because he had taken off his disguise, and his dog wasn't with him. On that day George swore he was through with politics!

CHAPTER

15

The great weakness in the structure of the sugar boom was labor. And for George Wilcox it was a problem of conscience as well as economics. He knew that the number of sugar plantations had doubled from about thirty-five to approximately seventy in the five years since reciprocity, creating twice the demand for workers. He knew also, since his father had worried about it so, that the Hawaiian population was shrinking at an alarming rate. There were less than 50,000 remaining of a nation of 300,000.

To meet the tremendous demand for workers, planters hired coolies under contract at low wages from Canton, China. But

George did not approve of the way many of the workers were treated. He was not alone. Sanford B. Dole and Albert F. Judd, both attorneys, denounced the system because it made refusal to work a criminal offense under the contract, punishable by fine and imprisonment. Dole thundered, "We are one hundred years behind the age!" Sam Wilder, shipping executive, and Sam Alexander, plantation owner, supported the system as necessary for the operation of the plantations. They argued that the coolie was far better off in Hawaii than he had ever been in China.

George preferred to hire local Hawaiians rather than itinerant Chinese because they were more apt to stay on the plantation. And there was also the matter of conscience. Every year the demand for labor brought more foreigners, crowding out the Hawaiians. An English travel writer, Isabella L. Bird, predicted that the Hawaiian race would be extinct by 1897.

There was a need for some way to halt the decline of the Hawaiian and to teach him to participate in the Islands' expanding economy. George took an active interest in a manual training school for Hawaiian boys started by a visionary teacher named Mueller in 1874. The school failed for lack of interest among the students. He set the teacher up in business and kept hoping for a way out of the dilemma. Finally, late in 1880, he convinced himself he had found the answer. He explained the theory to Carl Isenberg, Paul's younger brother who was now in charge at Lihue Plantation, as they waited on the beach for Kauai's contingent of new workers from the South Pacific to disembark from the schooner. "They're Pacific Islanders like the Hawaiians," George pointed out. "That's the important thing. Basically they have the same customs. They eat nearly the same food."

"Will they work?" growled Isenberg.

"Why not? The Hawaiian does, when he has a reason, and the best reason is because he lives on the land. He takes pride in it. These Gilbert Islanders will feel the same way once they get settled and start mingling with our natives. That's why we brought their women and children along. They'll be Hawaiian before you know it. And if they like it here, they'll repopulate the Islands with the kind of people who belong here." George paused for emphasis. He had saved the most convincing argument for the last. "And that will be the end of our labor problems!"

There were about 250 of them on the ship: proud, brown-skinned, bare-footed people, natives of the Gilbert Islands over 1,000 miles to the southwest. They were dressed in cheap, blue denim pants, cotton shirts, and cotton dresses. They carried leis of shells and wilted flowers. Their belongings were wrapped in bundles of lauhala matting. As the whaleboats unloaded their cargoes, Sam said dubiously, "They remind me of those country Hawaiians who used to come out of the hills to go to father's school."

"You know the lingo better than I do," George answered. "Talk to them. Find out which ones are assigned to Grove Farm. Sam quickly discovered that the Gilbert Islanders couldn't understand his Hawaiian and he couldn't understand them and neither could anybody else. The languages were similar but not the same. Everyone milled around in confusion. Just when he was about to give up a young Hawaiian came forward and began to chatter excitedly with the newcomers. They crowded happily around him.

"You see, I told you they'd mix with the Hawaiians," George told Sam.

Sam answered dryly, "He's Hawaiian, but that's Gilbertese he's talking. His father was a missionary down there. They sent the boy back because he kept getting into trouble."

The plantation owners finally sorted out their workers and started with them to their camps. George had built three new houses for his three families in the valley below the mill, where there was plenty of water, fruit trees, and space to grow taro. He got the new workers settled and went home. The next morning, as he made his rounds, he found all of the Gilbert Islanders crowded into one house, leaving the others empty. They were cold! George issued them extra blankets. But the next morning the whole colony was still sleeping in one house. No amount of argument would make them move. And Kipele, their chief, would not sleep with the others inside. Instead, he squeezed his huge frame into a storage shelf, with a door that came down over it, on the lanai. With a shrug, George gave up trying to change their ways.

Every day Pikau came to report, with a shake of his head, that the Kilipakis, as the Hawaiians called them, had to be taught how to use a shovel or a hoe. Or they couldn't seem to understand the principles of irrigation. Or none of them knew how to drive oxen. George sighed, "We had to learn, too, Pikau. Do the best you can with them."

*   *   *

Every issue of the newspaper brought more disturbing news. Sam would listen sympathetically as George complained of a new outrage in Honolulu. And Emma would caution, "don't get so upset." He couldn't help it, especially when the Moreno fiasco reached its climax.

Smarting from his rebuff by the foreign powers who refused to recognize his cabinet appointment, Moreno hatched a scheme to get even. He talked King Kalakaua into sending him as a secret emissary with letters to the governments of the United States, Britain, and France, demanding the recall of their Ministers in Hawaii.

When George read that he threw down his paper. "My God, what is he trying to do, start a war!"

The plot was discovered before it created an international incident. But George's confidence in the Kalakaua regime dropped lower than before. And it didn't help when Claus

Spreckels returned to hobnob with the King. The rumor was that Kalakaua was looking for another loan.

However, George didn't have much time to worry about politics. Grove Farm had grown to 1,200 acres. The plantation could produce 650 tons of sugar annually, and it employed fifty men. George kept experimenting with ways to increase his yield. In 1880 he tried a new variety of cane called Rose Bamboo imported from Queensland, Australia.

And he tried out a new theory to solve the labor problem. He hired a company of German farmers recruited in Europe by Paul Isenberg. With their experience in agriculture, Isenberg had promised, the Germans would each be able to do the work of several ordinary laborers. In a way, it worked. The new laborers were very industrious and thrifty. But they were also expensive and very demanding. At Lihue Plantation the Germans complained constantly. At Grove Farm George kept them happy, though it was a constant trial. First they were dissatisfied with their homes. So George built them better houses than he had for any of his other workers. Then they wanted vegetable gardens in order to supplement their income by raising their own food. George gave them each an acre of land and dug another mile of ditch to supply the gardens with plantation water once a week. Other plantation managers grumbled because he spoiled his workers.

George's investments also kept growing and demanding more of his time. He now owned interest in half a dozen coasting schooners, a steamship, Waianae Plantation on Oahu, Haiku Plantation on Maui, and Kekaha Plantation on Kauai, in addition to Grove Farm. He was constantly making personal loans to his friends, and on October 2, 1880, he helped found a telephone company on the Island of Kauai.

Oddly enough, it was King Kalakaua's extravagance which led to the single biggest windfall George enjoyed in the early 1880's. Ever since 1866 George, and Willie Rice, had been leasing land from a Hawaiian chiefess, Ruth Keelikolani, who lived in Honolulu. Princess Ruth, who weighed over three hundred pounds, was, with King Kalakaua, one of the few remaining descendants of the haughty old Hawaiian chiefs.

George and Willie never knew when to expect a summons for a couple of bullocks and a half a dozen pigs to provide the menu for a feast Princess Ruth had decided to give in Honolulu. The two men never refused, and, as a result, Princess Ruth considered them ideal tenants. However, she did envy Kalakaua his promotion to the throne, and when he built himself a palace, she insisted she must have one also.

In order to pay for it, she decided to sell the two royal tracts Willie and George had been renting. Honolulu real estate interests clamored for this valuable property. But Princess Ruth refused to sell to anyone but her haole "subjects," Wilcox and Rice. They paid a total of $27,500 for the property and divided the land between them.

Willie got two small tracts called Kipu and Kipukai. George received a pie-shaped section called Haiku, reaching from the mountains to the sea, about 10,500 acres. The purchase, completed on April 1, 1881, increased the acreage owned in fee simple by Grove Farm almost ten times more than the year before. Princess Ruth built her palace, an imposing mansion on Emma Street. But the next time George visited Honolulu he found that the chiefess was not living in her new home. She preferred to sit and admire the palace from the comfortable lanai of her old house not far away.

*　*　*

Hackfeld and Company was located near the waterfront on Queen Street, between Fort and Bishop, in a rectangular, box-like, two-story building constructed of coral slabs. This had once been a show place of Honolulu, the court house and legislative chambers, built in the 1850's, scene of the first fancy dress ball ever held in the Islands. Now the historic structure served as a warehouse for sugar and plantation supplies. The company offices were in front behind the small portico entrance.

Perspiring, George stopped to take off his coat before he started across the sun-baked dirt street to the meeting that most likely meant bad news. Two shabby coconut palms grew in the middle of the street. He walked up the steps. Inside he paused, sun-blinded, to let his eyes adjust to the subdued light of the outer office. Then he pushed open a door and entered without knocking. J. C. Glade looked up from his desk with a frown. When he saw George, he waved to a chair. He picked up a box from the desk and offered it. "Cigar?"

"Thanks," said George. He lit it, waiting. The calendar on the wall in back of Glade was turned to December, 1881.

Glade leaned back in his chair and cleared his throat. "Last year the entire crop of Island sugar went to Claus Spreckels' California Refinery. This year the other agents have again accepted his terms. Hackfeld holds the only major block of uncommitted sugar."

George nodded.

"Looking at the situation honestly, it may be the wisest course for us to go with Spreckels also," continued Glade. "He now operates the only sugar refinery on the Pacific Coast. This gives him a monopoly in that market."

George studied the tip of his cigar, waiting for Glade to make his point. The sugar agent arose and began to restlessly pace the room.

"But that is only the beginning. With his plantation on Maui, Spreckels is now the largest single producer of sugar in the Islands. His partnership with William G. Irwin last year gives him control of one of our largest sugar agencies. He has built his own line of sailing ships which carry his sugars at a cheaper rate than we pay." Glade threw himself into a chair. "The man is getting a strangle hold on these Islands. If we are going to fight him, we must do it now or it may be too late. Yet if we lose, he might freeze us out altogether."

"Let's fight!" said George bluntly.

Glade chewed on his mustache. "Most of the other planters feel that way, too. And we have an idea. But it might be risky."

"What is it?" George asked eagerly.

"Spreckels' control extends only as far as the Rocky Mountains. If we were to market our sugars in the East, it would make us independent of him. The most economical way to do this is to ship our sugars by sail around the Horn to New York."

"Do you think it would work?"

"There are several reasons why it should. By selling on the open market, rather than agreeing on a price beforehand with Spreckels, we can take advantage of high prices. And by shipping in the middle of the year when prices are high, we might do very well, indeed. If our calculations are correct, we could gain from three-fourths cents to one cent a pound. That would more than repay our shipping charges."

George sat forward in eagerness, but Glade held up a warning hand. "However, this is all speculation. The weakness of the plan is that we have no one in the Eastern market to look after our interests. If the sugar isn't sold promptly, and sits in a warehouse, we could lose a good deal of money."

"At least our sugar won't be going to Spreckels," George answered without hesitation. "I'm for taking our chances in New York!"

As they shook hands, Glade said, "perhaps, we can show Mr. Spreckels that we are no longer as backward as he thinks we are. We've come a long way in the last few years, especially you, George. I can remember when you didn't even have a book-keeper."

"I still don't have a bookkeeper," George admitted.

"Amazing! How do you manage?"

George grinned. "I get up early in the morning."

Glade shook his head in disbelief as George walked, in his shirt sleeves, out of the building and into the dusty, sun-scorched street.

Bark *George N. Wilcox,* wrecked on Molokai, 1894

Laysan Island in 1890's, showing guano deposits and
gooney bird population

Early photo of sailing ships
in Honolulu Harbor

Inter-Island Steam Navigation Company dock, Honolulu Harbor, about 1895

Left: Malumalu School for Boys, established 1890 for Hawaiian youth by Jared and Juliet Smith with support from George N. Wilcox

Center: "Hapai-ko," hand-loading sugar cane into cars at Grove Farm, 1890

Bottom: A Fowler steam plow, 1893

The bark *Adonis* cleared for New York in February, 1882, with 656 tons of sugar. In April, the *C. R. Bishop* sailed with 1,325 tons of Hackfeld sugar, the largest cargo of sugar ever to leave the port of Honolulu. That record was broken a few weeks later when the *Amy Turner* sailed for New York with a still larger cargo of sugar in her hold. Then the waiting began.

But there was plenty to keep George busy. For one thing, he was learning to know his Gilbert Islanders. He found they were susceptible to colds because the climate of Kauai was cooler and wetter than their own. So he was careful to call Dr. Smith before a bad cough turned into pneumonia. Under the contract, George was required to feed the workers. So he made sure they had fresh meat every day, twenty-one pounds a week, salmon on Sundays, and taro in addition to the vegetables they grew and the fish they caught. The children he sent to school.

Every morning, as he made his before-breakfast rounds, George received from the Kilipakis a daily ration of either amusement or frustration. He found that their chief levied tribute from his clan on pay day. Once they incensed the Hawaiians by going out to the sand dunes and digging up skulls of old Hawaiian burials to take back as trophies of battle. Another time George arrived at their camp on Monday morning to find the Kilipakis gleefully flying a kite. They were masters of the sport. This one was a beauty, about twelve feet long by three feet wide, and they had kept it up in the air for nearly twenty-four hours in the steady trade wind.

Before going back to breakfast, George rode by and told Pikau, "Leave one of those Kilipakis to tend their kite this morning. I'm curious to see how long they can keep it up there."

Every morning for a week, one of the Gilbert Islanders stayed home from work to tend the kite. Finally the wind failed, and it came down. By that time the story of George's eccentricity was all over the island. But he didn't care. So far

Lihue Plantation had lost, through dysentery, consumption, or pneumonia, twenty of its one hundred and three Gilbert Islanders. At Koloa plantation, five were dead; at Kealia, seven were dead. At Grove Farm all eighteen of George's Kilipakis were alive and healthy.

*   *   *

To George, it seemed that the 1882 Legislative Session set a record for irresponsibility. Claus Spreckels was on hand for the opening ceremonies. On May 19 Kalakaua's Cabinet resigned, and the King appointed Walter Murray Gibson premier. One of the first acts of the new Cabinet was to give Spreckels title to 24,000 acres of crown lands on the Island of Maui for a price of $10,000. Before the session ended, the Legislature appropriated twice as much money as there were taxes to pay for the appropriations.

There was still no news from New York, but George received a letter dated August 4, 1882, from Henry Baldwin on Maui that electrified him. Baldwin had just come back from a trip to the Pacific Coast where Spreckels was adding steamers to his shipping interests. "I was more impressed while at the Coast," wrote Baldwin, "that all this means besides our being obliged to sell our sugars to Spreckels, we shall soon be obliged to freight them over on his vessels and steamers and consign them to his agents. All this you can readily see will be too much power for him to have over us."

George had seen this for some time, now. But it was the solution proposed by Baldwin that excited him. The other planter wrote, "I think it will pay for us to have a refinery in San Francisco . . . I talked with several good businessmen at the Coast, and they said they would take stock in the refinery at once, just as soon as it was ascertained that enough planters had stock in the concern to supply the sugars."

Of course, that was the answer! If the Hawaiian planters owned their own refinery, Spreckels' domination would be over!

George's elation didn't last long. Early in September word came back from New York that the cargo of the *Adonis* had been held up by a complaint filed by Eastern sugar men who objected to competition from duty-free Hawaiian sugar. As the red tape piled up, 3,500 tons of Hackfeld sugar sat in a warehouse.

George was in a fighting mood when Baldwin's next letter, dated September 25, arrived at Grove Farm. The Maui planter wrote, "Your letters in regard to the new refinery were duly received. . . . Sam Alexander and myself are quite anxious to put the thing through as soon as possible and propose that we all meet a week before the Planters' Association meets in Honolulu, which will be the 16th of October. . . . It is important to fix things up as soon as possible before Spreckels knows of it and tries to break up the thing."

It was a determined little group that met in secret, the week before the general meeting in Honolulu of planters from all of the Islands. In addition to Sam Alexander and Henry Baldwin, several other Maui planters were there. George and his brother Albert completed the circle.

Henry Baldwin opened the discussion with optimism. "I was surprised to learn that a profit of one-fourth cent to one-half cent a pound is considered good in the refinery business. Spreckels is making about two cents per pound."

"You see why he wants to keep his hold on Hawaiian sugar?" said Alexander.

Baldwin continued enthusiastically, "That's why we should be able to undersell him and make money at the same time. The plan would be to put up a refinery that would cost about $250,000 with a capacity to refine 20,000 tons a year, enough to handle all of the sugars grown by the planters who want to take stock. It costs only one-fourth cent per pound to refine sugar. I feel confident the refinery can earn a dividend of $100,000 a year even if we make only one-fourth cent profit per pound."

"What would our investment be?" asked Albert.

Baldwin answered, "Sam Alexander and I are ready to put in $40,000. We'd like you and George to match that."

"We will," said George.

Some of the other planters were more cautious. One of them asked where the refined sugar would be sold if the grocers and jobbers on the Pacific Coast, all under Spreckels' thumb, refused to buy from the new refiner? There was a painful silence. And there was the question of control. Baldwin argued that someone from the Islands should be in charge of the operation. But which one of the group could qualify as manager of the new refinery?

Finally, they decided to sound out Pacific Coast investors more thoroughly before making a move. Judge Hartwell was assigned to draw up papers for a proposed corporation. George left feeling dissatisfied. He was elected vice-president of the new Planters' Labor and Supply Company, but it didn't ease his frustration. The growing power of Spreckels dominated the meeting.

The California refiner had already sunk $4,000,000 in his Maui plantation, the Hawaiian Commercial and Sugar Company, making it a model of efficient, up-to-date operation. Spreckels' engineers had developed a new five-roller mill that extracted an increased percentage of cane juice and permitted the cane stalks to be used as fuel without drying. Spreckels had installed a railroad system on his plantation, to bring his cane to the mill from greater distances in less time, and he was experimenting with a steam plow that would do the work in an hour that eighteen oxen did in a day. George listened to the reports with envy. He had to admire Spreckels' driving energy.

By the end of the year, the news was all discouraging. Hackfeld had done badly on its shipment of sugar to New York. The new refinery was nothing more than an optimistic dream. And Claus Spreckels was more firmly in the driver's seat than ever.

*   *   *

George took a sip of steaming coffee, gingerly holding the familiar mug without a handle as he lounged on the veranda by the cook house. Cows grazed peacefully in the valley below. Smoke from the mill stack rose lazily into the crisp morning air. This was his favorite time of day, just after dawn, when the earth was still expectant, waiting to receive the first seed of the morning, or feel the first bite of the plow. Unwillingly, he made himself listen to the story Sam was telling.

"Those Kilipakis almost caused a riot in Koloa Saturday night. The Chinese storekeeper wanted me to arrest them all. I never saw anybody so mad!"

"What happened?"

Sam chuckled over the memory. "The Kilipakis went into the Chinese store for a feed of bread and butter and coffee. You know how rancid the butter is in that store?" Sam had to stop laughing before he could go on. "Well, the Kilipakis really took to that butter. I guess it smelled like cocoanut oil because they smeared every bit of it into their hair. The Chinese storekeeper blew his stack! He kept yelling I should arrest the whole kit and caboodle for not putting the butter on their bread!"

Emma came hurrying out of the house. "Where's Gaylord?"

Sam and George looked guiltily at one another. "He was here just a minute ago."

"That boy!" exclaimed Emma.

The hunt began for small Gaylord, the most active of Sam and Emma's children. Ralph, a sober eight-year-old, went around the house to look in the lumber pile. Six-year-old Etta went the other way with her younger sister, Elsie, age five. They were hardly out of sight when the young Hawaiian yard boy, Kaaihue, came up the path out of the valley carrying Gaylord who was kicking with all his might.

"He likes to play in the stream down there," said Kaaihue as he handed the squirming bundle to Emma.

"Thank you, Kaaihue," she said. "Would you get the other children and have them wash their hands and feet before breakfast?"

With a sigh, George drained his mug and took it back to the cook house. It was so pleasant here during the morning "coffee hour." In a few hours he'd be off for Honolulu to help organize a new steamship company. That would be exciting. But thank God he had this to come back to.

*   *   *

Those moments of peace seemed to grow farther and farther apart. On February 19, 1883, George invested $30,000 for three hundred shares in a new corporation called the Inter-Island Steam Navigation Company. Albert bought three hundred shares in the new venture and Sam bought fifty. The only block of stock larger than theirs was owned by Captain T. R. Foster, president of the firm. George was elected auditor. The new shipping company operated four schooners and four steamers. The directors immediately made plans to build more steamers. Their chief competitor was the Wilder Steamship Company.

While George was in town, on February 12, King Kalakaua held his own coronation. He had ordered two crowns, a scepter, and a signet ring from England. Representatives of nearly every major power in the world were there for the event, held on the grounds of the Palace. For a week there were feasts, a regatta, canoe races, and a series of hula dances which delighted the Hawaiians and shocked the Mission community. George saw no objection to the hula dancing but he couldn't see the reason for spending $30,000 on the coronation of a king who had been in office for nine years.

More shocking to George than a few hula dances was the Spreckels silver coinage deal. King Kalakaua's government had given the California financier authority to mint $1,000,000 worth of silver coins for the Hawaiian Kingdom. Spreckels, who was now the chief creditor of the Kingdom, realized a profit of

$150,000 on the transaction, then opened his own bank in Honolulu.

With each new evidence of corruption in the Palace, George felt himself drawn back into the tangle of politics. He refused to hold office, but early in 1883 he became a member of a secret organization called the Committee of Nine dedicated to curbing the irresponsible use of King Kalakaua's power. On April 20, Sanford B. Dole was elected chairman, W. R. Castle became treasurer, and W. O. Smith was named secretary. George and Colonel Z. K. Spaulding of Kealia Plantation were assigned the job of quietly lining up support on Kauai.

But the Committee of Nine seemed to have as little chance of beating Kalakaua as the refinery group had of beating Spreckels. That fall George found himself once more in the office of Hackfeld and Company. J. C. Glade had become a silent partner. The man behind the desk was his brother, H. F. Glade, younger but similar in appearance, who had worked his way up on Hackfeld sugar plantations. George wondered how much mettle the young man had in him. He soon found out.

"As you know, we fared badly last year by shipping to New York," Glade said without apology. "This year we are in a bad spot, and Mr. Spreckels is well aware of the fact. Not only has he lowered his prices, but he will buy our sugars only if we agree to ship them in his bottoms. I don't like it. But unless we can find another market, we must accept his terms."

"Then let's find a market!"

Glade smiled. "I think we already have. The St. Louis Sugar Refinery has offered us as much for our sugar as Spreckels has. It will mean shipping the sugar by rail from the Pacific Coast across the continent. This is a major undertaking. The amount to be shipped will be 20,000,000 pounds of sugar valued at $1,500,000. Such a cargo should furnish tonnage for nearly forty-five regular freight trains. As a matter of fact, it would be much less trouble to sell to Spreckels at his terms."

"But if we give in, how do we know what his terms will be next year? I say fight him!"

"If the other planters feel as you do, we will fight," promised Glade. "I just hope, this time, we will win."

* * *

When the young Englishman appeared at the door of George's little office around the middle of October, 1883, the dogs raised a terrific din. George didn't even look up from his account books.

"Come in," he called. "They never bite an honest man."

He raised his head and saw that his visitor wore a neat suit that was frayed at the cuffs. George frowned, unable to place the man.

"My name is Purvis, sir, Robert W. T. Purvis," said the young fellow. He spoke with a well-bred English accent.

"Sit down, Purvis. What can I do for you?"

The man sat down carefully. "I came to ask you for a job, Mr. Wilcox."

"What kind of job?"

"I'm a bookkeeper."

George grunted. "You've come to the wrong place. I keep my own books. Everybody knows that."

The young man didn't give up. "You are a very busy man, Mr. Wilcox. If I took over your accounts, it would give you more time for other things."

George shook his head. "When I do it myself, I know exactly where I stand. That's one reason I make money. I know exactly where every penny goes."

Still the young Englishman would not leave. He paused, then said unwillingly, "I need a job badly, sir. My father isn't well, and I'm supporting my mother and sisters."

"Have you had any experience?" George asked.

"Yes, sir."

George looked annoyed. But the young man met his stare

without flinching. "Well, I suppose you might help out for awhile. Until you get on your feet. I'll pay you $100 a month. You can eat here with the family, if you like, until we see how it works."

Purvis proved to be an excellent bookkeeper, so good that George quickly stopped worrying about the accounts. It was more of a relief than he'd anticipated. Why not get somebody to do the worrying about the field work as well? For his plantation manager, George settled on a blustering, German ex-sea captain, Louis Ahlborn. And that hiring was as unorthodox as the other.

"Captain Ahlborn, I'd like you to take as much interest in this plantation as if it were your own," said George as they stood on the veranda that first day. "So I have a proposition to make to you. You can either take a straight salary, or I'll give you a living allowance plus fifteen per cent of whatever the plantation earns. That way we'll win or lose together."

Ahlborn was a heavy-set man with a round face and a small, dark mustache. "I'm willing to take a chance," he boomed. "I'll take the percentage."

"Good," George answered. "We'll call it profit sharing."

* * *

It became more and more obvious to George that the future of his plantation, as well as that of the whole Island economy, hung in the balance at Iolani Palace in Honolulu. So he spent more and more time in support of a Reform slate of candidates for the 1884 election. To his intense satisfaction, his work and that of the other members of the Committee of Nine proved effective. The Reform candidates, including Sanford Dole, were elected in strength to the Legislature. The Reformers gave Claus Spreckels his first major political defeat in the Islands.

Early in the session, the California financier had introduced a bill, written by his own attorney, that would permit Spreckels to establish a national bank of Hawaii authorized to issue paper money, own steamship lines and railroads, and carry on business without a license. The bill was designed to give Spreckels control of all business transacted between the Islands and the Pacific Coast. Spreckels returned to California boasting that he had the Hawaiian Legislature in his pocket. But this time he was wrong. A coalition of Reformers and Independents voted down the bill.

Otherwise, Spreckels had it all his own way. Hackfeld lost money on its shipment to St. Louis. In 1884 the company capitulated, and Spreckels bought at his own price every pound of sugar grown in the Islands. George agreed to the sale. But it infuriated him.

He came home from that disappointing conference to find an enraged bull terrorizing his workmen in the plantation yard. George ran for his rifle, hopped onto a bullock cart and ordered the driver to take him as close to the dangerous animal as possible. As the bull charged, George brought it down with a shot between the eyes. The Kilipakis watched open-mouthed.

The next day the chief brought their combined earnings and offered the money to George in exchange for his rifle. He refused to sell, but he told the chief he could buy rifles in Honolulu. The Kilipakis returned to their own Islands soon after, each proudly carrying a new rifle. The first thing they did on their return, George learned, was to charge into the next valley, singing Sunday School hymns they had learned in Hawaii, and exterminate an enemy tribe. That was the end of the noble experiment.

CHAPTER

16

George slapped his thigh with satisfaction when he heard the news. "This is going to be a good fight!" he said. It began late in 1884 when the American Refinery in San Francisco showed interest in expanding with Island capital to compete with Spreckels' giant California Sugar Refinery. American was a small company run by a former Spreckels man, E. L. G. Steele, whom Spreckels allowed to operate with inferior sugars in a restricted market. George immediately went to work trying to raise more money.

Judge Widemann was skeptical. "Yes, I've heard of the American Refinery. It is no competition to Mr. Spreckels."

"It's no competition because he makes sure American doesn't get any of our sugar. All Steele is permitted to buy is from Batavia, Java, and Manila, Philippines. If American can produce a quality product to compete with Spreckels, it would sell."

"I would like to believe you. But it isn't a matter of quality alone. Spreckels has the jobbers on the Coast under his thumb."

"And they don't like it!"

Judge Widemann sighed. "George, how much are you worth?"

"Oh, about $300,000 I suppose."

"There! You see how hopeless it is? Mr. Spreckels has a financial empire worth millions behind him. You have $300,-000."

The answer came at once. "But if enough of us stick together we can beat him. That's the important thing. We have to stick together!"

"I would be willing to help if I thought you could succeed," said Judge Widemann, shaking his head. "I am afraid you will only hurt yourselves."

George didn't give up. Cautiously, he and Henry Baldwin sounded out other planters. Paul Isenberg, who now owned a large interest in Hackfeld and Company, was in the Islands on one of his regular visits from Germany. He said simply, "Spreckels must be stopped. I am with you." It didn't help when a world surplus of sugar caused the price to slump. But on January 31, 1885, George made his first investment, $18,896.87, in the American Refinery. Sam Alexander, now living in California, and Henry Baldwin on Maui, came in. So did Albert Wilcox.

It was a beginning. Gleefully George read the story in the *Hawaiian Gazette* of February 25, 1885. "San Francisco, Feb. 10—A sugar war has broken out between Spreckels, of the California Refinery, and the American Refinery, which has the effect of reducing the price to lower rates than ever before ruled in this market. The American produces about one-fifth as much as the California."

"Opinion is divided as to the possible result. Some grocers think the California company will bring the American company to terms, but others maintain that the smaller corporation can stand the strain equally well. It is also asserted that as sugar cannot be manufactured at the present rates at a profit, the immense capacity of Spreckels' refinery will be a disadvantage to him."

As the price war on refined sugar continued in San Francisco, the price of raw sugar continued to drop around the world. Many planters cut back their acreage rather than risk a loss. George boldly planted more cane that he ever had before, extending his ditch system to get more water. He explained to Captain Ahlborn, "if the price goes down you have to grow more to make as much." The manager wasn't convinced.

The interest by Island planters in the American Refinery was still a secret when the heads of three large Hawaiian sugar agencies—Hackfeld and Company, C. Brewer and Company, and Castle and Cooke—sailed for San Francisco in July, 1885, to discuss a sugar contract with Claus Spreckels for the coming year. George waited impatiently for the result.

When it came it made headlines! Spreckels arrogantly refused even to make an offer for the sugar. After the meeting, the Honolulu men went to the American Refinery where President E. L. G. Steele gave them a three-year contract at the price Spreckels had paid the year before. The contract stipulated that Island planters could ship their sugars in any vessels they chose.

The three sugar agents hurried back to Honolulu to line up support. Within a few days they had signed up another major sugar agency, Theo. H. Davies and Company, besides two smaller companies, F. A. Schaefer and Company, and M. S. Grinbaum and Company. The combined product of these agencies represented nearly one half of the entire Hawaiian sugar crop. With the contract in hand, the American Refinery immediately announced an increase in capitalization to $1,000,-000 for expansion of the factory to handle the 55,000 tons of sugar expected during the next year. More Island planters took shares in the refinery. The *Hawaiian Gazette*, on September 8, 1885, called the sale of sugar by the independent planters to the American Refinery one of the most important events to happen during the past two or three years.

*   *   *

There just didn't seem to be a satisfactory solution to the labor problem, but the Hawaiian planters kept trying. In 1885 the Board of Immigration worked out an agreement with the Japanese government for workers there to take jobs on Island plantations. The Japanese were small and wiry and quite independent. Some of the plantations immediately reported desertions, especially those where lunas, or foremen, enforced their orders with fists or the tip of a hob-nailed boot.

Under the contract labor law, workers who ran away could be arrested and brought into court. The plantation manager usually paid the court costs which, with the amount of the worker's fine, were deducted from his wages. If the man refused to work, he stayed in prison until he changed his mind.

George was too immersed in refinery negotiations to give much attention to his new workers until one morning Captain Ahlborn reported that a Japanese field hand was missing. "Shall I round him up for you?" asked Sam who, as sheriff, spent much of his time tracking down deserters. "Don't bother," answered George. A few days later another worker ran away.

Captain Ahlborn was furious! "Those two have been trouble makers ever since they came," he blustered. "I'm going after them myself. And when I get my hands on . . . "

"Leave them be!" George said sharply.

"Leave them be? You might as well invite the whole bunch to run away! That's what's going to happen."

"I don't think so. Where would they run?"

Frustrated, the big German said, "Mr. Wilcox, the law says those two men belong in the fields or in jail and by God . . . "

George interrupted coldly. "I don't give a damn what the law says. If a man doesn't want to work, I don't want him on my plantation."

A week later, Captain Ahlborn met George on his morning rounds. "You'll never believe this, but those two deserters came into camp last night," Ahlborn said as he reined in his horse. "They want to go back to work. What shall I do?"

"Let them," George said, and rode on. The missing workers quickly told the others what they had discovered of conditions on other plantations. After that, Grove Farm had no problem with deserters.

* * *

George was unaware of his growing reputation as an unorthodox sugar planter though he added to it year after year. In 1885, a man named Haas, from California, made the rounds trying to sell a load of fish scrap fertilizer. Discouraged by refusals, Haas finally stumbled onto George who bought the whole shipment. He stored the fish scrap in an old building half a mile down the road from the Grove Farm house. The fertilizer smelled so bad the Hawaiians dubbed the store house "Hale Pilau" or "House of Stink." And when the rains loosed the stench of the first application to Grove Farm fields, George was the most unpopular man on the Island. But his next crop showed remarkable improvement.

From that time on, George bought from Haas a yearly supply of less smelly but equally effective bonemeal fertilizer.

Purvis, the bookkeeper, could have added to the lengthening list of George's eccentricities if he had been a less discreet employee. For example, one of his first entries in the Grove Farm books, on November 1, 1883, was to write off $1,300 in small loans George had made to his men over the past few years. In 1884, Purvis entered a total of $17,391.11 in donations made that year by George to Mission schools, churches of half a dozen different denominations, and to help young Hawaiians get an education.

Those figures remained buried in the books, but the story of George's killing in sugar in 1886 received embarrassing publicity. The world surplus of sugar in 1885 had frightened many planters into cutting back on production. As a result, a shortage soon followed, and in 1886 George, who had increased his acreage, almost doubled his income from sugar over that of the year before. The story that reached Honolulu was that he made $100,000. Actually, the figure Purvis entered in the books was only $21,846.75. But when Captain Ahlborn collected his fifteen per cent, it was twice as much as he had expected. George used part of his windfall to buy a piece of beach property on Nawiliwili Bay, called Papalinahoa, to be used as a mill site for Grove Farm just in case.

At the same time, he devoured every newspaper report of the refinery battle in California. But the news was not encouraging. The September 23, 1885, *Advertiser* reported that excavations for additional buildings at the American Refinery were suspended due to the law suits, and that the wharf, shed, and several thousand bricks had collapsed into the sea.

At the same time, Spreckels boldly increased the price of refined sugar from his factory to grocers two cents a pound. He caught the American Refinery with no reserve stocks of raw sugar and in the midst of expansion problems. Within a few months, Spreckels made a profit of about $1,000,000. Then, when the shiploads of Hawaiian sugar began to unload at the American Refinery, Spreckels dropped his price below the break-even point.

The price war was savage. American dropped its price to meet that of Spreckels. President E. L. G. Steele raised the pay of his men to keep Spreckels from raiding them. But nothing seemed to go right. By April 26, 1886, the American Refinery still wasn't able to process the enormous amount of sugar it had contracted for. Half a million pounds of raw sugar had to be shipped to New York. In June, Spreckels dropped his price another cent. The American Refinery followed suit. Some of the Pacific Coast investors began to grow panicky. On June 30, George invested another $44,182 in the refinery.

Meanwhile, to keep his hold on the shipping business, Spreckels lowered his freight rates. By spring of 1886 the rates had dropped from about five dollars to three dollars per ton by sailing ship and $3.50 by steamer between Honolulu and San Francisco.

"How long do you think it can last?" asked Sam.

"Until we beat Spreckels," George answered grimly.

The battle for control of the Legislature that year was just as fierce. This time King Kalakaua was determined to break the growing strength of the Reformers. He traveled to Kona on the Island of Hawaii to campaign against his old enemy, George W. Pilipo. The Lion of North Kona was defeated by a scant margin in an election that resulted in a conviction of fraud by Kalakaua's candidate. Of the legislators who sat in 1886, the majority of the members of the Palace party held government jobs given them by the King.

In firm control of the Legislature, Kalakaua began to push for a $2,000,000 loan with which to finance his dreams of empire. George followed the reports, growling his displeasure when Claus Spreckels offered to take the loan on condition that the Kingdom repay some $700,000 already owed him as chief creditor to Kalakaua's government.

George told Sam and Emma over the center table, "If that loan goes through, Spreckels will own us body and soul!"

Meanwhile, the Legislature passed a bill authorizing the sale of opium, and Kalakaua signed it into law. The appropriations bill came to $1,500,000 more than estimated revenues. One hundred thousand went for a gunboat, $15,000 to celebrate the King's birthday.

The comic opera Legislature dragged through the summer, the influence of Claus Spreckels hovering like an evil genie over the proceeding. In June he forced the resignation of the Cabinet. The next one, hand picked by Spreckels, contained two recent arrivals from California, a journalist and an attorney.

The next time George visited Honolulu he complained to Luther, "Who's king, Kalakaua or Spreckels?"

Luther smiled knowingly. "Spreckels thinks he is but he may be in for a surprise. They say the King is tired of taking orders. He's trying to float a loan in London to pay off Spreckels. If that happens, things will be different."

Luther was right. A London syndicate took the $2,000,000 loan after negotiations that smelled badly of graft. Nevertheless, even the Reformers favored the loan because it meant the end of Claus Spreckels' hold on the government. The California financier considered the action a slap in the face. He stormed into the Palace and flung down every decoration Kalakaua had given him during the past ten years. Then he took the first steamer for California swearing he would never return. It was the best news George had read all year.

* * *

The refinery battle dragged on. Spreckels never showed the faintest sign of weakening. The American Refinery struggled desperately to meet the competition. On September 6, 1886, the *Advertiser* reported, "There have been numerous complaints of the delay caused to shipping by the insufficient storage room and absence of landing facilities at the American Refinery, some vessels having to remain idle for weeks waiting their turn."

By 1887 H. F. Glade was worried. He glanced down at the figures on his desk, then looked up at George. "We can't go on losing money like this," he said shaking his head.

George's mouth was set. "Spreckels is losing money, too."

"Well, he can afford to lose more than we can . . . "

"That's what he wants us to think! It's the way he works. Scare the other man, bluff him, and when he knuckles under, make a killing! Well, he doesn't scare me!"

Glade smiled without humor. "It's not you we're worried

about, it's some of our Pacific Coast stockholders. If they sell out to Spreckels, we're finished."

"Will they sell out to us first?" asked George.

"That's what P. C. Jones is working on now. If you . . . "

George was half way out of his chair. "Why didn't you say so?" He clapped his straw hat on his head and hurried out of the door.

* * *

As the political situation became more intolerable, George was disturbed to hear that a secret, armed, anti-Kalakaua organization called the Rifles had sprung up in Honolulu in the spring of 1887. Then the movement spread to Kauai. Members were white businessmen and sugar planters. Some of them talked of overthrowing the monarchy and annexing Hawaii to the United States.

The King seemed unaware of the new, explosive nature of his opposition. He became more autocratic than ever. Late in the spring he sent an ancient copra steamer, fitted out as a gun boat, to Samoa in the South Pacific to display the naval might of his Kingdom. The voyage ended in fiasco when the captain and crew staged one drunken mutiny after another. George read a report on the expedition by author Robert Louis Stevenson, in Samoa at the time, who wrote, "The Kaimiloa was from the first a scene of disaster and dilapidation, the stores were sold; the crew revolted; for a great part of a night she was in the hands of mutineers, and the Secretary lay bound upon the deck."

But that wasn't what finally caused the explosion. Late in June a Chinese rice planter named Tonk Kee, alias Aki, announced that he had paid King Kalakaua and his Prime Minister, Walter Murray Gibson, a bribe of $85,000 for an opium license. Aki complained that after taking his money, the King had awarded the opium license to a syndicate headed by Chung Lung in return for another bribe of $80,000.

When the stories appeared in the newspapers, Honolulu erupted! There was talk of overthrowing the corrupt government and immediately applying to the United States for annexation. On June 30, 1887, all business houses closed. Citizens streamed to a mass meeting at the Armory on Beretania Street, where they voted that a Committee of thirteen wait on the King and demand that he dismiss Gibson and declare a new constitution that would severely limit his power. During the meeting, armed members of the Rifles guarded the doors.

In the face of such determined opposition, the King capitulated. The next day he sent a written reply agreeing to all demands. A few hours later he appointed a new Cabinet made up of staunch Reform party members. By nightfall the crisis was over.

But George's turmoil was only beginning. Between business conferences his friends in the Reform party urged him to run for the Legislature again. Two of his most persuasive visitors were Sanford B. Dole, an active Reform candidate, and Lorrin A. Thurston, the new Minister of Interior.

Dole was forty-three, five years younger than George, a tall, slender, erect man with a full, black beard that he combed into two points. "The elections are set for September 12," he said. "We want to field the strongest Reform ticket possible."

"You don't need me," George answered. "The fight is over."

"No, it's only begun," said Thurston. He was big and pugnacious, his gaze as direct as his manner. A close-cropped, dark beard covered his determined jaw, and his barrel chest always seemed to be straining the buttons of his coat.

"But the King is beaten," George argued.

Thurston waved his hand impatiently. "Only in this way. He's had to accept a government under the British system. Now he can no longer fire his Cabinet at will. Only the Legislature can do that by a two-thirds majority. And the Cabinet must approve bills before they become law."

"You've got him hog tied," said George.

"But I don't trust him," Thurston grumbled. "He still appoints the Cabinet. And if he gets control of the Legislature again we're right back where we started."

Dole's appeal was milder. "We've won a round, George, that's all. This constitution makes the King responsible to the Cabinet, the Cabinet responsible to the Legislature, and the Legislature responsible to the people. Now we must prove that the system will work, and we need your help to do it."

But it was Luther who made up George's mind for him. His usually light-hearted brother said soberly, "This new constitution puts the government in the hands of the haoles. Look at Thurston's Cabinet. All haoles! And the House of Nobles. Now, in order to be a candidate, you have to be worth $3,000. How many Hawaiians can meet that requirement?"

George nodded. "I know, but the reason for that is to see that responsible people fill those seats, not a bunch of wild-eyed . . . "

"Exactly!" said Luther emphatically. "And look at some of the wild-eyed Reformers who helped put over this new constitution! They were talking revolution, George! You heard them!"

"You always have a lunatic fringe," George told him.

"But it gets stronger every year. They're ready to kick the Hawaiians out. That's why you should run . . . "

"Luther, I'm not a politician. The whole rotten mess makes me sick!"

Luther answered in a tone their mother had often used. "I know you don't think much of Kalakaua. But remember there's Pikau and Josiah Kiawe and Punui and Kumaka and all the other Hawaiians who helped you get started. They deserve representation, don't they?"

George sighed heavily. "Yes."

He was elected easily to the House of Nobles, sitting with George Dole, also elected from Kauai. His brother, Albert, and Willie Rice won seats in the House of Representatives. When members gathered on November 3, George recognized Sam

Wilder, elected a Noble from Oahu, and Judge Widemann and Henry Baldwin, elected Nobles from Maui. Most of the faces were haole, and work proceeded with unusual efficiency.

Lorrin Thurston said happily, "At last, we have government instead of a side show."

* * *

The purchase of 2,000 shares of American Refinery stock, engineered by P. C. Jones of C. Brewer and Company, went through a few days after the election, giving Island investors control of the company. At about the same time, the hard-pressed refinery unloaded 5,000 tons of raw Hawaiian sugar in the New York market.

It was all very discouraging. So much so that George was dumbfounded by the unexpected piece of good luck that came in early 1888. P. C. Jones, a portly man with a small mustache, broke the news. "We've had an offer to sell the refinery," he said.

"You mean Spreckels wants to buy us out?" answered George, instantly suspicious.

"No, it isn't Spreckels. It's H. O. Havemeyer!"

George blinked. "The Eastern Sugar Trust!"

"That's right. He's offering a very good price."

"What does it mean?"

"It means Spreckels is finally going to get some real competition. And we'll come out of this with our skins. In fact, that refinery stock of yours may bring you a very handsome return! It pays to stand up and fight."

At first, George couldn't believe it. But the sale went through, and he made a thirty-three per cent profit on his investment in the American Refinery. He would have preferred to keep battling Spreckels to the end. As it was, he explained to Sam, "thirty-three per cent profit isn't bad for three years. And, besides, look at all the fun we had!"

CHAPTER

17

The owner of Grove Farm had never been so eager to get back to his plantation. From the time the special Legislative Session of 1887 began until the regular session of 1888 ended, the House had been meeting continuously for nearly twelve months. Finally, on May 29 it was all over. George took the first steamer for Kauai.

It wasn't only that he was homesick for the jagged mountain skyline and his fields of glistening cane. This time he had a special reason for wanting to go home. On the day before the session ended, he had paid $12,123.53 at Hackfeld and Company for a set of enormous Fowler steam plows and had them loaded on the steamer. George had never seen such beautiful machinery. He couldn't wait to try it out in his fields.

"Look at those boilers," he boasted to Sam as they examined the shiny, metal monsters parked outside the plantation yard. "The shells are five-eighths of an inch thick. No wonder they last so long. And those compound steam engines are as efficient as any ever built."

"They're big enough," said Sam.

George nodded in approval. "Twenty tons apiece. They're rated at forty-five horsepower, but that's conservative. They can pull a plow across a field at five miles an hour."

Sam whistled.

"For deep plowing the speed goes down to two miles an hour," George admitted. "That's still better than a span of eighteen oxen can do." He patted a cumbersome wheel. "It shouldn't be long before Lihue Plantation puts in a railroad for hauling cane to the mill. That will mean more expansion. When it comes, we're ready."

George was like a youngster with a new toy that first day they tried the steam plows out in the field. It was a spectacular operation. First, the two twenty-ton steam plowing engines lumbered onto one side of the field, one engine pulling a double-ended plow. Behind the engines came water wagons for the boilers and carts loaded with fire wood to supply the furnaces. Two men, an operator and a stoker, were required to run each engine, and four men rode the plow.

On the underside of each engine was a flat drum holding hundreds of feet of heavy, steel cable. At the edge of the field, the cable from one engine was hitched to one end of the plow, the cable from the other engine was hitched to the opposite end. Then one of the engines moved off, paying out cable as it went. When the engine reached the opposite side of the field, plowing could begin.

George explained eagerly, "The engine on the far side pulls the plow across the field by reeling in cable. Then the engine on this side pulls it back the same way."

He had to admit, however, that the plow was a ridiculous looking contraption. It was built like a teeter totter, a set of four plow shares bolted to a frame on each end of the teeter totter. The sets of plow shares faced one another. Weird or not, the contraption was efficient. It plowed forward or backward without turning around. As the plow moved across the field in one direction, the plow shares facing backward simply teetered up out of the way. When the plow moved in the opposite direction, these plow shares penetrated the soil while those on the opposite end lifted off the ground.

"Now watch," said George proudly.

Four men clambered aboard the plow, two to steer and two to regulate the depth of the plowing. The steam engine operator on this side of the field gave a toot on his whistle. An answering toot came from the other engine. Then the cable began to move, pulling the plow across the field. The plow made a swath six feet wide.

"Look at that!" George exulted. "Just look at that!"

Suddenly the plow bucked like a plunging horse, nearly throwing its riders. There was a lot of frantic shouting and arm waving. Plowing came quickly to a halt. George rode into the field where the plowmen were scratching their heads.

"It's a rock, a big one over a foot below the surface," one of the men said in disgust. "I don't think we can budge it."

They walked around the plow, then back again, wondering what to do. At last George told them, "Steer around it." The men climbed back into their seats and signaled to the steam engine operators. But the plow didn't move. Impatiently, George rode to the engine doing the pulling. "What's the matter now?"

The stoker hung his head. "I forgot to keep the fire up. We don't have enough steam pressure."

"Well, get some!" George snapped.

He rode back to where Sam was waiting, a grin on his face.

"Oxen may be slower," he said, "but they're a lot less trouble."

* * *

In 1890, the man behind the desk at Hackfeld and Company was Johannes Frederick Hackfeld, nephew of the founder of the firm, old Captain Henry Hackfeld. The nephew was a dapper, handsome man with wavy hair and a needle-pointed mustache. He glanced suspiciously at the grey substance in a small box on his desk, then picked up a sheet of paper and scanned its contents. Finally, he put the paper down and shook his head in indecision. "Mr. Wilcox, if anyone else came to me with a scheme like this, I would say he was crazy."

George puffed calmly on his cigar.

"I suppose you know that Captain Freeth has been trying to peddle this stuff to everybody in town." said Hackfeld with a wave of his hand toward the box. "You're the first to take him seriously."

"That's because I know something about guano. They don't," George answered.

Hackfeld leaned back in his chair and crossed his arms. "All right, what do you have in mind?"

George said eagerly. "Sugar men in these Islands are finally beginning to realize that you can't expect the yield to stay up if you plant cane in the same fields year after year without putting nourishment back into the soil."

The sugar agent nodded in agreement.

"The potential demand for fertilizer in the Islands is enormous. Here's my point. Right now we ship our bonemeal and all the rest of it from California. Why shouldn't we be supplying this demand ourselves?" George reached for the box. "The first thing I did with this sample was to take it to Dr. Albert Lyons, the chemist at Punahou. Lyons says the guano in this box is prime fertilizer. If there's enough of this guano on the island where Freeth found it, we're in business."

"I've heard of the guano trade," Hackfeld protested. "What

you want me to do is send a vessel to some God forsaken island . . . "

"I don't want you to do anything but listen! This sample comes from Laysan. That's in the Line Islands about seven hundred miles to the northwest. I intend to send Dr. Lyons up there at my own expense to take more samples and find out how big the deposits are. I'd go myself if the Legislature weren't in session. If there's as much guano on Laysan as I think there is, I'll organize a company to mine it and ship it here. Naturally, I'd like Hackfeld and Company to take a few shares and act as our agent."

Hackfeld shrugged. "Fair enough. It's your funeral."

Near the end of July, 1890, the Inter-Island Steam Navigation Company schooner, *Kaalokai*, commanded by Captain G. D. Freeth, sailed for Laysan Island with Dr. Albert B. Lyons as passenger. George hurried to the dock when he learned that the schooner had returned on Wednesday, August 20.

Lyons, small and brisk, was already busy with his lengthy report. His verdict: Laysan Island had large deposits of phosphates in the form known as guano. Now George found it difficult to concentrate on politics during his endless round of legislative committee meetings. His mind was on the new company that so few of his friends seemed to take seriously.

Luther was more diplomatic. He said, "George, you're the only man I know who could fall in love with fertilizer."

On October 15, 1890, George was elected president of the new North Pacific Phosphate and Fertilizer Company, capitalized at $100,000. George took the largest block of shares, three hundred at one hundred dollars each. J. C. Hackfeld, elected treasurer, and George's brother, Albert, both came in for 150 shares. After that, George was busier than ever outfitting an expedition that would establish a station on Laysan Island. He chartered the little Inter-Island Steam Navigation Company steam-sailer, *Pele*, and had her loaded to the gunwhales with lumber, provisions, railroad ties, and rails.

Captain Smythe scratched the stubble on his chin as he eyed the railroad cars chained to the deck. "We're way over the load limit already, Mr. Wilcox," he said diplomatically. "You ain't got anything more to go, have you?"

"Just a few passengers, Captain," George answered with enthusiasm. "You'll have to find room for about fifteen laborers."

The Legislature finally adjourned on Friday, November 15. An hour later the *Pele* steamed out of Honolulu harbor and turned her stubby bow to the northwest. George stood on the stern, dwarfed by the big Hawaiian seamen. He still wore his suit and his best straw hat, his legislative uniform, and his eyes sparkled with excitement.

Four days and seventeen hours later, the *Pele* anchored five miles off the western side of a bleak island that lay low in the water. A few ragged palm trees broke the monotony of sea and sand and sky. Huge combers rolled all the way to shore.

"I don't like it," said Captain Smythe.

George grinned. "Don't worry. It was almost as bad at Jarvis."

From then on it was just work: unloading the heavy rails and ties into the whaleboats, rowing through the surf, wrestling the materials onto the shore. Captain Freeth was put ashore with a rude house. George worked with the men. When there was nothing else to do he tramped by himself the six miles around the scrubby island, stepping carefully to avoid injury to the nesting birds, stopping to examine the plants he found. He counted about twenty varieties of low shrubs near the shore, red-stemmed portulaca inshore, and a false yam growing by the sea.

As the weeks passed, his short mustache and closely trimmed beard grew scraggly, and his skin toughened to the weather. Then one morning there was a shout on deck. The anchor chain had parted in a heavy gust of wind. The *Pele* narrowly missed piling up on the shoal and the captain, rather than risk another anchorage, sailed for Honolulu with some of her cargo still in the hold, leaving Captain Freeth and his men on the Island until spring.

They arrived in Honolulu Tuesday morning, December 9. The voyage took nine days and seventeen hours of endless rolling and plunging in rough seas. The captain of the *Pele*, who did the navigating, almost managed to sail past Oahu. But for George, it was a time of happy adventure. When he boarded the steamer to Kauai on December 10, 1890, he would much rather have been sailing back to lonely Laysan.

* * *

That was the year the Wilcox brothers and the Smiths and the Rices on Kauai made one more effort to help the Hawaiians on their Island step out of the Stone Age into the nineteenth Century. At Malumalu near Grove Farm, the missionary families put up a large, three-story boarding school. They hired teachers and brought books, set up wood working and black-smithing shops, cultivated acres of land for farming near the school, and then hopefully invited Hawaiian boys to come and learn the arts of civilization.

* * *

George knew something was wrong even before the S. S. *Mikahala's* whaleboat reached the pier. It was a little after 3:00 A.M., and lights from the steamer, anchored in the bay, moved in the darkness as she rolled in the swell. George often got up early, when he couldn't sleep, to meet the steamer. It gave him something to do. Now he waited as the whaleboat came out of the night.

A brawny Hawaiian seaman reached up to steady the boat against the pier. There were tears in his eyes. "King Kalakaua is dead," he said. The stevedores on the pier moaned softly.

George stayed only long enough to get a brief report from the purser. The King had traveled to San Francisco for his health. There he'd caught a cold which turned into pneumonia. His body had been returned aboard the United States cruiser

Charleston, her yards aslant, two days before. Princess Liliuo-kalani, his sister, had been proclaimed Queen.

While the *Mikahala* was loading freight, George rode home and packed a battered, leather suitcase. That afternoon he and his old friend, Paul Kanoa, sailed for Honolulu. There were twenty-four deck passengers. One old Hawaiian woman was wailing for the King, her voice rising and falling in a weird, endless sound of despair. That night George went to sleep with the wailing still in his ears.

They docked on Sunday, February 1, 1891. Honolulu was deep in mourning. The crisp white bulkheads of the war-ship *Charleston,* anchored in the harbor, were draped with black. On the waterfront the grand arch of triumph prepared for Kalakaua's return had been hastily covered with black cloth. As George went ashore, he saw black armbands. Portly Hawaiian matrons on the street wore black mother hubbards.

"It is a sad day for Hawaii, even for those who didn't like him," said George as he and Paul Kanoa parted on the dock.

The Hawaiian answered firmly, "It should be. He was our King!"

In the Government Building the next day, George found Minister of the Interior Lorrin Thurston staring moodily out of his office window. He looked up and waved to a chair. "Sit down, Wilcox. I'm glad you dropped by. You know what's happening, I suppose?"

"No."

Thurston banged on the desk. "Damn it, she wants to name a new cabinet! Do you know what that means?"

"The new Queen doesn't like you?" George asked mildly.

The Minister sighed. "Not any better than Kalakaua did, and for the same reason. Because my Cabinet has put an end to the wild spending, the incredible mismanagement." Thurston's jaw jutted with familiar determination. "Wilcox, have the last three years of government by Cabinet shown an improvement over government by Kalakaua?"

"They have," said George.

"Of course, they have! But Queen Liliuokalani apparently doesn't care about that. All she wants is her own way, and she knows she can't dictate to this Cabinet. She practically told Sam Damon she's going to try to kick us out so she can appoint her own men."

"Who are they?" George asked. "Maybe they'd be all right?"

"That's not the point," Thurston shot back. "It's the principle! Under the Constitution the Queen cannot dissolve the Cabinet. That is for the Legislature to do by two-thirds majority. At that time, the leader of the opposition will form a new Cabinet, present the names to the Queen, and she will appoint them. It's the English system of constitutional monarchy."

"I know. But this isn't England. Maybe if you . . . "

Thurston cut him short. "Wilcox, if the Queen is able to get around the Constitution this time, she'll do it again and again. Then we will be right back in the muddle we were in under Kalakaua. Is that what you want?"

George walked out of the office with a troubled frown on his face. And he felt even more uneasy after talking to Judge Widemann. The grey-haired man bristled at the mention of Thurston's name. "He wants to take Hawaii away from the Hawaiians and give it to the haoles," said Widemann flatly. "Under this Constitution of his, the Queen is no more than a figurehead."

George disagreed. "No, Thurston stands for good government. Kalakaua brought the Constitution of 1887 on himself."

Widemann flushed in anger. "I never imagined I would live to see the day when you would turn your back on the Hawaiian people."

"I'm not turning my back on them," George protested. But it did no good to reason with the old man. After the argument, George went for a walk on the waterfront, looking in vain for the tranquility that usually came to him there.

A strange mood had come over Honolulu. Business went on as usual. But there was an undercurrent of uneasiness. On

Thursday night, at Kaumakapili Church, George attended a meeting for the purpose of drawing up a statement of sympathy for King Kalakaua's widow, Queen Kapiolani, and of support for the new monarch, Queen Liliuokalani. Paul Kanoa acted as chairman. George noticed that the Hawaiian faces far outnumbered the haoles, among them B. F. Dillingham, W. O. Smith, W. G. Irwin.

And on Friday George took his place in the silent line of mourners moving slowly up the broad Palace steps. He could hear the wailing even before he passed between the double grey columns that supported the arched stone entrance to the first floor balcony. The wailing grew louder as the line moved into the gloomy reception room, which had crystal chandeliers hanging from the high ceilings and enormous, dark, oil paintings of European royalty lining the walls.

The wordless chorus of grief swelled to full volume as he entered the big throne room, all hung in gaudy red and gold. Magnificent feather kahilis stood against the walls. Beautifully carved calabashes, placed here and there on tables, gleamed in the soft light. The casket stood in the center, glossy black with gold handles, six on a side. On the casket was a feather cape and on that, a pillow holding Kalakaua's golden crown, scepter, and sword. Uniformed guards stood at each corner of the casket and twelve more men stood in stiff rows on each side.

The room was heavy with emotion. The King's widow, in somber black, sat at the head of the casket, wailing softly. On her right sat the new Queen, stout and solemn, her dark hair piled up and secured with a large Spanish comb. Her husband, John Dominis, sat beside her.

George bowed wordlessly to the sobbing Queen, then moved on. He nodded to Sanford Dole, recently appointed a Justice of the Supreme Court, as he sat all in black at the foot of the casket with other high government officials. By that time the wailing was beating at George's ear drums. It was like the primitive cry of a wounded animal, and it came from a group of

Robert W. T. Purvis, bookkeeper for George N. Wilcox from 1884 to 1917

Capt. Louis Ahlborn, Grove Farm manager from 1884 to 1893

Alfred Holly (Pele) Smith, Grove Farm manager from 1894 to 1902

E. H. W. Broadbent, Grove Farm manager from 1903 to 1935

native women who sat on the floor near the empty, ornate throne. The women sat with their eyes closed, their bodies rocking gently in sorrow, their voices rising and falling in ceaseless melancholy. George hurried away, glad to be free of the oppressive magnificence of Kalakaua's Palace. But it was a long time before he could forget the wailing.

* * *

Lorrin Thurston's battle with the Queen over the Cabinet went all the way to the Supreme Court. And the Queen won. On February 26, she appointed a new Cabinet that included Judge Hermann A. Widemann as Minister of Finance. But Thurston wasn't beaten. In the elections of 1892 he traveled to Maui, and in a slam bang campaign there got himself elected to the House of Nobles. Then he set out for the United States to arrange Hawaii's exhibit at the World's Fair in Chicago, Illinois.

George didn't see the energetic leader of the Reformers until after Thurston returned to the Islands on June 4, 1892. The Legislature had convened a few days before. When the two men did meet, George was in for a surprise.

Thurston explained, "As soon as I finished in Chicago, I went on to Washington to see what the attitude would be if these Islands were to ask for annexation. The attitude is favorable."

George tried not to show his surprise.

"I talked with Senator Cushing K. Davis, a member of the Committee on Foreign Relations, with Representative James H. Blount, chairman of the Committee on Foreign Affairs, with Secretary of the Navy B. F. Tracy, and Secretary of State James G. Blaine. They all listened sympathetically, and Secretary Tracy even brought me an encouraging letter from the President."

" Isn't that a little . . . premature?" asked George.

Thurston answered impatiently, "It may be. But it may also be our only means to bring sound government and a stable economy to these Islands. Unless Queen Liliuokalani acts within the Constitution, and there is no indication of that, I see nothing ahead but chaos!"

And there was chaos, both political and economic. The McKinley Tariff of October, 1890, removing many duties including sugar and nullifying the advantages of reciprocity, had thrown the Islands into a severe financial slump. Politically, no party held a clear majority in the Legislature. The result was a continual maneuvering for power. To make matters worse, George had heard rumors ever since the election that Queen Liliuokalani was preparing a new constitution. And the newspapers were full of charges of graft, gambling, and opium smuggling against the Queen's most trusted advisor, Marshall Charles B. Wilson, head of the police force.

But in spite of the chaos, Thurston quickly stopped talking about annexation. His most severe critic on the subject was Theophilus H. Davies, the sugar factor. Will Irwin, sugar agent for Spreckels, was also opposed. George knew that Paul Isenberg was against annexation. Henry Baldwin was opposed. George's brother, Albert, now a highly successful planter and a Representative from Kauai, felt the same way. "I'm satisfied with the Islands the way they are," he said one evening as they sat talking with Luther. "We can settle our own problems without any help from the United States."

Yet the problems multiplied week after week. On July 13, the fiery leader of the Liberal Party, Robert Wilcox from Maui, moved for a vote of want of confidence in the Queen's Cabinet. Wilcox was a spellbinding part-Hawaiian who had plotted an insurrection against the government earlier in the year and was jailed by Marshall Wilson for his pains. Since that time, Wilcox had waited for a chance to strike back. His first attempt to unseat the Cabinet failed. But on August 30 some Reformers, more and more exasperated by the Queen, voted with Wilcox's Liberals, and the Cabinet fell.

Naming a new cabinet was like trying to tie the arms of a

squirming octopus. The Queen insisted on her right to pick the men of her choice. Lorrin Thurston was just as determined to uphold the principle of cabinet selection under the Constitution. "The leader of the opposition shall form the new Cabinet!" he thundered. But none of the parties, including the Queen's Nationals, could muster enough support to keep a cabinet in office.

George watched the Legislature dissolve into a dozen squabbling factions. Work came to a standstill. It was not until September 14 that Thurston compromised his principle and permitted the Queen to choose her own cabinet. Three days later George saw the legislative chamber erupt into a bedlam of shouting and table pounding as the new Cabinet was voted out of office. But the Queen's supporters contested the vote. Finally, the Supreme Court rejected the want of confidence action, and the Cabinet remained in office.

"Now maybe we can get some work done," George growled to Henry Baldwin.

But on October 17, a coalition of Hawaiian members voted the Cabinet out again. This time Thurston refused to compromise. When one of the Hawaiian legislators, at the end of October, led in another Cabinet picked by the Queen, it was voted out in a little more than two hours.

George watched the fiasco with growing impatience. No work had been done in the Legislature for a month. Government employees, as a result, had gone without pay. Every day the Legislators met only to adjourn. There had to be some solution!

When it came, George was taken by surprise. Henry Baldwin and William Irwin suggested that he lead a new cabinet. George's initial action was one of embarrassment. "Get someone else," he said.

"I don't think there is anyone else," Irwin told him soberly. "We need a leader of the opposition who can satisfy Thurston's principle. And we need a man the Queen will accept. How many candidates can you name who meet those requirements?"

George appealed to Baldwin. "You know what you're asking? It's the most miserable job in the Kingdom!"

"And the most important right now," answered the Maui planter. "We need a man that everybody trusts, who can get support from all the parties. You can do that."

George's expression was one of distaste.

"I know you don't care for politics," Baldwin said hastily. "Well, I don't either. We're both in it to try to run a decent government for the Hawaiians as well as ourselves. We don't have government now, George. We've got anarchy! If it keeps on much longer we'll have a revolution on our hands."

"How soon do you want my decision?"

"Right away."

George bowed his head in thought. "I'd want to pick my own men."

"Name them."

George answered without hesitation, "Mark Robinson for Foreign Affairs; he's part-Hawaiian. Cecil Brown for Attorney General, and P. C. Jones as Minister of Finance."

Baldwin was pleased. "Very good. Now let's get these names to the Queen. I think we have finally found a Cabinet!"

* * *

While they waited for the Queen's decision, George sailed home for a short rest. He was in a glum, thoughtful mood. At the old house, Emma kept hushing the children, "Hush! Don't bother your Uncle George!"

The children were no bother, they were a relief from the selfish wrangling he had left behind in Honolulu. Breakfast was the best time of all, Emma at the head of the table, George and Sam facing each other at the sides, the younger children, those who weren't attending Punahou in Honolulu, spaced between. The baby, Mabel, was already ten years old and bright as a button, her brown hair streaming half way down her back. Charley, twelve, and Gaylord, eleven, seemed to spend most of their time teasing her or fighting each other. One afternoon George found them wrestling under the kamani tree in the front yard.

"Why don't you stand up and fight?" George suggested. The boys fell apart, their mouths open. "Go ahead, get up and box. Here, I'll show you how we used to do it."

He positioned Charley with his left arm extended, his left fist cocked beneath his chin. Next, George showed Gaylord his stance. "All right, go to it. That's the way! Jab with your left, then move in with your right!"

The commotion brought Emma out to the veranda. "George Wilcox, what are you teaching those boys?" she scolded. "Charley! Gaylord! You come inside and get to your lessons!"

The next morning, Saturday, November 5, a government messenger hurried importantly ashore with a sealed envelope for George. It was a summons from the Queen. Reluctantly he packed his battered bag and returned to Honolulu.

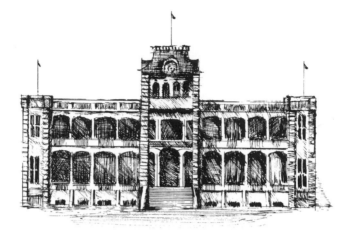

CHAPTER

18

George hurried up the Palace steps. As he strode into the reception hall, two uniformed attendants stepped up to bar his way. He stopped short, frowning. Then another Hawaiian in a glittering uniform came forward. "State your business, please," he said in a tone of official boredom.

Impatiently, George pulled the summons from an inside pocket and handed it to the Royal Chamberlain. The man opened the paper and read without hurry. When he looked up, his boredom had vanished. "This way, Your Excellency," he said smoothly.

For a moment, George didn't understand that the title was for him. Then he said, "Yes," with a curt nod and walked toward a tall, Gothic door on the left. The Chamberlain slipped ahead of him. "Your hat may go there, Your Excellency."

He pulled up short and hastily put his hat on a small table beside the door. With a quick look in the mirror above, he walked through the narrow door into the Blue Room. High windows looked out on the Palace entrance. The Queen sat at a small table, dignified but not unfriendly, her plump figure dressed in heavy silk with lace at the neck.

The door closed behind him. He stood uncomfortably, suddenly conscious of his dusty, travel-wrinkled suit. It had never occurred to him to change. He bowed stiffly and said, "I came as soon as I was able, Your Highness."

"That was kind of you, Mr. Wilcox," the Queen answered. "My country is grateful."

"It is also my country," George said quietly.

The Queen gave him a shrewd, measuring look. When she spoke, it was in a noncommital tone of authority. "It pleases me to appoint you my Minister of Interior. I will expect you to serve me and my government to the best of your ability."

The answer came slowly. "I will do my best, Your Highness, to serve you under the Constitution of our Kingdom. My goal is a sound government that will preserve the independence of this nation."

This time the Queen smiled. "You are a child of the land, Mr. Wilcox. Perhaps that will be enough." Then the curtain of authority came down once more. "I am also pleased to appoint the gentlemen whom, I believe, you proposed as Ministers of Finance, Foreign Affairs, and Attorney General. Will you so inform the Legislature?"

"Yes, Your Majesty."

"Good day, Your Excellency," said the Queen, closing the interview.

George bowed once more. He would have opened the door

himself if an attendant hadn't jumped to get there first. A few moments later he stood in the sunshine and took a deep breath. Now his troubles would begin!

Lorrin Thurston shook George's hand enthusiastically. "Congratulations, Wilcox. We finally have a strong Cabinet. It should last for years!"

"I wish I thought so," George answered with feeling.

At 1:40 P.M. on Tuesday, November 8, 1892, he stood outside the legislative chamber with the other members of his Cabinet: rotund P. C. Jones, the Minister of Finance; tall and stately Mark Robinson, Minister of Foreign Affairs; dapper Cecil Brown, Attorney General. George was the smallest member of the group. At fifty-two, his oval face was still unlined, but his mustache and short beard were snow white.

He squared his shoulders and opened the door. They were there, waiting, all the faces he knew so well. Most of them wore smiles. A few wore scowls of displeasure, and on some he saw polite suspicion. With the other Ministers, he walked to the four desks set apart from those of the Legislators. Then he turned and said, "it has pleased the Queen to appoint the present Ministry." The applause made him blink.

A few minutes later, the clerk took up a report from the Sanitary Committee on bills relating to repeal of the law compelling parents to have their children vaccinated.

For the first time in over a month the Legislature was back at work. It gave George a feeling of deep satisfaction. An hour flew by. He hardly noticed when Albert arose and made his way between the desks to the back door. Finally Luther left his seat and hurried to George's desk.

"What's the matter?" George asked.

"If we're going to go to Henry's wedding, we'd better hurry up. It starts at half past three."

"Oh, my God!" said George. His youngest brother, Henry, was marrying May Green, governess for the Rice and Wilcox children, this afternoon. If George missed the wedding, they'd never forgive him!

* * *

He didn't know which was the worse bother, buying a claw hammer coat or drawing up a statement of Cabinet policy. George had never owned a coat with tails. But Luther insisted he would need one for state functions. "And," he kept saying, "you're the Prime Minister, remember?" So George went down to McInerny Gent's Furnishing Store and had himself fitted for a claw hammer coat. It made him feel ridiculous!

The statement of Cabinet policy was even more difficult. Every day he got $1,000 worth of free advice. Robert Wilcox and his Liberals were adamant that the Attorney General fire Marshall Wilson. The Queen's Nationals wouldn't hear of it. Thurston's Reformers were fighting the lottery bill tooth and nail. The Queen supported it. Most of the Hawaiian legislators were in favor of a banking bill that would permit the Government to issue paper money. The very idea gave Honolulu businessmen apoplexy!

There was a controversial opium bill, supported by the Chinese and Hawaiians and opposed by missionary families. There was the question of leasing Pearl Harbor to the United States in return for a sugar trade agreement, supported by the business community, opposed by the Hawaiians. There was the everlasting labor problem. Sugar planters kept asking the Government to bring in more workers from the Orient. The opposition came from a strong coalition of skilled labor, dispossessed Hawaiians, and concerned community leaders including Lorrin Thurston.

When the Premier rose to a question of privilege on Monday morning, November 14, to read the Cabinet's policy statement, he knew it would not please everyone. But he had done the best he could. In a calm, unhurried voice he read what he had made up his mind to be the most sensible course.

"It will be the policy of Her Majesty's Government to maintain the autonomy and independence of the Kingdom." An old Hawaiian legislator nodded in approval. George continued, "to promote closer commercial relations with the United States to the end that the products of the Kingdom may be made remunerative to those engaged in their cultivation and production, and consequently insure to the benefit of the Kingdom at large." Some of the Hawaiians frowned.

George went on, "To assist in the passage of such laws that will, with proper restrictions, according to the classes of labor introduced for that purpose, tend to relieve the present want of labor necessary to carry on successfully the natural and special agricultural interests of the Kingdom."

Several sugar planters nodded decisively as George continued, "to carry on all branches of the Government in an economical manner. To see that the expenditures do not exceed the revenues of the Kingdom."

Now there was only silent waiting. "In regard to such measures as are non-ministerial and introduced hereafter, or that may now be pending, whether for the purpose of revenue or otherwise, Her Majesty's Ministers claim the right of acting and voting on such measures according to their several personal convictions, and not as a whole or as a Government matter."

For the first time, George paused. Then he read firmly, "This Cabinet cannot support any measure tending to legalize a lottery or license gambling. This Cabinet cannot support any measure that will interfere with or change the present monetary system of the Kingdom."

There was a stir of interest, but George did not pause. "To investigate and correct any and all abuses and corrupt practices in all departments of Government and to deal fairly and fearlessly with all officials in such investigations, and if necessary for the purpose of good government, take steps to secure the consequent removal of any official found wanting."

The Prime Minister sat down. He knew his last statement would not satisfy the Liberals who wanted a firm commitment to fire Marshall Wilson. But such a statement would immediately antagonize the Queen. There just wasn't a formula that would please everyone. George folded his hands and waited for the reaction. It was not long in coming.

Representative George P. Kaumaoha from the Island of Hawaii jumped up. He wanted to know if the desire of the Cabinet to establish closer commercial relations with the United States meant approval of a treaty to surrender Pearl Harbor, and if so, what was being done about it.

George rose to his feet. He looked directly at Kaumaoha as he spoke. "To the first question regarding the desire of the Cabinet to establish closer commercial relations with the United States, the Cabinet answers, Yes. In the negotiations of such a treaty, should the Government of the United States request, this Cabinet will favor the granting to that Government the exclusive right to enter the harbor of Pearl River on the Island of Oahu, and the right to establish and maintain there a coaling and repair station for the use of the vessels of the United States, and the right to improve the entrance to said harbor and to do all other things needful to the purpose aforesaid. Such rights to be co-terminous with such treaty, or to exist so long as Her Majesty's Kingdom enjoys the reciprocal rights granted by such treaty. No treaty or draft of treaty has yet been under consideration. Relative to sending a special envoy to Washington, the Cabinet says, No, as the Government has a Minister-in-Residence at Washington."

There were no more questions. The Prime Minister sat down again. Well, the die was cast! Now there was nothing to do but wait.

* * *

The editorial thunder that followed wasn't as bad as the Prime Minister had expected. The *Advertiser* criticized the new Cabinet for not dismissing Marshall Wilson but reacted favorably otherwise. Editor Henry Northrop Castle complimented the Queen for conceding to the principle of constitutional government and called the Cabinet "a strong one led by a premier who possesses the confidence of all parties."

Liberal editor John Bush, who published an English-Hawaiian newspaper called the *Ka Leo,* was not so kind. He reproached the Cabinet for not cleaning house in the Marshall's office and hinted at a secret agreement between the Queen and the Attorney General. The *Bulletin,* spokesman for the Palace party, wouldn't admit the Queen had conceded to anything, principle or otherwise, but agreed that the new Cabinet was an excellent choice.

"Well, it could have been worse," George muttered after he'd gone through the papers. "Now let's get to work."

The Legislators seemed to feel the same way. They quickly passed a bill providing payment for the long-suffering government workers. Then they settled down to the business of hammering out an appropriations bill. A labor bill went through. To spearhead an economy drive, the Cabinet members asked that their salaries be cut from $12,000 a year to $8,000. The Legislature compromised on $9,600.

On Thursday, December 15, the *Advertiser* finally conceded, "The cloud which has hung over Hawaii for so long a time has at last begun to lift a little, and there are signs of a better time coming."

The Premier had no such illusions. He had watched too many cabinets fall. The Bank Bill was due to come up soon. And the opium question was hanging fire. Every night he worked late, trying to keep abreast of the endless flow of official papers. Sooner or later, he knew, the shooting would begin.

When it came, it was over a bill no one had heard of before. The legislation would have set the salaries and hours and job specifications for government employees. To the Premier and his fellow Cabinet members, the bill interfered unnecessarily with the workings of the executive branch. The Ministers recommended to Queen Liliuokalani that she veto the bill. She did.

The storm was worse than anything George had expected because it came from his own party. Reformers as well as Liberals denounced the Queen. Lorrin Thurston saw the veto as a deliberate attempt by the Queen to show her disdain for the will of the people. Liberal leader C. W. Ashford thundered, "this is trampling representative government in the mud!" Albert was furious.

When George told Thurston he had recommended the veto, there was a stunned silence. Then they sat down to try to decide what to do. The word spread during the weekend, but there was no judging the mood of the Legislature as the members gathered on Monday. All day, George waited for the explosion. On Tuesday, December 20, it came.

Noble W. Y. Horner of Maui, Molokai, Lanai District asked the questions George had expected. 1. Did the Cabinet advise the veto of Bill 175? 2. Does the Cabinet intend to carry out or enforce the wishes of the majority of the House as expressed in Bill 175?

George stood and addressed the hushed chamber. "In answer to your first question, the Queen vetoed Bill 175 on the advice of the Cabinet. In answer to the second question, the Cabinet will execute the bill if it is carried over the veto."

He sat down and waited. It would be amusing, he thought with a wry smile, if his Reform Cabinet were to fall in support of the Queen. The voting began. Long before it was finished, George knew he had won. The final count was a decisive twenty-nine to fourteen upholding the veto. But it was not a pleasant victory. His brother, Albert, voted against George.

* * *

A month and a half had passed and the Wilcox Cabinet was still in office. They had beaten the Bank Bill. The Legislature was working hard and the Queen was still co-operative. George kept wondering how long it could last.

"I feel like a tightrope walker," he told Luther one day.

If he could just keep his feet during the rest of the session, the Cabinet would be safe until the Legislature met again in 1894. That would give tempers time to cool. The annexation fever would die down, and the Queen might lose her interest in a new constitution. But the tug of controversy continually threatened to jerk the rug out from under him. If that happened, the country would plunge back into angry confusion.

Each issue represented a new crisis, and the opium bill was the worst. An opium bill had been turning up like a bad penny in every session of the Legislature for the past fifteen years. By this time it was a political football. No responsible leader supported it. Yet, George knew several respectable businessmen in Honolulu who were reported to be making fortunes in smuggling the popular drug. Many Hawaiians used it and, by some perverse logic, had turned the issue into one of winning freedom from haole domination.

"It's a lot like the liquor issue," Luther observed. "Remember the big question a few years ago—should the Hawaiians have it or shouldn't they?"

"No," said George. "Opium is more vicious than whiskey. It's morally undesirable."

"I'm not so sure you can legislate morality," answered Luther. "Every day I see more opium cases brought into court. If it's against the law, why do so many people use it?"

"Does that make it right?" George insisted.

"No, I suppose not. But it doesn't make the law effective, either."

"Would it be more effective to license the sale of opium and try to control it?" George asked irritably.

Luther grinned at his brother. "That's a question I'm glad I don't have to answer. If you figure it out, let me know."

Unhappily, George had to figure it out. As usual, there was strong support for an opium bill from the same legislators who favored the Queen's pet scheme, a national lottery. George had already voted against them on the bank bill. He was on record as opposed to the lottery scheme. Now he hesitated to vote against the Hawaiians once more.

There were sound arguments for controlling the use of opium rather than prohibiting it. If opium were sold openly, smuggling would not pay. And the sale of it might actually provide more control than was possible now. Supporters of the bill always pointed to the British Colonies where the use of opium was common and perfectly legal.

In the end, George decided in favor of an opium bill that bristled with strict controls. The licenses would be limited to one per island, and use of the drug would be confined to the licensed premises where it was to be sold, as liquor is sold in a saloon.

On Friday, December 23, the *Advertiser* reported, "The House completed consideration of the Opium Bill yesterday, and it was passed for the third reading. If it is to be conceded that the principle of licensing the use of opium is a sound one, then it must be confessed that there is little to criticize about this bill. It is supplied with a very elaborate system of safeguards throughout."

But the brickbats were already flying. The wives of some of George's friends would not speak to him. Ministers expressed concern and dismay. Liberal leader John Bush, a recently converted Seventh Day Adventist, told his friends he would move for a vote of no confidence in the Cabinet.

George felt very much alone when the final reading of the opium bill came up on Saturday, December 31. Lorrin Thurston had stayed away. So had Henry Baldwin. Albert was there to vote against him. The bill carried thirty-two to nine. And when George looked around the room at the men he had voted with . . . the lottery crowd, Robert Wilcox, the rabble rouser, ludicrous Bipikane, the clown of the Legislature, who loved to roar like a bull, George half wished he had it to do over again.

The motion for a want of confidence vote came the following Wednesday. It made George feel better. The resolution mustered only nineteen votes, and the president had difficulty holding a quorum together during the debate. The *Advertiser* reported the next day, "The cloud-burst has passed and hurt nobody, and the Cabinet is safe." For George, that was worth the loneliness.

For the first time he began to feel optimistic. He looked up with a smile when Luther stopped by the following evening. "Well, tomorrow we will ask for the appointment of a committee to wait on her Majesty and request an end to the session," George announced. "When it's over, I can breathe again."

Luther slumped into a chair. "Have you heard about the meeting in Chinatown?"

"What meeting?"

"One of those nine-course Chinese dinners for legislators who need softening up. They say the want of confidence resolutions were flying faster than the liquor."

George chuckled. "Of course, they were. They've been flying ever since I took this job. Who's behind it this time?"

"I'm not sure. But I thought you ought to know," said Luther.

George was disturbed, however, when Attorney General Brown brought word that the Queen had become insistent over the appointment of a controversial attorney, Anton Rosa, to a circuit judgeship. "He won't do," said George. The Cabinet voted to overrule the Queen and appoint Walter Frear, another attorney, to the post. Attorney General Brown reported that

Queen Liliuokalani had not taken the news well. From that time on, George noticed a polite chill in her manner whenever he brought bills to the Blue Room for her to sign. And members of the Queen's National Party began to delay the closing of the Legislature.

But George still wasn't worried about the Cabinet until Luther brought him the news on Saturday that an old Hawaiian was circulating a petition on the streets asking for contributions to pay the expenses of delegates from the other islands to a constitutional convention. "I was hoping we'd put that headache behind us," George said, frowning. "A new constitution could cause all kinds of trouble."

"Especially for you if the Queen is behind it," Luther answered thoughtfully.

George shook his head. "No, she wouldn't do that. She promised to uphold this one. She's stubborn but . . . no, she's too smart to try that."

Luther leaned forward, his elbows on his knees. "I'm pretty sure she is trying it. And part of the plan is to get you kicked out of office!"

"But why?" George exclaimed in dismay. "I've tried to work with her, haven't I?"

"The Queen doesn't want a cabinet that works with her. She wants one that will work for her. She wanted Rosa. You gave her Frear. She wants the lottery. You won't sign it into law. She wants the old constitution back. You won't give it to her. So out you go!"

George still didn't believe that the Queen was scheming against him. But on Monday the *Advertiser* reported, "The intriguing which has been going on against the Cabinet for some days is a discredit to Hawaiian politics."

On Tuesday, the lottery bill, dead for so many weeks, popped up again and passed a second reading. The Reformers worked hard to block it, but on Wednesday the bill passed twenty-three to twenty. This time George was on the losing side.

That night when Luther came by George was working in the naked glare of an electric light bulb. From the expression on his brother's face, George knew the news was bad.

Luther sank wearily into a chair. "So far, I've heard that four of your friends have turned down bribes to vote against you tomorrow when they move the want of confidence resolution."

"Is it that bad?"

"I'm afraid so. There's even a story going around that the Queen went down on her knees to one legislator to get his vote."

George's shoulders sagged. Slowly, he straightened the papers on his desk into neat piles. Then he stretched. "I'll walk with you to Alakea Street," he said. He shrugged into his coat and clapped his straw hat on his head. Together they walked into the night.

A horse and rider clopped on the unpaved street. On the right, the ornate silhouette of Iolani Palace stood dark against the sky. The brothers walked slowly down the narrow sidewalk between the hitching rails and the wrought iron fence around the Government Building grounds.

"Luther, I never wanted this job in the first place," George said after they'd walked half a block.

"I know."

"God knows I've tried to keep everybody working together. For a while, there, I thought we'd pulled it off. I really thought so."

"So did I."

They stopped at the corner where George turned to go to Queen Street. "Well, we'll see what happens tomorrow," He said with a sigh. "Whatever happens, I'll be glad when it's over."

* * *

The skirmishing began in the morning. In spite of the rumors, members of the Reform Party were confident they had enough votes to save the Cabinet. As their opponents launched a barrage of criticism, Lorrin Thurston replied, "I can't blame Representatives Bush and Nawahi for making their last attacks on the Cabinet, as there are so few chances left for them to do so before the end of the session."

But Thurston was worried when the want of confidence resolution came that afternoon. George just felt numb. An old friend from Hawaii introduced the motion. He gave no reasons for the action. He simply said, "The Minister of the Interior and the Minister of Finance are good, charitable men, but I feel constrained to bring this resolution."

Another Representative, also from Hawaii, tried to explain. "These men of the Cabinet are able and honest men. There is no doubt they possess the confidence of the community. They are men of integrity who would be able to secure funds to carry on the Government." The native Legislator paused and his voice shook with emotion. "But will they carry out the wishes of our Queen? Will they do what the Queen and the Hawaiian people want them to do in regard to the lottery, the constitutional convention, appointments in government? That is the question we cannot answer. Will they do as the Queen wants them to do?"

There it was again, the complaint of the Hawaiian fighting for his land. And yet, George thought wearily, it was his land, too. He had worked for it, sweated over it, made it yield the wealth it held in its soil. Which of them was right? He didn't even listen as the debate became a wrangle. Finally, the votes droned in. It was close. The opposition mustered twenty-five votes, exactly a two-thirds majority.

The Queen had won. George felt as if a huge weight had been lifted from his shoulders.

* * *

The next day many of his friends were bitter. No haole Legislators even put in an appearance on the floor of the House. An *Advertiser* editorial reflected the mood of the business community: "The late Cabinet, as everyone knows, was removed by a combination of opium smugglers, disappointed office seekers, intriguing office holders, and haole haters, aided by the powerful influence of the Court and the Police Department and the free use of bribery."

George spent most of the day vacating his office for the new Minister of Interior. Queen Liliuokalani named Samuel Parker Minister of Foreign Affairs, W. H. Cornwell Minister of Finance, J. F. Colburn Minister of the Interior, and A. P. Peterson Attorney General.

On Saturday noon the Queen closed the Legislative Session, the longest in the history of the Islands, with a short speech. Few of the Reformers bothered to attend. Lorrin Thurston was busy trying to salvage a long neglected law practice. George was at loose ends waiting for the next steamer to Kauai. He visited friends and, after lunch, stopped by the office of attorney W. O. Smith on Fort Street just below Merchant. To his surprise, he found the place crowded. Albert was there.

"What's going on?" asked George.

Smith's deep-set eyes flashed with excitement, and he was a little out of breath. "The Queen is trying to shove a new constitution down our throats."

"She must be crazy!"

The lanky attorney nodded grimly. "We've alerted Captain Wiltse on the *Boston*. Thank God there's a United States warship in the harbor in case shooting starts. Both the American and the British Ministers have gone to try to talk some sense into the Queen. But Colburn says she's made up her mind."

George's face had set in anger. "That's illegal! Doesn't she know what this town will do if she pulls a stunt like that?"

There was no mistaking the mood of militancy that gripped the room. Lorrin Thurston was there, speaking insistently to a little group of men. More were arriving all the time. A few minutes later, Thurston raised his hand for silence. He looked haggard, but his jaw jutted as aggressively as ever.

"Gentlemen, the Queen is in revolt against the Government," he said bluntly. "This morning her new Minister of the Interior, John F. Colburn, came rushing into my office and said, and I quote, 'Lorrin, we've been having a hell of a time up at the Palace and have come to tell you about it.' Then he said the Queen was insisting that the members of the Cabinet sign a new constitution and that he had refused."

An angry mutter filled the room. Thurston went on, "I suggested that we talk it over with Judge Hartwell. So we did. The judge thought we should consult W. O. Smith, here. Well, all of us agreed that Colburn should stand pat against the Queen and that, meanwhile, we'd try to raise support for him downtown."

The crowd voiced its approval. Thurston's voice rose over the noise, "Now what I propose is that we draft a declaration here and now stating that the Queen is in revolution against the Constitution and the Government, and that the undersigned have pledged their support to the Cabinet in resisting her. Then we'll all sign our names."

The declaration was drafted on the spot. Men crowded around the desk to sign. By four o'clock almost one hundred signatures were scrawled on the paper, George's and Albert's among the rest. The office was jammed. There was no dissent in the group, only cold outrage. George could feel it gather momentum. The names on that list represented more power and influence than he had ever seen directed toward one purpose in the Islands before.

Shortly after four o'clock, two members of the new Cabinet squeezed through the crowd. They were Colburn and Peterson, both frowning and pale. They conferred hastily with Thurston. Then he called for silence.

"Here are the men who can tell you exactly what happened in the Palace today," he called out in a bitter tone. "Listen carefully, because you'll never know when the same thing will happen again!"

Colburn climbed on a chair and faced the crowd. "Well, the Queen has got it in her head that she's going to throw out the old constitution and put in a new one. This noon we argued with her for an hour. She must have planned it, because there was a big mob of Hawaiians outside the Palace waiting. Once she threatened to go out and tell them we were standing in her way." Colburn put his hand to his forehead. The crowd waited, grim and silent. "We stalled her and went out to get help. Frankly, I wasn't sure that if I went back, I'd come out alive. This afternoon we went at it again, hammer and tongs! She finally agreed to postpone the new constitution. But I don't know for how long. She might try to proclaim it tomorrow, for all I know."

An angry buzz followed Colburn's speech. Thurston jumped up on the chair. "It's obvious that unless we do something and do it right away this country will slide backwards twenty-five years. Frankly, I'm tired of going to bed at night wondering if, when I wake up, my liberties will be gone. I think what we need to do is to organize a committee to deal with this situation, to take whatever action is necessary to protect the peace and property and rights of the men in this room. I now move that Henry E. Cooper here be named chairman of the committee."

Thurston's decisive leadership carried the motion. Cooper, an ardent annexationist, named a Committee of Safety. Twelve of the men, including Thurston and Smith, were members of a group that called itself the Annexation Club. For his thirteenth member, Cooper chose Albert Wilcox. Then Cooper cleared the room for a secret meeting.

George waited impatiently for the meeting to be over. He walked with Albert to the house on Queen and Alakea Streets where they stayed during legislative sessions. "What happened?" George asked when they had passed out of earshot.

"Thurston moved . . . let's see, how did he put it, 'that it is the sense of this meeting that the solution of the present situation is annexation to the United States.' The others voted in favor."

George asked quietly, "And you?"

"I told them I wasn't opposed but that I hadn't really thought about it. I asked for a little time to think it over." Albert paused, his rugged face troubled. "How do you feel about it, George?"

"Until this afternoon I was against it," George answered slowly. "That's really why I let them talk me into being Premier. I thought I could hold things together. Now I'm not sure it's worth holding together. The Queen isn't interested in what's best for the country. All she seems to be interested in is having her own way. I think Thurston is right. If we don't stop her, she'll drag us back twenty-five years. Annexation is probably the best answer. At least, it would mean decent government. What we have now is rotten."

Albert nodded. "That's the way I've been thinking."

Sunday passed in a fever of meetings and rumors. Albert resigned from the Committee of Safety because he felt someone in Honolulu would be in a better position to do the work. But he attended the sessions. The Committee called a mass meeting at the Armory for Monday at 2:00 P.M. At 11:00 A.M., the Queen issued an assurance that she would abide by the present constitution. But it was too late!

On Monday afternoon, all businesses in Honolulu closed. George stood in the shouting, determined crowd of about 1,300 persons, most of the town's haole population. This time Thurston brought his annexation plan into the open. The crowd thundered approval. When Henry Baldwin got on the platform and suggested that they try to work with the Queen under the constitution, he was shouted down with cries of "No! No! No!"

George was caught up in the excitement with the rest. It was difficult to believe that this was actually happening in familiar Honolulu to people he had known all of his life. He listened as the crowd voted overwhelming endorsement for annexation to the United States.

Meanwhile, the Queen's supporters had called a mass meeting of their own. Threats of house burnings passed from mouth to mouth. That evening at 5:00 P.M. Captain Wiltse of the U. S. S. *Boston* landed United States Marines to protect the lives and property of Americans in the city. The Committee of Safety made feverish preparations to establish a provisional government, with Sanford Dole at its head, to rule until Hawaii could become a part of the United States. At the same time, Marshall Wilson barricaded his Police Station against attack.

It still didn't seem real when, on Tuesday afternoon, a little band of determined men walked unarmed up King Street to the Government Building. It was empty. From the steps of the building, committee chairman Cooper read the proclamation, to a nearly deserted street, declaring the Monarchy at an end. United States Minister John L. Stevens immediately recognized the new Government. A few hours later the Queen capitulated.

On Wednesday, the headlines screamed out at George as he opened his copy of the *Advertiser*, "THE NEW ERA! The Revolution Terminated by the Establishing of a Provisional Government. Citizens rise and seize the Government Building."

Well, it was done. Now he could go home. He packed quickly in order to catch the *Mikahala* when she sailed at 5:00 P.M. Before he left, he did one thing that gave him great satisfaction. He gave his claw hammer coat to the Japanese gardener.

PART V

The Family

CHAPTER

19

After breakfast, George paused on the veranda to light a cigar. He felt ten years younger in comfortable clothes and a pair of boots. But it was more than that! His eyes swept the wide, grassy yard with pride and tenderness. The barren bluff had become a garden, an oasis of serenity in a hectic world, and he had done it; every tree he had planted himself.

After the habitual rain-gauge check he walked briskly across the grass toward the little sand-colored wooden cottage, shaded by mango trees, behind his plantation office. Several horses tied to the hitching rail were switching flies with their tails. As George mounted the steps, Pikau opened the screen door and stepped onto the porch. George noticed absently that the foreman's beard was as white as his own.

"It is good to have you back, Keoki," said the Hawaiian, a wide smile splitting his brown, wrinkled face.

His office was a single, plain, well-lighted room furnished with a steel safe, bookcases, several small wooden tables and a large one, and a general scattering of chairs. The bare board floor was painted grey. A survey map of Grove Farm covered one wall. Here Purvis sat at one of the tables carefully making entries in an account book. When he looked up his smile was warm and genuine.

"It's been a long time," Purvis said, pushing the account book to one side.

George nodded pleasantly, but his mind was already busy framing questions. The last time he'd stayed away too long he had come back to discover that Captain Ahlborn was skimping on fertilizer in order to show a bigger profit. The manager had also knocked a Chinese workman to the ground with his fists for accidentally setting fire to a cane field with a lighted cigaret. So George had let Ahlborn go and had taken on W. O. Smith's youngest brother, Fred, as manager in January, 1892.

"Let's have the bad news first. What's the latest report on North Pacific Phosphate and Fertilizer?"

"I have it somewhere," said Purvis, fishing in a pile of papers. "Here it is. Not good, I'm afraid. To date, the company has only grossed $1,975.20 in sale of raw guano. The deficit as of November 30, 1892, is $39,949.91. Would you like to see the statement, Mr. Wilcox?"

"No, no," George answered. Something would have to be done about his guano venture or they'd all lose their shirts. Well, he'd worry about that later. "What about the plantation?" he asked.

"That's different," said Purvis in a happier tone. "Last year we netted $31,478.11. As for your total assets, Mr. Wilcox, they amounted to $662,325 on December 31, 1892."

George's head nodded once, quickly. He was doing well in

spite of the McKinley Tariff. Purvis seemed anxious to add something else but was cut short.

"Purvis, it's time to open a new account. The main ditch has needed straightening for a long time. Well, I'm going to start now. That ditch has got more twists in it per mile than a dog's hind leg . . . "

"Mr. Wilcox . . . " said Purvis eagerly.

"Tunnels, that's the answer," George went on. "Some of these new Japanese are A-1 tunnel men. They must have been miners at home, the way they take to tunneling. We can save enough water by straightening out the ditch to expand over into Aakukui . . . "

"Mr. Wilcox," Purvis burst out, "have you heard about the railroad?"

George blinked. "What's that?"

"It's the big rumor. The directors at Lihue Plantation have finally decided to retire their oxen and put in steam locomotives."

George whistled softly. "A railroad! That will mean expansion. It looks like I got back just in time." He pushed himself vigorously out of his chair. "If Fred Smith comes in, tell him I've gone up the ditch line."

He hurried to his own cottage for a straw hat, then untied his horse from the rail fence around the kamani tree. He swung eagerly into the saddle and turned the horse's head toward the mountains, his eyes alive with excitement for the first time in months.

* * *

The engineer who was hired for the ditch project was C. F. S. Dove, a tall, lanky fellow who had as his foreman young John H. Coney. George was at their elbows most of the time. They tramped over the ridges together, testing for rock strata, deciding on the best point of entry, making sure of the alignment.

Every day George came home happily spattered with mud. One morning in April, 1893, he crawled out of the mouth of a damp tunnel to find Henry Baldwin and Sam Alexander waiting for him. He held out his dirt-streaked hand.

"You're just in time," he told them. "We're going to blast in a few minutes."

"Something important has come up," said Baldwin. "Spreckels is trying to . . . "

"All right, but I can't listen now. Wait till I set off this charge of dynamite."

Later, they rode back down the ditch line. Baldwin didn't look happy. "Thurston's annexation scheme isn't working out the way he thought," the short, stocky planter said when they reached a place where they could all ride abreast. "The new administration in Washington has turned us down. It looks as though Cleveland wants to reinstate the Queen."

"I read about it in the papers," George answered. "That won't solve anything."

Alexander added impatiently, "But we have to decide which way we want to go. Spreckels is in town fighting annexation. The Queen is scheming to get her throne back. If the United States doesn't want us, what's the next move?"

"We have a government," George said bluntly. "Let's stand behind it."

"I hope you repeat that at the planters' meeting next week," said Baldwin. George's eyebrows lifted in surprise. The other planter explained, "Spreckels wants to meet with us to talk over the government situation. I don't exactly know what he's up to, but he holds a note against the Treasury for $95,000. And the government doesn't have the money right now to pay him back. He could cause a lot of trouble . . . "

"I'll be there," George promised.

The meeting was on Tuesday, April 25, 1893, at W. O. Smith's office. Fifteen sugar planters were there including Spreckels, a short, thick-set man with a German accent and an abrupt but not displeasing manner. He shook hands and chatted cordially before the meeting. But once it began he sat in aloof silence.

W. G. Irwin, the sugar agent, presented Spreckels' case in the form of a letter asking all the planters to sign in opposition to annexation. The contents of the letter did not annoy them so much as its arrogant tone. When Irwin sat down, George stood up. Everyone glanced around in surprise.

"I think we should thank Mr. Spreckels for his concern about our Islands," he said with studied courtesy. "But the truth is we got along pretty well before he came. Now he wants us to sign a letter opposing the stated aims of our government. It would be better if he talked about supporting that government. Until he does that, I am not interested in signing his letter."

Spreckels sat without moving as two more planters stood to oppose him. Too late, his attorney leaped to his defense. The opposition grew stronger. Finally, the attorney and Irwin asked that the letter be recalled. Instead, it was referred to a committee for consideration. When the meeting was over, Spreckels stalked out of the room.

"He won't forget this," said Baldwin.

"I hope not," George answered.

Spreckels struck back in late May when the Provisional Government was most vulnerable. A $30,000 interest payment on the London loan was due in July. On June 1, the notes for Spreckels' $95,000 loan came due. There had been no time for the new government to levy taxes. The treasury was bare. A few days before the deadline, Spreckels demanded payment.

George heard about it from Purvis who had gone to Honolulu on business at the end of May. He returned on the last day of the month bursting with news.

"Two days ago, Spreckels had a conference with the Queen," Purvis reported. "The reports are that he advised her that the Provisional Government cannot meet its bills and will soon fall to pieces as insolvent. I heard that Spreckels told the Queen to form a new cabinet and get ready to proclaim a new constitution."

George swore under his breath. He boarded the steamer for the return trip to Honolulu. By the time he arrived on June 2, the fun was over. On the day before the deadline for Spreckels' note, P. C. Jones had gone into the street and in half an hour raised enough money from Honolulu businessmen to pay off the loan.

Then Wilcox pledged $15,000 of his own money to the new government. Claus Spreckels was so angry he took the next steamer for San Francisco swearing he would not return to Honolulu until the grass grew in the streets.

"I hope he means it," said George.

* * *

Frank Damon was the most enthusiastic man George had ever known. He acted more like a school boy than a missionary. Now he tugged at George's arm as they neared the end of Chaplain Lane. "It will only take a few minutes, Mr. Wilcox, I promise you," Damon insisted, his bald head shining in the sun. "Just stick your head in the door and say hello. It isn't often a former Prime Minister comes to visit our school!"

They approached a long, low building with a veranda extending across the front. Vines climbed along the eaves and big-leaved, tropical plants grew along the shady walk.

"Right in here," said Damon, guiding his guest through the door. Then he was face to face with two dozen neatly scrubbed Chinese boys, each one wearing a high-necked, loose-sleeved coat. They stared at the newcomer from behind their school desks.

Damon said a few quick words in Chinese. The students smiled and chorused a welcome. He nodded in return. "Now we'll try it in English," Damon announced with equal enthusiasm. "How do you say it, class?"

Above: Grove Farm showing Stable Camp and Lihue Plantation Company mill, 1905

Left: First auto on Kauai, owned by George N. Wilcox, at A. S. Wilcox Hanalei house, early 1900's

Below: Harbor at Nawiliwili, Kauai, 1915

George Norton Wilcox, 1910

Lucy Etta Wilcox Sloggett, Grove
Farm director from 1922 through 1933

Henry Digby Sloggett, Grove Farm
director from 1924 to 1938,
treasurer from 1922 to 1937

Charles Henry Wilcox, 1914, general
manager of Grove Farm from 1913 to 1920

Ralph Lyman Wilcox, 1907, assistant
to George N. Wilcox from 1900 to 1913

First sled-type sugar cane planter, used at Grove Farm 1920

First wheel-type sugar cane planter, used at Grove Farm 1922

In ragged unison the students recited, "We'com to Meeus Institute."

Damon chuckled. "They have trouble with their 'l's', you see. I don't know if I'll ever get them to say Mills Institute correctly, but we'll keep trying." In the same cheerful tone, he spoke again in Chinese. The students immediately went back to their lessons.

"Impressive, isn't it?" asked the missionary.

"Yes, it is."

"Those boys are here because they want to learn, Mr. Wilcox. We didn't ask them to come." George looked up, interested. Damon explained, "My wife and I live close to Chinatown here, you know. It didn't take long for the families to learn that we have both worked in China and speak Chinese. Last year half a dozen boys came to the door and asked if we would teach them. Those ragged little fellows wanted an education."

"What's wrong with the public schools?" asked George.

Damon smiled disarmingly. "Oh, come now, Mr. Wilcox, you know better than that. These boys can't speak English, and we have no teachers who can speak Chinese. Yet these boys are pathetically eager to learn our ways. I have to laugh every time I hear someone criticize these people for not becoming assimilated. How can they when we don't give them an opportunity?"

The missionary continued eagerly. "It's amazing how intelligent these boys are, and how eager to learn. We started with half a dozen students. At the end of the year we had fifteen. Now it's up to more than thirty. We board them right here, you see, because most of them are so crowded at home there is no place to study. The only sleeping quarters we have that are big enough is the barn. But we have almost outgrown it already. Next year I'm hoping to find something bigger."

"Let's take a look."

The barn was fitted out with double-decker wooden bunks. It was very plain but neat and clean. Damon couldn't stop talking. "I can't help but marvel at the potential of this school. Do you realize, Mr. Wilcox, that here in Hawaii the East is meeting the West in a way that has never happened before? When I was in China, the Chinese had not the vaguest understanding about our Western world, about as little understanding as we have for them. But in this school that understanding is taking place." The missionary paused as reality forced itself into his dream. He sighed. "But it's so expensive, and I have so little to spend. I suppose I should make all of the boys pay the same. But you can't turn off a youngster's mind just because he's poor."

"Maybe I can help a little," George said hesitantly. So that year he increased the total of his donations by $2,000.

*   *   *

The annual sessions of Circuit Court at Lihue, usually early in the year, always brought excitement to Grove Farm. As sheriff, Sam played host to the Circuit Judge from Honolulu and to the company of attorneys, clerks, and interpreters who came along to try the cases. Since there were no hotels on the Island, the entire staff of the court stayed at Grove Farm. They filled the beds in the guest cottage, and the two extra beds in George's cottage. For weeks before the visitors arrived, Emma and the servants were busy boiling eggs and pickling them in brine spiced with cloves. By the time court convened, cooky jars were crammed; cakes were waiting on the shelves; and the pantry bulged with extra hams, freshly churned butter, and loaves of home-baked bread.

When court was in session, Kaipu was pressed back into service to help Johnny, the Japanese cook. Everyone ate breakfast and dinner at the plantation. But for lunch, the servants took big baskets loaded with pickled eggs, ham sandwiches, cookies, and cake to the court house.

Sometimes the visitors stayed for several weeks. One of the favorite diversions was quail shooting. George liked to go himself. When he couldn't, he would send his guests out with Kaaihue. During the 1894 session, Judge W. A. Whiting went quail hunting with Kaaihue. The Judge returned without any quail. He cut short his visit and left without ever discussing his failure to bring back some birds. It was Kaaihue who told George what had happened.

"The Judge took a couple of shots over by Malumalu School," said Kaaihue, looking uneasy. "Then that new blacksmith, the young haole from New Zealand, came out and said he would punch the Judge in the nose if he didn't stop shooting birds on the school grounds."

George let out a guffaw. "What did the Judge say?"

Now Kaaihue was grinning, too. "He climbed into the buggy and told me to drive away fast."

George roared. "Wait 'til I tell Sam! What's this blacksmith's name?"

"Broadbent," said Kaaihue.

"I'd like to have a look at him," George said, his eyes twinkling.

A few days later, he and Sam rode to the school. They found Broadbent with a gang of young Hawaiians working in the blacksmith shop. There was no mistaking the young New Zealander. He was a husky six-footer with blond hair and a ruddy face.

Sam said mildly, "I'm the sheriff, Sam Wilcox, and this is my brother, George."

Broadbent put down his hammer. "What can I do for you?" The Hawaiian boys looked frightened.

"I hear you chased Judge Whiting out of here the other day?" said Sam.

Broadbent answered without hesitation, "That's right."

"And you threatened to punch him in the nose?"

"He was shooting our birds. I'll punch anybody who shoots down our quail!"

"What did the Judge do?"

"He sputtered for a while, and then he left."

Sam looked at George who was trying hard to keep a straight face. "How old are you?" asked Sam.

"Twenty-one."

"Well, we don't want our judges getting punched if we can help it, especially after they come all the way from Honolulu," Sam said gravely. "So from now on we'll tell them not to hunt birds on the school grounds. Fair enough?"

Broadbent's square face broke into a grin. "Fair enough."

George had been eyeing a half-finished plow in the back shadows of the cluttered shop. It was all hand made and obviously of original design.

"That your work?" George asked.

Broadbent nodded. "I like to tinker," he said.

"You're good at it," George answered.

As the brothers rode back to Grove Farm, George said thoughtfully, "I like the way that young fellow handles himself. One of these days I think I'll ask him if he wants to learn the sugar business."

*   *   *

No matter how George tried to bury himself in the pleasant routine of Grove Farm, the world outside kept interrupting. First, there was the guano fiasco! After four years of grim labor, the new company had accumulated nothing but debts. Guano had become a joke among Honolulu businessmen, and some of George's directors were ready to quit.

Finally, a German chemist recommended that the company set up its own fertilizer plant in Honolulu to transfer raw guano and other materials into high grade fertilizer more saleable to the plantations. George's friends advised him not to throw good money after bad, especially since the construction of a plant would put the company more deeply in debt than ever. But he refused to quit and Paul Isenberg of Hackfeld and Company agreed with him. They doubled the capitalization of the company and, early in 1894, began building a fertilizer works in a district called Kalihi in Honolulu.

Politics was an even bigger headache. Since the Islands seemed no nearer to annexation by the United States, George agreed to run as delegate to a constitutional convention for the establishment of a Republic of Hawaii. With the other delegates, he sat in the Supreme Court chambers in the Government Building from May 30 to July 3 when they ratified the new constitution. It was proclaimed on the following day, July 4, 1894.

George had hoped that would end it. But W. O. Smith insisted, "We haven't won our point. We have to see this thing through! Here's the way I feel. I helped organize this government. So did you. The least we can do is stick with it until annexation. Then we'll both quit. How about it?"

Reluctantly, George agreed. He was elected to the Senate. Sanford B. Dole was proclaimed president of the new Republic. He appointed W. O. Smith Attorney General in the new cabinet.

Once more George became a commuter between his plantation and the capital and, as always, events piled up with bewildering rapidity. The railroad had, indeed, come to Lihue Plantation. George's new milling contract, signed April 10, 1894, called for replacing Lihue's forty-eight ox carts and the herd of 1,200 oxen with rail cars for hauling cane to the mill. In the following year, the first railroad tracks were laid into Grove Farm. More than ever, someone was needed who understood machinery. He remembered the young New Zealand blacksmith, and on September 1, 1895, Broadbent went to work as head luna on Grove Farm.

There was little time to admire the blacksmith's tinkering. During the 1895 legislative session, George was chairman of the Senate Education Committee, wrestling with the problem of requiring students to learn English in the public schools. There was strong resistance from some Chinese and Japanese parents, and Hawaiians saw the measure as one more way for the haole to control the Islands. In 1895 George also took a trip to New Zealand with W. O. Smith to study land laws there. The new government adopted some of their recommendations.

He always seemed to be hurrying from one meeting to another, and, although he owned stock in several dozen companies and was well on his way to becoming a millionaire, he had no opportunity to enjoy his wealth. He hardly got to admire the new Hackfeld and Company clipper ship named after him, the *George N. Wilcox*, before the trim vessel went aground on September 18, 1894, and broke up on the northeast coast of Molokai. From February 19 to June 15, 1896, he was back in Honolulu for the regular session of the Legislature wrestling with the problems of immigrant labor, the shortage of schools, the need for better roads.

Finally, the end seemed in sight. In 1896 McKinley was elected president of the United States, and the new administration fanned the hopes of annexation. George attended a special session of the Hawaiian Senate from September 8 to September 10, 1897, to ratify a treaty of annexation which President Dole had negotiated with the United States Minister. The Senate quickly approved the treaty.

After the adjournment, W. O. Smith was as exuberant as a school boy. He clapped George on the back. "Washington won't turn us down this time," he said with conviction. "How will it feel to live in the Hawaiian Islands, U. S. A.?"

George smiled. "I'll tell you when it happens," he said.

* * *

The war with Spain clinched it! On May 1, 1898, when Commodore George Dewey with six warships and one revenue cutter destroyed the Spanish fleet in Manila Bay, Philippine Islands, American citizens found that the remote Pacific was suddenly on their doorsteps. A few weeks later, troop ships began putting into Honolulu Harbor, bound for Manila, and the Republic of Hawaii became an American military outpost. Annexation was the next logical step. On June 15, the treaty passed the United States House of Representatives.

When the news reached Honolulu, about a week later, George felt more relief than elation. Often, during the past six years, he had doubted that his storm-tossed little nation would ever reach the safe harbor of annexation to the United States. Not until then would he feel his responsibility lifted so he could return to the kind of life that gave him the most satisfaction. Now, at last, the elusive goal seemed within reach.

Yet, he was troubled. He had been shuffling from one stuffy committee room to another in Honolulu since the Legislature had convened on February 16. Now he walked to the house on Queen and Alakea Streets to pick up a map. Then he made his way to the office of President Dole in Iolani Palace, renamed the Executive Building.

Dole's long, bushy beard, like George's short one, had turned white. The President of the Republic was as tall and erect as he had been at Punahou. The youthful intensity that once shone from his eyes had softened with experience. He was hard at paper work.

"Sit down, George, sit down," he said looking up quickly. "I'll just sign these and . . . there! Now, what's on your mind?" He leaned his tall frame back in the chair. "Exciting times, these, aren't they? We are moving in the stream of history. It makes one glad to be alive!"

George answered slowly. "This may not be important. But it's been bothering me since the news from Washington about annexation. If it goes through, shouldn't the United States annex all of us?"

"What do you mean?"

"I'll show you."

George unrolled the map, a chart of the complete Hawaiian chain including a line of uninhabited coral reefs and atolls that stretch over 1,000 miles away to the northwest. His finger moved up the map from Kauai as he ticked off the little-known islands. "This is what I mean. See, here's Necker, Laysan, French Frigate Shoals, Midway, Ocean Island . . . "

"Yes, yes, I know," Dole answered impatiently. "There is nothing on those islands but birds, and we already have title to the land."

"We have title to the islands you see here," George said. "What about the islands you don't see?"

Dole frowned. "Are you suggesting there are still islands we haven't claimed?"

"It's a possibility. Some of the old charts show a Byer, or Patrocino Island, about here, northwest of Midway, and another sighting listed as Morrill Island a little farther on." Dole studied the map as George continued. "There is a good chance that no such islands exist. But if they do, and we don't own them, it would be embarrassing to the United States to find some unfriendly country in possession. The sensible thing to do is check the title to our property before we deed it over."

"You're right," said Dole. "But how?"

George let the map roll shut. "Someone should go and investigate," he said.

The President's fingers drummed on his desk. "An expedition? That would be costly." He glanced thoughtfully at George. "Unless it were privately financed . . . by a shipping magnate from Kauai."

At first, George refused. But his sense of responsibility won. While his friends excitedly planned parades and parties for the visiting troops, he saw the steamer *Waialeale* into drydock and had her loaded with coal and supplies. The Legislature adjourned on July 7. At 11:00 A.M. on Wednesday, July 13, 1898, the *Waialeale* steamed out of Honolulu Harbor and swung her bow toward the northwest.

Once more George found himself surrounded by lonely ocean and limitless sky. They worked their way from one barren islet to another establishing indisputable claim to the land. Quickly the excitement of impending annexation became unreal. Here the realities were sharks and birds and beaches. They missed Midway Island in a rain squall and had to run back eighteen miles. At Ocean Island George scribbled into his little black notebook, "Saturday, July 23. The house erected by the Hawaiian Government about twelve years ago is all to pieces. Boards and galvanized iron scattered about. Iron tank rusted out. Cooking utensils scattered round."

Now the crew grew expectant. The "doubtful" islands lay just ahead. But they found nothing. As they passed over the position given for Byer Island, they saw only empty ocean. Where Morrill Island should have been, they sighted one mutton bird skimming the waves. The captain of the ship was crestfallen. "We've come on a wild goose chase. Wait till they hear about this in Honolulu. I'll never live it down!"

"It's not a wild goose chase," George answered. "Knowing those islands are not there is just as important as finding them."

So, after all of his concern and time and expense, George returned to Honolulu empty handed. Even the news that awaited them was an anti-climax. Luther hurried aboard when they docked on Monday, August 8, bubbling with excitement. "You just missed the big show. The *Waialeale* was hardly out of sight, in fact, I didn't even get home from seeing you off, when the *Coptic* signaled from off Diamond Head that annexation had passed the Senate. Did this town go wild! There must have been 1,000 people on the waterfront when the *Coptic* docked. The guns began saluting at four o'clock, 100 rounds. At 4:30 the whistle blew. I kept wishing that you had put off sailing just one more day."

"No matter," George said.

"At least, you got back in time for the official flag-raising ceremony. They've set it for August 12. I'm sure you'll get an invitation."

"You use it, Luther," George told him. "I have to get back

to Grove Farm, and besides, you know I hate celebrations."

As usual, the victory seemed less satisfying than he had expected. George went below to get his bag. At least, now he could retire from politics. He had fulfilled his obligation. This time, he told himself, he was going home to stay.

It wasn't until he stepped into the street that he noticed American flags flying from the buildings downtown. Suddenly he understood the enormity of what he had helped to accomplish. As he watched the crisp new flags fluttering in the trade wind against a blue Hawaiian sky, he realized that his Islands would never again be as he had always known them. His heart quickened, and he began to walk faster as he stepped into the future.

CHAPTER

20

George was on his way out of the door when he glanced into his mirror. So this is how he looked at sixty? The same shock of short, white hair, the oval face tilted quizzically sideways, the alert brown eyes, the neatly clipped grey beard and mustache.

"You're good for another twenty years, anyway!" he told the mirror.

There was no denying it, life had been good to him. Not always casy, but good! And from now on it should be easy as well. Purvis kept telling him he was a millionaire. Why shouldn't he enjoy it?

Yet, that wasn't the reason he felt like whistling on this sixtieth birthday. The real reason, he knew, was much more satisfactory than money. It was Ralph, his oldest nephew, back from business college as George had returned from engineering school so many years before. It was like seeing himself as he had been at twenty-three, small and shy and eager. He was starting the boy at the bottom. He would learn sugar planting as his uncle had done. And someday, when Ralph was ready . . . George hummed tunelessly as he pulled on his boots. It was as good as having a son of his own.

He felt jaunty as he stepped out into the cool, crisp morning. The mountains were clear of clouds. No rain today, he told himself automatically. He walked quickly along the path beside the new lily pond to the lanai overlooking the mill valley. Ralph was already there sipping a mug of steaming coffee.

"Johnny, bring my cup," George said briskly. The stocky Japanese cook grinned and reached for the old, white mug without a handle. George took it and sniffed with satisfaction. He turned to Ralph.

"I suppose you're going to finish furrowing out mauka today?" he asked, one planter to another.

Ralph shook his head. He was slender, with a boyish, tanned face. "I stayed on their tails and finished yesterday."

His uncle grunted, pleased.

"If it's all right with you, we'll start cutting seed cane today." Ralph asked.

"I'm not the manager. Take it up with him," George said curtly.

"Yes, sir. I didn't mean to go over his head."

George saw the hurt on Ralph's face. The rebuke had been unintentional. It was just that he had made up his mind never to show his nephew favoritism. Sometimes, like now, he knew he overdid it, and he began to soften the reprimand. Then he stopped. Ralph could take it.

Sam walked out onto the lanai and the moment passed. The two older men fell to reminiscing. Finally, Ralph stood up.

"I'll see you at breakfast," he said.

Sam smiled after his son. "It's good to have one of them home again," he said.

George nodded. "He's a fine boy, Sam. I envy you."

*　*　*

After breakfast, George headed for Palau Mahu, a straggling cluster of machine sheds and a blacksmith shop in a grove of trees northwest of the plantation yard. Since the coming of Broadbent, the big New Zealander, the Grove Farm blacksmith shop had held a particular fascination for George. Broadbent had never gone beyond grade school. But he was a born mechanic, and George delighted in watching those powerful fingers work magic with metal. The blacksmith shop was littered with the refuse of Broadbent's tinkering. This morning he was hammering rivets into a seam that joined the ends of a sheet of iron bent to form a large cone.

George watched for a moment, then swung deliberately off his horse. He wasn't as spry as he used to be. But when he heard one of the Hawaiian helpers call out in warning, "Here comes the old man!" he grinned.

Broadbent had taken off his shirt. There was a streak of grease on one burly shoulder. He looked up and shouted above the noise of his hammer. "Come in, Mr. Wilcox." He straightened, holding up the odd-shaped piece of metal. "What do you think of it?"

"I'll bite. What is it?"

"A fertilizer gun," answered Broadbent with pride. "We'll strap this metal cone on a man's back. A hand-operated valve will let out as much nitrate of soda as we want to apply to the furrow as he walks along. With this gun, one man should be able to do the work of two or three fertilizing by hand. And they don't have to breathe the stuff!"

George listened, his eyes alive with interest. He was examining the hand-operated valve when Fred Smith, the manager, rode up and dismounted from his horse. Smith was a slim, mild-mannered man. This morning his brow was furrowed with worry. "Mr. Wilcox, may I see you for a minute?" he said.

George followed him outside. They stood in the sun-dappled shade beside the horses. Smith looked around to see if anyone was listening. Then he said uncomfortably, "Those new Japanese families at Kahalehaka want me to build them a bathhouse."

"All right," said George.

Smith swallowed, then plunged on. "Do you think we should? They all bathe together."

"How's that?"

Smith nodded unhappily. "That's the way they do it. The men and women and kids, all at one time with no clothes on. What do you think people will say?"

George looked puzzled. "Are you sure they do it that way?"

"That's what they told me. They swear everybody bathes that way in Japan."

George's first confusion was turning into amusement. "Well, if they want to bathe together, let them. It's a lot better than not bathing at all."

Smith heaved a sigh of relief. "All right."

"Don't worry, Fred, I'll take the blame," George answered. He shook his head, grinning, as the manager rode away. There was never a dull moment on the plantation.

* * *

He first noticed the dimness around the end of 1901. One night after supper, he couldn't seem to get enough light on his newspaper. "If Tatsy would clean the chimneys on these lamps, maybe I could see what I'm reading," he grumbled.

"They look perfectly clean to me," said Emma, nettled over the criticism of her housekeeping.

As the dimness increased, George realized it was no fault of the lamps. Something was the matter with his eyes. He said nothing to Sam or Emma. But the next time he went to Honolulu, he stopped in to see a doctor. After a lengthy examination, the doctor assumed a grave expression.

To relieve his uneasiness, George joked, "I always thought I was too young for glasses. But I guess every man gets to be that age sooner or later."

The doctor shook his head. "Glasses won't help, Mr. Wilcox. Your problem is more serious." He hesitated, searching for the right words. "Do you know what cataracts are?"

It was so unexpected that George couldn't answer.

"How long have you noticed this condition?" asked the doctor.

"I don't remember," said George. "A few months, maybe."

"Or, perhaps, longer?" the doctor probed.

"I suppose so." George stared at the man, still trying to understand. "What can you do?"

Again the doctor hesitated. "There is nothing I can do."

"Then I'll go blind?"

"Not completely, perhaps, and probably not for some time. Cataracts often develop very slowly over a period of years . . ." George knew the doctor was taking refuge in technicalities. He hardly heard the medical diagnosis. Only at the end, the doctor's words penetrated his consciousness. " . . . one hope, although there is considerable risk. The operation is still in an experimental stage. There have been successes. But, in all honesty, I must tell you there have also been failures."

"What happens in case of failure?" George asked.

"Permanent blindness," the doctor said gently.

"No!" George answered in horror.

The cataracts changed everything. For the first time, he felt like an old man who had outlived his usefulness. As usual, he carried his burden of worry alone. Each night he would sit with the newspaper spread futilely in his lap.

Now and then Emma would say with quiet tact, "Why don't you let Elsie read to you?"

And he would answer, "I can see all right."

The bright spot in his life was Ralph. The young man had a mind that pounced on a problem like a terrier on a bone. He was fast becoming a first-rate sugar planter. And to make it perfect, he began courting one of Willie Rice's girls, Anna Charlotte. Everyone called her Daisy.

"It doesn't seem possible, does it?" said Sam one night as they smoked their after dinner cigars on the lanai. "Just yesterday she and Mabel were attending school in pigtails."

"She'll be good for Ralph," George answered quietly.

The girl reminded him of her aunt, Maria. She was so gay and attractive, like sunlight on a leaf. And Ralph was like himself, shy and serious.

The dimness gradually increased, drawing a grey curtain between himself and the world. In 1902 he found a doctor in San Francisco who promised to cure his blindness by means of eye exercises. He grasped at the new hope and wrote to Ralph on September 3, 1902, "I am under treatment here, but it is too soon to expect results."

The results never came but the doctor's fees amounted to about $1,000 a month. Finally, George faced the grim truth. The man was a quack. Reluctantly, he returned to Grove Farm. He wasn't aware at what point he decided to have the operation. Or exactly why, except that he had never given up before without a fight. Once he had made up his mind, he felt better. But there were a few details to take care of first. He looked forward to them with pleasure.

On February 17, 1903, Daisy and Ralph were married under a bower of daisy chains and maile at Halenani, the home of Mr. and Mrs. William Hyde Rice in Lihue. The ceremony took place at noon and the Rev. Hans Isenberg, younger brother of Paul Isenberg, read the marriage vows. Ralph and

Daisy lived in the beach house at Papalinahoa on Nawiliwili Bay while he was having a new house built for them near Grove Farm on a bare expanse of cane field. "Don't worry, it won't look so bleak once the trees start to grow," George promised.

Etta was married on June 3 to handsome Henry Digby Sloggett, whose parents came from England. George got back from San Francisco just in time to attend the ceremony. But, this time, his pleasure was diluted with pain. And all because of a careless accident.

That spring Luther, now the district magistrate in Honolulu, had pared a troublesome corn from his toe with a razor. The wound did not heal properly. Luther, who had never been sick a day in his life, paid no attention. Now he lay seriously ill. The infection had turned to gangrene. On June 20, doctors amputated the toe. A few days later, they removed another toe. On July 7, in desperation, they amputated the leg below the knee. But it was hopeless. During the last week, George stayed beside his brother's bed, trying to match Luther's unfailing good humor. On July 12, Luther died.

George bowed his head and let the tears come. He had never realized that growing old would be like this, watching younger men die. But why Luther who had brought so much laughter into the world? At last George straightened his shoulders. There were funeral arrangements to be made.

It was the largest funeral Honolulu had seen for many years. The line of carriages extended from Kawaiahao Church more than a city block past Capital Square. Flags on all of the government buildings were at half-mast. All judges closed their courts that day. The church was packed and the names of the dignitaries who attended filled half a column of small type in the *Advertiser*. But by far the greatest number of mourners were Hawaiians.

When the service was over George emerged into the sunlight

on the broad church steps. The Royal Hawaiian Band struck up a funeral hymn. He felt a hand at his elbow. It was Sanford Dole, now Governor of the Territory of Hawaii, U.S.A.

"I wish we had a dozen more like him," the Governor said slowly. "There are so few men who can bridge the gap between the Hawaiian and the haole."

George nodded as one of his brothers guided him down the steps. He was too full of sorrow to speak, and his clouded eyes were too full of tears to see.

There was one more thing he had to do. This year, for the first time in its history, Grove Farm would show a loss. Part of the problem was the handicap of his blindness. Part of it was the low price of sugar. Some of it was due to a plague of insects called leaf-hoppers, which were ravaging the cane. In any event, George felt it was time to reorganize. In August he moved Broadbent up as plantation manager, replacing Fred Smith, and put Ralph in charge of the ranching operation that his father had handled up to now. Now he was ready.

The doctor in Honolulu directed him to a specialist in New York, Dr. Frank N. Lewis, at 35 West 36th Street. Gaylord, the youngest of Sam's sons, just back from two years of sugar technology at Louisiana State, made the trip with his uncle. They arrived in December.

It was a bewildering, unpleasant experience for both of them. But Dr. Lewis put them at ease. "There is nothing mysterious about this operation, Mr. Wilcox," he explained. "As you know, a cataract is a disease of the lens. Blindness is caused by a milky fluid that forms within the lens capsule. The object of the operation is to remove that fluid."

"I see," said George. It sounded simple enough.

"Can you make out this chart, Mr. Wilcox? Good. As you see here, the lens capsule is located here behind the pupil. In order to remove the fluid within the lens capsule, we make an incision here through which the fluid can be removed. Then we rupture, or tear, the lens capsule and massage the eye forcing out the undesirable fluid. Do you understand?"

"I think so," George answered.

"There is one more complication," the doctor continued. "A diseased lens usually becomes opaque, or cloudy, by the time a cataract is fully developed. As a result, you still will not have clear vision even after the removal of the fluid. For this reason, we puncture the lens to enable light to activate the retina. In order to focus this light properly, you will need to wear glass lenses to substitute for your own. I cannot promise you perfect vision. But I feel we can make a vast improvement."

"All right," said George. "Let's get on with it."

They decided to operate first on only one eye. A second operation could be made later if the first proved a success. It was soon over, much more quickly than had been anticipated. The waiting was the worst. He lay under the bandages, summoning all of his patience to remain still. Would the eye see again? Or would it look out upon total darkness?

The glasses produced a miracle. The first thing George saw was Gaylord's face, drawn with worry and staring at him. Why, his nephew was a full grown man already! With startling clarity he saw the firm jaw, the steady grey eyes. He looked around the room and the objects sprang at him.

"I can see!" he burst out.

The following November came his second operation. This time another nephew made the trip with him: Charley, now bookkeeper at Koloa Plantation. The second operation was as successful as the first.

"You are a very lucky man, Mr. Wilcox," the doctor in Honolulu told him. "If it were I, I'm not sure I'd have had the courage to go through with it."

George soon discovered that he could see clearly only directly in front of him. The thick lenses distorted his vision into a meaningless blur around the edges. As a result, he often passed friends on the street without seeing them. And he formed the disconcerting habit, when someone caught his attention, of swinging about abruptly and staring into the startled person's eyes.

Strangers began calling him a crusty old man. George didn't know this. All he knew was that he had taken a very long gamble and won. He had never felt so grateful in his life.

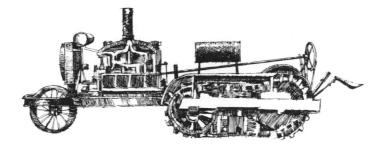

CHAPTER

21

George looked around to admire the big yard as he approached the house. Ralph and Daisy had their lawn in and trees well started. The dogs began to bark as he walked his horse up the drive. Daisy came out on the big, front porch to see what was happening. She was a tall girl, slim and very fair. When she saw George on his white horse, her face lit up and she waved exuberantly.

"Uncle George, come in. You're just in time for a fresh cup of coffee!"

"Already had mine this morning," he said, swinging off the horse.

"Well, for goodness sake, you can have one more," Daisy laughed. "I haven't had a chance to visit with you for almost a week."

George tied the reins to a hitch rail and walked up the steps. He handed Daisy a bulging paper sack. "Sweet corn down in the valley is getting just about right," he said.

Daisy beamed. "And you stopped to pick some for us."

George said, "Humph!" He looked carefully around the yard. "Are you taking care of that monkeypod tree the way I told you?"

"It's growing like a weed," Daisy answered cheerfully. "Now, you come in and keep me company. Ralph is out making his rounds. I don't have a single person to talk to and you know how I love to talk!"

George permitted himself to be seated at the table, protesting that he didn't have time although they both knew that was why he had come. He told her the latest news of Charley and Gaylord, both working at Koloa Plantation now. "Hard to choose between 'em," he said proudly. "Pat McLane tells me they're both bright as whips!"

But Daisy was more interested in hearing about Elsie and Mabel's trip to the East. In the next fifteen minutes, George learned about the party Daisy and Ralph had given the weekend before, which plantation families were expecting new babies, what the minister said in church the Sunday before, who was going to run in the next election. At last he rose to go.

"Old men shouldn't overstay their welcomes," he said as he put on his hat.

"Uncle George, you are not an old man. We wish you would come see us more often."

She waved at him as he rode away. Daisy had that rare talent for letting people know they were wanted.

* * *

Once more George awoke to greet each new day with eagerness. There was plenty to keep him busy. Early in 1905 the sugar planters of Hawaii pooled their resources and purchased the Crockett sugar refinery in California, a big new plant standing idle. George took 126 shares and committed his sugar to the refinery. This time Spreckels, whose enormous plantation on Maui had already been sold to Island interests, could not beat down the competition. The new operation, organized as the California and Hawaiian Sugar Refining Corporation, flourished almost from the start. At about the same time, Island money helped establish Matson Navigation Company to ship sugar to the new facility.

"At last, we've won our independence," said George.

On February 23, 1906, he signed a new milling contract with Lihue Plantation. The agreement gave Grove Farm a three-fourths share of its manufactured sugar, increased Grove Farm acreage for planting to 1,000 acres, and provided for new miles of railroad tracks to reach the new fields.

As if he didn't have enough to do, he plunged the same year into construction of a new irrigation ditch which would send, at a profit, surplus Grove Farm water to Koloa Plantation.

The harder he worked, the younger he felt. In 1907 he bought one of the first automobiles on his Island, a two-cylinder horseless carriage that steered by tiller like a sailboat and attracted crowds of visitors to Grove Farm. In an unusually gregarious mood, the owner announced a day for a public demonstration of the mechanical marvel. The first spectator to arrive was John Ashton Hogg, a jack-of-all-trades who ran the telephone company. Hogg, an inveterate tinkerer, immediately began to fiddle with the engine. When it was time for the demonstration, the car wouldn't start.

Flushed with exasperation, George flared, "Damnit, Hogg! You've ruined it already!"

His friends advised him to get a horse. Meanwhile, the mortified Hogg kept on tinkering until the temperamental engine coughed into action. But George soon lost patience with his new toy and, in the end, gave it to Hogg for whom it worked like a charm.

In the same year, an ex-Army engineer named Joe Moragne came to Kauai. George took an immediate liking to the soft-spoken, quietly competent man who talked the language George understood. He hired Moragne, who had taken a job as county engineer, to draw up plans for extensions to the Grove Farm railroad. Moragne built the first re-inforced concrete bridge in the Islands, across the Huleia River, opening up new acres of cane land in an area called Aakukui. George hired Japanese immigrants to work the virgin soil and, to save transportation time, laid out a new plantation village convenient to the far flung fields.

In Honolulu, most of his business associates were retiring. On almost every visit, somebody urged him, "Why don't you slow down, G. N.? You've made your pile! Relax and enjoy it!"

He tried. In October of 1907 he set out with Elsie and Mabel on a two-month tour of the Orient. But the moment he returned he went to work on negotiations for another milling agreement with Lihue Plantation for more favorable terms.

Frank Damon's dream of a school in Hawaii that would bridge the gap between East and West kept growing, and George's interest grew with it. In 1906 Mills School for Chinese boys began taking Japanese students from a school started in 1896 by the Rev. Takai Okumura, a Christian missionary among plantation workers. So many Korean students applied for admission, in the same year, that Frank Damon added a Korean department. By that time the school was hopelessly overcrowded.

In 1907 the school merged with the Kawaiahao Seminary for Hawaiian girls to form Mid-Pacific Institute. The first step was to get land for a campus, then money for buildings. In 1908 the bulk of George's donations to charities, $136,859 that year, went toward establishing an endowment fund for Mid-Pacific.

It never entered George's mind that a gift of $100,000 would be of interest to anyone not concerned with the school. And he was much too modest to talk about his giving. As a result, there had never been a breath of publicity about any of the nearly half a million dollars he had already given away during his lifetime.

When the first publicity came, late in 1908, he was extremely embarrassed. The Salvation Army in Honolulu was trying to raise $15,000 to build a rescue home for orphaned and neglected children. The fund drive sputtered along fitfully. It had not quite reached the $3,000 mark when Mr. Wilcox heard about it. He pledged $5,000. The Salvation Army went straight to the newspapers.

"Ridiculous!" he snapped when he saw the headlines.

No matter how much he gave away, his wealth seemed to grow. By the end of 1909 Purvis' meticulous accounts showed George to be a millionaire twice over. By the end of 1910, he was worth well over $2,500,000. So whenever Purvis would question the size of a donation, George would shrug and answer, "You might as well let them have it. The more I give away the richer I get."

* * *

George had two visitors in 1910, Major E. E. Winslow and Major W. P. Wooten, Corps of United States Engineers. He greeted both men with unusual enthusiasm.

"Is it true that the Engineers are seriously considering Kauai for a new deep water harbor?" he asked eagerly.

"Yes, that's true," said Major Winslow. "I'd like to make our position clear. Major Wooten and I are authorized to make a survey of the possible sites for an all-weather, deep-water harbor on this Island. However, we are not empowered to decide where the harbor should go."

"I understand," said George.

Major Winslow continued, "As you know, President Theodore Roosevelt was the first to recognize the military advantages of having an all-purpose harbor on each of the major Hawaiian Islands. The harbor at Hilo on the Island of Hawaii is now undergoing extensive improvement. We are developing a harbor at Kahului on the Island of Maui. But here on Kauai there is no facility for handling ocean going vessels."

"Major, that's something we've needed for years," George

answered emphatically. "Without it this Island can never develop its potential."

"We are aware of your interest in shipping, Mr. Wilcox," said Major Winslow. "What we are here to ask, if you have the time, is to give us your opinion of the port possibilities on the Island."

George spoke without hesitation. "There is only one place to put a deep-water harbor on this island and that's at Nawiliwili." He jumped to his feet and went to the wall map. Pointing with his finger, he began ticking off the locations. "Hanalei, there, is the best natural harbor on Kauai. But our freight is sugar and Hanalei is the farthest possible distance from most of the plantations. Kilauea Bay is too small. Anahola is badly exposed, Kealia too small."

He paused. The two engineers were listening intently. "Starting at the other end, there's Waimea Bay, a roadstead, nothing more. Hoanuanu and Hanapepe are both small and cramped. Gentlemen, that leaves two locations right here in the area most accessible on this Island to cargo. First, there's Hanamaulu Landing where Lihue Plantation ships its sugar. Some call the place Ahukini. It's adequate for our small coasting vessels. But it's much too small ever to be a major port. The last possibility is Nawiliwili Bay: roomy, centrally located. Build a breakwater across the mouth of the bay and you have a land-locked, all-weather harbor. Do a little dredging and Nawiliwili Bay will be deep enough to handle any ocean liner or battleship."

"Thank you, Mr. Wilcox," said Major Winslow. "I think . . . "

"One more thing," George said, holding up his hand. "There are private interests promoting nearly every one of these locations as the site for a major harbor. That's because various plantations and sugar agencies have spent quite a lot of money to build facilities for loading sugar in these places. I'm not trying to argue the merits of those claims. My opinion is based mostly on what I've learned from sea captains."

"This has been very interesting," said Major Winslow, getting to his feet, "I'm sorry that we took so much of your time."

"It's been my pleasure. I've dreamed for fifty years of a good, safe harbor for this Island. It's high time we're getting one." He paused. "You're going to take a look at these sites yourselves, I suppose?"

"Of course."

"Why don't you let me show them to you?" asked George eagerly.

The engineers looked at each other in surprise. "We'd be flattered, Mr. Wilcox," said Major Winslow.

George clapped his hat on his head. "I'll be right back. I'm going to get a handful of cigars," he said, hurrying out of the door.

Winslow and Wooten stared after him. "He's an amazing old man," said Major Wooten.

Purvis looked up from his ledger at a table across the room and said quietly, "Don't let him hear you call him an old man. He'll never forgive you."

* * *

Some day soon, George promised himself, he would turn the plantation over to Ralph. But not just yet. Ralph had plenty of years ahead of him. So George indulged in the luxury of playing gentleman farmer. Broadbent was such a good plantation manager that he often anticipated George's orders. Ralph had a thorough grasp of George's business affairs. With the future of Grove Farm in such capable hands, George permitted his old habits of frugality to relax a little.

He developed a weakness for travel. No one ever knew when he would drop everything for a trip to Honolulu. At least once a year he sailed for San Francisco. Since he was president of the now highly successful Pacific Guano and Fertilizer Company and a director of Inter-Island Steam Navigation Company, the First National Bank of Hawaii, and half a dozen other corporations, he never lacked an excuse to go on business.

By 1910 he had extensive investments in sugar plantations, shipping, railroads, real estate, utilities, banks, oil wells, and the fertilizer plant. Once he even sunk $400 in an ostrich farm. He never saw the money again. But not long after, he sold his Kewalo property in Honolulu for which he had paid $10,000 in the 1870's, for $100,000 in C. Brewer and Company stock.

Yet, his first love always remained the plantation. He was happiest when he and Broadbent were planning a new ditch or trying out a new piece of equipment, like the fertilizer spreader George brought back from San Francisco in 1912. The machine held three hundred pounds of fertilizer in a mule-drawn hopper that released the fertilizer in controlled amounts along the furrow. Best of all, the driver rode the machine instead of walking behind it.

"That means the spreader will move at the speed of the mules, not the speed of a man. You can cover more ground that way," George explained.

Broadbent nodded in immediate understanding, his mind already busy with plans for reinforcing the frame so it would last longer.

* * *

Frank Damon unrolled the plans, impatiently putting paper weights on the ends to hold them down. His voice glowed with pride. "There it is, Mr. Wilcox. That's the building we have planned for the new Mills School."

George leaned forward to study the sketch.

"Beautiful, isn't it?" Damon said with enthusiasm. "Grey lava rock walls, enough room to house two hundred students and twenty-two teachers. Fourteen classrooms, each one with outside exposure on at least two sides to let in plenty of light. That's the reason the building is designed in the shape of an "H." The manual training workshop will be in the basement with the agricultural laboratory. We'll have our own laundry, two kitchens, a hospital . . . "

George looked up. "It's quite an ambitious plan," he observed.

"That's what makes it such an exciting concept. Just think of it! Some of our students have gone back to China to take government jobs there! Others have been accepted at universities on the United States mainland. "We're spreading understanding already, Mr. Wilcox. I tell you, the potential for international good will that can be fulfilled in this building is unlimited."

George nodded. "I'll take care of it," he said.

The building, second largest in Honolulu at that time and the land around it, cost George $115,000. It was dedicated in 1912, but another six years passed before officials of the school persuaded him to agree that the building be called Wilcox Hall.

* * *

He sailed for San Francisco about the first of May, 1913, looking forward to a little hunting in the mountains. While waiting for the steamer in Honolulu, he had written to Ralph with directions about having the plantation houses along the Grove Farm road wired with electricity. By the time George returned, he knew that his nephew would have the job done. Sometimes he wondered how he had ever gotten along without Ralph.

When the cable arrived on Sunday night, July 12, it didn't seem real. Ralph was dead! He had drowned while swimming at Haena on the north coast. The funeral would be over before George could get back. He was stunned! At first, there was only the pain of personal grief. His heart ached for Daisy.

Slowly the whole meaning of the tragedy came to him. "What will happen to Grove Farm now?" he asked himself again and again on the way home. He was seventy-four years old. He had only a few more good years left. Then what?

He felt old and tired when he landed in Honolulu. Why, he wondered, must contentment always elude him? Sam had it. Luther had it. But for himself life was one long prodding of responsibility. And at the end, where was his reward? The lucky man, George told himself, left behind children to dignify his struggle on earth, to remember his good deeds and applaud his success. His child was a sugar plantation.

He rode out early on his first morning back, out of the green seclusion of the plantation yard onto the plain where the cane stood tall and thick. He stopped once, just to listen to the musical murmur of water as it hurried down the ditch. He stopped again to dismount and take the moist soil in his fingers. His land! The jagged green mountains embraced it all: his past and his future, the land that had held his love for fifty years. Somehow he must make his plantation live on after him. Ralph's death had been a cruel blow. Now he must try again with Charley.

* * *

It wasn't easy. At thirty-three, Charley had been manager of Koloa Plantation for four years. He had made his own success and he was proud of it.

"I'm happy where I am, Uncle George," he explained carefully. "I guess I've gotten sort of used to being my own boss."

George bowed his grey head. "I've always regretted not putting Ralph in charge before . . . " He stopped to clear his suddenly constricted throat. "Old men sometimes get selfish," he said bitterly.

"No, Uncle George," said Charley. "If it's anything you aren't, it's selfish."

George sighed. "Charley, I don't know how to ask this. But you're the oldest son now and I think of you as my own." He made a stern effort to keep emotion out of his voice. "I need you at Grove Farm, Charley."

So Charley came. George built his nephew and family a comfortable house near the old Grove Farm house. Charley and his wife, Marion, planted royal palms along the curved drive.

George put his nephew in complete control of the plantation as his general manager and executive assistant. From the beginning, Charley showed his mettle. He not only knew every phase of sugar planting, but he had an amazing head for figures. Best of all, he understood the complex new income tax laws passed by the Woodrow Wilson administration. George never could figure them out.

The months passed and George's anxiety passed. Charley seemed happy. Once more the future began to look bright. George felt tremendously grateful.

*   *   *

He had always been fascinated by machinery. In 1915 he bought two Model-T Ford trucks. The first time one of those box-like vehicles clattered into view, a mule bolted in a nearby field dragging a cultivator half way to the mountains. When they were loaded, the trucks had a bad habit of tipping over backwards, especially on steep hills. As soon as the front wheels left the ground, the vehicle would start turning in crazy circles. But the trucks were much speedier than ox carts, and on the new roads which Joe Moragne was building all over the Island, the funny-looking contraptions worked well.

In California a man named Benjamin Holt had invented a novel type of tractor that crawled along on endless tracks instead of wheels. Holt called his machine a "caterpillar." The first gasoline powered model weighed eight tons and was terribly clumsy to steer. But, within a few years, Holt developed a smaller, more maneuverable model. George saw it demonstrated at the Panama Pacific Exposition in San Francisco in 1915. He bought two of the new machines.

Broadbent and his shop foreman, Carl Nelson, quickly modified the tractors and put them to many uses. They were excellent for plowing on hilly land where the Fowler steam plow would not function. They were even better for pulling the cane cars that ran on portable track from the main line into the fields during harvest. Before, oxen had pulled these cars into the fields for loading, then back to the main track where the cars were hitched to the steam locomotive for their trip to the mill. Ox teams moved one car at a time at one mile an hour. A Caterpillar tractor could move half a dozen cars at several miles an hour.

Nelson and Broadbent also designed and built in the blacksmith shop hitches for pulling the heavy-duty furrowing plows behind the Caterpillars. Before that, it took a team of eight mules to pull one plow. Broadbent hitched two plows in tandem behind a Caterpillar, thereby doing double the work in much less time. The new operation had one major drawback. The man who walked behind the plow could not keep up with the tireless tractor. Broadbent put swing men on either end of the field to relieve one another. But still the machine drove the men to exhaustion.

"We'll have to build a hitch that will control the plow from the tractor," Broadbent said as he and George squatted with Nelson on the dirt floor of the shop. Broadbent's thick forefinger traced a tentative design in the dust. Then he rubbed it out. "What I'd really like to do is combine several operations, say plowing and planting in one."

George grinned. "That would be some plow. Why don't you teach it to do the fertilizing at the same time?"

Broadbent nodded thoughtfully. "That's not a bad idea."

*   *   *

George N. Wilcox at ceremony
marking connection of Koloa
and Grove Farm Company's
railroad systems, 1930

George N. Wilcox's first airplane
flight, between Oahu and
Kauai (Port Allen), 1928

S. S. Mikahala on the Kauai run, 1915

S. S. Hualalai entering Nawiliwili Harbor at opening of port, July 22, 1930

Plaque at Nawiliwili honoring George N. Wilcox for his part
in development of harbor

THAT NAWILIWILI HARBOR HAS BECOME ESTABLISHED
THAT SHIPS COME AND GO THAT PASSENGERS AND CARGO
ARRIVE AND DEPART IN SAFETY IS LARGELY DUE TO THE
VISION AND AID OF
GEORGE NORTON WILCOX
AND IN APPRECIATION THIS TABLET IS ERECTED BY THE
KAUAI CHAMBER OF COMMERCE
1936

As he approached his eightieth birthday, George counted his blessings and decided he was a very lucky man. He had always taken a secret pride in the accomplishments of his nieces and nephews. Every year they pleased him more. Young Gaylord, at the age of thirty-three was manager of Makee Plantation at Kealia up the coast, as independent as George had ever been. Mabel had spent three years studying nursing at Johns Hopkins Hospital. Now she had come back to pioneer public health nursing on Kauai. She was assigned to the tuberculosis program and often asked her father to go with her to translate for her among Hawaiian families where the disease struck hardest. Etta was busy bringing up a family. Elsie was occupied with community service projects.

His life amidst that energetic family moved in a comfortable, well-ordered pattern. He had everything he wanted. The house had grown with Sam's family. A completely new two-story addition was put up in 1915 to replace the four rooms built in 1877.

George was pleased that Sam and Emma wanted to keep the original old house, though they did remodel it in 1915 to widen the verandas and make three large rooms out of the many small ones. Now and then George thought of buying a yacht of his own. But something else always seemed to be more important.

In November, 1915, he turned over to Mid-Pacific Institute stocks worth $355,810. He made the gift with only one stipulation: that there would be no publicity about it. As Purvis made the entry in the Grove Farm books, out of curiosity he tried to figure up how much George had given away so far. His total came to $1,500,000. Purvis smiled, then crumpled the paper and tossed it into the waste basket.

The accustomed routine of George's life was interrupted when Purvis retired in 1916. Edward S. Swan took charge of the books. The next time George went to Honolulu, he deposited $35,000 in Purvis' bank account as a retirement bonus.

That same year George visited the Salvation Army home for neglected girls in Honolulu. When he learned there was an even greater need for a boy's home, he said, "I'll take care of it." His $50,000 donation made the front page of the *Advertiser*. "Why can't they leave a man alone?" he complained when he saw the story.

The World War interrupted once more the comfortable pattern of life at Grove Farm. Mabel left for France in 1917 as a Red Cross nurse. Elsie was busy organizing volunteer corps of women to combat the food shortage. Charley had the workers plant corn and potatoes for the war effort. Broadbent designed cultivators for the new crops and Nelson worked overtime in his blacksmith shop to build a corn grinder.

Then the war was over and Mabel came home with a decoration from the Queen of Belgium for front line bravery while caring for Belgian refugees. Gradually, things settled back to normal. George sighed with thankfulness. He was an old man, he told himself, and he wanted to live out the rest of his life in peace.

* * *

More than anything else, the plantation gave George constant satisfaction. It couldn't have been in better hands. Charley had the business and executive ability; Broadbent knew how to handle men and machinery. And both had aggressive ideas for expansion.

Before the war they decided to make major improvements in the ditch system. With Joe Moragne in charge, and assisted by Edward Palmer, they began work on a new main "upper ditch" on the slopes of Kilohana. The project included a huge new reservoir that would hold water against times of drought. The cost of the project was enormous. But it greatly increased the amount of irrigation water on Grove Farm.

On May 12, 1917, Grove Farm entered into a new milling agreement with Lihue Plantation. This time Charley sat through the negotiations with his uncle. They won an eighty-one per cent share of sugar and molasses milled from Grove

Farm cane and almost unlimited acreage. Charley was jubilant. "Nothing can stop us now!" he exulted.

George was almost as pleased when Gaylord in 1918 became vice-president at American Factors, a new corporation built upon what was left of Hackfeld and Company, forced by the government to dissolve during the World War because of its alien German ownership. American Factors became the agent for Grove Farm sugar, and George invested in the new company.

In spite of the triumphs, George was constantly aware of the shadow of sadness that more and more filled the corners of his life. Albert died in 1919, about a month before George's eightieth birthday. At least once a month the name of an old friend would appear in the obituary columns. But George refused to stay depressed very long. Whenever the feeling came over him, he had only to ride out among the tall, leafy forests of cane. Or watch the tender new shoots as they drank in the sun. Or turn a trickle of water into a thirsty furrow. Here in the fields there was no growing old, only constant rebirth. George knew that as long as Grove Farm remained, his life would have meaning.

One morning a new attendant brought George's horse to the kamani tree. As George walked around the house in his black coat, boots, and straw hat, the attendant asked, "Should I hold his head while you get on, Mr. Wilcox?"

George jerked the reins out of the attendant's hands. "Of course not!" he said.

He put one foot into the stirrup and swung nimbly into the saddle. Then he turned the horse's head and rode, erect as a ramrod, out of the plantation yard with five dogs gamboling at the horse's heels.

* * *

The Harbor Committee of the Kauai Chamber of Commerce came to call during the Legislative Session of 1917. George peered hopefully at the visitors through his thick glasses. After seven years of fruitless effort, his Island still remained without a safe, convenient harbor.

"Well, what happened?" he asked eagerly. "Is Nawiliwili still a political football?"

"No, I think we have a chance this time," said the spokesman of the group. "Representative Coney feels we can get a bond issue for the harbor improvement through this session if this Island will take the bonds; and if we can show the United States Congress and the Territorial Legislature that we're ready to shoulder part of the expense, Coney thinks we have a good chance of getting work started," the spokesman explained.

"How big is the bond issue?" asked George.

"It's for $200,000, to be used for breakwater construction. We've had a meeting of the Chamber and voted unanimously to endorse Nawiliwili as the harbor site. What we're trying to do now is round up enough financial support to underwrite the bond issue."

"Do you think that this will work?" George asked thoughtfully.

"It better!" said the spokesman impatiently. "Kauai is the only major island in the Territory without a deep-water harbor. Until we get one, we can count on losing out on the tourist business, we'll stop loading sugar every time the wind comes up, and we'll pay higher freight rates. It's got to work!"

George nodded. "All right, I'll guarantee purchase of the bonds."

That year the Territorial Legislature passed the $200,000 bond issue for Nawiliwili Harbor.

* * *

George usually sailed for California during the summer in order to avoid being home for his birthday on August 15. If he stayed, someone inevitably arranged a celebration for him, and he hated having a fuss made over him.

When he set out in 1920 he hardly felt his eighty years. Seldom had the future looked more rosy. The price of sugar was soaring to record heights. At last his pet project, the harbor at Nawiliwili, seemed to be getting underway. And with Charley and Broadbent running things at home, he really didn't have a care in the world.

So the tragedy struck when he least expected it. A cable arrived late Sunday night, June 20. Charley had been killed in an auto accident while driving his family home from an outing in the mountains above Waimea. A niece was also dead and Marion and her daughter, Lois, were in the hospital with injuries.

"Oh, no! Not Charley, too!" he groaned.

At first, he was numb. After that, there was only grief for Marion and defeat for himself. This time, he told himself, he was too old to fight back. When he returned to Grove Farm, he was bent under the weight of his years. For the first time when George was at home, his horse remained tied to the little rail fence around the Kamani tree.

They all tried to cheer him. But he drew a wall of reserve around himself they dared not break. As always, he fought his battle alone. What would happen now to Grove Farm when he was gone? Twice he had tried to pass on the reins of control. Now they were heavier than ever in his hands.

Should he try to start all over again with Gaylord? Dare he try again to entrust this dream to a single successor? Or was there a better way?

The answer eluded him and so, at last, he turned to the place where he could think best. When he announced the next morning that he was going to take a ride around the plantation, Sam smiled with satisfaction. More slowly than before, but with a firm step, George made his way to the tree and untied his horse. As he rode away toward the fields of waving cane, Emma said, "He'll be all right now."

* * *

It was a long way out of the depths of his despair. The first step was a trip to Honolulu to see Gaylord, Sam's third son, now vice-president of American Factors. George told his nephew, "I lost Ralph. Then I lost Charley. Now I need you." But it was not that simple.

Gaylord was as independent as George, proud of making his own success. The younger man agreed to act as his uncle's executive assistant in financial affairs and to sit in his place when necessary on boards of directors. Gaylord also assumed a position as consulting manager of Grove Farm in policy matters. But he would not move away from Honolulu, and he would not resign his important post at American Factors.

So George's long-range problem remained unsolved. Meanwhile, a host of smaller ones kept him busy. On other plantations, labor unrest was becoming a more and more serious problem. On Grove Farm there was little trouble, and George tried to keep it that way by providing attractive living and working conditions. He supplied wood for the workers' cooking stoves and kerosene for their lamps. Broadbent invented a wood cutter and splitter so the workers didn't have to make their own kindling. Other plantation managers made the usual complaint, "You're spoiling your men!"

About 1920 George began construction of a completely modern camp at Puhi in the heart of the expanding plantation. Instead of building houses haphazardly as new families moved in, a complete village was laid out with streets, a playground, room for gardens, and lawns. The houses had proper kitchens equipped with running water and enough bedrooms for each family depending upon the number of children.

The Nawiliwili Harbor project continued to be an anxiety. Inertia and petty rivalries always prevented action on the breakwater. In Honolulu, officials of Alexander and Baldwin, a large agency with heavy investments in Kauai plantations, refused to support Nawiliwili as a harbor site because the company had built its own loading facilities at Port Allen and wanted the harbor to be put there. Governor Charles McCarthy finally went to Kauai to look the situation over for himself. After a precarious landing by whaleboat in heavy seas, he returned to Honolulu convinced that the Island of Kauai most certainly needed a safe, all-weather harbor. He agreed that Nawiliwili was the best site.

But it was 1919 before the United States Congress finally appropriated money for a breakwater. And that appropriation bristled with conditions that must be met before work on the harbor could begin. The most important condition required the sugar plantations of Kauai to link their railroads so that cargo from any point on the Island could reach Nawiliwili Harbor by rail. George and the other planters immediately promised to comply with the condition.

On January 27, 1921, George fulfilled his pledge and bought the entire block of Territorial bonds providing $200,000 in funds to match the Federal appropriation. Construction on the breakwater began soon after. On October 28, the Kauai Chamber of Commerce arranged a ceremony during which George laid the cornerstone.

The requests for money to finance worthy projects never ended. On January 19, 1922, George gave $32,000 for a unique Salvation Army undertaking. The plan was to build an attractive restaurant in a romantic setting in suburban Manoa Valley in Honolulu where girls in residence could be taught the skills of cooking, waiting on tables, preparing menus, and housekeeping. Since the restaurant would be open to the public, profits could be used to pay the girls' wages and to finance other Salvation Army projects. The name chosen for the airy, lava rock building with comfortable lanais was Waioli Tea Room in honor of George's old home in Hanalei.

Later that year, he gave another $300,000 to build a Salvation Army Boys' Home in a district called Kaimuki in Honolulu.

Always in the back of his mind he was thinking about the future of Grove Farm. It was near the end of 1922 when, reluctantly, he made his decision.

*   *   *

The team of attorneys listened as George explained his intention. Then one of them said, "As I understand it, Mr. Wilcox, you wish to transfer management of Grove Farm Plantation to a corporation consisting of your nieces and nephews."

"That's correct, I want the plantation to pass on to the family when I die," said George.

"What is the structure of management now?" the attorney asked.

"I run it."

Patiently the attorney said, "Yes, I know. What I mean is, who else owns stock in the company. Who is on your board of directors?"

"There is no stock," said George quietly. "I don't need a board of directors. It's my plantation."

"You are the sole owner?" the attorney asked, incredulous.

"Of course. I have been so for fifty-seven years," George answered.

"Isn't that rather unusual?"

"That's beside the point. Is it possible to set up the company?"

"Yes, it is possible," the attorney replied quickly. "Quite easy, in fact. You must understand, however, that such an action will dilute your control."

"That's the reason I'm doing it," George told him. "I want the family to be in a position to assume full control when I'm gone."

"Very well," he said. And they went to work. They evolved a corporate structure under which George divided about one-fourth of the shares of the new company among his nieces and nephews, and their children, from Hawaii to California. He retained three-fourths of the stock to be voted in trust after his death by Sam's children: Etta, Elsie, Gaylord, and Mabel. Upon their deaths, the stock in the trust would be distributed among all the descendants of George's brothers in equal amounts.

The attorney pointed out, "When that happens, Mr. Wilcox, there is no way to prevent control of the corporation from slipping away from the family if enough members care to sell their stock. Any outsider who buys enough shares will control the plantation."

George sighed, "I know that. But I'm hoping, by that time, every one of those Wilcoxes will take enough pride in Grove Farm to want to keep it in the family."

The attorneys gathered up their papers and took their leave. George sat for a while before he got up to go. It was done, the best way he knew how.

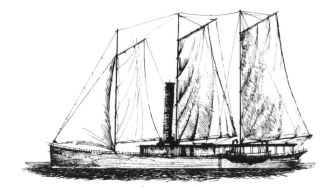

CHAPTER

22

Elsie watched her uncle as he stepped onto the lanai, ready to go out. She was a small woman with alert brown eyes and a ready sense of humor. But she never made fun of Uncle George. And she never, never told him what to do. Yet, she did hope that this morning he would not take pity again on the pineapple farmers.

"Oh, Uncle George," she reminded him as he walked briskly to the Studebaker. "We have plenty of pineapples today."

He didn't answer. Making his rounds in an automobile was less satisfactory than from the back of a horse. The automobile closed him in away from everything, the crisp morning air and the good smell of the soil. He couldn't follow a whim in an auto as he had on his horse, up the ditch line or straight across a field to look at a new planting. Well, there was no help for it.

Manuel Souza held the car door open for him. He was Portuguese, comfortable with the familiarity of long association. He had started as a field hand.

"Let's see if the cane at Kealia is any better off than ours," George said, settling back into the seat. He took a cigar from his lapel pocket, pulled off the wrapper and efficiently bit away the tip.

They drove out of the yard, past the rain gauge which had been moved from the back of the house, and turned right onto the road, bordered by sugar cane on one side and trees on the other, that had once been the barren horseback trail to Grove Farm. Suddenly he took the cigar from his mouth.

"Pull up, Manuel," he said.

The car came to a stop and he stepped nimbly out into the road. He crossed over, clambered down into the ditch and up the other side to a dripping water tap. With a quick turn of the handle, he stopped the dripping. Then he scrambled back through the ditch and into the car.

"All right, go on," he said.

He couldn't stand to see water being wasted. It always made him think of that first meager ditch and the pitiful trickle he had worked so hard to bring from the mountains. Now Grove Farm had sixteen miles of modern ditches that delivered twenty-six million gallons of water every day. But the old habit remained.

The road dipped into the valley, and more memories crowded into his thoughts. How the mill had grown! There was no trace of the smooth, shimmery mill pond or the old water wheel, no raw-boned oxen hitched to clumsy carts. Now the mill yard was criss-crossed with railroad tracks.

Ahead, walking by the side of the road, was an old Chinese. Manuel was told to stop. The Chinese looked up and when he recognized George his wrinkled face broke into a wide smile. George rolled down his window.

"You go hana hana this morning?" he called.

The old Chinaman grinned at the joke. "Me all samee you, no hana hana."

George grinned back. "Everything all right?"

The Chinese nodded vigorously.

"You boy stop Honolulu? He do all right in his store, eh?"

"New baby five time now," said the old man proudly.

Manuel drove on while George's mind turned back the years to the day a young Chinese, awkward in his graduation suit, had come to thank him for his scholarship to Mid-Pacific Institute. George still had a clear impression of those quick, shrewd eyes, the precise English. That had been money well spent!

As they drove through the growing town of Lihue, now laid out with paved streets and stores and a county court house, George found himself living in the past. The road up the coast was so smooth! But he saw it as the rutted, dirt trail he had repaired again and again as road supervisor fifty years before. There was hardly a bend in the highway that did not set off a new train of association. The Wailua River made him think of the scow that had carried passengers across until he had finally secured an appropriation from the Legislature for a bridge in 1892, the year he'd been Premier. How proud he'd been of that first bridge! What a leap forward it had been for the Island! Now hardly anyone remembered it.

Farther on a young Japanese farmer was arranging fresh pineapples on display at a roadside stand. "Stop, Manuel," said George. The farmer glanced up hopefully as the car stopped beside the stand.

"How's the pineapple business today?" he was asked.

"Not so good," the farmer answered. He was a small, wiry, sunburned man with a thick shock of black hair.

"What's the matter?"

The farmer shrugged. "Same as yesterday and the day before. I can't give them away."

"Well, I'd like to buy some this morning," George said

cheerfully. "Manuel, put three cases in the trunk. And be sure to get good sweet ones."

As they drove away, Manuel asked, "What are you going to do with them this time, Mr. Wilcox?"

"We'll make a few stops on the way," George answered briskly. So they gave a case to the Moragnes and the Hoggs and a Portuguese family with a dozen children.

* * *

For months Broadbent had been working with Carl Nelson, shop superintendent, and George Jottmann, head blacksmith, to develop a mechanical cane planter that would also plow and fertilize in one operation. The machine was to be designed for unirrigated fields in areas of heavy rainfall where furrowing was not necessary. There were sugar growers who laughed at such a preposterous scheme.

Since the very beginning, sugar cane had been planted by hand, one worker to a row, dropping the two-foot lengths of seed cane onto the ground from a bundle carried by a mule. Another team of workers followed from behind with hoes to cover the seed cane with earth. Ten men working fast could plant an acre of cane a day.

George was as excited as Broadbent about the project. Every day he stopped by the blacksmith shop to see how the work progressed.

"What started me thinking was a crude cane planter I saw once at Kilauea Plantation," Broadbent explained as they stood amid a pile of old machinery parts. "That was just a sled loaded with seed cane. They hitched the sled behind a plow. One man rode the sled, dropping seed cane into the row as they went along. It's better than planting by hand but not much."

George nodded.

"Here's my idea," Broadbent continued. "We'll mount the whole unit on the wheels of an old Fordson tractor. The chassis will be an angle iron frame. We'll bolt two plows to the frame with extra holes so we can adjust for plowing at different depths, then we'll mount a chute just behind each plow. The seed cane lengths will slide down the chutes into the rows. This disc attachment will cover the cane almost immediately with dirt; and those rollers, they weigh seventy pounds each, will come along behind and press down the soil. I haven't worked out an attachment to drop fertilizer into the rows along with the seed cane, but I don't think it will give us too much trouble."

"How many men does it take to operate?"

"Two men to drop the seed cane into the chutes and two men to keep them supplied. With the man on the tractor, that makes only five men. I figure they can do what it takes fifty to do now."

"If the planter works."

It did. Broadbent's planter, pulled behind a Caterpillar tractor, was capable of plowing and planting six acres a day. Soon managers from other plantations were visiting Grove Farm to learn how to build similar machines of their own.

* * *

One seemingly permanent frustration was the Nawiliwili Harbor project. The harder he worked at it, the slower it went. In 1923 the Kauai Chamber of Commerce asked the Territorial Board of Harbor Commissioners in Honolulu to make a survey of the harbor site to determine the location of wharves. The Commissioners reported there was no money available to make the survey.

"We'll make our own survey!" said George.

It took one year. On July 30, 1923 the Kauai Chamber submitted plans that called for the filling in of part of the bay to provide land for harbor installation: piers, sugar loading machinery, parking. Before work could begin on the fill, it would be necessary to build a retaining wall to hold the fill in place. Since the harbor was to be deepened by dredging anyway, the most economical filling material would be that dredged from the bottom of the bay. Therefore, construction of the retaining wall should begin as soon as possible in order to make use of this fill when dredging operations began.

George waited impatiently for the next meeting of the Harbor Board in August. At that meeting, the Commissioners refused to take action on Nawiliwili Harbor until they had more information on the amount of freight that would be shipped at the new terminal.

"They've had five years to get that information," Broadbent said bitterly. "What's the matter with them, anyway!"

"Politics," George answered.

It was very discouraging. On September 20 the Harbor Board wanted to know whether the Federal government or the Territory of Hawaii would own the land created by filling and who would have riparian rights to the new land in front of the G. N. Wilcox property now bordering the bay. George immediately waived all such rights to the land. But he knew that the land issue was only a smoke screen. The real opposition to Nawiliwili Harbor had not yet come into the open.

"Don't worry, we're not licked yet," he told Broadbent. "Tell those fellows at the Chamber of Commerce to get busy on a freight report."

*   *   *

In May, 1924, George Wilcox was elected president of Inter-Island Steam Navigation Company. He showed no sign of slowing down. As president of the new Grove Farm Company, he presided over the quarterly meetings of board of directors. Every weekday morning after breakfast he looked in at the office to open his mail and plan the day's plantation activity with Broadbent. No one ever knew when he would be leaving for Honolulu. Once or twice a year he and Swan sailed for San Francisco, always in time to avoid a birthday celebration at home. By this time he had come to know his California nieces and nephews, the children of his older brother Charles, so well it was like having more than one home.

To the amusement, and sometimes despair, of his nieces he insisted on doing things exactly his own way. In spite of modern plumbing, he still had his bath in the same large round wooden tub he had used for half a century. He cleaned his pipes with the wing feathers of hen chickens, explaining that tail feathers were too soft. He carried a small box to meals for saving scraps of meat that he took back to his cottage and fed to the little gecko lizards that scampered across his screens.

As he passed his mid-eighties, he realized that young people sometimes stared at him as a stranger from another world. He clung to the ways of the past. Yet, when the minister one Sunday morning defended from the pulpit George's right to bathe in an old fashioned wooden tub, he was half amused, half annoyed. "Bathing is no subject for a sermon!" he remarked.

* * *

In 1924, the pendulum swung back in favor of Nawiliwili Harbor. Matson Navigation Company President E. D. Tenney reported that his company would send its vessels into Nawiliwili. Matson freighter skippers testified in favor of the harbor project. On July 9, 1924, the Board of Harbor Commissioners received legal opinions that cleared up the land questions. The Territorial Legislature had appropriated $100,000 to begin work on the new terminal. At last, construction on the retaining wall could begin.

The Harbor Board dropped its bombshell at the August meeting. The Commissioners approved a resolution that read: "Owing to the fact that this Board has been definitely informed by certain of the large shippers of cargo on Kauai that they will not use the proposed wharf at Nawiliwili if constructed and that other large shippers have given no assurance that they will use the wharf if constructed, this board feels that it cannot authorize the expenditure necessary for a retaining wall until the Board has the assurance of the shippers of Kauai that the tonnage that may eventually pass over the wharf will warrant the expenditure necessary to complete the project."

Almost immediately, the United States Engineers announced that they would hold up construction of the breakwater, now nearing completion, until the Board of Harbor Commissioners went ahead with the terminal. In a twinkling, the whole project had collapsed.

On Kauai there was shocked disbelief, then dismay. Just when it seemed that success would crown their years of effort, they had met defeat. More than one member of the Chamber of Commerce shook his head and said, "It goes to show, you can't fight an arbitrary bureaucracy."

To George Wilcox, that attitude was treason. "This is not the time to give up," he said indignantly. "Now we've got to fight harder than ever." To anyone who would listen, he explained his theory. "This is a political battle. The Commissioners are under pressure to relocate the harbor. We all know that pressure is coming from the big sugar agencies in Honolulu who have built their own port facilities in other locations, especially at Port Allen. Our job now is to apply our own pressure. The United States Engineers are on our side. The sea captains are on our side. The Legislature is on our side. We have the whole Island of Kauai behind us. Let's go down there and show them!"

The answer was always, "If only we could get one big shipper behind us."

And George would reply, "Don't be too sure we can't."

Under a sudden wave of protest from Kauai, the Board of Harbor Commissioners called a public hearing to be held September 3, in Honolulu, on the Nawiliwili Harbor issue. George, as usual, stayed behind the scenes. But the Kauai Chamber of Commerce sent a strong, determined delegation to the meeting. They got support from the newspapers, from holdover legislators, and both Inter-Island and Matson Navigation Company sea captains. The surprise witness was a representative of American Factors, a company that had so far refused to commit itself, who declared that the sugar agency did not oppose Nawiliwili Harbor and, furthermore, expected ultimately to use the new harbor for loading sugar from the Kauai plantations it represented.

Impressed by such solid opposition, the Harbor Board reversed itself and appointed its own engineer to survey the harbor site. The survey was highly favorable. On January 14, 1926, the Kauai contracting firm of Hobby and Coney received the bid for a two-year contract to build the retaining wall. To make sure nothing would go wrong again, George signed the contractor's bond for the project, guaranteeing completion of the retaining wall.

"Now that we're finished with the politics, let's get on with the work," he said with satisfaction.

*   *   *

He was only vaguely aware of his reputation as the richest man in Hawaii. Charlie Fern, the energetic editor of Kauai's weekly newspaper, the *Garden Island*, claimed that G. N. Wilcox had recorded one of the nation's highest incomes in the year 1920 when the price of sugar had reached record proportions. Actually, George's income from investments as well as sugar in 1920 was less than half a million dollars. In normal years, it was hardly a fourth of that.

Yet the enormous sums he donated to charities each year had built the legend of his wealth. By this time he had lost track of the amount of money he had given away. But it was probably well over $3,000,000.

George's giving was always highly personal. One morning he surprised Tokio Fuji, his new driver, by stopping to deliver a fish net to a needy Hawaiian family. "Do them more good than money," he explained brusquely. Every Christmas he sent checks to friends, destitute families, churches of all denominations, schools, hospitals, missions, and orphanages. He set up a trust, in memory of his father and mother, for non-ordained missionaries and placed it under the jurisdiction of the American Board of Commissioners for Foreign Missions.

* * *

The breakwater was completed by the United States Engineers on March 30, 1926. On March 16, George watched as a power shovel started an excavation near his beach house to uncover rock that would build the retaining wall. His grey suit and straw hat soon became a familiar figure at the construction site.

In the beginning, the work seemed to go very well. By fall, Charlie Fern's *Garden Island* reported that eight thousand tons of rock had been placed in four hundred feet of wall. But to George there appeared to be a great deal of misdirected motion.

That winter the work slowed to a snail's pace. The contractors explained, "We have to make a fill out into the bay in order to get a crane in position to lay the outer wall. And we've had to open a new quarry to get boulders big enough to stand the pounding on that wall. But we'll be on schedule again soon."

As the months went by, it became more and more obvious that the contractors were not on schedule. In October, 1927, they threw in the sponge. They had run out of money. The job was not quite half finished. Once more the harbor project ground to a halt.

To some of the members of the Kauai Chamber of Commerce, this was the final straw. It seemed that the Island was doomed to remain without a modern harbor. Everyone sympathized with Mr. Wilcox. The contractor's failure had left him, as bondsman, with the unpleasant task of finishing the retaining wall at his own expense.

He was neither discouraged nor vindictive. He simply called

for Broadbent and, with the familiar gleam of excitement in his eyes, told his manager, "See if the Commissioners will give us a year's extension on that deadline. Then we'll show them how to build that retaining wall!" The Commissioners granted another 350 days.

He was eighty-eight years old when he took charge of the construction of the mammoth wall. He pulled out the surveys he had hired Joe Moragne to make for him years before. Moragne had suggested taking rock from the other side of the bay beyond the lighthouse where large boulders were plentiful.

They built a road to get to the boulders. Then a fleet of trucks from Waimea Stables began hauling rock around the bay. Less determined men said it was too long a haul. But, in spite of heavy rains, the trucks delivered enough rock to keep two cranes working at capacity placing boulders in the wall.

During the first month, Charlie Fern reported that the new construction crew laid 226 feet of rock. On January 17, 1928, Broadbent told a meeting of the Kauai Chamber of Commerce that the retaining wall had reached a point where filling could begin. On February 25 the crews set a record, placing 468 tons of rock in one working day. In June, three months ahead of schedule, the retaining wall was finished.

* * *

More and more things reminded George that he was growing old. It had seemed only yesterday that Joe Moragne's boy, Bill, had worked as rod boy for his father during the summer on surveying jobs. Suddenly the boy had become a man with an engineering degree. In 1928 George put him to work modernizing the lower main ditch. "I want it straight no matter how much you have to tunnel," George ordered, "and I want the whole thing lined with concrete." The young man tackled the job with his father's quiet efficiency.

Sam died on May 23, 1929, while George was visiting San Francisco. On the way home, aboard the *S. S. Maui*, he celebrated his ninetieth birthday. It was a lonely feeling for he was no longer among people he knew. They were all gone: Sanford Dole, Henry Baldwin, Sam Alexander, W. O. Smith.

When Mabel's friend, Ethel Damon, author and school teacher from Honolulu, congratulated him on appearing so young, he held up his hand and said, "Don't make a fuss about it or Father Time will hear you. I've cheated him a long time, you know."

* * *

No one could talk George out of making the first trip by steamer into the new harbor. So he was aboard the *Hualalai*, Inter-Island's newest vessel, when she sailed from Honolulu Harbor late in the afternoon on July 21, 1930. The ship was loaded with dignitaries eager for an excuse to celebrate. In fact, they began celebrating before the ship ever left the dock and didn't stop all the way to Kauai.

But George went early to his stateroom. Before dawn he was getting his own coffee in the main cabin when the officer on watch discovered him. Three stewards immediately materialized to serve the president of the company in proper style.

When he came out on deck, Kauai was dead ahead, her jagged outline purple-grey in the early morning haze. The ship was beginning to stir. People passed by and spoke to him. He stood at the rail, alone with his thoughts.

There was no one to tell what he was thinking because they would not understand how unreal this moment seemed. He was remembering another trip to Kauai, in 1860 when he'd come back from Jarvis Island in January. Edward and Albert had just started their three-week, mid-semester vacations at Punahou and were waiting for the steamer *Kilauea* to make her monthly trip to Kauai. George talked them into sailing, instead, on a little schooner bound for Moloaa, a tiny landing on

Kauai, where the schooner captain traded for salt beef which he sold to whale ships.

First the wind had died, then turned contrary. What was normally a twelve-hour sail, lasted one day, two days, then three. The boys had run out of their provisions and ate the crew's poi. When that was gone, they broached a sack of potatoes in the hold and roasted them by building a fire on a coil of chain on deck. The schooner finally landed them at Nawili-wili, half way around the Island from their destination. A week-and-a-half late, the boys arrived home on borrowed horses.

Now the deck was crowded with laughing, jostling passengers, eager to go ashore and begin celebrating again. George didn't hear them. A vivid picture had popped into his mind, of big Paul Isenberg riding the back of a Hawaiian from the beach to the whaleboat. That would be very near the spot where the *Hualalai* would dock today.

A strange object in the water caught his eye. "What's that?" he asked, pointing. The man at his elbow answered, "The Navy sent a submarine from Pearl Harbor to give us an escort." Two columns of fishing sampans advanced from the mouth of the new harbor to take positions alongside the *Hualalai*.

At six o'clock the *Hualalai* slipped into the channel and entered the calm, land-locked harbor. It all looked so raw and new. His beach house now stood on the edge of barren fill. The retaining wall obliterated the spot where Sam had landed with his bride.

George stared at the strange landscape, hardly aware of the confusion about him. He knew that very few men are permitted such moments of victory. He stared, his heart full. He had lived to see his dream become reality.

Then he was moving down the gangway, firm hands guiding each elbow. A string of firecrackers let go, deafening him. A voice close to his ear shouted over the racket, "That's for you from the Japanese Chamber of Commerce." He gave his quick nod.

Now they brought him to a stop before an enormous crowd of people. J. T. Moir of the Kauai Chamber of Commerce stepped forward and put a flower lei over his head.

A group of girls in hula costumes began to sing and George saw the older Hawaiian women advancing toward him. He wished he could get away. But he stood erect, his grey head tilted a little to one side, waiting. He knew the women, every one of them. The oldest was almost as ancient as he. She came to him, her wrinkled face serene, the mokihana lei of Kauai in her gnarled hands.

"Aloha, Keoki," she said softly in a voice that had lost none of its musical magic. "I speak to you from the Hawaiian people. Wear this lei in the spirit of Mother Rice who also did so much for our island." Then she gently laid the lei on his narrow shoulders and kissed him gracefully on both cheeks.

Behind their lenses, George's eyes filled with tears. He tried to speak but he could not. It was all he could do to make his lips stop quivering.

* * *

Later that year, Inter-Island Steam Navigation Company added a subsidiary called Inter-Island Airways. So, at the age of ninety-one, on October 31, 1930, George took his first ride in an airplane, a Sikorsky amphibian, on the inaugural flight from Honolulu to Kauai. When they landed, he told reporters, "It was simpler than I thought it would be."

Now there was a new reason for him to travel, and he used it as often as he was able because the old restlessness often came over him. At home there was less and less for him to do. He went riding with Tokio and fed his cats and played cribbage with his nieces and the nurse they had brought in to help him. The doctor tried to make him cut down on his cigars.

So George would give Swan the high sign and off they would go. They took a trip to San Francisco late in 1930, and on the way back George met his new assistant manager, W. P. Alexander, an expert agriculturist who had been hired from an assignment in Cuba by Grove Farm.

The doctor told George he had cancer, and the pain began. He grew a little more unsteady. But not too unsteady to enjoy a trip to Honolulu. In January, 1933, he felt restless again. But this time his strength failed shortly after Swan and he arrived at the Alexander Young Hotel. For three days the doctors treated him in his suite because he was too ill to be moved. He died quietly at 1:00 A.M. Saturday morning, January 21.

In an editorial, the *Advertiser* said, "A mighty tree has fallen."

* * *

The rain came down in a steady, uncompromising drizzle as they began to gather Tuesday afternoon on the grassy bluff overlooking the mill where Maria had been buried so many years before. Today the huge mill was silent although the grinding season was at its height. The bluff, once so barren, was beautifully landscaped.

The people kept coming by the hundreds to wait quietly in what was now a downpour: the Governor of Hawaii, presidents of the largest corporations in the Territory, field hands, oriental shopkeepers, Hawaiian fishermen. An enormous shipment of flowers from friends in Honolulu lay banked against the pile of raw earth.

It was four o'clock when the funeral procession arrived. Gaylord, now the head of the family, carried the urn. There was no sermon, only a short eulogy and a prayer. The Lihue Hawaiian Church choir sang "Malu Ia Iesu" and "Jesus Lover of My Soul" in clear, four-part harmony.

Then the members of the family and close friends came forward to place their wreaths upon the grave. One by one they stepped up to say good-by. A little Oriental man waited until the last. He had no wreath like the others, only a bouquet of flowers he must have picked in his own garden. When everyone else had finished, he came shyly forward and placed his little bouquet upon the grave. Then he turned away, tears streaming down his face. No one seemed to know who he was, and he got away before anyone thought to ask his name. Finally, they all went away and the bluff was silent again except for the lonely sighing of the wind in the ironwood trees.

PART VI

The Plantation

CHAPTER

23

A calendar on the wall of the old plantation office read March 6, 1934. Broadbent sat attentively in his straight-backed wooden chair, heavy arms folded across his deep chest, as he glanced around the table at the members of the Board of Directors. Gaylord, greying and business-like, sat in the chair as President of the Company. Broadbent didn't change his loyalties easily, but he had a grudging respect for this nephew who, at fifty-one, displayed his uncle's uncanny combination of business and farming sense. Gaylord's sisters, Elsie and Mabel, sat on either side of him and Etta's husband, Digby Sloggett, who managed the ranch, filled out the table.

It was very different with G. N. gone. Yet the ruddy-faced manager often told himself that it was a good thing the old gentleman died when he did. George Wilcox wouldn't have approved of a lot of things that were happening in the world. Over in Europe it was Hitler and Mussolini and the Bolsheviks. In the United States it was the Depression. Every time Broadbent opened a newspaper that fellow Roosevelt was starting up another government agency. But it didn't seem to do any good. The whole world was going crazy and Broadbent couldn't make sense out of any of it.

The only sane place left was Grove Farm. Broadbent always enjoyed retreating to the familiar contemplation of the plantation. Young Moragne's new ditch was bringing down enough water to irrigate even during dry spells. The fields, well supplied with fertilizer, were producing 4.68 tons to the acre. He was ready to expand the acreage anytime now.

Gaylord's voice cut his musing short. "Would Mr. Broadbent please give us his manager's report?"

Broadbent pushed himself to his feet and passed around copies of his annual report for the year 1933. When each director had a copy, he read the report in a dry, matter-of-fact tone, stopping sometimes to explain a paragraph more fully.

"This matter of labor unrest among the Filipino workers was caused by the interpreter," the manager said, departing from his text. "Those men don't speak English. So we are required to hire a man who acts as a go-between for the laborers and the plantation. He makes their requests, handles their beefs, things like that. Well, the interpreter, it turns out, was playing favorites. And he charged each man a fee to do his interpreting. No wonder they got mad! When we found out what was going on, I fired the interpreter. The men seem satisfied now."

Broadbent went back to his report. He finished reading, then made a last comment.

"In the matter of a new plantation office, I feel this is a very pressing problem. We're all crowded up in here. My assistant manager, Will Alexander, and I share this table. Hib Case, the bookkeeper, uses that table over there. Bill Moragne and two timekeepers work in that room on the side. There isn't any place at all for the supervisors to fill out their time sheets for their crews. They have to do it at home or sit out on the porch.

"We need new stables for our horses and mules. Also, we urgently need a new shop. The one we have now is really a blacksmith shop, you know. It's too small. And it's not equipped to do the work any more. When we strip down a truck or a tractor, we have to do it outside. That's hard on machinery parts. Then, too, the plantation is growing away from this office. The new Puhi camp is two miles from here. Aakukui Camp is five miles away. The logical place for plantation headquarters is close to the center of operations. I think that's all I have to say."

Broadbent sat down. Now he'd have to wait for the Board of Directors to discuss his recommendations and vote on them. It wasn't easy to get used to running the plantation this way. Under the old system, they just talked it over and that was that. But Broadbent knew he had no reason to complain. Some Boards of Directors never let the manager make a move unless he asked permission. Once these Wilcoxes had set the policy, they expected him to use his own judgment in carrying it out.

They voted to build a new office and shop and stables at Puhi in the heart of the plantation. Broadbent thanked them all in his gruff way as they left. Then he stood at the window looking out over the green quiet of the plantation yard. He couldn't help it. He was homesick for the days when Mr. Wilcox and he ran the plantation.

*   *   *

The new plantation headquarters was a snug, concrete building with grey-white walls and a Hawaiian style roof of grey cement shingles. Broadbent and Alexander shared a room almost as big as the entire old office. Time keepers had the main room, the bookkeeper a space for himself. The engineering department worked in another small room and supervisors had desks for filling out reports.

Nearby, across the compound, young Bill Moragne was busy erecting an all electric-powered plantation repair shop. By the end of 1935, Grove Farm would be the most modern, best-equipped plantation in the Territory of Hawaii.

Broadbent knew he should be contented but he wasn't. Almost every day brought a new outrage. Lihue mill had shut down to enlarge the factory. As a result, grinding had started two months late. By the time it would be finished, some of the cane would be rotten, the sucrose content of the juices would be down, and the rats would multiply in the uncut cane. To complicate things, many of Grove Farm's best workers had completed their labor contracts and were taking their savings back to the Philippines.

Broadbent's greatest exasperation was the Jones-Costigan Act, an agricultural relief measure of the Roosevelt Administration. The act was full of restrictions. The worst limited the number of acres each plantation was allowed to harvest. Hardly a day went by that Broadbent didn't growl his displeasure at this injustice to Will Alexander across the room. It was always worse when the big New Zealander was making out his quarterly reports. Toward the end of March, he threw down his pencil in disgust.

"It's against common sense," he grumbled, staring at what he had just written. "When the price of sugar goes down, you don't cut back on production, you plant more to make up the price difference."

Alexander, leaner and not so tall as Broadbent, nodded sympathetically. He had too much respect for the ruddy-faced manager's success to argue the point. But at forty-two the younger man had grown up in a different world. Broadbent was sixty-five.

Elsie Hart Wilcox, 1951, Grove Farm director from 1922 to 1954 and vice president from 1933 to 1954

Mabel Isabel Wilcox, 1951, Grove Farm director since 1922 and vice president since 1956; secretary from 1922 to 1942

William Patterson Alexander, Grove Farm Company manager from 1937 to 1953, vice president from 1948 to 1953

A. Hebard Case, 1953, Grove Farm treasurer from 1938 to 1959 and vice president from 1953 to 1959

Koloa mill, 1948

Lihue Plantation Company mill, 1958

Grove Farm rock-crushing plant at Half-way Bridge, 1958

Grove Farm limestone quarry, Mahaulepu, Koloa, 1952

Mauka portion of Grove Farm fields, Haiku Division, from plantation headquarters and Puhi Village to Knudsen Gap

Makai portion of Grove Farm fields, Haiku Division, from plantation headquarters and Puhi Village to Nawiliwili Harbor

Grove Farm Koloa mill, 1958

"Quotas!" Broadbent said in disgust. "The government says we can't produce any more than 9,032 tons of sugar. Just when we're ready to expand! What if we produce 12,000 tons this year? Are we supposed to feed 3,000 tons to the pigs?"

"I guess we'll have to try to keep production down to the quota," the assistant manager said diplomatically as he got up to leave.

Alexander did not have Broadbent's rough edges. The friendly assistant manager had specialized in chemistry at Yale and held a Master's degree in sugar technology from the University of Hawaii. He'd spent five years as a researcher in the Hawaiian Sugar Planters' Association Experiment Station before going to Ewa Plantation as Director of Agricultural Research and Control and then taking charge of a group of plantations in Cuba. Now his chief interest was in scientific agriculture, and his biggest problem, at the moment, was rats.

With a last smile of sympathy for Broadbent, he hurried out to his dusty Model A coupe. He wore puttees to protect his shins, khaki pants, a long sleeved shirt, a tie, and a pith helmet. It was late afternoon, and he had just time to make a couple of stops before knocking off for dinner.

First he drove to the new shop, a long, roomy shed with sliding doors to let in air and sunlight. Moragne was there, twelve years younger than Alexander, his face a rich brown from the sun.

"How's it going, Bill?" asked the assistant manager.

The engineer grinned. "It's going fine. We're putting in the traveling crane. Wait till you see how she operates. We'll be able to lift a motor out of a chassis and move it to the work bench without straining a muscle. There isn't another plantation in Hawaii that has an outfit like this!"

Alexander nodded in approval. "If you aren't careful, the other shop foremen will be jealous."

"They are already," said Moragne, pleased.

The assistant manager stepped back into his car and slammed

the door. A few moments later he was driving slowly along a smooth graveled road that led like a narrow canyon between fields of ten-foot high sugar cane. Alexander was anxious to check on his latest attempt at rat control.

At last he recognized the spot he was looking for. He stopped the car and strode across the road. At an open place in the jungle of cane stalks, he forced his way inside. It was stifling in that leafy thicket, and saw-tooth edges on the leaves cut his face. He pushed on, as the sour smell of rat-damaged cane filled his nostrils. Quickly he found what he was looking for. It was a poison torpedo. And it had been nibbled on.

He bent closer, pleased that the rats were taking his bait, but he did not touch the torpedo because the rats would be back. Smiling, he pushed through the stalks on his way out. The torpedoes were easy enough to make, poisoned grain wrapped in toilet paper and dipped in paraffin. The workers simply threw the torpedoes into rat infested fields and waited.

Now he'd have to hurry or he'd be late for dinner. He turned the car and headed back to the office. Instead of stopping he drove to the county highway just beyond and turned right toward Lihue town. The plantation's social hall, a combination auditorium and gymnasium built for the workers, stood nearby. Alexander could hear shouting inside as he approached. In spite of his hurry, he stopped the car to investigate.

Inside he found a boxing match in progress. Two of the young, single Filipino field hands were flailing away at one another while a group of excited spectators crowded around shouting encouragement. Alexander watched with interest until the end of the fight.

"Those fellows are pretty good," he said to the worker nearest him, an irrigation foreman. "How long has this been going on?"

"Quite a while," said the foreman.

"You know, they have a boxing team over at Kekaha," said Alexander thoughtfully. "They're looking for competition."

The other workers closed in, listening. "Let's get up a team," one of them suggested. "How about it, Mr. Alexander?"

"I think we could furnish some equipment," he said.

The irrigation foreman shook his head. "We wouldn't have a chance without a coach. These boys are strictly amateur."

"I know a stevedore at Ahukini who fought professionally in Honolulu," one of the boxers said eagerly. "He'd coach us."

Alexander asked, "If we rustled up a little lumber and some rope, do you boys think you could build yourselves a ring?"

They all nodded emphatically.

The assistant manager grinned back at them. "All right, I'll get to work on it tomorrow. That Kekaha bunch will be in for a surprise." Then he glanced at his watch and, with a hasty wave of his hand, hurried home to dinner.

* * *

Ever since his uncle had died three years before, Gaylord Wilcox had assumed more and more responsibility in the management of Grove Farm and his uncle's many investments. Gaylord finally decided he could not do justice to so many jobs. On July 31, 1936, he resigned his position as vice-president of American Factors in Honolulu. Shortly thereafter he moved his family to Kauai, living in one of the guest cottages at Kilohana not far from Grove Farm headquarters. During that time a new residence was being constructed on the site of the old Albert Wilcox home.

Gaylord continued to give his manager a free hand in running the plantation, but he liked to stop at the office now and then to keep in touch. Broadbent wasted no words explaining his biggest problem.

"It's labor," he said with a worried frown. "Within the last six months we've lost 137 men. Mostly they're the single Filipinos going to Honolulu where it's more exciting. So far, we've had seventy hires but that still leaves us sixty-seven men short of what we were a year ago. And the new men are a poor lot compared to those who quit."

"It's the same story on all the plantations," Gaylord answered looking glum. He was a man of medium height, erect as a gatepost, with square shoulders and a firm jaw.

Broadbent sighed. "Well, we'll just have to figure out how to get along with fewer men." Gaylord nodded in agreement.

That became the never ending problem. There was always so much to do and never enough men to do it. The three of them, Broadbent, Alexander, and Moragne, stayed awake nights trying to invent ways to save man hours. Hoeing was a good example.

Of all the tasks on the plantation, weed control was the most time consuming. From the moment of planting until the cane grew thick enough to shut out sunlight, preventing further weed growth, it was hoe, hoe, hoe! Sometimes, after prolonged rains, the entire labor force had to turn out to keep the weeds from choking the young cane.

With his background in chemistry, Alexander suggested spraying non-poisonous chemicals on the weeds. Broadbent was dubious. "What if the chemicals injured the men?" "We'll give them gloves and face masks," answered the assistant manager.

So they tried chemical weed control. Alexander fitted out a group of men with small pressure tanks of weed killer carried on the back. Each tank was equipped with a hand pump to force the chemical out in a spray. With these "knapsack sprayers" the men walked along the rows of young cane, spraying the weeds with herbicides. The men suffered no ill effects and, in fact, proudly called themselves the Sabidong Gang. The chemicals sharply reduced the need for hoeing, releasing men for other jobs.

When Moragne saw how well the knapsack sprayers worked, he said thoughtfully, "Maybe we can design a machine that will do the job in less time."

The shortage of labor was always most acute during harvest.

On some plantations, cane rotted in the field because there were not enough men available to cut it and load it upon the cane cars that carried it to the mill. Harvesting was the most strenuous and unpleasant work on the plantation. For that reason, it paid better than any other. Still there were never enough men to cut the cane, gather it into piles, and load it upon the cars.

Again and again Alexander had watched the picturesque scene, trying to figure a way to make it easier. First came the cutters, bent nearly double, swathed in gloves and long sleeves to protect against irritating cane fuzz, their heavy knives flashing wickedly in the sun as they sliced each stalk at its base, then lopped off the cane top at the other end.

The cutters left the field littered ankle deep in stalks, then came the pilers, often wives of the loaders, who gathered the stalks into small piles for their husbands who did the loading. Finally, the hapaiko men who had the most strenuous job of all, moved up to carry the cane into the railroad cars.

They were incredible, those loaders. Will never tired of watching. A man would stoop for an armload of cane, anywhere from one-hundred to two-hundred pounds in an armload, then trot off to the cars where narrow ramps of planking, cleated to give footing, provided walkways into the cars. With the enormous load on his shoulders, the man would trot up the walkway balancing as he went, heave the stalks into the car, and trot back for another load. Some of the men could work like that all day, day after day, loading ton after ton of cane.

But others could not. The Japanese were generally more muscular than the Filipinos and made better loaders. But the Japanese who had remained at Grove Farm were growing too old for loading. Their sons didn't like the work. Every year, the problem grew more acute.

This time Moragne came up with a solution. He had seen cargo slings used for loading sugar cane on other plantations. "Let's try it," he urged. "We still have those tractor cranes

G. N. inherited from the Nawiliwili Harbor job. I can rig them for loading cane in no time."

So they tried slings. After the cutters had finished a section, the pilers would lay a piece of cable. When the pile was ready, the ends of the cable were pulled together cinching the load. The crane lifted the sling and swung it over one of the cane cars where a worker from below pulled a rope that released the snatch block. The cane tumbled into the car.

But Moragne wasn't satisfied. "The slings wear out too fast," he said, shaking his head. "And too much cane gets spilled out on the ground when the sling lets go over the cars. We'll have to think of a better way."

* * *

The labor shortage was growing steadily worse when Broadbent retired at the end of 1936. On January 1, 1937, William P. Alexander became manager of Grove Farm. The new manager explained his philosophy of operation to the supervisors who bossed the irrigating, cultivating, planting, harvesting, and maintenance crews. "The government controls our acreage," he told them, "and there's not much you and I can do about the price of sugar. But we do have control over the way this plantation is run and my job is to see that it is run as efficiently as possible."

To try to keep workers, especially the younger men, to stay on at Grove Farm, the new manager stepped up his activities program. By this time boxing had become the single most popular sport on the Island. Charlie Fern played it up big in his weekly newspaper, as a circulation builder among plantation workers, and Grove Farm developed a champion of Golden Gloves caliber. Head bookkeeper Hib Case and statistician Tsutao Sato coached an active baseball team. Personnel man Fred Weber had a soccer football team. Alexander helped start a Filipino band and promoted family vegetable gardens. At the suggestion of Elsie and Mabel Wilcox, he hired a part-time nurse to help the immigrant wives learn about hygiene and nutrition.

With his interest in scientific farming, Alexander paid particular attention to things like biological control of insect pests: the army worm, the mealybug, the leaf hopper, the cane borer, and the Chinese grasshopper. The development of new and better-producing cane varieties resistant to diseases which attacked older varieties was also an important problem. The new manager also introduced a rapid method of testing the soil with chemicals to determine the exact fertilizer requirements for each field.

The idea for loading with grabs instead of slings came from Ewa Plantation on Oahu where Will Alexander had watched the new operation. He sketched it for Moragne.

"The cranes were fitted out with grabs, like this . . . " Crudely, the manager drew an iron claw resembling a pair of ice tongs. "The pilers stack the cane in piles. Then the crane operator picks up the piles with his grab and dumps the cane into the cars. It's faster than sling loading and saves on manpower."

Moragne studied the sketch. "The hard part is right there, the grab. It'll have to be built to take a beating. Well, we'll get to work on it."

The engineer was right. Designing and building a quick acting, heavy duty grab resulted in several bad starts before Moragne and his ingenious shop foreman, George Jottmann, got the machine they wanted. By spring it was ready. Alexander watched anxiously as the crane moved into position before a huge pile of cane stalks. The great claw opened. Down it came. The claw snapped shut. Swiftly it lifted almost two tons of sugar cane and swung toward the waiting railroad cars. The claw opened and the cane stalks crashed into a car. Still open, the claw swung back to pounce again on the piled up cane.

"It works," said Moragne with a sigh of satisfaction.

But the next day a new problem developed. When Will

Alexander stopped in the field on his morning round, he found the crane idle and the workers standing in a knot, arguing with their supervisor. The manager came hurrying up.

"What's the matter?" he asked.

The supervisor, his face flushed in anger, answered, "These men refuse to work."

"Why?"

"They don't like the new grab. If you ask me, that one over there is the troublemaker."

Alexander turned to a defiant little man with a flat, brown face and flashing eyes. "Why don't you like the new grab?" he asked.

"I no like cheat!" said the little man, shaking his fist.

"Who's cheating you?"

"How you count my load, eh? How you count cars, eh? How you count slings, eh?" the little worker insisted.

Then the manager understood. Always before, the men had worked in small teams. It was easy enough to count the number of cane cars or the number of slings each team loaded per day. The men were paid accordingly. Now the only method of measuring labor was the tonnage each crane loaded per day. The pay had to be divided among the large crews, a dozen or more, piling cane for each crane.

"I know it's different," the manager explained, "but we're not cheating you. Actually, you'll be able to earn more money and not work so hard."

"You say," the worker answered suspiciously.

"All right, I'll give you a choice. If you want, you can work for regular plantation day rates. Or you can try this new system and divide the incentive pay among you. It doesn't matter to me. But I think you'd be foolish not to at least try the new way."

The piling crew finally agreed. As the manager had predicted, they earned more than they had before, even though the work was easier.

Early that summer, Moragne and Jottmann finished tinkering with a boom spray weeder. They mounted the unit on a small caterpillar tractor. The booms extended about thirty feet from each side of the tractor. Set on each boom were spray attachments for applying weed killer to the rows of young cane. The unit worked far better than Alexander and Moragne had hoped, except in strong winds when the spray blew into the operator's face. And the machine could do the work of a dozen men on foot carrying knapsack sprayers.

"By golly, Bill," said Alexander happily, "we're not licked yet."

* * *

There was never any end to the complications of running the plantation. One day early in 1939 a pleasant young man named Dorsey Edwards came in to talk with Will Alexander. The visitor proposed an unorthodox idea that made so much sense Alexander felt a surge of excitement.

"Just a minute," he said, "I want Moragne to be in on this." When the engineer was seated in the office, the manager explained, "Dorsey wants Grove Farm to grow pineapples for his cannery."

Moragne's eyebrows went up. "That's a new wrinkle."

Edwards answered quickly, "I realize that no other sugar plantation has ever gone into pineapples. The two crops would strengthen each other."

"He's right," said Alexander. "Rotation of crops makes sense from an agricultural standpoint."

"Except that we don't know the first thing about growing pineapples," Moragne pointed out.

"You could learn," argued Edwards. "You're planters, aren't you? Any good farmer can learn how to grow pineapples."

Before long Moragne was just as excited as Alexander about the new project. With the approval of the board of directors, they made an experimental fifty-acre planting of pineapples. Other plantation managers shook their heads dubiously.

From pineapples, Grove Farm went into the manufacture of hollow tile blocks in order to develop a more economical way to build termite proof homes for its workers. Then a contractor asked to quarry rock on plantation property and Alexander found himself in the crushed rock business. Probably his most unusual job was setting up a Filipino restaurant in the village to satisfy his unmarried workers.

"It's a good thing I don't have a license," he told his wife one evening over dinner. "They'd put me to work performing marriages, too!"

*   *   *

A new blow fell on February 13, 1940, when Lihue Plantation abruptly announced cancellation of the grinding contract that had been in force since 1917. The notice made clear that Grove Farm would receive a smaller share of the sugar from its crop under the new contract. Gaylord handled negotiations.

"What they're asking could cost us $30,000 to $40,000 a year," he told Will Alexander after a discouraging session with Lihue officials.

The manager frowned. "That will hurt! Wages are going up. Machinery costs are going up. Everything goes up but the price of sugar."

"We aren't beaten yet," said Gaylord doggedly.

The negotiations continued to go badly. As the months went by, Gaylord grew more discouraged. Once he ordered plans for a new mill. Then he abandoned the idea. When the new cost plus contract went into effect on January 1, 1941, the manager knew that Gaylord was far from satisfied.

*   *   *

The labor shortage grew more severe as war clouds gathered over the United States. By June, 1941, Grove Farm had lost eight men to the National Guard mobilization and twenty-five more to defense plants in Honolulu. The labor force was lower than it had been since 1927. By winter, thirty per cent of the field laborers were in defense work. The payroll in one short year had dropped from about 450 to 350.

It didn't seem possible that so few workers could cut and pile almost 130,000 tons of sugar cane. But Alexander and Moragne refused to give up. The manager had sent his engineer out to scout other plantations for labor saving ideas. Moragne came back with a design in his head for a push rake that could replace the big crews required to pile the cane by hand. He explained the new idea to Alexander.

"We can build a rake attachment to fit on the front end of a Caterpillar," the engineer said. "With a little practice, that Caterpillar operator should be able to rake the harvested cane into windrows for the grabs to pick up."

Alexander nodded. "Let's try it!"

There were problems. The bulldozer pushed up rocks and dirt as well as cane stalks. Before the cane could be milled, Lihue Plantation had to add a cleaning plant to its factory. And Grove Farm needed more tractors. All of these things cost money. But in spite of the cost and the headaches, the new method of piling worked well enough to bring in the crop at what would eventually be a saving.

By the end of November, 1941, Will Alexander began to breathe more easily. He and his wife flew to Honolulu the last week in November to relax a bit. Will planned to attend a meeting of the Hawaiian Sugar Planters' Association on Monday, December 8. He and his wife, Alice, stayed with Will's parents in shady Manoa Valley, a suburb of Honolulu. During breakfast Sunday morning, Alexander noticed that the paper hadn't arrived. He sent his son, Bill, out to fetch it.

The young man came back looking puzzled. "Somebody's shooting off a lot of big guns," he said. "There's smoke in the sky like anti-aircraft fire."

Will's father waved away his grandson's worry. "It's a drill. They've been doing it a lot lately."

"It sure looks real to me," said Bill. He went to the radio and flicked the knob. "Maybe the news will have something."

A few moments later the familiar voice of Webley Edwards, a well known Honolulu radio personality, brought them up short. He spoke in deadly earnest, "Japanese aircraft are bombing Pearl Harbor. I repeat, this is not a drill. This is the real McCoy.

Japanese planes are bombing Pearl Harbor . . . "

They all stared at one another in disbelief. But the voice went on, giving instructions for all military personnel to report to duty stations immediately. Will put down his fork.

"I think I'd better get back to Grove Farm right away," he said quietly.

CHAPTER

24

A week of nightmare went
by before the plantation manager was able to leave Honolulu.
During those seven hectic days, the Islands were put under
martial law and the military immediately clamped a ban on
inter-island travel. Rumors flew. A newspaper headline thundered, "Invasion Threatens." Alexander heard hysterical stories of sabotage by local Japanese. These later proved untrue.

Will didn't know what to believe. Like most people in
Hawaii, he understood better than other Americans the com-
pleteness of the Japanese victory at Pearl Harbor. Now the
Hawaiian Islands, 2,100 miles from the nearest United States
port, lay helpless before the enemy. If an invasion came, Hawaii
would have to fight the battle alone.

On the Sunday following the bombing of Pearl Harbor, the plantation manager and his wife flew back to Kauai in an inter-island plane that had been blacked out with heavy paint over the windows. As he stepped from the gloomy interior of the airplane, he realized that the war had gotten to Kauai before him.

Work at Grove Farm had come almost to a standstill. Moragne was spending most of his time as assistant director of the Office of Civilian Defense under newspaper editor Charlie Fern. They were busy organizing beach patrols and setting up emergency fortifications in case of attack. Hib Case had been given the job of Food Administrator for the island. Every young man on Kauai was trying to enlist.

At the Grove Farm office, Will Alexander wasn't sure where his responsibility lay, or what he should do about it. He went inside and sat at his familiar desk. He was at loose ends. What should he do first? He was still pondering when the telephone rang. It was Charlie Fern.

"Will, I've got a job for you," said Fern crisply.

"Shoot!"

"We're trying to get evacuation camps ready for civilians in case the Japanese invade. How about taking some of your men up in the mountains back of Hanamaulu and clearing a camp site for us? We'll need latrines and fireplaces. Can you do that?"

"I'll be glad to."

"Pick a spot near a water supply, Will. Let me know when you find a good place."

"All right," said Alexander, hanging up.

But before he could move out of his chair, an Army Colonel walked in. He seemed impatient as he shook hands with Will. "I understand that this plantation owns a rock crusher," the Colonel said without sitting down.

"You understand correctly. It's the only large one on the island."

The colonel looked relieved. "Good. I didn't think we'd

be so lucky. It's Mr. Alexander, isn't it? Well, I'm with the Army Engineers. We have an airstrip and gun emplacements to build, and we don't have time to waste. I'm going to ask if you can give us the entire output of that crusher on an around the clock basis?"

"We can do that," answered Will promptly.

"How about hauling the stuff? We don't have enough . . . "

"We'll do the hauling," said Will.

The Colonel thrust out his hand. "I can't tell you how much better I feel," he said in gratitude. "You're going to save us weeks of wasted effort."

"It's our pleasure," said Will.

The officer had hardly gone when Moragne hurried in. "Welcome home," he said cheerfully.

Alexander tried to sound displeased. "Fine thing! Just when I need you most you get yourself a soft government job."

Moragne grinned. "Next week I'm going to ask them for a raise . . . to five cents an hour." Then his tone grew serious. "Will, the plantations are all pooling equipment to help the Army Engineers until they can get their own stuff over here. Grove Farm has a couple of bulldozers the engineers can put to good use. How about it?"

"Take them," Will answered. "If the Japanese beat us, we won't be using bulldozers."

"And we need men. Especially equipment operators. Can do?"

"All right, Bill. Thank the Lord we're in a slack season. Take whomever you need."

Moragne hurried out. By this time Will felt a little breathless. The phone rang again. This time Alexander recognized Case's slow drawl on the line. "Will, I suppose you know that the military has taken over all shipping in the islands?"

"I know."

"There may be a food shortage before this is over, especially if the Japanese start sinking supply ships from the West Coast.

We have orders to be as self-sufficient as possible. So I'm asking all plantation managers to cooperate by planting other food crops as well as sugar from now on. I'm working up a planting program now that should keep us fairly well supplied. In the meantime, you'd better get about ten acres ready for something like corn, beans, and potatoes."

"All right, Hib."

Alexander replaced the telephone and sat for a moment, trying to collect his thoughts. He felt much better now that the indecision was over. Well, he'd better get to work and help win the war!

* * *

Gas rationing quickly went into effect. And food rationing. The blackout immediately became a nightly annoyance. With nothing else to do in the evenings, Will and Alice usually turned in around sundown.

Besides, those first few days were exhausting. Every night Will would tumble into bed, worn out from the feverish preparations for war. Plantation bulldozers quickly cleared the evacuation centers in the mountains. Grove Farm workers were laying stone fireplaces and digging latrines. Several acres of cane land had been planted to string beans and Irish potatoes. School children were hoeing the weeds after class. At Will's house, the home G. N. had built for his nephew Charles, there was a freshly dug air raid shelter under the big mango tree in the yard. Assigned to the shelter were the plantation manager and his wife and the yardman and his wife, Mr. and Mrs. Shima, who lived on the edge of the yard. At the sound of the mill whistle, they jumped out of bed and hurried into the shelter. The planes never came. But one scare followed another.

Will awoke after 1:00 A.M. on December 30, 1941. He thought he'd heard an explosion. Then it came again, a double concussion. There was another one! Suddenly he realized what it was. Shell fire!

He scrambled out of bed and ran into the yard. In back of

the house he saw a glow in the sky. The cane was on fire! The shelling continued in regular bursts from the direction of Nawiliwili Harbor. Will ran for the car. By this time Alice had come out. They drove through the darkness.

The parachute flare startled them both. It lit up the whole countryside. Ahead they saw fire trucks. Will parked the car and ran ahead. Firemen were hastily running a hose into the cane field. Moragne was there, shouting orders.

He saw Alexander. "One of those flares set the cane afire," he explained hurriedly.

"What's going on?" asked Will.

"There's a Japanese submarine sitting off the harbor. I think they're trying to blow up the fuel tanks."

Another man came running up. "What can we do about it?"

Moragne answered hopelessly, "We can't do anything. We don't have anything to shoot back with."

In thirty minutes it was all over. The submarine slid back into the dark water. On the Island, the people wondered when the invasion would come.

*   *   *

By March 31, 1942, Grove Farm had produced 8,633 pounds of string beans and 4,195 pounds of Irish potatoes. An airstrip had suddenly appeared on the beach at Barking Sands, on the western tip of Kauai. Enough crushed rock from Grove Farm quarry had gone into the construction to build a road fifteen miles long.

But for Will, harvesting was the major effort. Every man, woman, and child on the plantation helped in some way. Still there were not enough of them to get in the crop. Luckily, Moragne's Civilian Defense duties had eased with the arrival of regular troops. He put into operation a technique for cutting cane that Will had seen at Kekaha. Bulldozers, equipped with low slung cutting knives, sheared off the cane and pushed it into windrows for the grabs to pick up.

To Will's great relief, the technique proved successful, though a new worry kept nagging at him. Workers were still finding unexploded shells fired from the Japanese submarine in the fields above the harbor. Alexander had nightmares that one of the shells would be pushed into a windrow, loaded into a cane car, and sent to the mill where it would blow the factory sky high.

With the complete mechanization of the cane harvest, the manager had to depend more heavily on the bulldozers, battered from overtime construction work. The tractors were wearing out, and parts were difficult to buy. New machines more difficult still. "Keep them together with bailing wire if you have to," Alexander told his men.

* * *

The fear of invasion hung like a gloomy cloud over everything they did. All over the Pacific the news had been bad. The Japanese were fanning out scoring spectacular victories. Bataan had fallen, Corregidor. All over Hawaii the people constantly wondered, will we be next?

Will was sitting at his desk on June 3, listening to the radio station Charlie Fern had added to his newspaper interest, when a special bulletin came on.

"We have just received word that a Japanese fleet has been sighted in the North Pacific near Midway Island. Reports indicated that the armada includes aircraft carriers, battleships, and transports in addition to supporting craft. The fleet is believed to be heading . . . "

Abruptly the radio went dead. Will waited. There was only silence. Impulsively, he dialed Charlie Fern. The explanation was curt and unsatisfactory. "We've been ordered off the air," said the newspaper publisher.

In the outer office, the plantation manager saw frightened faces. Alice had the same look when he stepped into the house. "This may be it," he told her gently.

Now the Honolulu radio stations had gone dead, also. The day dragged on with no news. Then the next. Everyone tried to act as though nothing were happening. But it was like smiling at a funeral. Another day dawned. Will and Alice went to a wedding. The strain showed on all of the guests.

The reception was half over when a late arrival hurried in with a fresh rumor. "Carrier planes are landing at Barking Sands airstrip," he said breathlessly. They've got bullet holes in them. There must be a big battle going on."

That night was the most nerve-wracking of all. They waited for news. But none came. Only the ominous rumor of planes battered in a distant battle. Finally, the next day, radio stations broke silence.

"United States Naval forces have scored a decisive victory over the Japanese at Midway in the North Pacific. Four Japanese aircraft carriers have been sunk. The Japs have also lost an estimated 250 planes and 3,500 men. American losses are one aircraft carrier, 150 planes, and 300 men . . . "

Will put his arm around Alice. "We owe those boys our lives," he said softly.

* * *

With the threat of invasion past, Alexander concentrated his energies on the production of sugar, pronounced a necessary food by the War Production Board. The draft boards deferred sugar workers as essential to the war effort. Every time Alexander heard of a new victory on the battlefront, he tried to match it with a modest victory of his own.

The battle of Guadalcanal began August 7, 1942. Meanwhile, on Grove Farm, a much less heroic battle was going forward against wasted sugar in the form of broken cane stalks left in the field after the mechanical harvesters finished. These short lengths of cane stalks represented tons of sugar. To prevent the waste, Moragne and his boys in the shop built a rake that hitched behind a small tractor and pulled the broken pieces of cane into piles. The men called the new piece of equipment a Liiliiko rake.

In 1943, American soldiers and marines moved on to Attu, Bougainville, and Tarawa. On Grove Farm the soldiers were boys and girls who wielded hoes, helped spread fertilizer, and replanted seed cane by hand in places where the stools, or clumps, had died out. The biggest problem was to keep the old, worn out tractors running.

June 6, 1944, brought D-Day to Europe. The same year brought a new crisis in labor on the plantation. Since the beginning of the war, workers had been frozen to their jobs and prohibited from traveling to Honolulu. Many of the men were disgruntled with the regulation. When the travel restriction was lifted on August 6, 1944, there was an immediate exodus to Honolulu. Some of the men didn't like the big city and returned to the plantation. But freedom of travel meant fewer workers in the long run. To help meet the emergency, Moragne's crew developed a replanting machine that did away with this time consuming hand operation.

In 1945 American armies crossed the Rhine and the marines took Iwo Jima. Germany surrendered to the invading Allies on May 4. On Grove Farm a different kind of invasion was taking place. Quietly, the International Longshoremen's and Warehousemen's Union was organizing the workers. In June, Grove Farm laborers formed a bargaining unit and voted to be represented by the ILWU. Alexander made no attempt to interfere with the Union. "They're within their rights," he said.

The final victory came on August 14 when the Japanese surrendered. Will was jubilant. At last, it was over. Along with the exciting war news came an item of local interest. In the Philippines, 6,000 laborers had signed up to work in Hawaii. Within a few months, the shortage in plantation labor should ease off.

"Now you can take a vacation," Alice told him. "You've earned it."

"Wait a few more months until things get back to normal," he told her.

* * *

"Back to normal" never came. First, the Union strenuously objected to bringing in new workers. Then, after they finally arrived, Grove Farm received the wrong men. On the advice of old timers on the plantation, Alexander had carefully made up a list of applicants who were related to men already working at Grove Farm. But in the last minute rush of labor recruiting, the list never got to the right place, and Grove Farm's applicants were sent to other plantations. Of the eighty-eight men who were sent to Grove Farm, fifty of them left almost immediately to be near relatives. Only twenty-six were re-hired from other plantations.

From the moment the war ended, Union leaders began agitating for higher wages and, especially, a change in relationship between sugar workers and their bosses: no more free housing, free medical service, free fuel. Instead, the Union asked that the plantations pay their men wages high enough to pay their own rent, medical bills, and other living expenses.

Will Alexander knew that the time was ripe for Union demands. For long years during the war, the men had become increasingly impatient with the travel restrictions. The sugar workers kept comparing their wages with those paid in defense plants. The comparison hurt, especially if you didn't take into account the low cost of living on a sugar plantation. But Union leaders called the plantation fringe benefits paternalism.

The walkout on all sugar plantations in Hawaii began on September 1, 1946. Will knew that most of his workers, the old timers in particular, were as confused and frightened as he was. The first day, Shima came furtively to the door and said, "I cannot do the yard work now, Mr. Alexander. They won't let me."

"I know," said Will heavily. From then on with Alice's help he did it himself.

A few of the supervisors, who were not in the bargaining unit, sneaked into the fields during the first few days and opened the gates in the irrigation ditches. A couple of the more militant Union members threatened to beat up the supervisors.

"Don't provoke them. We don't want violence," Will told his foremen.

At a meeting of the plantation managers on Kauai, the question came up, "Shall we let striking workers stay in our plantation houses? We have every right to kick them off our property!" Will voted against such a move. "What purpose would it serve to kick them out?" he reasoned. "When this is over, we'll want them back again."

He marvelled at the efficiency of the Union leaders who kept their members busy planting gardens to grow food, organizing fishing and hunting parties. There were Union activities to keep the wives busy and even programs for the children.

Yet, it was difficult to be reasonable when, day after day, Will watched the cane die a little more, the supple green leaves turn brittle and yellow. He watched the weeds choke out the tender young shoots of sugar cane. There was nothing he could do about it but wait as negotiations continued in Honolulu between Union officials and representatives of the sugar industry. The irrigation ditches remained dry, and the soil turned to dust. Week after week, Will grew more deeply discouraged.

The charges and counter-charges flew faster as the strike dragged on. Union leaders called the sugar planters paternalistic, power hungry. Sugar spokesmen accused the Union of having communistic leanings and wanting to wreck the economy. The Union claimed that the plantations could easily pay higher wages since the price of sugar was at its highest point in history, $111 a ton. Industry leaders answered that costs had risen as high as the price of sugar, and that they were faced with the need of replacing expensive equipment worn out during the war.

By early November there had been violence and rioting on

some plantations. At Grove Farm, an uneasy peace prevailed. But two thousand tons of sugar had already been lost. By mid-November Will found himself wondering if the strike would ever end. The workers showed no signs of giving in. Industry spokesmen were just as obstinate. At last, the break came. And on November 19 the men went back to work after a settlement in which the Union won for its members the highest agricultural wages paid anywhere in the world.

"I just hope we can afford them," Will muttered when he heard the news.

The workers on Grove Farm seemed as eager to go back to work as the manager. By February 1947, the weeds were under control once more. The old team was back again, functioning smoothly: Bill Moragne, now assistant manager; Hib Case, office manager; Fred Weber, who handled employee relations; George Jottmann in the shop.

Will finally decided it was time for him to take a vacation, his first in over six years. In April, he tidied up his desk and said good-by to his staff. Then he got behind the wheel of his mud-spattered sedan and drove home.

But it was hard to let go after so long. As he drove out of the plantation headquarters he glanced at the rows of new machines he had helped to develop. He turned into the highway. Puhi Village was on his left, a rental unit now with all workers covered by the Union Contract. So much had happened since he'd come to Grove Farm. He would miss the excitement, even for a little while.

CHAPTER

25

The old plantation yard was serene and still when Gaylord drove his Buick slowly through the wide entrance and across the broad lawn, his uncle's rain gauge still standing in the center. A middle-aged Japanese gardener looked up from where he was hoeing out crabgrass near the kamani tree. No one else was in sight. The old frame office was locked now, and the venerable Grove Farm house seemed to doze in the sun, the slanting roof sweeping gracefully toward the sky. As Gaylord stepped out of the car, he felt sure G. N. must be watching from the veranda of his cottage, a big cigar in his hand. He walked briskly up the steps and knocked, hoping his uncle would approve of what he was about to do.

Elsie, his sister, answered the door, and Mabel was waiting

inside. The family resemblance was strong in all three of them. They greeted one another warmly but not effusively. Then Gaylord took a chair as Elsie and Mabel sat down on the over-stuffed sofa near the fireplace. Gaylord watched them as he tried to frame what he had to say so that they would both understand.

Generally they took his advice about plantation policy. But he knew from uncomfortable experience that both women had minds of their own. His sisters had carved their own careers, and sometimes he wondered how they found time to undertake all of the projects they were constantly getting into. Neither had married. Instead, Elsie had gone into education and politics winning a long-term appointment as Kauai Commissioner of Public Instruction for the Territory of Hawaii and two elections to the Territorial Senate. Meanwhile, Mabel had been just as busy directing Nursing Service of the Health Department on Kauai, then the Welfare Department, and, later, serving six years on the Territorial Board of Health.

"Well, now, what's this mysterious matter you want to take up with us?" asked Elsie, her lips curved faintly in a teasing smile.

Mabel reached for a cigaret. "I hope you haven't unearthed a family skeleton," she said with the same wry humor.

Gaylord was used to their teasing. It was a Wilcox trait. So he ignored it and said, "I came to talk about the future of Grove Farm." His sisters became instantly alert. "It doesn't look bright," Gaylord continued bluntly. "Oh, we've done all right so far. But time is running against the small plantation. Hana has gone under. So has Waimanalo and Waianae. There's a reason."

"We're listening," said Elsie.

Gaylord continued, "We're feeling the pinch already. The new grinding contract with Lihue was at our expense. Now that the men are organized, we can expect wages to keep going up. Equipment costs more every year. But the price of sugar has not kept pace with these costs. A small plantation is no longer efficient. In order to bring the cost factors in line, you need a large operation. Sugar's become a big man's game."

"Then why don't we expand?" asked Mabel.

"It isn't that simple," Gaylord answered. "To get maximum efficiency, we need as much control as possible over every phase of the operation. That includes manufacturing the sugar, and we don't have a chance of controlling that as long as Lihue grinds our cane. What we need is our own mill to give us independence and a big enough crop to make it pay. Otherwise our costs will eventually catch up to our income, and that will be the end of Grove Farm. Not tomorrow or for quite a few years. But if we don't think ahead in time, I believe the plantation might eventually have to go under."

Elsie asked crisply, "What do you suggest?"

Gaylord answered with care. "This has been on my mind for quite a few years. Now I think I've found a way for us to double our acreage and get a mill of our own all in one stroke." He hesitated, then went on. "It would require a merger."

"With whom?" his sisters asked in one voice.

"Koloa Plantation."

Elsie and Mabel stared at him in disbelief. It was Elsie who said, "Hasn't Koloa been losing money for quite a few years?"

Gaylord nodded. "That's why they are ready to merge. They need someone to assume about $1,000,000 in obligations."

Mabel asked, "Where in the world would we get that much money?"

"We have the fund that G. N. put away for a mill we never built. And we can borrow the rest," said Gaylord.

They all sat in silence for a few moments. Then Elsie said, "Do you really believe this is a good move?"

"I do," he answered firmly. "The first thing we need is a mill. Koloa has one. The next thing we need is more land.

Koloa is about the size of Grove Farm. By combining the two small plantations into one we can eliminate duplication in manpower, equipment, administrative costs. Believe me, such a merger would put us in a much better competitive position."

"But it's quite a risk, isn't it, borrowing so much money?" asked Mabel quietly.

"Yes, it's a risk," said Gaylord.

Mabel put another question. "Do you think all of the family stockholders will approve?"

"No, I don't suppose they will," Gaylord answered honestly. "Taking over Koloa will strain our resources for quite a few years. There may not be very much left for dividends for a while. But G. N. left his stock in trust to us. It's up to us to decide what he'd do."

"What do you think he'd do?" asked Elsie.

Gaylord answered without hesitation. "I'm sure he'd take the risk. That's one thing that never frightened him when the odds were in his favor. He always did what was best for the plantation."

"Then I'm willing," said Elsie.

"Yes, so am I," said Mabel.

Gaylord got to his feet. "Good. Frankly, nothing may come of this and I want to get more information before we make a final decision. And we might not even be able to make a deal. But I think we have a chance. I'll tell Bill Moragne and Hib Case, of course, and Will Alexander when he comes back. No one else will know, so keep the information to yourselves."

* * *

Bill Moragne was sitting at his desk in his shirt sleeves when Gaylord broke the news. The assistant manager sat bolt upright, his eyes alive with excitement. Gaylord watched the younger man, pleased by his enthusiasm.

"Well, Bill, what do you think of the idea?"

"I like it," said Moragne, trying to keep the excitement from showing in his sun-browned face. "We'd double our cane production and add a mill besides."

Gaylord nodded. "Right! The big question though is, can we turn Koloa into a paying proposition. It's a sorry mess now. What do you think?"

The assistant manager didn't hesitate. "I don't see why Koloa can't be put on a paying basis. But we should find out what's wrong and how to correct it before we make up our minds."

Gaylord nodded again. He had learned to place a good deal of confidence in the younger man's judgment. "All right, see what you can find out, and let me know. Meanwhile, don't breathe a word of this to anyone."

That night Moragne could hardly sleep. The bold concept left him breathless. His wife Jean sensed his excitement and knew he would be the first to tell her when the time was right. It was seldom that an assistant plantation manager had the opportunity to take part in such a challenging project, and now, with Will Alexander away, the responsibility rested squarely on Moragne's shoulders. He had come a long way from his days as a rod boy on his father's surveying crew.

After his 5:30 cup of coffee the next morning, Moragne drove his dusty sedan away from plantation headquarters through the cane fields toward the knife-like mountain ridges that separated Koloa Plantation from Grove Farm. His engineering instinct told him that this natural barrier would be the greatest obstacle to a profitable merger of the two plantations.

He parked the company car at the end of the road at the edge of the last field. Then he got out and began hiking up the jungle-covered slope. Quickly, the ascent became more rugged. But the morning was still fresh and he climbed steadily, breaking his own trail, breathing deep of the crisp, mountain air.

He was forty-five minutes reaching the highest ridge. Panting now, his boots drenched with dew, he sank gratefully down on a jagged rock and turned his head to see how far he had come.

Grove Farm lay spread out in a vast panorama below, an undulating green-brown carpet that stretched from Nawiliwili Harbor to the foothills, 3,041 acres of sugar cane. Moragne felt a surge of pride as he saw how carefully tended the fields were, now smooth and free of rocks, how proper fertilization made them uniformly green. His eye could follow the railroad tracks that bisected the plantation. But he was more interested in the new roads that neatly linked field after field. He knew that meant freedom from the expense and cumbersome operation of the railroad. In a few more years, Grove Farm wouldn't need the rails at all!

At last, Moragne turned his face to the other side of the mountain. The contrast was startling. From the spiny mountain ridges, the land sloped toward a grim, beautiful, lava-bound seacoast. In the distance the fields were studded with rocks. Cinder cones from the last volcanic activity on Kauai made brown, arid islands in a sea of green.

No wonder Koloa was losing money. Those rocks would make junk out of mechanical harvesting equipment within a matter of days. The only way to harvest in such fields was by expensive hand labor. The fields could be cleared of rocks. But it would be a terribly expensive operation.

He looked for roads but found only a few. Koloa was just starting to haul cane by truck but was mostly dependent upon an old-fashioned railroad to bring cane to the mill. Maintenance costs must be fantastic. The plantation needed a whole network of new roads. The expense of such an undertaking staggered him.

Yet, the prize was worth the battle: 3,755 acres of fertile cane land in a hot, dry climate that was ideal for producing sugar. And the greatest prize of all, small and toy-like in the distance far below, was the mill. No more limitations on acreage. No more waiting a turn to have the crop ground. No more second-rate status.

With this prize came the biggest obstacle of all. How to get Grove Farm cane to Koloa mill. Moragne measured the distances with his eye. To go around the mountain Grove Farm trucks would have to drive anywhere from fifteen to twenty-five miles on each round trip to the mill. It cost four cents per mile to haul a ton of cane, and Grove Farm's crop had come to nearly 150,000 tons. The hauling bill would come close to $100,000. Would such an operation be economically sound?

On the dizzy height of the mountain, Moragne remembered Gaylord's words. "I think the real key to this merger may be a tunnel through the mountain. At least, it would give us a short-cut to the mill." It was a sound idea. Such a tunnel would need to be about half a mile long. It would have to be large enough for the biggest trucks. Digging a tunnel like that would be fantastically expensive.

Still, the logic of the idea remained. A tunnel would cut from two to ten miles from the distance between Grove Farm fields and Koloa mill. In only one year the short-cut could save the company up to $42,000. And the tunnel would eliminate the need for building maybe seven extra miles of heavy-duty road around the mountain. At last, Moragne climbed down from his high perch. His mind churned with ideas. The tunnel was the most exciting of all.

* * *

Gaylord called the moves with all of his uncle's cool daring. First he beat back an attempt by another plantation to take Koloa away. On December 5, 1947, he won approval in principle for his plan at a stockholders meeting. But a militant minority with 2,200 votes opposed him.

Stockholders weren't his only critics. Managers at other plantations made jokes about the merger to Will Alexander. "You'll lose your shirt on that mill alone," they told him. "It's nothing but a coffee pot!"

"I know what condition the mill is in," said Gaylord, unperturbed. "It can be modernized."

With Case, the statistician, providing cost estimates and financial statements, Gaylord began negotiating for loans. To the amazement of quite a few skeptics, he quickly arranged to borrow enough money to meet Koloa's $1,000,000 in accumulated debts.

On January 5, 1948, the board of directors put the merger into effect. They named Will Alexander, general manager of the combined plantations; Bill Moragne, manager of operations; Karl Berg, assistant manager of operations.

"Well, we did it," Gaylord told them soberly. "Now let's make the plan work."

* * *

From that moment on there was a crisis every hour, and there were never enough hours in the day. Will Alexander had his hands full trimming the labor force to avoid duplication of jobs. He met almost daily with ILWU Regional Director Jack Hall, or members of his staff, to negotiate an agreement with the Union. Before they had finished, the payroll was cut from 710 to about 580.

Moragne's job, under Will's direction, was to integrate the physical operation of the two plantations: seed cutting, planting, weeding, harvesting, irrigation. The mill was a coffee pot, all right! It broke down constantly. But Moragne's evil angel was a sky hook salesman.

He had bustled into the office one day smoothly quoting statistics to prove that he had the perfect answer to Grove Farm's problem of hauling cane to the mill. As he talked, he brought out charts and diagrams and illustrations to make his points.

"Gentlemen, you are gazing upon a revolutionary new concept in freight transportation," he told them grandly. "The principle is that of the cable car. As you know, this amazingly safe and simple device has been used for years to carry passengers over difficult terrain. Now the same principle has been applied to freight hauling."

"Are you suggesting that we use this gadget to carry our cane to the mill?" asked Moragne in surprise.

"Exactly! Up and over the mountain, the shortest distance between the fields and the mill. The Sky Way is almost completely automatic, thus reducing personnel costs to a minimum. This unit is coming into increasing use in the lumber industry. Onomea Plantation on the Big Island has installed one."

"We've been thinking in terms of a tunnel," said Moragne doubtfully.

The salesman shook his head in annoyance. "Tunneling through that mountain would cost you up to a million dollars. I can install a Sky Way for a quarter of that."

There was no getting rid of the man. He hounded Will. He made life miserable for Moragne. He forced himself on Gaylord, even after they learned that the operating costs of the unit at Onomea Plantation were prohibitive.

In spite of their annoyance with the salesman, one awkward fact made them listen. The successful merger of the two plantations depended in large part on a solution to the problem of quick, cheap transportation of harvested cane to the mill. A cable car over the mountains was one solution. In spite of Moragne's insistence on a tunnel, the Sky Way cost much less to install. So the board of directors appropriated $10,000 to get Moragne started on plans for a tunnel and another $5,000 for a survey of the Sky Way plan.

* * *

In February 1948, the operations manager sat at his desk staring at the figures he'd written on his scratch pad. The figures were estimates by construction company men of what they

Grove Farm's bulk seed cane planter, 1962

Aerial view of mechanical equipment used on Grove Farm, 1963;
plantation headquarters near center at flag pole;
Puhi Village in background

Grove Farm harvesting operation, 1964. *Top:* Pushing cane into windrows. *Center:* Loading by cane grab into 30-ton trailer. *Bottom:* Hauling sugar cane from field to mill.

Grove Farm Koloa mill, 1964; land reclamation in progress
in right foreground

Nawiliwili Harbor, 1964, with Grove Farm's Haiku Division in background

William Middleton Moragne, 1954,
Grove Farm manager since 1953,
vice president since 1953

Gaylord Parke Wilcox, assistant to
George N. Wilcox from 1921
to 1933, president of Grove
Farm Company since 1933

Wilcox home at Grove Farm, 1958

might charge for putting a tunnel through the mountain. Not one estimate was below half a million dollars. If only there were a cheaper way!

With a sigh, Moragne reached for his mail. Among the letters he saw a new surplus bulletin. Eagerly he picked it from the pile. He enjoyed poring over the catalogues. Honolulu since the war had been full of Army and Navy surplus of all kinds. Already he had bought a dozen bargains in machinery which he'd converted to plantation use.

He leafed idly through the bulletin until an unusual item caught his eye; Tunnel Car, five cubic yard capacity, Mokuleia, Oahu. He felt excitement grip him! Of course, why hadn't he thought of it before? The Army must have used tunneling equipment to build its underground installations!

On the next line he read, "Tunnel Locomotive." Then, "Mucking Machine." Then "Air Blowers with Compressors." Here was a complete set of tunneling equipment. His eyes shone! Why, with equipment like this, he could build the tunnel himself! Hastily, he read on. The equipment would come up for bids in three weeks.

He couldn't wait that long. The next morning he stepped off an airplane in Honolulu. In a rented car, he drove across the Island to an area named in the bulletin, Mokuleia, a narrow wilderness of thorny kiawe trees between an endless strip of tawny beach and a range of sharp, spiny mountains. Here the army had built an air field. Now he could see only empty barracks among the kiawes. There was no sign of tunneling equipment.

He drove to the gate keeper's shack and explained his problem. The man said, "I've never seen any tunneling equipment around here. But you're welcome to look if you want."

"Are there any underground installations in those cliffs?" he was asked.

"Yep! You'll find an old command center over back of them trees. But it's dark as pitch in there."

"I brought a flashlight," said Moragne.

Following the man's directions, he drove to the foot of the cliffs that rose dramatically from the jungle. He got out and scouted until he found the face of the tunnel. Slowly he entered. The sunlight didn't penetrate very far. He snapped on his flashlight and pushed on.

The tunnel, he saw, was being used as a storage area. Boxes were piled along the walls, machinery stood covered with dust. But he saw no sign of a locomotive or the mucker. He went on, stumbling in the thick darkness.

His flashlight showed him that the floor was littered with old pieces of cable and odd scraps of iron. Then the beam splashed against a looming object that stood higher than his head. The mucker! Moragne's heart thudded against his ribs. And there were the tunnel cars. He moved the beam of the flashlight in a slow arc. He saw an electric railroad engine. Then another. He couldn't resist climbing into the locomotives. The batteries were dead, but otherwise, the locomotives seemed almost new. Best of all, he found an enormous stack of spare parts.

Now he was ready. He couldn't wait to put his plan to Gaylord, who listened carefully, as Moragne, trying not to show his enthusiasm, outlined his idea.

"That equipment is worth at least a quarter of a million dollars new. I think we can get it for a fraction of that. After all, there's not much demand for tunneling equipment in the Hawaiian Islands. With that equipment, we can build the tunnel ourselves at half of what we would have to pay a contractor."

Gaylord eyed Moragne shrewdly. "You're a good engineer, Bill, but have you ever put through a vehicular tunnel?"

"I've put through plenty of irrigation tunnels," Moragne answered evenly. "I don't think it will be very different."

The older man smiled, pleased. "I like your spirit, Bill. Go ahead!"

Three weeks later, through a surplus dealer, a bid of ten

cents on the dollar was made for the equipment, and the whole lot was brought for $26,000.

* * *

The Grove Farm tunnel project, when it was announced, caught the imagination of the whole sugar industry. No one had ever heard of boring through a mountain just so cane hauling trucks could have a shortcut to the mill. Suddenly the merger seemed practical.

Yet, Moragne was worried. He knew that Gaylord and the other directors were appropriating enormous sums for mill repairs, new roads, replacement of machinery, clearing rocks from the fields. He had to push the tunnel through with the least possible cost. There could be no mistakes!

He laid his plans with care. "The trick is to avoid tunneling through dirt pockets. That means cementing in," he explained to Will Alexander. If we can tunnel through solid rock the whole way, it will save time and money."

"How do you avoid hitting dirt pockets?" Alexander wanted to know.

"We do a little drilling first."

So Moragne and his crew spent months boring holes from the top of the mountain along the projected tunnel bore to make sure it would not strike dirt. At last, the engineer was satisfied.

In September of 1948 a tunneling crew was hired which had just finished a job on west Kauai and began drilling into the mountain from the Koloa side. By that time, interest in the project had subsided. In fact, few people were aware that the work had started. Moragne didn't mind. He was more interested in the absolute accuracy of the tunnel alignment, worked out by active, grey-haired Elbert Gillin, an old timer from Koloa Plantation. And he was overjoyed with the way the tunnel locomotives, with fresh batteries, worked as good as new.

* * *

By 1949 Grove Farm had borrowed $2,000,000, mortgaging all sugar now owned or hereinafter produced and owned by the company. In that year, the board of directors appropriated almost $400,000 for road building and new equipment. Early in 1950, another $300,000 went for modernization of the Koloa division. Will Alexander watched expenses mount with growing concern. He knew Grove Farm faced more years of spending before Koloa would support itself.

Luckily, because of Moragne's ingenuity, the tunnel would cost only a little more than $200,000, less than half of the original estimates. And that wasn't all. Every truckload of rock that came out of the tunnel was put to use as a base for the wide, heavy duty road that connected the tunnel and the mill. Also, every rock that came off the Koloa fields was put to work as a foundation for more of the new roads that crisscrossed the old plantation. Nothing was wasted.

Yet, in 1949, for the first time in its history, Grove Farm Company paid no dividend. There was grumbling from some of the minority stockholders. But Gaylord didn't seem worried. So Will gritted his teeth and hung on.

*   *   *

He didn't remember when the pressure began to ease. It happened gradually. Dividends were resumed. The tunnel was completed April 29, 1949. By that time the hectic process of making one plantation out of two had tapered off. Now the new Grove Farm was a smoothly functioning unit. At the end of 1950, the Korean War pushed the price of sugar to the high World War II levels.

"I think the worst is over," Will told his wife one day.

But Grove Farm wasn't the same. It was not just bigger but different. The easy familiarity wasn't there. Things were more business-like. With a start, Will realized that this is the way Broadbent must have felt before him. Perhaps it was time to let younger men take over.

So, near the end of 1952, with no regrets, Will Alexander submitted his decision to retire. One of the last jobs he completed on the plantation was his annual report. He was meticulous, as usual, carefully drafting the manuscript in long hand because he had never learned to use a typewriter.

Yet, as he put down the dry statistics, his mind ranged back over the years that had been so exciting: the depression, then the war, the merger! He had been lucky to live through so much! He smiled to himself with pride as he realized that G. N. would hardly recognize his plantation now. Grove Farm had just produced a record crop of 30,400 tons of sugar on four thousand acres. Better still, each acre had produced 7.73 tons, almost three tons more than when he had taken over as manager. Already the new mill was grinding seventy per cent of the Grove Farm crop, Lihue mill the remainder. A network of new, all-weather, rock-based roads linked the fields to the mill. And every day dozens of trucks rumbled straight through a hole in the mountain, the biggest miracle of all.

He stacked the handwritten pages neatly into a pile. On his way out of the office, he gave them to the secretary for typing. Then he stepped outside. At last, it was over. And it wasn't as difficult as he'd expected, not with Moragne to step into his place. That fellow was one of the best sugar men in the Islands. "He should be," Alexander told himself with secret satisfaction as he climbed into his dusty sedan. "I've trained him for twenty-two years."

CHAPTER

26

Moragne took a small vial from his desk drawer. He pulled the cork and carefully shook out a small heap of white powder upon a clean sheet of paper on his desk.

"Go ahead, taste it," he said.

Gaylord took a pinch of the stuff between his fingers and touched it to his tongue. "Sweet," he said. "Did our chemist make this?"

"From Grove Farm ti," said Moragne proudly.

"It's the best yet." Gaylord settled himself comfortably in a chair. "Bill, I think we're ready to try commercial production, don't you? I want you to step up our plantings. How many acres of ti do we have in now?"

"A little more than three and a half."

"Well, let's put in double that much this year," said Gaylord briskly. "And I think it's time to set up our own factory. We might start by borrowing some of that experimental equipment the HSPA Experiment Station is using."

"Yes, sir," said Moragne.

Gaylord gave his manager a shrewd glance. "Don't you think it's time to get into levulose?"

"The possibilities sound very good," said Moragne carefully. "But it's too early to make a firm decision."

Gaylord answered with a bit of impatience. "I know that, Bill, but it isn't too early to begin experimenting. We're in the sugar business, aren't we? Well, here's a brand new sugar product! Levulose, one of the most chemically pure forms of sugar known to man. So pure it can be used for intravenous injections. Think of it! The only levulose now sold commercially is a very expensive product. We've proved that we can extract levulose in its natural form from the old Hawaiian ti plant. At $27 a pound, why shouldn't we explore the possibility of producing a better product at a lower cost than anyone else?"

"I said the possibilities look good," Moragne answered quickly.

Gaylord hardly heard him. "Besides, ti will grow on land we can't plant to sugar. And if we can get a factory going, we might be able to farm out contracts to small planters and start a new industry on this Island. What's wrong with that?"

"Nothing, Mr. Wilcox," said Moragne. "I'll tend to the planting and the factory equipment right away."

"Good," answered Gaylord. He pushed himself to his feet. "The cane looks good this year?"

"Very good," Moragne answered happily. "I think we'll have another record crop."

"That's fine. Well, good day." said Gaylord, picking up his straw hat and walking out of the office. The manager smiled to himself. The "Old Gentleman" was in a class by himself. He wasn't satisfied with doubling the size of Grove Farm. Now he wanted to start a whole new industry. "It must run in the family," Moragne said to himself as he sat down to complete the list of improvements he wanted to make on the mill.

* * *

The new manager had expected the excitement to wear off after a while. But it didn't. That first year, in 1953, Grove Farm set a new record in sugar production. In 1954, using a widened plantation road as an airstrip, a small plane began scattering fertilizer pellets and spraying weed control chemicals by air to Grove Farm fields faster than he had ever dreamed it could be done. By 1955, a Grove Farm program of home ownership for workers had taken hold. Already, 177 employees were living off the plantation in their own homes.

When a visitor asked why the plantation was breaking with the traditional system of housing its workers in rented, plantation camp cottages, Moragne replied, "The rentals we get for those cottages hardly pay for their maintenance. Besides, when a man owns his own home he's more likely to stay on the Island."

In 1956 office manager Hib Case revolutionized the accounting system by introducing a new electronic system called IBM. It eliminated the need for entering each item into the ledgers by hand. With the new equipment, the accounting was done in less time with four fewer men than before.

Every day Moragne awoke in anticipation of a new challenge. And he was seldom disappointed. Most of the challenges came from the mill where he had been pushing the tired machinery to the limit. The manager always knew by the sound of the factory superintendent's voice when something had gone wrong.

It was almost always the same, rocks picked up by the mechanical harvesters were creating havoc in the mill machinery. Because of the rocks, grinding capacity dropped from forty-seven tons an hour in 1953 to only forty-four tons in 1954 in spite of costly improvements to the mill. Moragne knew the problem would have to be solved before Grove Farm could be completely free of Lihue.

So he called in Victor Vargas, the factory engineer and a brilliant design man. Vargas was born in the Philippines of an excellent family. He'd graduated from the University of Detroit and worked for the Ford Motor Company in an effort to find a place in the world which he liked. Finally, he'd found it in Hawaii.

"I suppose you know those rocks are killing us at the factory," Moragne told him bluntly. "Do you have any ideas?"

Vargas obviously did. "I've been experimenting with the mud bath principle and I think I have an idea that will solve our problem, if it works."

"Show me," said Moragne.

The mud bath principle had been applied successfully at Pioneer Mill Company on Maui. The basic idea was simple. Sugar cane was too heavy to float on water. But when the water became muddy, thus increasing its density, cane stalks floated on the surface. Therefore, the cane was dumped for cleaning into a huge tank of water, mud, rocks and all. The rocks sank to the bottom of the tank. Water washed the mud from the cane stalks as a conveyor moved them out of the bath into the factory for crushing.

Vargas talked as he sketched a design of a mud bath cleaning plant. "The big drawback to this type of cleaning operation is the tendency of the cane stalks to get all tangled up in the tank. When that happens, rocks ride across the bath in the tangle and create havoc in the mill."

Moragne looked thoughtfully at the sketch. "You know, Vic, if the water was flowing, instead of standing still, it might carry the cane along . . . "

"That's it!" said Vargas, his dark eyes sparkling with enthusiasm. Rapidly he added to his sketch. "We could add a circulating system! Look, like this. We'll run troughs along the outside of the tank to carry the water around. In each trough, we'll put electrically powered propellers to suck the water out of the tank at the far end and pump it around through the troughs into the end where the cane comes in. If we can keep that water moving, I'll bet the cane moves with it."

"We'll give it a try," said Moragne.

Vic Vargas and his able assistant Mac Inouye designed and built the new cleaning plant and the circulating system during the off-season of 1955 with the help of Shige Kashima and his construction men who were carpenters skilled in steel erection. That year the capacity of the factory jumped from forty-four to fifty-one tons per hour. A year later, Vargas reported that the mill was averaging nearly sixty-six tons of cane per hour. Moragne smiled with satisfaction. But that wasn't all. The rocks were hauled off and made into roads. The mud and cane trash from the cleaning plant were used to build up new acres of productive land.

* * *

Gradually, the staggering expenditures for improvements eased off: from $645,100 appropriated in 1954, to $212,850 in 1955. In 1956 the amount dropped to less than $150,000. In the same year, Grove Farm harvested the largest crop in the history of the plantation. By 1958 the mill capacity had jumped to seventy-four tons per hour, and in that year, for the first time, Grove Farm ground its entire crop in its own factory.

Just when it seemed that Moragne could relax, a triple blow dashed his hopes. In December 1957 a hurricane, named Nina by the Weather Bureau, slashed across the cane fields of Kauai leaving wreckage that resulted in a loss of nearly 1,000 tons of sugar to Grove Farm.

On the following February 1, 1958, sugar workers throughout the Islands went on strike. The new Union contract added in 1959 an estimated $60,000 to Grove Farm's labor costs. By the time the strike was over 126 days later on June 9, the cane was almost dead, and the working capital was exhausted, requiring heavy borrowings.

That wasn't all. A year later, on the evening of August 6, 1960, hurricane Dot roared out of the south leaving a trail of broken cane stalks. Sugar losses from both hurricanes were estimated at 6,444 tons. Combined estimates for both strike and hurricanes indicated the loss of one complete crop over the 1958, 1959, and 1960 period.

The experimental levulose program ground to a halt. A new irrigation tunnel, intended to bring more water to the dry Koloa fields, had to be discontinued. Road building and field clearing activities were sharply curtailed. A crowning blow was the announced closing of the second of Kauai's pineapple canning factories. Reluctantly, Moragne phased out Grove Farm's successful pineapple operation.

"Don't worry, Bill, there's no way to avoid our share of bad luck," Gaylord told him. "We'll just pull in our belts and wait it out. The important thing is to be in a position to take advantage of good luck when it comes along."

The good luck followed quickly. From a heart-breaking crop in 1960, the second smallest in almost twenty years, Grove Farm ended in 1961 with the largest harvest in its entire history, 370,251 tons of cane that produced 37,870 tons of sugar. The levulose program took on new life, and the tunnel crew pushed 4,288 feet into the mountain.

That was just the beginning. In the following year, Grove Farm produced 400,703 tons of sugar cane. Moragne had expanded the harvest to 4,197 acres. A world shortage of sugar, largely caused by lack of production in unsettled Cuba, sent the price of sugar soaring. The manager reported a gross profit of $1,013,223 for the year. The factory was grinding cane at a record 80.7 tons per hour.

By this time, the Grove Farm crew was setting production records only to break them twelve months later. In 1963 the plantation manufactured an all-time record of 41,458 tons of sugar from 400,826 tons of cane. Even more impressive, the fields of both divisions of the expanded plantation yielded an impressive 9.38 tons of sugar per acre, a new record. Office manager and treasurer Fred Lawrence reported earnings before Federal and State taxes of $1,911,091. And the limit hadn't been reached. In 1963 Gaylord and Moragne negotiated a long term lease with the Eric Knudsen Estate for nine hundred additional acres of cane land.

When Moragne assembled a list of statistics for a progress report to Grove Farm stockholders in California, he was amazed to find that there had been built, since the merger, twenty miles of new heavy duty road with rock bases averaging four feet thick, and fourteen miles of new cinder-based road. In addition, 650,000 tons of rock had been removed from 1,900 acres of cane land and 350 new acres cleared for planting.

Over the same years, Grove Farm trucks had hauled 1,225,-000 cubic yards of cane trash and soil from the mill cleaning plant to improve 130 acres of barren lava flow that had been completely unproductive before. Most plantations simply dumped the trash into the nearest gully. Another 550,000 cubic yards of thick, fertile mud had been used to cover 400 acres of thin soil spots in existing fields.

During 1963 as many as twenty sugar men from other plantations visited Grove Farm every month to study new machinery being developed there. As a result of almost total mechanization, Grove Farm had been able to triple the wages of its field workers while keeping its total labor cost static.

Best of all, the enormous debt was paid off. It seemed incredible: over $2,000,000 in less than seventeen years. In addition, during the same period, Grove Farm had installed and paid for $8,000,000 worth of permanent improvements. And the Koloa division, once so hopelessly mired in problems, was now a better producer than its neighbor across the mountains. In 1964, as Grove Farm approached its one hundredth birthday, the future had never looked brighter.

In the heart of the plantation, in the little office off the main house at Kilohana, Gaylord Wilcox sat at a roomy desk from where he had been guiding the destiny of Grove Farm for almost forty years. His uncle Albert had once lived there, long ago in the days of ox carts and hand harvesting, when Kilohana was a country home surrounded by wilderness. In 1936 when Gaylord moved from Honolulu to make his home, he replaced the old house with a new home surrounded by great spreading lawns and majestic shade trees.

As he often did when he sat there alone with his cigars and stamp collection and memories for company, he planned for the second hundred years of the plantation as he knew his uncle George must have planned for the century just completed.

First there was land, unused land. In Gaylord's thought there were 1,500 marginal acres on Grove Farm that would some day be producing sugar. A professor at the University of Hawaii had been trying, without success, to interest plantation managers in a new chemical treatment of soil, until Grove Farm agreed to install test areas which showed promise of a substantial gain. The secret ingredient was common slag, a useless by-product of the phosphate industry. It made productive soil of marginal areas never used before.

Gaylord also thought of water, enough even to supply arid Koloa in times of drought. And that was already coming true. In 1964 on the Koloa side of the mountains Grove Farm was drilling artesian wells for irrigation. Each well would produce four to five million gallons a day and would supply water during drought periods.

These would be expensive plans, but the plantation would gradually die without them. Overhead irrigation was a perfect example. The only major hand operation left on the plantation was the opening and closing of irrigation ditches. Younger workers preferred other tasks. In a few years, when the old-timers were gone, who would irrigate the fields? The answer was more mechanization, including giant overhead sprinklers.

Installation costs were fantastic but so was the saving from erosion and seepage of water in the old fashioned ditches. Already, Grove Farm was testing several kinds of sprinklers to see which ones worked best.

Another of the plans, just as revolutionary, was only a matter of time. Since the beginning of sugar plantations in Hawaii, juice from the stalks had been extracted by squeezing the cane through rollers. After years of improvement of the machinery, the percentage of extraction had gone up to about ninety-five per cent of the juice in the stalks when harvested. That seemed to be the limit until an inventor from the Mainland had come around with a way to apply the principle of diffusion, used to extract sugar from beets, to the milling of sugar cane. Instead of being put through rollers, the stalks were shredded and put through a bath which extracted the sugar. Gaylord had contributed ideas to the first design. There were fewer moving parts to wear out in the new unit and the percentage of extraction was an incredible ninety-seven to ninety-eight per cent. Better still, fewer operators were required to run the machinery. He hoped to have a unit in operation within a very few years.

Then there was levulose, the product of ti which might replace pineapples as a second crop. There was also the big, new electric plant for the plantation that would probably not only supply Grove Farm with all the electricity its expanding facilities would require for years to come, but also provide a profit from excess electricity sold to public utility companies.

There was a new mechanical harvester that would pick up the stalks of cane, clean them of leaves, and cut them into shorter lengths. The harvested cane would then pass into a dry cleaning plant at the mill instead of the old-fashioned mud bath where the stalks lost a substantial per cent of their sugar into the bath water. That saving of sugar would soon pay for installing the new equipment.

There were more plans, of course, and Gaylord smiled when he thought of what his uncle would say if he could hear them.

He would listen with his head tilted a little to one side, that alert look in his eyes. When he had heard enough he would give his quick nod and move on. For Gaylord was satisfied that his dreams were the same practical, hard-headed kind that had served Grove Farm during its first one hundred years.

* * *

The day began, crisp and clear, as the June sun chased the damp shadows from Kauai's jungle-covered mountains. It was a golden day as are so many days in Hawaii. The clouds floated serenely overhead. The sugar cane fields, thick with long leaves, or brown with newly plowed earth, made a pattern on the land. Cloud shadows moved slowly over that broad pattern, then slipped noiselessly across the jagged peaks of the surrounding mountains, bold and picturesque against the washed blue sky.

It was June, 1964, and the harvest and factory crews were hard at work in the twenty-four-hour day of sugar production. In the office only one man was stirring. He was short, dark, and stocky, and his eyes twinkled with good humor. Erich Spillner, research agronomist for the plantation, often let himself into the office long before anyone else arrived. On this day, at sunrise he quickly collected several notebooks. Then he set out on his rounds driving a well-worn Chevrolet sedan.

His eyes darted everywhere as he drove, his mind recording half a dozen impressions at once, each one meaningful in the complicated life cycle of sugar cane. For Spillner had many responsibilities.

One of his jobs was to keep a constant check on the moisture content of the soil so that he could tell the irrigating crews which fields needed water. In the romantic days of George Wilcox, when Spillner's grandfather had come from Germany to work on Grove Farm, a farmer simply picked up a handful of soil and felt it for dampness. That method was no longer exact enough. So once every week his crew of men under assistant agriculturist Masao Ono took readings from the moisture blocks buried at regular intervals all over the plantation. The blocks were chunks of plaster of paris with electrical wire plugged into each side. In wet soil, the plaster of paris absorbed a great deal of moisture which conducted electricity through the block. In dry soil, the block absorbed only a little moisture, making a very poor conductor. By measuring the amount of electricity being conducted through the block on a meter above the ground, the agronomist knew exactly how much water was in the soil, and he relayed this information to Kiyoshi Shintani who was in charge of all irrigation.

There were other tests, of course, for Spillner constantly tested the welfare of the sugar cane like a doctor taking the pulse of his patient. By snipping off pieces of leaves from plants in different parts of the plantation, then by having the samples analyzed in Brewer and Company's Hilo laboratory, Spillner could tell how much nitrogen, phosphate and potash the plants were getting. This information he passed along to the assistant manager and the cultivation superintendent.

His restless eyes moved about. He was constantly on the lookout for rat damage, since he was in charge of the 180,000 or more rat poisoning stations set out each year on the plantation. He worked closely with Ono in testing new varieties of cane that might increase the yield. In 1950, Spillner's experiments helped in the development of a new variety called 39–7028 which increased by several tons of sugar per acre the yield on Grove Farm. He was in charge in September when the cane was sprayed to prevent it from the tasseling which reduces the yield. His advice counted most when it came to planning when a field should be harvested, ratooned, or planted.

In the shady old town of Koloa amidst fields that had been growing cane continuously for over a hundred and thirty years, daybreak saw another man on his way. He was Lyle Van Dreser, assistant manager and Moragne's right-hand man, a Midwest school teacher turned cane farmer. The men all called him Van. He was not tall, but heavily built, and did his job

Samuel Whitney Wilcox, director
from April 20, 1942, secretary
from April 20, 1942 to April 17, 1947,
vice president from April 16, 1964

Richard Henry Sloggett, Sr.,
director from March 6, 1934

Gerald Wilcox Fisher,
director from May 5, 1939

Albert Hart Wilcox, substitute director
for G. W. Fisher from April 23,
1948, alternate director from April 15,
1953, director from April 8, 1954,
secretary from April 17, 1947

Office of Grove Farm Company, Inc., Puhi, Kauai, 1964

Grove Farm Company Board of Directors, 1963. *Left* to *right:*
Front: Albert Wilcox, Mabel I. Wilcox, Gaylord Parke Wilcox, C. Hutton Smith.
Back: Richard Sloggett, Harold C. Eichelberger, Gerald Fisher,
Sam W. Wilcox, William M. Moragne

with quiet competence. This morning he stepped out of his house and into his company sedan.

His mind was busy planning the day as he drove through Koloa, past the false-fronted stores to the old butcher shop where the men of the Koloa division were waiting. Some of them wore baseball caps, some straw hats. Their shirts were plaid, faded blue, military suntan; and their trousers were just as varied. But they all wore heavy shoes. Van Dreser got out of his car and exchanged a word with his supervisors.

If Spillner was the plantation nurse maid, Van Dreser was its doctor. He kept in his mind an endless list of machinery to be repaired, fields that needed fertilizer, the abilities and weaknesses of his men. It was Van Dreser who had to see that the tractors ran, that the harvesting crews stayed on schedule, that the weeds didn't get out of hand. This morning he gave his orders in conversational tones. There was a decision to take some of the men off weed control and put them to replanting.

The day's field work set, Van Dreser drove to the mill. There he checked the records against breakdowns during the night. Satisfied, he went back to his car and headed toward the tunnel. He slowed down before he came to the portal, turned on his lights, then proceeded cautiously into the dark interior of the mountain. As Van emerged from the tunnel he heard someone calling "car two," Van's signal on his mobile radio. The voice was that of Ernie Warner, the cultivation superintendent and Van's right arm in the field. Warner was reporting excellent results of an improvement he had suggested and asked Van to meet him later in the planting field.

The sun rose higher that June morning as Van Dreser drove toward plantation headquarters. Casually, he waved to a man on a huge, squarish, big-wheeled, bright yellow machine. The man was George Makaneole, a husky young Hawaiian who was very proud of his job. It was the only one of its kind on the plantation. For Makaneole ran the new seed cutter, and he ran it alone, just as his father before him had spent thirty years running a Grove Farm locomotive, tending it like a baby, greasing it, polishing it, tinkering with it.

However, the seed cutter was considerably more complicated than the old, primitive locomotives had been. Makaneole knew every inch of his strange looking machine. If a part broke, he knew how to weld it together. If the engine coughed, young Makaneole knew how to fix it.

So he rode the seed cutter proudly that June morning for he knew that his machine did the work of twenty men cutting seed cane by hand. All alone, just the machine and he, they cut the cane, cut the green leaves from the stalks, then neatly sliced the cane stalks into planting lengths and blew the trash onto the ground. When the hopper was full, Makaneole dumped his load into an empty truck parked nearby.

He had just finished filling the truck with seed pieces when another drove up. Out jumped a slim, middle-aged Filipino, Larry Serraon. He waved at Makaneole and slipped behind the wheel of the loaded truck. Expertly, he wheeled the vehicle onto the road, leaving behind the empty he had brought for filling.

The sun had reached a third of the way into the sky when Serraon maneuvered his truck alongside the seed treatment center in the plantation compound. He hopped briskly out of the cab and started the pump which filled the watertight truck body with a fungicide solution. He drained it quickly and, within a few minutes, was on his way again, completing an operation that had formerly taken hours.

Van Dreser drove to another part of the plantation where he found Ernie Warner watching another strange-looking machine at work on a hillside. This was the planter, one man driving, two men feeding seed cane into the chutes. They stopped long enough to take on another load of seed cane, then moved on, furrowing, planting, fertilizing, covering, all in one operation. Those three men and their machine could easily plant twelve acres a day.

Warner watched the performance of the planter with pride. He knew that a great many sugar men before him would have said machine planting on such a steep hillside would have been impossible. It had been his suggestion to put longer tracks on the tractor for balance. Today the machine was getting its first real hillside test, and, sure enough, the extended tracks held the tractor to the slope with ease. The sunburned planter driver, Bernard Augustin, stopped at the end of the furrow near Van Dreser and Warner. "I've been driving a planter for twenty-three years," Augustin called from his high seat, "and I've never seen one that sticks to a pali like this one!" They waved back with satisfaction.

Here in the freshly plowed field the earth was moist and pungent. The soil lay bare, waiting to be impregnated once more. Mynah birds fluttered down, far away from the planter, to look for worms. Only a few fields away the scene was completely different as Van Dreser drove past. Here a harvesting crew was at work stirring up dust, smashing down the tall, stately cane; sweeping the field clean.

The harvester was an enormous D—8 Caterpillar, one of the largest made, with a huge rake, more than eighteen feet across, attached to its front. Roaring with power, the tractor marched through the field, mowing down three rows of cane at one time.

A young man in suntans stood beside his dusty, company sedan on the edge of the field. He was the harvesting superintendent, Bill Moragne, Jr., who had his father's love of machines. He never tired of watching them work. Now he studied the performance of a snorting, grumbling cane-grab as it picked up several tons of cane at a time, dropping the stalks into the bright yellow cane-hauling trailers, each big enough to hold thirty tons. It was young Bill who had worked out Grove Farm's efficient hauling system and kept it running smoothly.

He watched as a heavy-duty truck tractor roared to a stop and unhooked an empty trailer. The driver hitched the cab to a loaded trailer, and with a wave of his hand to young Moragne, headed his mammoth machine toward the tunnel in the mountain. Fifteen minutes later, Moragne knew, the driver would pull up at the mill, unhook his loaded trailer, hitch up to an empty, and start back for another load.

Everywhere on the plantation on this June day in 1964 there was system and planning, the application of special skills developed over one hundred years of hard won experience. And yet the scenes from field to field varied dramatically. The machines had not conquered completely. Roaring diesel trucks on the way to the mill passed middle-aged men with leathery, brown faces, walking patiently with hoes riding on their shoulders. They made picturesque figures, these men clad in faded denim. It was their job to open by hand the gates of the irrigation ditches to bring water down the rows where it seeped to the thirsty roots. Most of the ditches were dirt, a few were aluminum by this time, or lined with concrete, and the gates were of metal or wood. Yet they all needed to be opened and closed by hand, and in a few places, cane trash still served to hold back the water. These old-time irrigation men were the last of their breed for their sons were not satisfied with such humble labor. They preferred to operate machines.

The newest machine of all, a sprawling metal giant painted gleaming yellow, was at work in a nearby field where the stubble of a freshly harvested crop of sugar cane remained to grow a second "ratoon" crop. For one hundred years men had walked down the rows of such fields, slowly replanting by hand the places where there were gaps in the stubble. But on the June day in 1964, the sprawling machine, that spread over four rows at once, did the work of seventeen such men. Steadily it moved along the symmetrical rows, one man driving the Caterpillar, four more men riding out on the flanks, each man sitting directly over a row of stubble passing below. When one of the men came to a blank spot in the row, he pressed a lever with his foot. A hydraulically powered plow plunged into the dirt below, dug a furrow, and left a seedpiece where it was immediately covered by the machine.

The endless cycle of plowing, planting, cultivating, irrigating, and harvesting went on as the sun rose higher in the sky, each part of the cycle taking place somewhere on the plantation at the same time. Middle-aged and swarthy Manuel Rosa, his sun-wrinkled eyes protected by goggles, sat at the controls of an enormous, growling D—9 Caterpillar that pulled a heavy disc plow. That plow relentlessly ripped up the earth to a depth of two feet at a speed that prepared twenty acres a day for planting. Once Rosa looked up to wave at a man driving by in an auto. His teeth flashed white in the sunlight for the man in the car was his son, Bernard, field equipment overseer, a job that made him his father's boss.

By this time Van Dreser had returned to the plantation headquarters. He nodded pleasantly to Freddy Bukoski, the weed control superintendent, as they passed in the parking lot. Short, balding old timer Kiyoshi Shintani, the irrigation superintendent, drove up at the same time. Van stopped to compare notes with him and listened closely because Kiyoshi knew more than most plantation men knew about sugar cane, and everyone could depend on his good judgment.

And still the bewildering list of tasks required to operate the plantation were not ended. Two men stood that day on a shady mountain slope, talking earnestly beside the damp, raw portal of a new tunnel. One of them was a short, black-haired Japanese, Henry Oshima. The other, tall and lean, was Carl Minium. They were tunnel supervisors, each in charge of digging one end of the new irrigation tunnel, comparing progress to date.

On the other side of the mountains, a crew was at work at strange tasks in the factory. There was Frank Zimmer, a Dutchman from Indonesia who had fled the Communists there. At middle age, Zimmer had ended his trek nearly around the world at Grove Farm, where his skill in sugar chemistry had increased the recovery of sugar from molasses by two and one-half per cent. On this June day he was carefully squinting through a microscope at a batch of sugar crystals from the vacuum pan to make sure the boiling procedure was being properly handled. If it wasn't, Zimmer would promptly explode at the shift sugar boiler.

In the mill office, Fred Hebert, who had helped wrestle the factory into shape, was working over his desk plotting the percentage of extraction, his greying-blonde head bent over his work. Victor Vargas worked in a nearby building drafting a design for a super heater for a steam generator that would meet the demands of the expanding mill. In the same building, seventy-year-old engineer Elbert Gillin was instructing his new assistant Donn Carswell in the technique of determining pipe capacity requirements for a new overhead irrigation system that must deliver 5,000,000 gallons of water per day through each sprinkler.

Now the sun was high overhead and limousines loaded with coconut-hatted tourists sped along the highway, passing the fields of glistening sugar cane, the plantation office, and the workers' village. In the limousine, a tour guide rattled off some impressive statistics about the sugar industry in Hawaii. But the visitors sped away hardly sensing the achievement that lay all around them.

Not one of them had even noticed the nondescript, shed-like building across the plantation compound where much of the magic at Grove Farm had taken place. This was the shop, plain and functional. It was here that shop superintendent Lloyd Nelson and his crew took ordinary tractors and made them into machines that planted, weeded, harvested, replanted. Nelson was the key to the whole mechanization program, like his father who had been shop superintendent under Broadbent when they developed the first cane planter.

Even if the tour car had stopped, the passengers would probably not have understood what was going on nor who the actors were in this drama. On the plantation there was no obvious sign of rank. Three men stood in the shade of a machine shed. One of them was assistant manager Van Dreser. With him were Joe Arruda, head electrician, and Shige Kashima, veteran carpenter, talking over a work schedule for the installation of a new evaporator station at the mill. From the way they dressed, no one could have guessed which was the assistant manager and which the carpenter.

The only men who wore ties on the plantation, and then not all the time, were those who worked in the main office. There Fred Lawrence, in his quiet way, supervised one of the two fully equipped IBM plantation offices in Hawaii. He was talking to his assistant Bill Coots. Together they were digging out some financial statistics for Gaylord. At a nearby desk, old timer Tsutao Sato, hired by George Wilcox himself, was calling for an airplane ticket that would take Manager Moragne to Honolulu on a business trip. Down the hall in another office, grey-haired Fred Weber, employee relations chief, sat at his desk patiently explaining to a field worker how to buy his own home. They were interrupted by Dick Tom who edited the *Grove Farm Plantation News*. Tom wanted a story about the new home owner. In the same office, Toki Fujii, who had once been George Wilcox's driver, was issuing safety goggles to a tractor driver.

So the work of the plantation went on, 480 men applying the 480 different skills that produced the miracle of sugar. Two of these men sat at the far end of the hall in a large office under a portrait of George Wilcox who seemed to be smiling down on them in understanding. The two men were grey-haired Gaylord, his cigar in hand, and Manager Moragne, his hair thinning a little but his face as tanned as ever.

Gaylord puffed at his cigar as he told Moragne his latest ideas for a new sprinkler method of irrigation and a diffusion method of sugar extraction. "To keep abreast of the times," he said firmly, "we must try new ideas."

So every man on the plantation went about his work as the sun climbed in the sky. When the sun was directly overhead, in the fields and the forests, the machines and the men paused in their unusual tasks: George Makaneole on his outlandish seed cutter, Victor Vargas at his drawing board, Manuel Rosa aboard his giant tractor, Toki Fujii in the office.

Then this unique assortment of men sat down with lunch pails, or drove home to dinner. Some of them had jelly sandwiches, some had rice balls for lunch, some had Chinese noodles. Some of them chatted in Filipino, some in Japanese. They gossiped in the earthy language of laboring men, in the precise terms of mathematical equations, in the sophisticated jargon of finance.

Yet none of these men, eating their polyglot lunches on a tiny volcanic island in the middle of the Pacific Ocean, thought of himself as unique. Nor that his job was out of the ordinary. No more so than the shy, energetic man in muddy boots who had dreamed one hundred years before that this barren plain might one day bloom with waving sugar cane, if only he planned and worked hard enough.

PART VII

The Heritage

CHAPTER

27

The second hundred years at Grove Farm began very much like the first hundred ended. But there were small, telltale changes. Only one of George Wilcox's nieces remained to look after his historic old homestead. Miss Mabel's hair had gone completely white. She was small and frail and slightly stooped, a gentle woman of quiet humor and good taste. Her concern for people and lack of pretension made her a legend on the island. At age eighty-two, she was entirely alone in the house once Hisae Mashita, the cook, and Dorothy Bonilla, the maid, cleaned up and went home after dinner. There was not even a telephone at her bedside. To make a call, she had to get up and go down the hall.

Four times a year, Miss Mabel took a dust rag and walked across the broad lawn to her uncle's little, frame plantation office. A Spartan room where George Wilcox had felt at home in muddy boots was still used for quarterly meetings of the Grove Farm board of directors. Miss Mabel took her responsibilities as a director very seriously. So, before every board meeting, she dusted the room and set out the ashtrays on her uncle's termite-scarred, koa worktable.

Miss Mabel smoked unfiltered Camel cigarettes in disregard of the warning on each package that they were a danger to one's health. No one had the courage to scold her because she had done more to improve the health of people on Kauai than any other human being. After graduating from the Johns Hopkins School of Nursing in 1911, she had gone into plantation camps as Kauai's first public health nurse to work with babies, mothers, and midwives. World War I found her on the battlefields of France with the Red Cross. She emerged with decorations from the Queen of Belgium and the Mayor of La Havre. Back on Kauai, she supervised the pioneer public health program there from 1925 to 1934 and spearheaded the founding of a tuberculosis hospital in 1917 as well as the first general hospital on the island in 1938.

Since her sister Elsie's death in 1954, she had been the only woman on Grove Farm's board of directors. The only special consideration she asked for herself was the cane-bottomed chair. Gaylord's ashtray went in the middle. The others, mostly family, ranged around the small table. There was Gerald Fisher, married to Margaret Sloggett, a daughter of Miss Mabel's older sister, Etta. Jerry was president of Bishop Trust Company in Honolulu. Next came Sam Wilcox, Miss Mabel's nephew, vice president of Bishop National Bank and manager of the Lihue branch. On the other side sat another nephew, Richard Sloggett, who had been in charge of the plantation ranch. There were chairs for Bill Moragne, the manager of Grove Farm, for Lyle Van Dreser, his assistant, and for additional members

Gaylord ran the show. Jerry Fisher wasn't afraid to speak up but his opinions didn't have much impact since Gaylord, Miss Mabel, and Sam were trustees of the George N. Wilcox Trust, which owned fifty-one per cent of the stock in Grove Farm Company, Incorporated, and Miss Mabel generally supported her brother in his proposals. Before the board meetings, he would drop by to chat and to discuss the agenda, and then lapse into a long Wilcox silence. Finally, Gaylord would get to his feet and leave.

"He had his sitting pants on today," Miss Mabel would say to herself with a smile.

* * *

As he grew older, Gaylord leaned more and more on his nephew, Sam Wilcox. Sam had his hands full at the bank. He also had a heart condition, so he and his wife, Edie, talked it over. They didn't need the money, and he had been with the bank twenty-three years. Why not step down, take it easy, and live longer? His retirement party at the Kauai Surf Hotel in January 1964 was the largest ever held on the island. But, as vice president of Grove Farm, Sam couldn't seem to retire from the plantation. His uncle needed him. Owing to a drop in the price of sugar, the plantation reported a loss of $164,565 that year. Fortunately, a $425,133 gain on sale of stock and $164,124 in dividends turned the loss into a net profit of $486,685, which was equivalent to $2.32 per share. The next time Sam went to Honolulu, he dropped by to see Jerry Fisher in his ground floor office at Bishop Trust on King Street.

"It hasn't been a good year at Grove Farm," he said carefully.

"We came out of it better than most," answered Jerry. "Kilauea lost $82,838 in spite of a record harvest. My concern is our pre-occupation with sugar. I'd like to diversify."

"There's levulose," Sam said.

"Which isn't going anywhere. The real potential now is residential or resort development. Look what Amfac is doing at Kaanapali. That's going to be very profitable."

"Have you mentioned this to Gaylord?" asked Sam with a wry smile.

Jerry grinned back. "It wouldn't do any good."

"Well, we're not Amfac," said Sam. "Gaylord is a sugar man. You can't blame him for sticking with what he knows."

A year later, sugar prices rose again and Grove Farm bounced back with a net profit of $420,000. In 1966, the net dropped to a still respectable $323,000. Yet, Sam worried about Grove Farm stock held by Amfac, formerly known as American Factors. Amfac owned some 37,500 shares. Sam worried more after a conversation with Gaylord the following year. Gaylord, senior director at Amfac, had returned from Honolulu after their annual stockholders meeting.

"They voted in a new man named Harry Weinberg," reported Gaylord. "He's been buying up Amfac stock."

"I read about it in the paper," said Sam. "It said he's got 100,000 shares."

"That's right."

Weinberg was a self-made financier who had exploded on the Honolulu scene after moving in and taking over Honolulu Rapid Transit Company before anyone knew who he was. Then they learned he had taken over companies in Maryland, Pennsylvania, and Texas. Now he seemed to be moving in on Amfac.

"They figure he's already invested about three and a half million," said Gaylord.

"Why do you think he's doing it?"

"Well, he says he has confidence in Amfac management and that he believes the company's assets are valued way below their true amount," answered Gaylord. "That's probably right. Kaanapali must be worth twenty-five million by now."

"I wish Amfac didn't own so much of our stock," said Sam.

A year later, his concern proved justified when he opened his *Honolulu Advertiser* on February 12, 1967 and read, "Harry Weinberg, chairman of the Honolulu Rapid Transit Co., moved yesterday to assume partial control of Amfac Inc. Weinberg who was elected to Amfac's board of directors a year ago, said he will seek to have three directors of his own choosing elected at the next stockholders meeting March 22. He also said he will attempt to gain a seat on the board of directors of Lihue Plantation Co., an Amfac subsidiary."

If Weinberg succeeded in moving in on Lihue Plantation, he might also move in on Grove Farm. Sam immediately conferred with his uncle and Jerry Fisher. They decided to buy back as much stock as possible, starting with family members on the mainland, under the assumption that the mainland relatives didn't really care what happened to the plantation. That assumption proved wrong. Sam was firmly rebuffed by his mainland relatives, who considered themselves very much a part of Grove Farm. Meanwhile, Weinberg's take-over move also failed. Amfac stockholders ousted him from the board by reducing the number of directors from fourteen to seven.

But there was more bad news. That year, 1967, Grove Farm reported a net loss of $30,000.

"I don't understand it," said Jerry Fisher.

"The drought and rats and cane borers have cut sugar production," Sam answered.

"But the statement says we made a gross profit of $2,498,000 on the sugar operation. Something's wrong." He ran his finger down the statement. "We spent $628,000 for services to employees. I wonder what that means?"

"We could use a better accounting system."

"Exactly. What we need is budgeting, cost control. Do you think Gaylord would object if I suggested that to the board?"

"He'll probably grumble, but I don't think he'll fight it. I'll talk to him. I'm also going to see if we can't buy back those shares from Amfac."

On April 22, 1968, Sam reported at the annual stockholders meeting that he had succeeded in buying back all of Amfac's Grove Farm stock in exchange for the stock Grove Farm held in Lihue Plantation, Kekaha Plantation, and Amfac. A letter from Jerry Fisher to the board resulted in a new accounting system. In addition, the board retained a team of experts headed by A. Douglas Ednie from C. Brewer & Co. Ltd. to make an operational survey of the plantation. The survey, to be completed by July, would explain how to improve operations in the face of lower prices and rising costs.

Finally, by unanimous vote, Sam was elected president of Grove Farm Company, and Gaylord moved up to chairman of the board. He gave Sam his blessing but grumbled about the cost of the survey.

"It's a waste of $10,000," he snorted. He fought back when the directors phased out levulose, giving in only after they had argued back and forth. Even then he was convinced it would pay if only they gave it more time.

* * *

The Ednie report on Grove Farm's operations did not make comfortable reading. Van Dreser stayed up all night going through it. The more he read, the madder he got. "They don't think we did anything right," he muttered to himself. That wasn't fair, of course. Van Dreser had a great deal of respect for the men who did the survey. Doug Ednie, a retired Brewer plantation manager, was a wizard with figures. R. G. "Tom" Watt, an Amfac engineer, ranked with the best mill men in the nation. Dr. Harry Clements, at the University of Hawaii, was a crackerjack agronomist. They had merely put down in black and white the management problems Grove Farm, or any other plantation, would have to solve to meet a sharply rising cost curve. Their recommendations included modernized methods, different fertilizers and varieties of cane, an improved irrigation system, and new equipment, all at horrendous expense.

Sam's reaction to the report was more worry than anger. To him it was a danger signal. The improvements would cost millions that would have to be borrowed at a much higher interest rate than Gaylord had paid when he financed the Koloa merger. Even if they invested in the improvements, there was no guarantee the return would make the investment worth while. No one could predict sugar prices.

The Ednie report taught Sam a greater respect for G. N. Wilcox and Gaylord. He realized how vulnerable a small plantation like Grove Farm was and that their fields had never enjoyed exceptional productivity because they were located on the wet, windward side of the island. Kekaha Plantation, on the dry, leeward side, regularly produced thirteen to fourteen tons of sugar per acre. In contrast, Grove Farm in a top year produced little more than nine tons per acre. The break-even point stood somewhere around eight tons per acre. That left very little margin for error to a small plantation with limited financial resources.

So Sam studied the methods G. N. and Gaylord had used to survive. One method was the introduction of more efficient methods of growing sugar cane. The Ednie report took care of that. Another method was expansion, which increased the rewards for efficiency. Sam saw now that Gaylord's merger with Koloa had been a master stroke. The huge investment had paid handsome dividends. But even with 10,000 acres in cane, Grove Farm was not a large plantation. And they were hemmed in now by Lihue, McBryde, and the mountains.

"I've got an idea," Sam told his uncle one day.

"Shoot."

"Maybe we ought to merge with McBryde."

"I was wondering how long it would take you," said Gaylord.

Sam answered carefully. "It would have to be a merger with Alexander & Baldwin for the purpose of combining operations with McBryde Plantation. That would give us about 15,000 acres in cane."

"Grove Farm has always been independent," barked Gaylord. "If I were doing it, I'd buy out McBryde."

Sam stood his ground, aware that this was a crucial decision.

"We bought out Koloa and that gave us twenty profitable years," he said. "But look ahead at the next twenty. Say we did buy out McBryde. How long would that give us before we'd have to expand again? The way costs are going up, I'd say ten years. A small, independent plantation can't make it pay. We're in a strong position now. That's the time to get out."

He searched for a way to make it easier for his uncle, then added, "We'll keep the Grove Farm name."

Gaylord wasn't fooled. "All right, but it won't be the same."

It wasn't the same for Moragne, either. Like Gaylord, he was of the old independent school. The veteran plantation manager had been with Grove Farm for forty-one years. He decided it was a good time to retire, so, in the midst of negotiations with Alexander & Baldwin, he stepped aside and Van Dreser took his place.

Sam explained the merger proposal in a letter to stockholders dated May 22, 1969. He was busier now than he had ever been at the bank. For six months he shuttled between Lihue and Honolulu. Both Grove Farm and Alexander & Baldwin hired consultants. The accounting firm of Peat, Marwick, Mitchell & Co. and planners Belt, Collins and Associates, both of Honolulu, developed a value for Grove Farm lands not only in sugar but in their potential in residential, industrial, and resort development. A&B had a study made by a New York investment banking firm, F. Eberstadt & Co.

Meanwhile, the outlook at Grove Farm improved as budget and cost control programs came into effect. In spite of a drop in sugar prices of $3 per ton, the company was headed for a profit of nearly half a million compared with $15,000 in 1968. So Sam was not prepared to give anything away. By December, the negotiations had bogged down. Sam explained why in a letter to stockholders:

"One of the main obstacles encountered has been the difference in size of the two companies; A&B with nearly ten million shares outstanding, and Grove Farm with less than two hundred thousand. Another was that divisions other than sugar, namely rock and land development, play such an important part in Grove Farm's operations. During the past week the directors of first, Grove Farm, and then A&B have met and the decision has been made to discontinue explorations of a consolidation at least for the present."

To his son-in-law, David Pratt, one of the rising young men in the Amfac sugar department, he confided, "There was another stumbling block, our land value. We never did get close on that."

Cheered by the substantial profit, the Grove Farm board of directors voted to continue as a fully integrated company. At that meeting, Jerry Fisher's chair was vacant. He had died on October 15, 1969 after a long illness. The directors voted to seat Van Dreser as an alternate until a permanent director could be named. They also voted to move the board meetings from around G. N.'s battered koa table in the old plantation office to the air-conditioned luxury of a conference room at the Lihue branch of First Hawaiian Bank. Sam was in full control now. His retirement had turned out to be an illusion. His health hadn't improved, and he didn't know how long he could keep up the pace.

CHAPTER
28

Sophie Cluff moved to Grove Farm in January 1968. Miss Mabel and Sophie had gotten along famously since Sophie first visited Grove Farm more than a year before. As librarian for the Hawaiian Mission Children's Society in Honolulu, she had come to collect the papers of author Ethel Damon, who had lived with Miss Mabel until her death in 1964. Both Miss Mabel and Sophie loved books, they shared an interest in history, and they both came from missionary families.

The move to Grove Farm was, for Sophie, like stepping back into a slower-paced period of Hawaii's past. The first night she asked for the key to lock the front door.

"Oh, I don't bother," said Miss Mabel mildly.

"But you've been alone in the house at night," protested Sophie.

"This isn't Honolulu," Miss Mabel reminded her. "But if you want to lock the doors, go ahead."

Miss Mabel ran a household that had changed little since her uncle's time. She permitted Hisae to order staples and bulk items like toilet paper, light bulbs, laundry supplies, fertilizer for the garden, chicken feed, and Lysol from Yoneji Store because they delivered. But Miss Mabel did the grocery shopping herself, and she always selected the best New York cuts or legs of lamb, which she shared with the servants.

Mrs. Kikunyo Moriwaki, the laundress, arrived from her cottage across the lawn at 7 A.M. every Monday to light the wood fire under a big kettle in the wash house. When the water was hot, she poured it into the spinner washing machine. The sheets were put to boil in what was left. Mrs. Moriwaki, who was nearly eighty, insisted on scrubbing out stubborn dirt stains on an old, hardwood washboard she had been using since coming to work at Grove Farm in 1921. She smoothed out bed linens at the same mangle she had always used. Tactfully, Sophie suggested to Miss Mabel that it would be easier for Mrs. Moriwaki if hot water were piped into the laundry room, and it was done. But the feeling of history persisted.

"I don't think there is another home like this anywhere," Sophie mused as she and Miss Mabel sipped Scotch and water on the lanai before dinner.

Miss Mabel chuckled. "Probably not. This one just grew around us like Topsy."

"That's what makes it so special, a hundred years of life."

"What will happen to the place when I'm gone?" mused Miss Mabel.

"Wouldn't it be wonderful if it could be preserved as a museum?" said Sophie.

Miss Mabel did not answer right away.

"It meant so much to Uncle George and to my parents. In many ways, it means a great deal to the people of Kauai. Perhaps it is presumptuous of me, but I look on this old homestead as a symbol of Hawaii's plantation heritage."

She seemed glad of the opportunity to express herself this way. Sophie encouraged her to do so. Before long, after similar conversations, her concern had turned into resolve.

* * *

Miss Mabel wasted no time, once she had made up her mind to preserve Grove Farm Homestead as a museum to tell the story of sugar in Hawaii. First, she consulted her nephews, Sam Wilcox and Dick Sloggett, for financial advice. They promised to help her transfer ownership of the homestead from Grove Farm Company to Waioli Mission, the family foundation that operated the old mission house in Waioli as a small museum.

Next, Miss Mabel floated her idea at an annual stockholders meeting. Most of the relatives were enthusiastic. The board of directors were more cautious once the old homestead had been appraised at $750,000. They hadn't realized the price of a museum came that high, but they voted to sell the homestead to Miss Mabel. She didn't blink an eye.

Family members on Kauai formed a museum committee headed by Dick Sloggett. Grandnieces Patsy Sheehan and Gale Carswell began researching old Grove Farms files. Dick Sloggett found an album of old Grove Farm photos. Friends pitched in to help.

Stacks of papers on Miss Mabel's desk in the writing room grew steadily as she composed letters asking for advice from museum experts. She hired an architect who, with Sophie's help, supervised restoration of the moss-stained fernery just beyond the porte-cochère, and the tea house, a gazebo overlooking the valley. When a storm blew down the old shed where oxen had been hitched to carts during her girlhood, she insisted on putting the building back up.

She grew frailer every year and needed more help to manage both the house and museum planning. But her enthusiasm flagged only in attendance at board of directors' meetings. For her, it just wasn't the same now that they met in the bank instead of her Uncle George's old Grove Farm office. She knew why the change had been made. The men wanted their comfort—air-conditioning and uphol-stered chairs. Then, too, ripe mangoes had made a distracting thump when they fell on the roof of the old office. And the table *was* a little small.

Miss Mabel sighed as she waited for Van Dreser to pick her up for the meeting on June 15, 1970. She sat through the discussions silently, dismayed by the decisions the directors were making. Uncle George had taught her never to sell land. Yet, Sam and the others were negotiating with Alexander & Baldwin, C. Brewer, Grosvenor-Davies, and Kaiser Aetna, all of whom were interested in buying land for a resort development at Maha'ulepu. The board had hired planners to look into development of Puhi. But how could she pro-test? The sugar crop was short again.

On the way home, her reserve broke down. "Mr. Van Dreser, it goes against my grain to sell land," she said.

That was the last board meeting Gaylord Wilcox attended. The old pioneer died the next day, a link with the past broken. He had begun his sugar career in the boiler house of Lihue Plantation in 1900, then landed a job as corporate secretary for the old Hackfeld company, predecessor to American Factors; he had survived the re-organization to become vice president and, in 1933, had become president of Grove Farm. He had been a fighter, tenacious, daring, outspoken. His greatest memorial was the solid financial condition of Grove Farm. No one grieved more for the veteran sugar man than his sister. She had never felt more alone. Time was running out for her generation.

* * *

The idea of drafting David Pratt as the next president of Grove Farm Company, Ltd., occurred to more than one person. Maybe Sam thought of it himself. Dick Sloggett suggested that Doug Ednie had put the bug in somebody's ear. Van Dreser denied this, saying that he gave Sam the idea and that Sam had said, "Leave me out of it. I can't go to the board and ask for my own son-in-law. But if you want to take the initiative, go ahead." So Van Dreser took David to lunch at the Pacific Club and offered him a job as his administrative assistant. Then he added, "Nobody but family has ever headed up Grove Farm. We think you're the logical candidate."

That's why Pratt, grandson of former Grove Farm manager Edward Broadbent, found himself in Van Dreser's office with other members of the plantation's management team on Tuesday, July 11, 1972.

"You all know that, after two good years, the bottom has dropped out of sugar again," said Van Dreser. "We may be headed for a big loss. A very big loss."

That was not news to anybody.

"We're not the only plantation on the ropes. Kahuku on Oahu went under last year. Kilauea here on Kauai will close at the end of this year. Kohala on the Big Island will shut down at the end of the grinding season next year."

That was not news either. But what followed left them stunned.

"Van and I have just come back from meetings in Honolulu," said Sam. "We met with Eddie Holroyde, Alexander & Baldwin's vice president for sugar, and with Karl Berg, Amfac's vice president for sugar. What we talked about was combining sugar operations. If it works, we may go out of the sugar business."

They all waited for Sam to continue in his methodical way.

"The proposal we made was for either Lihue Plantation or McBryde, or both, to lease our sugar land. It's the only way either of them can expand. It would solve a lot of their problems, especially for McBryde. Their old mill needs modernizing. But they can't pay off an investment like that unless they expand."

"If they took over our mill, they wouldn't have to modernize their own," somebody said. "With some work, ours would have all the capacity they'd need."

"That's right," said Sam. "And by leasing our land, we would avoid the complications of a merger."

"What happens if we go out of sugar?" asked someone else.

"We concentrate on land development, rock crushing and our housing projects, which are profitable."

"How did the talks go?"

"Karl Berg made several suggestions. One was for Amfac to lease all of Grove Farm and turn Lihue into a super plantation. Eddie Holroyde wasn't too hot for any proposal other than a grinding contract with Grove Farm. But I think he'll come around. He needs us more than Amfac does."

Sam was right. By August 18, after another meeting, Holroyde had assigned Phil Conrad, his plantation manager at McBryde, to work up a report on a number of possibilities including the take-over of both Lihue and Grove Farm plantations by McBryde. Sam and Van Dreser brought David along to the meetings that followed. For him, it was a lesson in diplomacy and patience. On October 3, a Tuesday, he drove over to McBryde to see how Conrad was coming with his report.

"Well, what did he say?" asked Sam when David returned.

"Conrad likes the idea of taking over the mill and getting our Koloa land," said David. "But he's cool about getting involved in planting on this side because it's windward."

"Good. Now let's talk Amfac into taking the rest of our cane land."

Unfortunately, it wasn't that simple. David didn't attend the next meetings with Amfac and A&B in Honolulu, but he heard all about them when Sam and Van Dreser got back.

"The question is who gets to be king of the mountain," explained Sam. "Neither Amfac nor A&B wants to give in to the other. I wish we could talk them into splitting it up. But nobody is willing to make the first move."

"What chance is there?"

"Well, right now we'd better see if we can make our sugar operation break even for another five years."

"Is it that bad?"

"The only chance I can see is to work on A&B. They need our mill and their manager isn't interested in being king of the mountain.

If we can talk Holroyde into making a solid proposal for our mill and our Koloa cane land, I think Amfac will take the rest."

The campaign to convince Holroyde began on January 4, 1973. Meeting followed meeting; January 18, February 12, February 23. On March 15 Holroyde agreed to ask his board of directors for approval to take over Grove Farm's mill and to lease Grove Farm's Koloa cane lands. On his next visit, he explained the verdict. The board had approved the concept in principle but there were still a great many details to be ironed out before the deal could be consummated.

That was the understatement of the year. During the next twelve months, Sam, Van Dreser, and David commuted between Grove Farm and Honolulu. Amfac fell into line, as Sam had predicted, and agreed to the land division. But that proved to be only the first step. Four hundred seventy-five workers were employed at Grove Farm: field laborers, mill workers, machinists, clerks, accountants, tractor drivers, supervisors, crane operators, and an irrigation crew. Dividing them between A&B and Amfac was more difficult than the land division.

The first meeting of industrial relations directors to allocate the workforce convened on April 5 with Amfac, A&B, and Grove Farm represented. By May the negotiations had become so complicated that Grove Farm hired Harold Hee of C. Brewer Company to represent the plantation in dealing with the union.

Sam, Van Dreser, and David sat in on meetings with Valdemar Knudsen of the Knudsen Estate concerning a lease of Knudsen land between Grove Farm and McBryde plantations. McBryde would take over the lease from Grove Farm and McBryde cane trucks would cross this land on their way to the Koloa mill. So McBryde officials wanted to make sure they would not be held up for ransom by the Knudsen Estate when the lease expired. They solved the problem by having Grove Farm exchange land with Knudsen Estate so that Grove Farm would own the haulcane road connecting its land with McBryde's.

Summer rolled around. Sam, who kept close check on the progress of negotiations, asked his son-in-law, "How is it going?"

"The people problem is the worst," David answered. "Lihue and McBryde don't want to take all of our workers and the union won't sit still for lay-offs. Housing is another snag. McBryde and Lihue will have nothing to do about housing the workers they do take from us."

The negotiations went forward without publicity until Grove Farm sent a letter, dated August 21, 1973, to its stockholders and the media, informing them of the plan. Two days later *The Advertiser* carried a story that read:

"McBryde Sugar Co. and Lihue Plantation Co. will lease sugar cane land now farmed by Grove Farm Co. under a plan formally announced yesterday. McBryde, a subsidiary of Alexander & Baldwin, Inc., will lease 7,200 acres of Grove Farm and Knudsen Estate sugar land as well as the Grove Farm factory and adjoining shop. Lihue Plantation, a unit of Amfac, Inc., will lease approximately 2,800 acres."

The story explained that the leases would give Lihue 17,500 acres and McBryde 13,163, and that Grove Farm would go out of sugar production on January 1, 1974. The president of A&B was quoted as saying some twenty per cent of Grove Farm personnel would have to be laid off although the remainder would be assured of continued employment.

As David had predicted, the International Longshoremen's and Warehousemen's Union flatly rejected any plan to lay off twenty per cent of the workers. The union put the lay-off issue at the top of the agenda for upcoming industry-wide negotiations for a new sugar contract. Grove Farm was caught in a union-industry battle that threatened the leasing agreement. David grew more frustrated at meetings through September, October, and November.

"McBryde and Lihue seem to think we're overstaffed," he explained to Sam. "I try to tell Phil Conrad how good one of our workers is and he acts as if I'm selling him deadwood."

"Can we add a few more men to our rock crushing operation?"

"We've already done that. And some of the men are taking early retirement. That still leaves about two dozen. The union wants to protect the men. They're arguing that Lihue and McBryde will lose workers by attrition during the next year or two, so why not hire experienced men while they can right now. It's like talking to a stone wall."

Tension grew during December. Lihue and McBryde continued to balk at hiring more men. Marathon sessions took them through January 1, 1974 without an agreement. On January 5, David wrote in his notebook, "Whole deal cooling off." It appeared that a year of effort had been wasted. The issue remained stalled during four days of futile negotiations through January 10.

"We can't play this game forever," said Sam in disgust on their way back to Kauai.

"What's the alternative?" asked David. "I'll call Berg and Holroyde tomorrow and set a deadline for January 18. If they don't come around by then, the deal is off."

Negotiations began again on January 14, a Monday, and continued through Thursday with no agreement. By this time the union had brought in Louis Goldblatt, secretary-treasurer of the ILWU, in an attempt to reach a settlement. He proposed a lower retirement age and that the ceiling be lifted on reparations of workers on all three plantations. Both Lihue and McBryde agreed to take a few more workers. This whittled down the number of lay-offs to those workers who refused to take jobs they were offered.

Union negotiators received the proposal on the morning of January 18 in a conference room at Alexander & Baldwin in Honolulu. They took it to ILWU headquarters for ratification or rejection. Negotiators for the sugar industry waited through the morning, and then through lunch. It was after 4 P.M. when the union negotiating committee returned, smiling and cheerful.

"They're going to sign," said Sam when he saw their faces.

By 4:30 P.M. it was done. Grove Farm ended its career as a sugar plantation. An article in *Hawaii Business* magazine, commenting on the agreement, said the pattern of small plantations phasing out of sugar had become familiar and that the settlement between Grove Farm and its neighbors had been rumored for months. Yet, when it came, it sent a shiver through the state's sugar industry.

"Part of the reaction was sentimental, the sort of thing that happens with the passing of a landmark," the article explained. "But part of it too was tinged with a very real and growing concern for the industry itself. For Grove Farm had a long-standing reputation for survival in the face of crisis, and its decisions have more than once foreshadowed things to come. It may be reasoning of this sort, as well as a touch of nostalgia, that prompts one long-time Kauai plantation man to concede, 'One thing about Grove Farm; no matter what they did, it turned out to be the right thing so often that you got the feeling they knew something you didn't know.' "

Sam frowned thoughtfully when he read the article. "Everyone knew what we knew," he said to himself. "We just acted on it."

* * *

But not everyone was pleased. Mabel Wilcox no longer attended board of directors meetings. She did not criticize or complain. She simply stopped being part of it. Her nephew, Dick Sloggett, explained to a friend, "Aunt Mabel felt very strongly that Grove Farm should remain a sugar plantation. I believe she feels useless now. I guess she doesn't want to sit there in those meetings and listen to the younger generation make decisions she doesn't like. For her, it's over."

In another way, it was just beginning.

At age ninety-one, she realized that her dream of turning the old Grove Farm Homestead into a museum was approaching reality with increasing speed and complexity. She kept wishing she had more strength. Little by little, she turned over to Sophie more of the management of the house and museum planning. But there was still too much work for them. A young man named Robert Schleck, who took a part-time job working on the inventory, turned out so well that Miss Mabel made him a permanent employee. There was still much to do. How to go about it?

Mabel I. Wilcox at Waioli Mission House, 1970.
(Photo courtesy of James L. Amos, National Geographic Magazine.)

Grove Farm Company Board of Directors, 1981. *Left to right:* Pamela W. Beck, Samuel A. Cooke, Richard H. Sloggett, Sr., William C. Corbett, Sr., Gaylord H. Wilcox, Campbell W. Stevenson, John H. Moskowitz, Jr., Randolf G. Moore, David W. Pratt, John Hubert Mee, Jr., Wilcox Patterson.

In January 1973, Miss Mabel invited Dr. Barnes Riznik, museum vice president of Old Sturbridge Village in Massachusetts, to visit Grove Farm and Waioli Mission House and advise her about how to proceed. Sam Wilcox and Dick Sloggett came around on Sunday afternoon to hear what he had to say.

"I'm quite excited by what I have seen," he told them all. "There is excellent potential here for a museum that can tell the story of a pioneer sugar plantation and this unusual family. My advice would be to begin by defining a philosophy. There are many ways to treat an historic site. At Sturbridge we have restored the buildings and farmland to an early historic period, just as you have at Waioli Mission House. But you should leave Grove Farm as it is. Everything here has its place and is part of the continuity of Grove Farm's history."

The Wilcoxes liked what they heard. Miss Mabel invited Barnes Riznik back in 1974 and 1975 to help with the museum planning. As Bob Schleck made slow but steady progress on his inventory, it all began to come together.

Meanwhile, Sam Wilcox reorganized Grove Farm Company. Some of his stockholders had objected when he offered 200 acres of prime cane land to the University of Hawaii for a community college. But Sam insisted the location of the college would draw development toward Puhi to the future benefit of Grove Farm. He was already thinking about building a shopping center on that side of Lihue.

But he concentrated now on operations already underway. Sam increased the output of Grove Farm rock quarries at Halfway Bridge, between Lihue and Koloa, and at Maha'ulepu near Koloa. These two facilities, and a portable rig at Kilauea, supplied all the rock used for construction on the island of Kauai. He also expanded the old plantation program of building, from houses for workers to commercial house building, and added grading and installation of utilities for house lots. The carpenters were kept busy during slack periods repairing old plantation supervisors' homes for rental. Then there was the shop at Puhi where mechanics and metal workers now fabricated machinery for other plantations instead of Grove Farm. Sam even got a few clients to hire time from the Grove Farm computer.

The shift over from sugar went smoothly. Best of all, it was profitable. For the first time since he had taken the reins from his Uncle Gaylord, Sam felt that Grove Farm had a future.

* * *

Nineteen seventy-four proved to be a year of transition. Barnes Riznik had been so helpful at the museum that the family wanted him as director, and indications were that he was willing. But they needed an organization to support him. Dick Sloggett and Sam Wilcox reorganized a small family foundation that had been set up in 1952 to run Waioli Mission House. Now it became Waioli Corporation, a public, nonprofit educational foundation which required a board of trustees that included members outside the family. There was Sophie, of course. But who else? It was decided the board should represent as wide a range of community interests as possible. Dick and his aunt spent hours going over names. Armed with a list, he got on the phone.

By the time he was finished in December, a unique group of individuals had agreed to serve on the board: Ralph Daehler, State District Forester; Donna Marie Garcia, Kauai Regional Librarian; Clyde French, banker; Gabriel I, public school Hawaiiana teacher; Maili Yardley, author; Winona Sears, public school science teacher.

Most of the family members represented the new generation of Wilcoxes: Nancy Goodale, Pamela Beck, and Gale Carswell. The board elected Dick Sloggett president, Sam Wilcox treasurer, and Sophie Cluff secretary. One of their first actions in 1975 was to offer the job of museum director to Riznik. He accepted with enthusiasm.

By this time, Sam felt his work was finished. He had successfully phased the family business out of sugar, the company paid dividends, and there was not much more he could do for the museum. For all these reasons, he had stepped aside the year before. David Pratt had been elected president and chief executive of Grove Farm Company,

Inc. on October 18, 1974. Now Sam decided to take the vacation with his wife he had always promised himself. A few weeks later, on May 15, 1975, he died of a heart attack on the mainland. He was sixty-five years old.

* * *

Miss Mabel fell and broke her hip in 1975. Confined to a wheel chair, she grew more and more frail. She tired easily and seldom went out. On November 2, 1978, her ninety-sixth birthday, she did attend the fortieth birthday party of the G. N. Wilcox Memorial Hospital, which she had helped found. She was too weak to sit through the long program. Pam Beck, her great-niece, wheeled her in for the cutting of the *maile lei*. A hush descended over the crowd as the tiny, white-haired woman came forward.

It was her last public appearance. She died on the morning of December 27, 1978. Her death came as a shock to people all over the state to whom she had seemed, somehow, indestructible. Newspapers, television, and radio carried the news. Editorials listed her accomplishments.

The crowd at the cemetery grew larger and larger. People came from all islands, from all walks of life. There were retired nurses and children of patients Miss Mabel had treated for TB; plantation workers stood elbow to elbow with the elite of *kamaaina* society. Members of the Order of Kamehameha from all over the state brought a huge floral tribute and sang Miss Mabel's favorite song, "E Kolu Mea." The simple ceremony concluded with a hymn by the Waioli Hui'ia Church Choir. Afterwards, the family gathered at Grove Farm in the tradition she had fostered. They had always retired there after funerals at Miss Mabel's invitation because family had meant so much to her.

Two more busy years passed with her nephew, Dick Sloggett, heading the museum board in developing Grove Farm Homestead Museum. Maps and artifacts had to be sent to the conservation center at the Bishop Museum for cleaning; more than a dozen buildings were repaired; the catalogue of books, paintings, tools, furniture, trees, and plants, and Grove Farm and family papers kept growing. The plantation records, now housed in an archive vault, were already in use by scholarly researchers. Barnes Riznik recruited an enthusiastic group of local persons who concentrated on a twelve-week course in history as preparation for work as guides. By October 1, 1980, they were ready to begin leading tours through the buildings and grounds.

A few days before, the trustees hosted a reception to open the museum to the public as a gift from Miss Mabel to the people of Kauai. It was time for remembering the woman who had made it all possible and her Uncle George, who had created the prosperous sugar plantation. Surely, thought Dick, he would have been pleased and grateful had he known that Grove Farm Homestead would be preserved and shared with all people.

Family and *kamaaina* friends from every island and walk of life gathered on the lawn under the shady, spreading tree beside the house. All had vivid memories of Grove Farm, and they felt that the spirit of G. N. Wilcox was still alive around them.

Epilogue

If G.N. were to travel home today to his beloved Kauai, he would arrive by airplane at the Lihue Airport about two miles from Nawiliwili where travelers landed by ship in the early days. He would recognize the Nawiliwili Harbor and the breakwater that he built as the plane made a wide sweep onto the runway. Instead of green fields of sugar cane that had for many years surrounded the runway on either side, he would see weeds of African tulip, Christmas berry and Guinea grass – for sugar cane is no more. The demise of sugar in the second half of the twentieth century occurred more rapidly than its rise that had begun more than a century earlier.

Moving into the 1980s the spreading Kukui tree that became Grove Farm's logo was seen in numerous venues, signaling a new, more diverse Grove Farm Company that was operating in an economy ever more dependent on tourism. Revenues came from lease rents and ongoing operations such as rock crushing. Development replaced sugar as the focus of the company – it held the potential for significant profits as well as the risks that went with it. Grove Farm worked with the state and county to develop a long-term vision for residential, commercial and industrial growth. In accordance with these plans, the company expanded its employee-housing program, which had operated on a break-even basis, and opened residential tracts *Ulu Kukui* (candlenut tree grove), *Ulu Mahi* (farm land) and *Ulu Ko* (sugar field) to the general public. The University of Hawaii chose to accept the donation of Grove Farm's Puhi land over a Wailua site, and the Kauai Community College now sits across the main road to the west of the company's historic office building. On the other side of the office, former plantation support buildings no longer needed were rented and lots were developed for industrial use. Kukui Grove opened in 1982 as the island's first shopping mall. Sitting on the western outskirts of Lihue, Kukui Grove was popular with shoppers. A few years later lots were developed around it for office buildings and light industrial uses.

Tourism was doing well, the population was expanding and the future looked bright in 1989 when Grove Farm announced its six hundred acre Lihue/Puhi Project to be built on former sugar lands between the two towns. The third largest development proposal in Kauai's history, it would be comprised of various housing projects surrounding a new golf course on well situated land. With new roads and utilities requiring massive infrastructure expenditures, this was a long term project stretching out for several decades, and demanding large bank loans.

On September 11, 1992, an unusual event occurred in Hawaii. A fierce storm was tracked on weather screens heading for the Hawaiian Islands. Residents watched closely on television as the storm moved rapidly southwest and then took a sudden "J" turn and set a course straight for Kauai. At 1:20 PM on Kauai's own 9 / 11, the electricity went out island wide. By 7 PM the skies cleared and a full moon appeared lighting the wreckage. The island was denuded, broken, and without power or water. The island was completely quiet. Every resident on Kauai learned a new word which would never be forgotten – *Iniki* (piercing wind).

The timing could not have been worse for Grove Farm. Tourism disappeared for months, then revived slowly and came back over the years. A short-lived construction boom fueled by insurance payouts kept certain sectors of the economy going, but after a couple of years the economy on Kauai slumped to a halt. Well into its Lihue/Puhi Project, interest and principal payments on Grove Farm's debt were running high, and without a healthy economy there were no buyers for the house lots to provide the cash needed to repay the loans.

Various steps were taken to get the company on a sound financial footing – dividends were stopped, employees laid off, maintenance deferred and a number of pieces of property put up for sale. Cash flow improved, time was bought, but the housing market failed to recover and the debt load continued to mount. The Board took a hard look at the figures and agreed that the company was heading toward bankruptcy. Presented with the figures, the majority of shareholders in 1999 indicated a willingness to sell "to the right buyer."

On December 1, 2000, the shareholders of Grove Farm Company, Inc., voted to sell all their shares to Steve Case, the Hawaiian born and raised creator of America On Line. Grove Farm now belonged to a new entrepreneur, a different kind of pioneer, in a new age. Case's interest in the company had a personal touch. Young Steve's grandfather Hib Case had worked for 40 years for Grove Farm Company, retiring in 1959 as treasurer. Case soon thereafter purchased an additional 18,000 acres of neighboring Lihue Plantation, all being managed by Grove Farm Company.

* * *

While Grove Farm Company has kept its eye on the future, Grove Farm Homestead Museum has worked equally diligently to preserve the past. The quiet opening in 1980 was as Miss Mabel wished, and her influence can still be felt in the policies and procedures that guide the operations. The decision to open only three days a week with small tour groups, the retention of the worker camp houses, and a willingness at times to purchase nearby properties to protect view planes all reflected this philosophy.

Iniki was a major blow to the museum properties and provided Director Barnes Riznik and his staff with the challenging work of authentically restoring broken buildings, sodden *ohia* floors, and naked foliage. After the work was completed successfully in 1995, Barnes Riznik decided to retire after twenty years, having led the museum from its infancy. Bob Schleck was chosen to move up from his Curator position to take over as Director. Having been at Grove Farm Homestead for over 30 years, Bob knew "what Miss Mabel would want" better than anyone.

Miss Mabel would probably be pleased with her museum legacy. Living on in the Waioli and Grove Farm family homes are the values, commitments and personalities of Mabel herself, her sister Elsie, her parents Sam and Emma, her grandparents Abner and Lucy, and uncle George. The quiet charm remains. One can almost see Miss Mabel sitting on the *lanai* overlooking the valley and the sea beyond.

* * *

One hundred and fifty years have passed since Lucy and Abner led the first four of their eight sons, who would be born in Hawaii, from their canoe at the Waioli River to their new home in Hanalei. The family has now grown to over 250 members and most have chosen to remain in Hawaii. The name will no longer continue, however, for there were no Wilcox sons born in the sixth generation.

Today a new century on Kauai is unfolding. The economic future of the island and Grove Farm looks brighter in the new millennium. Kauai residents look toward Steve Case with interest to see where he will take this large and beautiful land in the future. The forty thousand acres of land provide opportunities in agriculture, commerce, education, shopping and recreation. Luxury residential homes are in demand. Kauai provides a safe, beautiful tropical climate in which to live and work. The Lihue and Hanamaulu ditches and tunnels restructured by George Norton Wilcox in 1869 and 1897 respectively, bringing precious water from Mount Waialeale to *makai* lands for sugar cane, now irrigate banana and other crops. A new ecotourism venture has recently been started by young descendents of Lucy and Abner. Adventurers on all terrain vehicles, horses, kayaks, or bicycles travel on the former sugar cane field roads that provide beautiful mountain and river vistas formerly hidden by the waving cane. Adults and children now float the waterways on rubber tubes. During a tour's quiet picnic lunch one might hear a *kamaaina* guide tell the story of his great-great-grand Uncle George – the engineer who built a plantation on Kauai called Grove Farm.

PAMELA WILCOX DOHRMAN

2003

The Wilcox Family

Abner and Lucy Hart Wilcox had eight sons. Three of them, Charles, Albert, and Samuel, continued the Wilcox family. Following is a list of four generations of the Wilcox family. The direct descendants of Abner and Lucy Wilcox are in capital letters. Divorces and deaths are not indicated.

CHARLES HART WILCOX (married—Adelaide Van Mater)
    ELLA LENORE WILCOX (m—Galen Merriam Fisher, Jr.)
        GALEN MERRIAM FISHER III
        GERALD WILCOX FISHER (m—MARGARET ELLERY SLOGGETT)
            GERALD WILCOX FISHER, JR.
            CHARLES TALCOTT FISHER (m—Barbara Lee Perry)
            MARGARET GALE FISHER (m—Donn Atlee Carswell)
        ELEANOR TALCOTT FISHER (m—Robert Gordon Johnston, Martin Pence)
            MERRILL JOHNSTON
            THOMAS GALEN JOHNSTON (m—Margot Gosse)
            ANNE DRUSILLA JOHNSTON (m—O. D. Pinkerton, William H. D. King III)
            SUSAN HART JOHNSTON (m—Harvey K. Low, Fred M. Hemmings, Jr.)
        RALPH HART FISHER (m—Sally Eleanor Waters)
            GALEN MERRIAM FISHER IV (m—Christine Frances Smithers)
            JONATHAN WATERS FISHER (m—Molly L. McClaskey)

TIMOTHY WILCOX FISHER (m—Kathleen Kolb)

ANTHONY HART FISHER

LUCY ELIZA WILCOX (m—Herbert Clifford Cheek)

EDITH CHEEK (m—Clifford Wm. Nelle, Robert B. Bartlett)

CARLA NELLE (m—Thomas Frederick Jordan)

LINDA NELLE (m—Robert James Moore, Jr., Thomas L. Coleman)

MARION CHEEK (m—Frederick Loring Winsor)

DIANA WINSOR (m—Alexander Baldwin McAllister)

JULIA WINSOR (m—Peter Blair Mara Eby, Charles Edward Medland)

ELINOR CHEEK (m—John Hillis Moskowitz)

JOHN HILLIS MOSKOWITZ, JR. (m—Mary Kathryn Bowles)

ANNE MOSKOWITZ (m—John David Boquet)

PETER HOLLAND MOSKOWITZ (m—Charlotte Maria Lilling)

SALLY BEATRICE CHEEK (m—Neil Cedric Cornwall, John Hubert Mee, Jr.)

JOHN HUBERT MEE III (m—Miri Moyal)

NANCY MEE (m—Dennis Eugene Evans)

CATHERINE MEE

CHARLES HART WILCOX, JR. (m—Grace May Davis)

DOROTHY ELIZABETH EDEN WILCOX (m—William Donald Patterson, Jr.)

WILLIAM DONALD PATTERSON III (m—Naomi Fay Loveridge)

WILCOX PATTERSON (m—Pamela Anne Cranmer, Virginia Lee Gilmore)

GEORGE NORTON PATTERSON (m—Janis Maria Paulsen)

GRACE MAY PATTERSON (m—Gerald Leslie Green)

EDEN PATTERSON (m—John Burdette Charles)

HELEN HART WILCOX (m—William Colver Corbett, Jr.)

HART WILCOX CORBETT (m — Mary Joe Kidd)

WILLIAM COLVER CORBETT III (m — Joan Elizabeth Rice

MARJORIE GRACE WILCOX (m — Herbert Edward Michels)

    GEOFFREY WILCOX MICHELS

    CATHERINE GRACE MICHELS (m — William Robert Dunham)

    HERBERT EDWARD MICHELS, JR. (m — Louise T. Yardley, Mary A. Sumpf)

NORTON EDWARD WILCOX (m — Grace Bradley Cheek)

MIRIAM GRACE WILCOX

GEORGE NORTON WILCOX

EDWARD PAYSON WILCOX (m — Mary P. H. Rockwell)

ALBERT SPENCER WILCOX (m — Luahiwa, Emma Kauikeolani Napoleon Mahelona)

Ethel Kulamanu Mahelona Wilcox (m — GAYLORD PARKE WILCOX)

    ALICE KAUIKEOLANI WILCOX (m — Christian Lawrence Ecklon)

    ALBERT HART WILCOX (m — Dorothy Louise Shingle)

        GAYLORD HART HAALILIO WILCOX (m — Carol Lee Morse)

        ALICE PATRICIA KUAIHELANI WILCOX (m — Michael Guard Sheehan)

Mary Kaui Wilcox (m — Archibald Andrew)

    Archie Wilcox Andrew (m — Mapuana Rowena Mossman)

    Albert Spencer Andrew

    Maryly Kaui Andrew (m — Andrew Bruce Hayes)

        Geoffrey Bruce Hayes

        Michael Andrew Hayes (m — Janice Dean Heiner, Jan Diger)

        Maryly Kaui Hayes

        Susan Lilikoi Hayes

Allen Clessen Mahelona Wilcox (m — Florence C. Mugridge, Jacqueline Bond, Lillian Norfleet)

    Allen Clessen Mahelona Wilcox, Jr. (m — Barbara Anne Stevens)

Allen Clessen M. Wilcox III (m—Carolyn L. Hyberg, Maxine Suder)

Steven Clark Wilcox

Anne Irene Wilcox (m—Kim Irish Milner, Peter Thomas Young)

SAMUEL WHITNEY WILCOX (m—Emma Washburn Lyman)

RALPH LYMAN WILCOX (m—Anna C. "Daisy" Rice)

Eunice Hyde (Scott) Wilcox (m—Rogers Lee Hill)

Ralph Leroy Hill

Rogers Lee Hill, Jr.

Martha Lee Hill (m—Thomas John Van Dyke)

Mary Anne Hill (m—John Carmine Pette)

Robert Scott Hill

LUCY ETTA WILCOX (m—Henry Digby Sloggett)

RICHARD HENRY SLOGGETT (m—Susan Frances Reynolds, Anna Bishop)

NANCY WILCOX SLOGGETT (m—Holbrook March Wichman Goodale)

RICHARD HENRY SLOGGETT, JR. (m—Barbara Eleanor Burkett)

SALLY REYNOLDS SLOGGETT (m—Mark Auerbach, Frederick Peterson)

MARGARET ELLERY SLOGGETT (m—GERALD WILCOX FISHER)

GERALD WILCOX FISHER, JR.

CHARLES TALCOTT FISHER (m—Barbara Lee Perry)

MARGARET GALE FISHER (m—Donn Atlee Carswell)

ANNA DOROTHEA SLOGGETT (m—William Harrison Rice Cooke)

EDITH EMMA SLOGGETT (m—Charles Montague Cooke III)

CHARLES MONTAGUE COOKE IV (m—Mary Sue Reasoner)

SAMUEL ALEXANDER COOKE (m—Jean Mary Moragne)

ARTHUR CHARLES SLOGGETT (m—Diane Hayden Armitage, Natasha Trip, Lydia Mundy)

> ARTHUR WHITNEY SLOGGETT (m—Meridee Shane Zander)
>
> ANNE HAYDEN SLOGGETT (m—Charles Cheever Hardwick III)

ELSIE HART WILCOX

CHARLES HENRY WILCOX (m—Marion Butters Waterhouse)

> MARGARET LOIS WILCOX (m—Frederick Wm. Klebahn, Jr.)
>
> > MARION ISABELLE KLEBAHN (m—Robert C. Redfield)
> >
> > HUGH WALKER KLEBAHN (m—Rosemary Stock Hoggard)
>
> SAMUEL WHITNEY WILCOX II (m—Edith Anne King)
>
> > DEBORAH WILCOX (m—David W. Pratt)
> >
> > PAMELA WILCOX (m—Nichols C. Beck)
> >
> > JUDITH WILCOX (m—Michael Bryan, Charles G. King)
>
> MARTHA MARION WILCOX (m—Guy St. Clair Combs, Jr.)
>
> > GUY ST. CLAIR COMBS III (m—Candace Gilbert)
> >
> > CHARLES WILCOX COMBS (m—Bonnie Anne Browne)
> >
> > MARION WILCOX COMBS

GAYLORD PARKE WILCOX (m—Ethel Kulamanu Mahelona Wilcox)

> ALICE KAUIKEOLANI WILCOX (m—Christian Lawrence Ecklon)
>
> ALBERT HART WILCOX (m—Dorothy Louise Shingle)
>
> > GAYLORD HART HAALILIO WILCOX (m—Carol Lee Morse)
> >
> > ALICE PATRICIA KUAIHELANI WILCOX (m—Michael Guard Sheehan)

MABEL ISABEL WILCOX

WILLIAM LUTHER WILCOX (m — E. Kahuilanuimakehaikalani)

CLARENCE SHELDON WILCOX

HENRY HARRISON WILCOX (m — Mary T. Green)

Compiled by *Pat Palama*

Glossary

akamai—smart, wise
aloha, Keoki—Hello, George.
auwai—water ditch

hala seed—seeds of the pandanus or puhala tree
hana hana—work (pidgin Hawaiian)
haole—white man, foreigner
haole nui—big white man
haole liilii—little white man
hau bark—bark of *Hibiscus tiliaceus,* a large-leaved, lowland tree found near water
holokus—fitted Mother Hubbards with trains

imu—underground native oven

kanaka—a native Hawaiian
keiki—child
Kilipakis—workers of the Gilbert Islands
koa trees—native hardwood tree (*Acacia koa*)
koa settee—wooden bench seat made of koa, a native hardwood
kukui—candlenut tree (*Aleurites moluccana*)
kuleana—a Hawaiian family homestead

lanai—open air porch
lauhala leaf—leaf of the pandanus or puhala tree (*Pandanus odoratissimus*)
lauhala mat—mat woven of pandanus leaves
leis—garlands of flowers
liiliiko—small pieces of cane (plantation pidgin Hawaiian)
luau—Hawaiian feast
luna—supervisor

mahalo—thank you
mahele—division of Hawaiian land in 1848
maile—fragrant mountain vine (*Alyxia olivae-formis*)
malo—Hawaiian breechclout
Mokihana lei—garland woven of the berry of the Mokihana bush (*Pelea anisata*)

Nu Hou—something new or strange

o'o—blubber spade, a tool adapted by the Hawaiian farmer from the whaling industry
ohia wood—wood of the ohia tree grown on upper mountain slopes
okolehao—whiskey made by distilling ti root

pali—cliff
pilikia—trouble
poi—a paste made by mashing taro, common native food
poi dog—mongrel
puka—hole
pupule—crazy

ratoons—successive crops of sugarcane grown from the original stools
rial—coin of a value of about 25¢

sabidong—a Filipino word meaning weed poison

ti root whiskey—see okolehao
ti leaves—leaves of the ti plant (*Cordyline terminalis*)

Index

* indicates illustration

A

Adonis (ship), 209, 211
Ahlborn, Capt. Louis, 217, 221, 222, 224, 240*, 268
Aholo, the Hon. L., 197
Alexander, Sam, 46, 89, 95, 101, 162, 185, 189, 202, 211
Alexander, Brother William, 14
Alexander, Prof. William D., 48, 73, 88, 113
Alexander, William P., 327-73, 336*
Alexander and Baldwin, 189, 310, 401, 402, 406, 408, 409
Aliiolani Hale, 195
American Board of Commissioners for Foreign Missions, 27, 28, 323
American Factors (Amfac), 307, 310, 322, 339, 397, 398, 399, 408, 409, 410. *See also* Hackfeld & Co.
American Guano Co., 75, 76, 84
American Refinery, 219-22, 224, 226, 230
Amfac. *See* American Factors
Amy Turner (ship), 209
Anderson, Dr. Rufus, 27, 36, 38
Annexation, Hawaii, 162, 228, 241, 254, 262, 263, 270, 279, 281, 282
Argo (ship), 79
Arruda, Joe, 391
Ashford, C. W., 253
Augustin, Bernard, 387

B

Baker, James Hoapili, 196, 199
Baker's Island, 83
Baldwin, Dr. Dwight, 35
Baldwin, Henry P., 74, 101, 185, 210, 211, 220, 230, 242, 244, 255, 263, 270, 325
Beck, Pamela, 413*, 414, 415
Belt, Collins and Associates, 402
Beckwith, Edward, 51, 75
Berg, Karl, 367, 407, 408
Bipikane, 256

Bird, Isabella L., 202
Bishop, C.R. (ship), 209
Bishop National Bank, 396
Bishop Trust Company, 396
Bonilla, Dorothy, 395
Boston (ship), 260, 264
Brewer, C. & Co., 221, 230, 300, 384, 399, 409
Broadbent, Edward H. W., 240*, 275-342, 407
Brown, Cecil, 244, 248, 256
Bukoski, Freddy, 389
Burbank, Sam, 101
Bush, John, 252, 255, 259

C

California and Hawaiian Sugar Refining Corporation, 295
California Sugar Refinery, 219, 220
Cambridge (ship), 97
Carswell, Donn, 390
Carswell, Gale, 405, 414
Case, A. H. (Hib), 336*, 342, 350, 351, 352, 359, 363, 367, 376
Castle & Cooke, 89, 104, 221
Castle, Henry Northrup, 252
Castle, Samuel Northrup, 31, 32, 34
Castle, W. R., 215
Catlin, Nellie, 102
Chamberlain, Levi, 75, 78, 79, 83
Charleston (ship), 238
Chung Lung, 227
Clements, Dr. Harry, 400
Cluff, Sophie, 403, 404, 405, 412, 414
Colburn, J. F., 260-62
Committee of Nine, 215, 217
Conde, Samuel, 50
Coney, John H., 269, 308
Conrad, Phil, 408, 410
Cooke, Pattie, 101
Cooke, Samuel A., 413*
Cooper, Henry E., 262, 264

431

Coots, Bill, 391
Coptic (ship), 281
Corbett, William C., Sr., 413*
Cornwell, W. H., 260
Croton (ship), 31, 34

D

Daehler, Ralph, 414
Damon, Ethel, 325, 403
Damon, Frank, 272, 273, 296, 300
Damon, Samuel, 239
Davies, Theophilus H., 242
Dillingham, B. F., 240
Dole, Charlotte C., 43-45
Dole, Daniel, Rev., 34, 43, 47, 48, 50, 142, 143
Dole, George, 101, 141, 170, 229
Dole, Sanford B., 50, 101, 162, 194, 200, 215, 217, 228, 240, 264, 277-80, 290, 325
Dominis, John, 240
Dove, C.E.S., 269
Drysdale, Dr. R. H., 79, 80

E

Eberstadt, F., & Co., 402
Ednie, A. Douglas, 399, 400
Edwards, Dorsey, 345
Edwards, Webley, 348
Eichelberger, Harold C., 385*
Emelia (ship), 3, 4, 5, 7, 8, 9, 12, 13
Emerson, Nathaniel, 50
Ewa Plantation, 337, 343

F

Fern, Charles, 322, 323, 324, 350, 354
Fisher, Gerald Wilcox, 384*, 385*, 396, 397, 398-99, 402
Fisher, Margaret Sloggett, 396
Foster, Captain, T.R., 187, 214
Frances Palmer (ship), 89
Frear, Walter, 256, 257
Freeth, Captain G. D., 234, 235, 236, 237
French, Clyde, 415
Fujii, Tokio, 322, 327, 391, 392

G

Garcia, Donna Marie, 414
Germanic (ship), 182
George N. Wilcox (ship), 208*, 278
Gibson, Walter Murray, 196, 198, 199, 210, 227, 228
Gillin, Elbert, 371, 390
Glade, J. C., 181, 182, 187, 188, 189, 190, 207, 208, 215
Goldblatt, Louis, 411
Goodale, Nancy, 414
Goodale, Warren, 152
Gosport (ship), 84
Green, May (Mrs. Henry Wilcox), 248
Grinbaum, M. S. & Co., 221
Grove Farm Homestead Museum, 405-6, 412-14, 415-16
Grove Farm Plantation;
  Aakukui area opened, 296
  accounting by IBM, 376, 391
  airplane for spraying and fertilizing, 376
  bridge over Huleia River, 296
  Ednie survey, 399-401
  electric plant, 382
  ends sugar production, 409-12
  Filipino restaurant, 346
  first mill purchased (1876) and sold to Lihue, 180-84
  fish scrap fertilizer, 223
  Grove Farm Homestead preserved as museum, 405-6, 412-14, 415-16
  Haiku, 206, 337*
  home ownership plan, 376
  Hurricane Dot, 379
  Hurricane Nina, 378
  incorporated (1922), 312, 313
  irrigation water,
    artesian wells, 381
    first ditch, 107-11
    first tunnel, 130, 131
    Kilohana reservoir, 306
    overhead sprinklers, 381, 382, 390
    surplus to Koloa Plantation, 295
  Knudsen estate lands, 380, 409
  Koloa Mill, 336*, 337*, 366, 368, 373, 376, 378, 401
  labor,
    Chinese, 166, 213
    Filipino, 356

German, 205
Gilbert Islanders (Kilipakis), 203, 204, 209, 210, 218
Japanese, 222
organized by ILWU, 356
strikes, 357, 378
leafhopper infestation, 290
leased by G. N. Wilcox, 108–16
lease to McBryde Sugar Company and Lihue Plantation, 407–12
levulose production, 375, 379, 382, 397, 400
mechanization, 209*, 231, 273*, 285, 300, 303, 304, 317, 345, 356, 368*, 369*, 380, 382, 386–89
merger with Koloa Plantation, 362–67, 400, 401
mill cleaning plant, 377, 378, 380
milling contracts with Lihue Plantation, 121–24, 184, 277, 295, 306, 307, 346
pineapples, 345, 379
plantation houses, electricity installed, 301
proposed merger with McBryde Plantation, 401–2
Puhi, 310, 335, 336, 385*, 406, 413
railroad tracks laid, 277, 304*
road system, 365–68, 372, 380
road to tunnel, 366–73
rock quarry, 336*, 346, 413
sheep, 124, 136
Sky Way plan, 368
slag tested for fertilizer, 381
Ti plant grown for levulose, 374, 375
tile building blocks, 346
tunnelling equipment bought, 369–71
World War I, 306, 307
World War II, 346–56
Gulick, Charles, 39
Gulick, Rev. P. J., 35
Gulick, Willy, 89

H

Hackfeld & Co., 112, 134, 140, 146, 149, 181, 182, 187, 190, 206, 207, 209, 211, 212, 215, 218, 220, 221, 231, 234, 235, 276, 278, 307
Hackfeld, Captain Henry, 234
Hackfeld, J. C., 235

Hackfeld, Johannes Frederick, 234
Haiku Plantation, 179, 185, 189, 205
Hall, Jack, 367
Hana Plantation, 361
Hanamaulu, 183, 184, 298, 350
Hart, Albert, 54
Hart, Miles, 54
Hartwell, Judge Alfred, 169, 189, 212, 261
Havemayer, H. O., 230
Hawaiian Commercial & Sugar Co., 212
Hebert, Fred, 390
Hee, Harold, 409
Hogg, John Ashton, 295, 317
Holroyde, Eddie, 407, 408, 409
Holt, Benjamin, 303
Horner, W. Y., 253
House of Nobles, 229
Hualalai (ship), 305*, 325, 326
Hutchinson, Captain, 79, 84, 86

I

I, Gabriel, 414
Inouye, Masato, 378
Inter-Island Airways, 327
Inter-Island Steam Navigation Co., 214, 235, 300, 319, 322, 325, 327
International Longshoremen's and Warehousemen's Union, 410, 411
Iolani Palace, 217, 258, 279
Irwin, William G., 207, 240–43, 271
Isenberg, Carl, 202
Isenberg, Rev. Hans, 288
Isenberg, Paul, 102, 119–22, 132–35, 145–49, 155, 158, 161–64, 168, 171, 178, 179, 182, 183, 185, 190, 196, 202, 205, 220, 242, 276, 288, 326
Ives, Rev. Mark, 35

J

Jarvis Island, 75, 188, 325
Johnson, Brother, 13–30
Jones, P. C., 227, 230, 244, 248, 272
Josephine (ship), 76–80, 82, 83, 87
Jottmann, George, 317, 343, 345, 359
Judd, Albert F., 202
Judd, Dr. Gerrit P., 26, 75
Judd, Charles, 75, 78–83

K

Kaaihue, 213, 214, 275
Kaalokai (ship), 235
Kaimiloa (ship), 227
Kaipu, 130-39, 166-68
Kalakaua, King, 188-240
Kamahalo, Solomon, 147
Kamehameha III, King, 3
Kanoa, Paul Puhiula, 193, 238, 240
Kapiolani, Queen, 240
Kashima, Shige, 378, 391
Kaumaoha, George P., 251
Kawaiahao Seminary. *See* Mid-Pacific Institute)
Kealia Plantation, 210, 215, 315
Keelikolani, Princess Ruth, 179, 205, 206
Kekaha Plantation, 190, 205, 353, 399, 400
Kekuanaoa, M., 3
Kellet, Captain, 13
Kiawe, Josiah, 229
Kilauea Hou, (ship), 188, 189
Kilauea (ship), 325
Kilohana, 306, 339, 381
Knudsen Estate, 409, 410
Knudsen, Valdemar, 409
Koloa Plantation, 69, 101, 210, 291, 294, 295, 302, 362-67, 400, 401, 409
Kuaea, Rev. M., 197
Kumaka, 229

L

Lane, Chaplain, 272
Laweleka, Kahele, 170
Lawrence, Fred, 380, 391
Laysan Island, 235, 280
Lewis, Dr. Frank N., 290
Lihue Plantation, 108, 115, 121-24, 180, 190, 202, 205, 210, 232, 269, 277, 295, 296, 346, 347, 408, 409, 411
Likelike (ship), 189
Liliuokalani, Queen, 238-72
Lovell, Joseph, 134
Lyman, Sarah J., 17, 18
Lyons, Dr. Albert, 74, 234, 235

M

Makaneole, George, 385, 386, 392
Makee Plantation, 305

Malumalu School, 209*, 237, 275
MaMagia, Ignacio, 92-95
Marshall, James F. B., 152
Mashita, Hisae, 395, 404
Matson Navigation Co., 295, 320, 322
Maui (ship), 325
McBryde, Duncan, 107
McBryde Sugar Company, 401, 407, 408, 409-11
McCarthy, Charles, 311
McLane, Pat, 294
Mee, John Hubert, Jr., 413*
Mid-Pacific Institute, 296, 305, 316
Midway Island, 280, 281, 354, 355
Mikahala (ship), 237, 238, 264, 305*
Mills Institute, 273, 296, 300. *See also* Mid-Pacific Institute.
Minium, Carl, 389
Mirrlees, Tait & Watson, 181, 190
Moir, J. T., 327
Mokolii (ship), 189
Moore, Randolf G., 413*
Moragne, Joseph Hughes, 295, 296, 303, 306, 324
Moragne, William M., 324-91, 369*, 385*, 396, 401
Moragne, William M., Jr., 387, 388
Moreno, Celso Caesar, 198, 199, 204
Moriwaki, Mrs. Kikunyo, 404
Morse, Captain, 79
Moselle (ship), 181
Moskowitz, John H., Jr., 413*
Mott-Smith, J., 197

N

Nawahi, James, 196, 259
Nawiliwili Harbor, 272, 298, 305*, 308, 310, 311, 318-22, 326, 353, 368*
Nelson, Carl, 304,317
Nelson, Lloyd, 390
Neuman, Charles, 142
North Pacific Phosphate & Fertilizer Co., 235, 268
Norton, W. A., 91
Nu Hou, 144*, 145*, 152, 369*

O

Okumura, Takai, 296
Ono, Masao, 383
Oshima, Henry, 389

P

Pacific Guano & Fertilizer Co., 300
Palmer, Edward, 306
Parker, Samuel, 189, 260
Patterson, Wilcox, 413*
Peat, Marwick, Mitchell & Co., 402
Pele (ship), 235-37
Peterson, A. P., 260, 261
Pikau, 126-31, 138, 147, 152-56, 171, 204, 209, 229, 267
Philipo, George W., 196, 198-200
Polynesia (ship), 79, 80
Pratt, David, 402, 406-7, 408, 409, 410, 411, 413*, 414
Prevost, Victor, 59, 62, 96
Punui, 229
Purvis, Robert, W. T., 216, 217, 223, 240*, 268, 269, 271, 283, 297, 305
Purrington, Edwin, 91

R

Rhodes, Hon. Godfrey, 197
Rice, Anna, 61, 65
Rice, Anna Charlotte (Daisy) (Mrs. Ralph L. Wilcox), 288, 293, 294, 301
Rice, Emily, 61
Rice, Maria (Mrs. Paul Isenberg), 60-62, 65, 66, 102, 119, 120, 154, 155, 157, 288, 328
Rice, Mary, 61
Rice, Mrs. Mary S. (Mother Rice), 50, 61, 68, 120, 147, 158
Rice, (Brother) William Harrison, 46, 47, 52-72, 102
Rice, William Hyde (Willy), 61, 65, 134, 139, 141-43, 147, 157, 162, 184, 192, 205, 206, 229, 288
Riznik, Barnes, 413, 414, 416
Robinson, Mark, 244, 248
Rosa, Anton, 256
Rosa, Bernard, 389
Rosa, Manuel, 389, 392
Rowell, Rev. and Mrs. G. B., 13, 14

S

St. Louis Sugar Refinery, 215
Sally (ship), 155, 156
Salvation Army, 297, 306, 311

Sato, Tsutao, 342, 391
Schleck, Robert, 412, 413
Sears, Winona, 414
Serraon, Laureano (Larry), 386
Sheehan, Patsy, 405
Shima, Mr. and Mrs., 352, 357
Shintani, Kiyoshi, 384, 389
Sloggett, Henry Digby, 272, 289
Sloggett, Richard Henry, 384*, 385*, 396, 405, 406, 412, 413*, 413, 414, 415, 416
Sloggett, Margaret, 396
Smith, Alfred, (Fred) 170, 285, 286, 290
Smith, C. Hutton, 385*
Smith, Charlotte (Lottie), 142-44, 147, 154, 155, 157, 163, 169
Smith, Emma, 142
Smith, Dr. Jared K., 17, 184, 185, 186, 209
Smith, Marcia, 46, 47
Smith, W. O., 192, 215, 240, 260, 261, 270, 277, 278, 325
Souza, Manuel, 315-17
Spaulding, Charley, 95
Spaulding, Sarah, 102
Spaulding, Col. Z. K., 215
Spillner, Erich, 383-85
Spreckels, Claus, 190-230, 242, 270-72
Steele, E. L. G., 219, 221, 224
Stevens, John L., 264
Stevenson, Campbell, 413*
Stone, Captain W. C., 76, 77
Swan, Edward S., 305, 327, 328

T

Tatsy, 191, 286
Tenney, E. D., 320
Theo. H. Davies & Co., 221
Thurston, Lorrin A., 228-30, 238-43, 248-55, 259-63
Thurston, Lucy, 35
Titcomb, Charles, 13, 19-23, 29, 52, 64, 96
Tom, Richard M. D. (Dick), 391
Tonk Kee (alias Aki), 227

V

Van Dreser, Lyle, 384-87, 389, 391, 396, 400, 402, 406
Vargas, Victor, 377, 378, 390, 392

W

Waialeale (ship), 280, 281
Waioli Corporation, 414
Waioli Mission, 5–8, 12, 15, 17*, 23–28
Waioli Tearoom, 311
Walker, Allen & Co., 158
Warner, Charles Ernest (Ernie), 385, 386
Watt, R. G. (Tom), 400
Wawra, Dr. Heinrich, 164, 165
Weber, Frederick W., (Fred), 342, 359, 391
Webster, William, 109, 110
Weinberg, Harry, 398–99
Welton, Charles, 95
Weston, D. M., 60
Whiting, Judge W. A., 275
Widemann, Judge Hermann, 29, 64,
    104–16, 121, 129, 134, 149–53, 162, 163, 170,
    177, 187, 190, 194, 219, 220, 230, 239, 241
Wilcox, Abner, 16*, 5–45, 73, 88, 89, 91, 99,
    100, 151, 159
Wilcox, Albert Hart, 384*, 385*
Wilcox, Albert Spencer, 5, 6, 25–27, 30–40,
    97–99, 103, 114, 158, 183, 190, 211, 220, 229,
    235, 242, 248, 253, 255, 260–63, 307
Wilcox, Charles Hart, 6, 7, 9, 10, 12, 18,
    25, 31, 37, 43, 46, 49, 50–54, 97, 159, 320
Wilcox, Charles Henry, 244, 245, 272, 294,
    302, 306, 307, 309
Wilcox, Edie, 397
Wilcox, Edward Payson, 9, 10, 11, 18, 23, 25,
    30, 43, 91, 92, 95, 159
Wilcox, Elsie Hart, 213, 288, 294, 296, 305,
    306, 313, 314, 333, 336*, 342, 361, 362, 363,
    396
Wilcox, Emma Lyman (Mrs. Samuel W.),
    176–78, 183–86, 191, 204, 213, 225, 244, 245,
    274, 287, 288, 305, 309
Wilcox, Etta, 396
Wilcox, Gaylord Hart, 413*
Wilcox, Gaylord Parke, 213, 244, 245, 290,
    294, 305, 307, 309, 310, 313, 334, 339, 340,
    346, 360–75, 369*, 379–83, 391, 396–97,
    398, 399, 400, 401, 406
Wilcox, George Norton,
    appointed Minister of the Interior (Prime
        Minister), 244
    at Punahou School, 44–52, 80*
    at Sheffield Scientific School at Yale, 80*,
        88–96
    becomes member of Committee of Nine,
        215
    builds Grove Farm's first tunnel for
        water, 130, 131
    childhood, 1–40
    death, 238
    delegate to Constitutional Convention,
        277
    elected to House of Nobles, 229
    elected to House of Representatives, 194
    endows Mid-Pacific Institute, 296, 301,
        305
    ensures purchase of Nawiliwili Harbor
        bonds, 308, 311
    First National Bank of Hawaii, 300
    first jobs and pioneering on Kauai,
        97–106
    first plane ride, 304*, 327
    gifts to Salvation Army, 297, 306, 311
    goes to Europe to purchase mill, 180–182
    goes to New York for eye surgery, 290
    guano expeditions:
        to Jarvis Island, 75–87
        to Laysan Island, 235–37
    incorporates Grove Farm, 312
    invests in American Refinery, 220
    invests in California and Hawaiian
        Sugar Corporation, 294
    invests in Inter-Island Steam Navigation
        Co., 214
    invests in North Pacific Phosphate &
        Fertilizer Co., 235
    leases Grove Farm, 81*, 114–16
    leases Haiku land, 179
    Nawiliwili Harbor, 305*, 311, 318–22, 326
    North Pacific Phosphate & Fertilizer
        Co., 235, 268, 276, 277
    pets; dog "Smut", 19, 20, 23
        Galapagos turtle, 11
        horse "April Fool", 54, 56, 64
    Planters' Labor & Supply Co., 212
    purchases first automobile, 272, 295
    purchases Grove Farm, 163
    purchases royal land, 206
    purchases steam plows, 231
    sells mill to Lihue Plantation, 184
    supervises construction of retaining wall
        at Nawiliwili, 324
    supervises Grove Farm's first water
        ditches, 107–11*, 128–35

supports Mills Institute, 272–74
tours Orient, 296
visits New Zealand, 278
youth, 43–116
Wilcox, G. N., Memorial Hospital, 415
Wilcox, G. N., Trust, 396
Wilcox, Henry Harrison, 101, 151, 159, 160, 183, 248
Wilcox, Lucy Etta (Mrs. H. D. Sloggett), 213, 272, 289, 305, 313
Wilcox, Lucy Hart (Mrs. Abner), 5, 7–14, 16*, 17, 18, 24–45, 74, 101, 102, 152, 153, 159
Wilcox, Luther. See William Luther
Wilcox, Mabel Isabel, 244, 288, 294, 296, 305, 306, 313, 333, 336*, 342, 361–63, 385*, 395–97, 403–6, 412, 412*, 415–16
Wilcox, Marion Waterhouse (Mrs. Charles H.), 303, 309
Wilcox, Ralph Lyman, 184, 186, 187, 213, 272, 283, 284, 288, 290, 293, 294, 299, 301
Wilcox, Robert (not same branch Wilcox family), 242, 249, 256
Wilcox, Samuel Whitney, 24, 25, 30, 39, 43, 101, 141, 152, 159, 163, 175, 176–78, 183–86, 190–92, 203, 213, 222, 232, 233, 244, 274–76, 284, 285, 287, 288, 305, 309, 325
Wilcox, Samuel Whitney II, 384*, 385*, 396, 397, 398, 399, 401, 403, 405–15
Wilcox, William Luther, 30, 101, 151, 159, 183, 188, 189, 194–98, 226, 229, 235, 248, 249, 254–58, 281, 289
Wilder, Samuel G., 75, 78, 83, 84, 86, 162, 188, 202, 230
Wilson, Charles B., 242, 249, 264
Wiltse, Captain, 260, 264
Winslow, E. E., 297–99
Wooten, W. P. 297, 299
Wundenberg, G. F., 29
Wyllie, Robert C., 96, 103

Y

Yankee (ship), 54
Yardley, Maili, 414

Z

Zimmer, Francis, E. (Frank), 389, 390

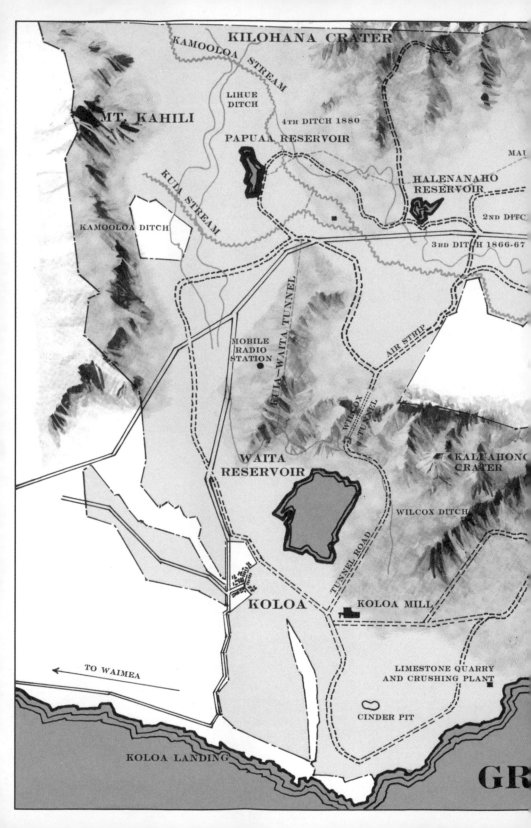